British Psychoanalysis

British Psychoanalysis: New Perspectives in the Independent Tradition is a new and extended edition of *The British School of Psychoanalysis: The Independent Tradition*, which explored the successes and failures of the early environment; transference and counter-transference in the psychoanalytic encounter; regression in the situation of treatment, and female sexuality. Published in the mid-1980s, it had an important influence on the development of psychoanalysis both in Great Britain and abroad, was translated into several languages and became a central textbook in academic and professional courses.

This new, updated book includes not only many of the original papers, but also new chapters written for this volume by Hannah Browne, Josh Cohen, Steven Groarke, Gregorio Kohon, Rosine Perelberg and Megan Virtue. Addressing and reflecting on the four main themes of the first collection, the new papers discuss such subjects as:

- a new focus on earliest infancy
- new directions in Independent clinical thinking
- the question of therapeutic regression
- the centrality of sexual difference in Freud.

They also highlight the connections between and the mutual influence of British and French psychoanalysis, now a critical subject in contemporary psychoanalytic debates.

British Psychoanalysis: New Perspectives in the Independent Tradition will be important not only to psychoanalysts and psychoanalytic psychotherapists and the full spectrum of professionals involved in mental health. It will be of great value in psychotherapy and counselling training and an important resource for teaching and academic activities.

Gregorio Kohon is a Training Analyst of the British Psychoanalytical Society. His psychoanalytic publications include *Reflections on the Aesthetic Experience: Psychoanalysis and the Uncanny*, published by Routledge in 2016.

THE NEW LIBRARY OF PSYCHOANALYSIS
General Editor: Alessandra Lemma

The New Library of Psychoanalysis was launched in 1987 in association with the Institute of Psychoanalysis, London. It took over from the International Psychoanalytical Library which published many of the early translations of the works of Freud and the writings of most of the leading British and Continental psychoanalysts.

The purpose of the New Library of Psychoanalysis is to facilitate a greater and more widespread appreciation of psychoanalysis and to provide a forum for increasing mutual understanding between psychoanalysts and those working in other disciplines such as the social sciences, medicine, philosophy, history, linguistics, literature and the arts. It aims to represent different trends both in British psychoanalysis and in psychoanalysis generally. The New Library of Psychoanalysis is well placed to make available to the English-speaking world psychoanalytic writings from other European countries and to increase the interchange of ideas between British and American psychoanalysts. Through the *Teaching Series*, the New Library of Psychoanalysis now also publishes books that provide comprehensive, yet accessible, overviews of selected subject areas aimed at those studying psychoanalysis and related fields such as the social sciences, philosophy, literature and the arts.

The Institute, together with the British Psychoanalytical Society, runs a low-fee psychoanalytic clinic, organizes lectures and scientific events concerned with psycho-analysis and publishes the *International Journal of Psychoanalysis*. It runs a training course in psychoanalysis which leads to membership of the International Psychoanalytical Association – the body which preserves internationally agreed standards of training, of professional entry, and of professional ethics and practice for psychoanalysis as initiated and developed by Sigmund Freud. Distinguished members of the Institute have included Michael Balint, Wilfred Bion, Ronald Fairbairn, Anna Freud, Ernest Jones, Melanie Klein, John Rickman and Donald Winnicott.

Previous general editors have included David Tuckett, who played a very active role in the establishment of the New Library. He was followed as general editor by Elizabeth Bott Spillius, who was in turn followed by Susan Budd and then by Dana Birksted-Breen. Current members of the Advisory Board include Giovanna Di Ceglie, Liz Allison, Anne Patterson, Josh Cohen and Daniel Pick.

Previous members of the Advisory Board include Christopher Bollas, Ronald Britton, Catalina Bronstein, Donald Campbell, Rosemary Davies, Sara Flanders, Stephen Grosz, John Keene, Eglé Laufer, Alessandra Lemma, Juliet Mitchell, Michael Parsons, Rosine Jozef Perelberg, Richard Rusbridger, Mary Target and David Taylor.

For a full list of all the titles in the New Library of Psychoanalysis main series as well as both the New Library of Psychoanalysis 'Teaching' and 'Beyond the Couch' subseries, please visit the Routledge website.

THE NEW LIBRARY OF PSYCHOANALYSIS

General Editor: Alessandra Lemma

British Psychoanalysis

New Perspectives in the Independent Tradition

Edited by Gregorio Kohon

Routledge
Taylor & Francis Group

LONDON AND NEW YORK

First published 2018
by Routledge
2 Park Square, Milton Park, Abingdon, Oxon OX14 4RN

and by Routledge
711 Third Avenue, New York, NY 10017

Routledge is an imprint of the Taylor & Francis Group, an informa business

© 2018 selection and editorial matter, Gregorio Kohon; individual chapters, the contributors

British Library Cataloguing-in-Publication Data
A catalogue record for this book is available from the British Library

Library of Congress Cataloging-in-Publication Data
Names: Kohon, Gregorio, 1943– editor.
Title: British psychoanalysis: new perspectives in the independent tradition /edited by Gregorio Kohon.
Description: New and extended edition. | New York: Routledge, 2018. |
Series: New library of psychoanalysis | Revised edition of The British school of psychoanalysis, c1986. | Includes bibliographical references and index.
Identifiers: LCCN 2017036621 (print) | LCCN 2017038178 (ebook) |
ISBN 9781351262880 (Master) | ISBN 9781351262873 (Web PDF) |
ISBN 9781351262866 (ePub) | ISBN 9781351262859 (Mobipocket/Kindle) |
ISBN 9781138579040 (hardback: alk. paper) | ISBN 9781138579057
(pbk.: alk. paper)
Subjects: LCSH: Psychoanalysis – Great Britain – History. | Psychoanalysis – Great Britain.
Classification: LCC RC503 (ebook) | LCC RC503.B75 2018 (print) |
DDC 616.89/1700941 – dc23
LC record available at https://lccn.loc.gov/2017036621

ISBN: 978-1-138-57904-0 (hbk)
ISBN: 978-1-138-57905-7 (pbk)
ISBN: 978-1-351-26288-0 (ebk)

Typeset in Bembo
by Florence Production Ltd, Stoodleigh, Devon, UK

To the memory of my psychoanalytic teachers:
Enid Balint, Nina Coltart, André Green, Paula Heimann,
Adam Limentani and Harold Stewart, all of them truly
independent people.

Contents

PART III
EARLY ENVIRONMENT: SUCCESS AND
FAILURE 73

PART IV
THE PSYCHOANALYTIC ENCOUNTER:
TRANSFERENCE AND
COUNTERTRANSFERENCE 131

Contents

Biographical notes

Michael Balint (1896–1970). Born in Budapest. He moved to Berlin to escape anti-Semitism in Hungary, where he started his training with Hanns Sachs. Before completing his training he went back to Budapest, where he finished his training, with Ferenczi, in 1926. He moved with his wife, Alice, to Manchester in 1939, when the political persecution in his own country had become intolerable. After Alice's death, he moved to London. In 1948 he joined the Family Discussion Bureau, whose leader, Enid Flora Albu, was later to become his wife. He wrote seven books and over 100 papers. His most important contributions include *Primary Love and Psycho-Analytic Technique* (1956) and *The Basic Fault* (1967). The influence of Michael Balint and his wife, Enid Balint, on the organization and practice of the probation services, social work in general, the work of general practitioners, and the development of brief psychotherapy in Britain has been very great.

Christopher Bollas. Born in the United States. He was Visiting Professor in Psychoanalysis at the Istituto di Neuropsichiatria Infantile, University of Rome; Visiting Professor of English Literature, University of Massachusetts; and Director of Education at the Austen Riggs Center. He published 15 psychoanalytic books and a number of novels and plays. He is a Fellow of the British Psychoanalytical Society, a member of the Los Angeles Institute and Society for Psychoanalytic Studies, and Honorary Member of the Institute for Psychoanalytic Training and Research. His latest book is *When the Sun Bursts: The Enigma of Schizophrenia* (2016).

Hannah Browne. Born in South Africa. She did her medical training at the University of Cape Town. After qualifying, she moved to London, where she trained as a Child and Adolescent Psychiatrist at the Tavistock Clinic. She is a Member of The British Psychoanalytical

Society. She now lives in Belfast and works in the NHS in a service for young people with gender dysphoria and also has a part-time private psychoanalytic practice.

Patrick J. Casement. Having graduated from Cambridge in theology and anthropology, he worked for ten years as a social worker. Before becoming a psychoanalyst, he trained with the British Association of Psychotherapists. He is a Fellow of the British Psychoanalytical Society. He was formerly a Training Analyst, having been in full-time private practice for many years, and has now retired. He lectured widely around the world. He is the author of numerous publications, including his most famous, first book *Learning from the Patient* (1985).

Josh Cohen. He is a Fellow of the British Psychoanalytical Society. He is also Professor of Modern Literary Theory at Goldsmiths, University of London. He is the author of five books on psycho-analysis, cultural theory and modern literature, including *How to Read Freud* (2005) and, most recently, *The Private Life: Why We Remain in the Dark* (2013). He has also contributed with many book chapters and written a large number of papers. He is on the Editorial Board of the *International Journal of Psychoanalysis*. He is currently working on a study of inertia in psychic and cultural life. He works in private practice in London.

Nina E.C. Coltart (1927–1997). She took her first degree in modern languages at Oxford, before doing her medical training. She became a training analyst in 1971 and was Director of the London Clinic of Psychoanalysis for ten years. Through her professional and clinical influence, she was one of the most important Independent training analysts of her generation. Her last book, published before her death, was *The Baby and the Bathwater* (1996).

Steven Groarke. He is a Member of the British Psychoanalytical Society and Professor of Social Thought at the University of Roehampton. He is the author, most recently, of *Managed Lives: Psychoanalysis, Inner Security and the Social Order* (2014). He served as Honorary Archivist of the Winnicott Trust from 2011 to 2016 and has held honorary appointments with Central and North West London Mental Health NHS Trust at Parkside Clinic and St Charles Hospital. He is on the Editorial Board of the *International Journal of Psychoanalysis*. He works in private practice in London.

M. Masud R. Khan (1924–1989). Born in Pakistan. Was Editor of the Psycho-Analytical Library, the Hogarth Press, and Associate

Editor of the *International Journal of Psychoanalysis* for many years. He was also *Coredacteur Etranger* of the *Nouvelle Revue de Psychanalyse* and Director of Sigmund Freud Copyrights Ltd. His first two books are acknowledged as his most important psychoanalytic contributions: *The Privacy of the Self* (1974) and *Alienation in Perversions* (1979).

John Klauber (1917–1981). Took a history degree in 1939, obtaining his medical qualification in 1951. He started work in private practice as a psychoanalyst in 1953 and gained full membership of the British Psychoanalytical Society in 1959. He was also a Member of the British Psychological Society and a Foundation Fellow of the Royal College of Psychiatrists. At the time of his death, in 1981, he had been President of the British Society for a year, and was about to take up the post of Freud Memorial Visiting Professor at University College London. His papers were collected in *Difficulties in the Analytic Encounter* (1986).

Gregorio Kohon. Born in Argentina. He is a Training Analyst of the British Psychoanalytical Society and works in London in private practice. He moved to England in 1970, and qualified as a psycho-analyst in 1979. From early 1988 to December 1994, he lived in Australia, where he co-founded (together with Valli Shaio Kohon) and directed The Brisbane Centre for Psychoanalytic Studies. He edited *The British School of Psychoanalysis: The Independent Tradition* (1986); *The Dead Mother: The Work of André Green* (1999); and, together with Rosine Perelberg, *The Greening of Psychoanalysis: André Green's New Paradigm in Contemporary Theory and Practice* (2017). He is the author of *No Lost Certainties to be Recovered* (1999), *Love and Its Vicissitudes* (co-authored with André Green, 2005), and *Reflections on the Aesthetic Experience: Psychoanalysis and the Uncanny* (2016). His novel *Papagayo Rojo, Pata de Palo* [*Red Parrot, Wooden Leg*] (2007/2008) was a finalist in the 2001 Fernando Lara Prize. He published four books of poetry in Spanish, and in 2015, he co-authored a collection of short stories, *Truco Gallo*. He participated in many anthologies of Argentinian literature, the latest being *Argentina Beat* (2016).

Adam Limentani (1913–1994). Born in Italy. He was forced to emigrate to England in 1938, soon after graduating from medical school. He became a psychiatrist, and later trained as a psychoanalyst, qualifying in 1953. He worked as a consultant for the London Clinic of Psychoanalysis for many years. He was a Fellow of the Royal College of Psychiatrists and Honorary Consultant Psychotherapist, Portman Clinic, London. He was the President of the British Psychoanalytical

Society from 1974 to 1977, and he served as President of the Inter-national Psychoanalytical Association from 1983 to 1986. A collection of his papers was published under the title *Between Freud and Klein* (1989).

Juliet Mitchell. Born in New Zealand. She is a Fellow of the British and International Psychoanalytical Societies. She was a lecturer in English Literature at the universities of Leeds and Reading (1962–1970). In 1966, she published the path-breaking *Women: The Longest Revolution*, and, in 1974, *Psychoanalysis and Feminism*. After subsequently qualifying as a psychoanalyst in 1979, she worked as a clinician in both private and public practice. At the same time, she continued her academic engagements, holding posts and visiting professorships in numerous institutions, including Yale, Cornell, and Princeton universities, the Courtauld Institute of Art, Cambridge University (where she founded the Centre for Gender Studies), and the Psychoanalysis Unit at UCL, where she devised and directed the PhD programme in Theoretical Psychoanalysis and where she continues to teach today. She has delivered over 200 keynotes and public lectures in 30 countries and written and co-edited a number of books on both feminism and psychoanalysis. She is continuing her work on siblings and their lateral social heirs from *Mad Men and Medusas . . .* (2000), and *Siblings, Sex and Violence* (2003) with a collection of her essays, *The Sibling Trauma and the Law of the Mother*, and a book on *Siblings and Shakespeare* (for which she was awarded a Leverhulme Emeritus Fellowship). A special number of *Psyche* will print 'Siblings and the Horizontal Axis' (2017). Her writings have been translated into 21 languages. She is Professor Emeritus at Cambridge University, Fellow Emeritus at Jesus College, Professorial Research Fellow at UCL and Fellow of the British Academy.

Rosine Jozef Perelberg. Born in Brazil. She is a Training Analyst of the British Psychoanalytical Society, Visiting Professor in the Psychoanalysis Unit at University College London and Corresponding Member of the Paris Psychoanalytical Society. She completed a PhD in Social Anthropology at the London School of Economics. Her publications include *Psychoanalytic Understanding of Violence and Suicide* (1997), *Female Experience: Four Generations of British Women Psycho-analysts on Work with Women* (1998, 2008) and *Freud: A Modern Reader* (2006). In 2017, she edited, together with Gregorio Kohon, *The Greening of Psychoanalysis: André Green's New Paradigm in Contemporary Theory and Practice*. She is the author of *Time, Space and Phantasy*

(2008), and *Murdered Father, Dead Father: Revisiting the Oedipus Complex* (2015). In 2007, she was named one of the ten women of the year by the Brazilian National Council of Women. She works in private practice in London.

Harold Stewart (1924–2008). He was born within the sound of Bow Bells, which, he liked to say, made him one of the few Cockney psychoanalysts in Britain. He qualified in medicine in 1947. The following year, he became a GP and practiced as such for 17 years; during this time he became interested in the use of hypnosis, and later on in psychoanalysis. He qualified in 1961, becoming a Training Analyst four years later. He was Clinical Assistant in the Department of Psychological Medicine, University College Hospital, then Consultant Psychiatrist at the Paddington Centre for Psychotherapy, and finally Consultant Psychotherapist at the Tavistock Clinic until his retirement from the NHS in 1989. He wrote two books, *Psychic Experience and Problems of Technique* (1992), and *Michael Balint: Object Relations Pure and Applied* (1996).

Neville Symington. Born in Portugal, of British parents. He studied Philosophy and Theology and became a Catholic priest. Later, he studied Psychology, took a degree in Clinical Psychology, and trained as a psychoanalyst. He is a Fellow of the British Psychoanalytical Society. He held a senior staff position in the Adult Department of the Tavistock Clinic from 1977 to 1985. In 1986, he moved to Sydney, Australia, where he was Chairman of the Sydney Institute for Psycho-Analysis from 1987 to 1993, and President of the Australian Psychoanalytic Society from 1999 to 2002. He is the author of 14 books and many papers. In 2016, he published *A Different Path: An Emotional Autobiography*.

Megan Virtue. Born in South Africa. She is a Fellow of the British Psychoanalytical Society. After reading Humanities, she trained as a Clinical Psychologist and, later on, in Adult Psychotherapy at the Tavistock Clinic. Since 2001, she has worked in the NHS and for nine years has been Consultant Clinical Psychologist in Psychotherapy at St Mark's Hospital, working with patients with gastrointestinal disorders. She teaches psychoanalytic theory at University College London and works as a psychoanalyst in private practice in London.

D.W. Winnicott (1896–1971). Qualified as a doctor at St. Bartholomew's Hospital in London and worked for many years as a Paediatrician at Paddington Green Children's Hospital. He trained as a Psychoanalyst in the late 1920s, qualifying as an Adult Psychoanalyst in 1934, and a year later as the first male Child Psychoanalyst in Great Britain. As a member of the British Psychoanalytical Society, he was always very involved in its scientific as well as its administrative life, participating in many committees. He also lectured on Child Development at the Institute of Education, University College London, and at the London School of Economics. He was President of the British Psychoanalytical Society on two occasions: 1954–56 and 1963–65. He practised both as an Adult Psychoanalyst and as a Child Psychiatrist until his death. His prolific writings, which started in 1931, included scientific papers, reviews, journal articles, and correspondence, and he also gave radio talks designed to introduce psychoanalytic ideas about the family to a non-specialist audience. Winnicott's contributions constitute a major development in psychoanalysis, recognized on an international scale. *The Collected Works of D.W. Winnicott*, a 12-volume set (edited by Lesley Caldwell and Helen Taylor Robinson), was published in 2017.

Acknowledgements

The following papers are reproduced by kind permission of the *International Journal of Psychoanalysis,* the *International Review of Psycho-Analysis* and their publisher John Wiley & Sons, Inc.: 'The Transformational Object', by Christopher Bollas, *International Journal of Psychoanalysis* (1979) 60: 97–107; 'Fear of Breakdown', by D.W. Winnicott, *International Review of Psycho-Analysis* (1974) 1: 103–107; 'Affects and the Psychoanalytic Situation', by Adam Limentani, *International Journal of Psychoanalysis* (1977) 58: 171–182; 'The Analyst's Act of Freedom as Agent of Therapeutic Change', by Neville Symington, *International Review of Psycho-Analysis* (1983) 10: 283–291; 'Some Pressures on the Analyst for Physical Contact During the Reliving of an Early Trauma', by Patrick Casement, *International Review of Psycho-Analysis* (1982) 9: 279–286; 'Problems of Management in the Analysis of a Hallucinating Hysteric', by Harold Stewart, *International Journal of Psychoanalysis* (1977) 58: 67–76; 'Reflections on Dora: The Case of Hysteria', by Gregorio Kohon, *International Journal of Psychoanalysis* (1984) 65: 73–84. 'The Concept of Cumulative Trauma' (1963), by M. Masud R. Khan, was first published in *The Privacy of the Self* (Hogarth Press, 1974); the book was later published by Karnac Books in 1996, and it is reprinted here with kind permission of Karnac Books. 'Elements of the Psychoanalytic Relationship and Their Therapeutic Implications', by John Klauber, was first published in *Difficulties in the Analytic Encounter* (Jason Aronson, 1981); the book was later published by Karnac Books in 1986, and it is reprinted here with kind permission of Karnac Books. 'The Question of Femininity and the Theory of Psychoanalysis', by Juliet Mitchell, first published in *Women: The Longest Revolution* (Virago, 1984). 'The Unobtrusive Analyst', by Michael Balint, was first published in *The Basic Fault* (Tavistock, 1968). The paper by Nina E.C. Coltart, ' "Slouching towards Bethlehem . . ." Or Thinking the Unthinkable in Psychoanalysis', was first published at my request in the 1986 original collection. It was later reproduced in her book, *Slouching towards Bethlehem . . .: and Further Psychoanalytic Explorations* (first edition: Free Association Books, 1992). A revised version of Patrick Casement's paper, 'Some Pressures on the Analyst for Physical Contact during the Reliving of an Early Trauma', was included in *On Learning from the Patient* (first edition: Tavistock, 1985).

Epigraph to Part I: W. R. Bion, 'Evidence' (1976), in *The Complete Works of W. R. Bion, Vol. X*, edited by Chris Mawson. London: Karnac, 2014, p. 131. By permission of The Marsh Agency Ltd on behalf of the Estate of W. R. Bion. Epigraph to Hannah Browne, 'Regression: Allowing the Future to Be Revisited': 'Going Home' from *MAP: Collected and Last Poems*, by Wislawa Szymborska, translated from the Polish by Stanislaw Baranczak and Clare Cavanagh. English copyright © 2015 by Houghton Mifflin Harcourt Publishing Company. Reprinted by permission of Houghton Mifflin Harcourt Publishing Company – All rights reserved.

I would like to express my gratitude to Eric and Klara King for their invaluable help with the editing of the manuscript. My gratitude to Valli for her permission to use her 'Conversation' (2014) for the cover image.

PART I

AN INDEPENDENT
TRADITION

Nobody can tell how you are to live your life, or what you are to think, or what language you are to speak. Therefore, it is absolutely essential that the individual analyst should forge for himself the language which he knows, which he knows how to use, and the value of which he knows.

Wilfred R. Bion, 'Evidence' (1976)

1

THIRTY YEARS LATER

Looking back into the future

Gregorio Kohon

It is hard to believe that thirty years have passed since the publication of the first edition of *The British School of Psychoanalysis: The Independent Tradition*. When, in 1983, four years after qualifying as a psychoanalyst, I first suggested the book to a senior member of the Publications Committee of the British Psychoanalytical Society, I was met with a wry smile as he said, 'Quite a task, to put together a book about a group that refuses to be a group.' This was true: there was a group of psychoanalysts who, at some point in the history of the British Psychoanalytical Society, had refused to belong either to Anna Freud's B group or to the Kleinians, wishing to remain in the 'middle'.

My colleague's response to my suggestion only made me more determined to carry on with the project – although there were unforeseen difficulties. For example, I was not given permission, for what seemed arbitrary and rather capricious 'administrative' reasons, to include papers by Paula Heimann, Pearl King and Marion Milner – three women analysts who had contributed significantly to British psychoanalysis. Otherwise, the support from the majority of my Independent colleagues was unconditional.

It was for both organizational and political reasons that the 'Middle Group' later became the 'Group of Independent Psychoanalysts'. However, the name of 'Middle Group', originally so described by Edward Glover during the Controversial Discussions (Riccardo Steiner, in King and Steiner, 1991, p. 681), persisted for a while.

3

At one point, Glover referred to it in terms of the 'English Freudians' (King and Steiner, 1991, p. 136), and Barbara Low called it 'the "Middle" Party' (King and Steiner, 1991, p. 83). While Michael Parsons thought that the final name was agreed upon around the 1950s (Parsons, 2014a, p. 184), John Keene suggested that this occurred in the 1960s (Keene, 2012, p. 4). Throughout the 1960s and 1970s there was also a rather hostile description of the group as a 'muddled' group. During my training (1975–1979), I heard a number of senior Independent analysts commenting on this, but for them it was a compliment, an achievement, rather than a failure, denoting the Independents' refusal to be associated with dogmatic attitudes or unjustified certainties.

I believe that the 1986 edition of the book made *Independent tradition* a widely accepted description. Afterwards, other books dealing with this particular tradition followed the same principle of avoiding reference to a 'group'. In 1991, Eric Rayner published *The Independent Mind in British Psychoanalysis*. In 2012, Paul Williams, John Keene and Sira Dermen edited a collection of papers that they entitled *Independent Psychoanalysis Today*. The emphasis of the titles was not on the 'group' but on the individuality of its members.

More recently, Michael Parsons has written,

[The concept of] the Independent traditon does not coincide with the Independent Group. There is a large overlap, in that the majority of analysts who have exemplified and developed the tradition have been part of the Group. However, there are members of the Independent Group that do not stand within the Independent tradition. Conversely, the Independent tradition is not limited to the Group, or even to the British Society.

(Parsons, 2014a, p. 187)

This distinction, between an organizational and political group, on the one hand, and a tradition, on the other, is very important. As can be seen from Parsons' quotation above, the very concept of a 'tradition' is a complicated one: within one given tradition there might be many different strands, perhaps coexisting in disagreement, all parts of a paradoxical and complex whole. This does not apply just to one particular professional, political, religious, or any other type of group of individuals. In psychoanalysis, naming one tradition helps to recognize and distinguish it from any others; in fact, the distinction only makes sense if considered in contrast with and compared to other traditions. Although, in social terms, naming a group represents a way of identifying people, the differentiation rarely takes place on exclusively fair and accurate assumptions; frequently, it may also be based on unconscious prejudice, false perceptions, and/or tactics of relatively conscious active discrimination. Naming and describing a group can also fairly easily turn into the creation of misleading stereotypes – not an uncommon event in the psychoanalytic world.

The present book does not aim to give a historical view of the institutional changes in the British Psychoanalytical Society, nor to give an account of the British Independents' clinical and theoretical contributions of the last thirty years. For this, I would refer the reader to the collection of papers brought together and edited by Williams, Keene and Dermen (2012), already mentioned above. Given the existence of a relatively new Association of Independent Analysts within the British Psychoanalytical Society and the annual meetings organized by them under the heading of *The Cambridge Convention*, there may be in the near future the opportunity for a new volume of collected papers written by younger contemporary Independent analysts.

This is a *new* book and should not be considered a re-presentation, nor is it an updated edition of the original 1986 publication. From the beginning of this project, my wish and intention were to make a personal selection of the 1986 original papers, following somewhat idiosyncratic criteria: a subjective appreciation of their theoretical and clinical value for my present way of thinking psychoanalytically. In making such choices, I was aware of excluding very important papers, not unlike the editing process at the time of the 1986 edition. Then, I did not include papers by Marjorie Brierley, Edward Glover, John Bowlby, John Rickman, Ronald Fairbairn, Ella Freeman Sharpe, Sylvia M. Payne, and, of course, many others. Looking back, I especially regret the exclusion, besides Paula Heimann, Pearl King and Marion Milner, of Marjorie Brierley's work on affects (1937), Sylvia Payne's comments on technique (1943), and Ella Sharpe's contributions (1958). This is somewhat restored, if not fully rectified, by Steven Groarke's references to their work in his chapter in this volume (pp. 133–147 herein).

Once the present choice of papers was made, my ideas about the book changed: I wanted to invite analysts from a younger generation to present *their own thoughts* about the papers selected. Instead of

5

elaborating on the importance of these papers for me, I became rather curious and more interested in discovering the possible impact, if any, that these writings from the past may have had on a small group of younger colleagues, who had trained and qualified at different times during the last thirty years.

When the 1986 edition was published, two unexpected comments were made to me by colleagues from the Independent Group: first, that it had taken a foreigner to come up with this idea, and, second, that my writing was not really representative of their group. The text of my Introduction and my Dora paper were both 'too *French*' – most definitely, some of them argued, *not* 'Independent'. I came to realize that there were good reasons for this comment, to which I will return.

The Society has always been very welcoming to overseas students and analysts. In fact, the group of students in training during my years as a candidate included, apart from Welsh, Scottish and English students, Greek, Chinese, Australian, Peruvian, South African, Chilean, New Zealander, Argentinian, North American, Mexican, Spanish, Italian, German, Swedish, Irish and French candidates – and a 21-year-old Brazilian trainee who was pregnant at the start of her training. In terms of the present average age of candidates, times have certainly changed.

I have always considered the British Psychoanalytical Society my psychoanalytic home, and, come rain or shine, it has always remained so. After returning from Australia in 1995, I was made a training analyst two years later; this was the only constitutional moment when a member was required to declare his/her allegiance to a group in the Society. I then became a member of the Independent Group of Training Analysts. However, in 2003, I resigned from it, which meant I no longer belonged to any group that was part of the Gentlemen's Agreement. Not belonging to a group is not the same as being 'non-aligned' (thus, neutral, impartial, uninvolved, unattached, uncommitted, sitting on the fence, etc.).

As stated in my Prefatory Remarks (pp. 21–24 herein), 'independent' can be understood as 'not depending upon the authority of another, not in a position of subordination or subjection; not subject to external control or rule; self-governing, autonomous, free' (*Oxford English Dictionary*). I believe that this remains a valid and reasonable description. Nevertheless, any individual, group or nation wishing to be independent has, tacitly or not, to acknowledge and take on board the need for others. In this sense, members of the Independent

6

tradition have never felt deterred from recognizing their indebtedness to authors from different theoretical traditions. Look at the bibliographies included in the writings by Independent authors during the last six decades.

In the 1986 edition, I referred to 'tradition' as implying, '. . . a certain continuity in time, a body of experience, principle and/or laws, a complex of customs and beliefs that are rooted in the past and that link a certain group of people (e.g., professionals, artists) across generations' (p. 21 herein).

Thirty years later, Steven Groarke, in his 'Making Sense Together: New Directions in Independent Clinical Thinking' (p. 133 herein), asserts the need to pay respect to the authority of the past, to become 'trustful guardians' of a well-regarded legacy. Paradoxically, this goes together with the crucial need to renew that legacy in the present: to develop, change and enhance what has been passed on from that past. This entails, in Groarke's description, becoming the inevitable 'oedipal usurpers'. Paying due respect to the past is not just a blind act of faith nor a meaningless and repetitive duplication of sterile and withered ideas; on the contrary, tradition can only be kept alive if exposed to 'the retrospective influence of new ideas'.

One might want to argue that only the weak and insecure fear artistic, literary or scientific traditions: we greatly benefit by responding to the challenge of making sense and further use of valued past experiences. To respect tradition, to accept being part of it, is not equivalent to being a political 'traditionalist', a right-winger, a reactionary, a conservative who resists change.

In a well-known essay, T.S. Eliot writes,

> In English writing we seldom speak of tradition, though we occasionally apply its name in deploring its absence. We cannot refer to 'the tradition' or to 'a tradition'; at most, we employ the adjective in saying that the poetry of So-and-so is 'traditional' or even 'too traditional.' Seldom, perhaps, does the word appear except in a phrase of censure. . . . You can hardly make the word agreeable to English ears . . .
>
> (Eliot, 1921, p. 1)

Poets may be praised or admired for those features of their work considered individual and original, that is, *not* traditional, the term implying a certain disapproval. In contrast, Eliot claims,

... if we approach a poet without this prejudice, we shall often find that not only the best, but the most individual parts of his work may be those in which the dead poets, his ancestors, assert their immortality most vigorously.

(Eliot, 1921, p. 2)

In considering the value and significance of tradition, Eliot argues that it is not a matter of mere sycophantic imitation, a passive repetition of what has already been achieved, a resistance to change. A legacy needs to be taken possession of, through hard work and challenging critical labour. This demands what Eliot calls a 'historical sense', involving a particular perception, 'not only of the pastness of the past, but also of its presence . . .'. For Eliot, tradition is not fixed and static: it is constantly changing, growing and becoming different from what it was. Tradition is affected *nachträglich* – although, most likely, Eliot did not know this concept: the past guides the present but this present also modifies the past; when a new and original poem is written, Eliot argues, it can actually change the concept and the view of the literary tradition to which the poem belongs.

In the case of the Independents, they are not united by sharing particular beliefs and analytic doctrines. I described them (p. 23 herein) as being comparable to '. . . a school of painters, by virtue of *a shared set of problems and sensibilities*' (Greenberg and Mitchell, 1983, italics added). There is nothing essential about the Independent tradition: people can and do widely disagree about certain issues. In his 'Psychic Life: A New Focus on Earliest Infancy' (pp. 75–87 herein), Josh Cohen describes, in a particularly insightful way, the subtle and yet important disagreements among Independent authors concerning the privilege of external reality over unconscious phantasy.

The attention centred on the influence of the early environment in the development of the individual was a specific result of the theory of object relations: it was argued that an individual was formed, from the very beginning, following the vicissitudes of the relationships with objects. This implied the mediation of some kind of self, or ego, present from very early on in life. Different authors developed similar notions resulting from the interest in the relationship between mother and baby. They attempted to describe particular characteristics found in the treatment of disturbed patients: premature ego development (James, 1960); cumulative trauma (Khan, p. 104 herein); basic unity (Little, 1960); true and false self (Winnicott, 1960b); basic fault (M. Balint, 1968). They all tried to account for 'something missing'

8

in the patient's life: it was seen not as a conflict to be resolved, or a trauma to be uncovered; it was a 'fault', something wrong in the mind, a kind of deficiency that must be put right (M. Balint, 1968).

Cohen brings to light the presence of *nachträglich* temporality in the three papers in this section – a temporality in which the earliest events in life are not given linear causal priority, something theoretically assumed by most Independent writers until very recently. This is just one instance of many theoretical and clinical differences of opinion within this one particular tradition; I could also mention a lack of consensus about the importance of the drives, or the frequency of the interpretations, or the emphasis given to reconstruction as opposed to the relevance of constructions in the here-and-now, or the clinical understanding and theoretical place of the oedipal conflict, or what is meant by 'intersubjectivity'. The variations and discrepancies between the members of the same Independent tradition may be as important as those between the different groups. In fact, this may well be an internal feature of other groups too.

There is nothing dogmatic about the ideas of Independent analysts, no specific truth that is passed on from one generation to the next. This may be seen, for example, in questions of clinical technique: referring to specific problems with patients in psychoanalysis, Michael Parsons writes, '. . . no technical prescriptions are possible'; the *how* to proceed will rest on '. . . an availability that depends on the inner silence of the analyst's listening' (2012, p. 84). This inner silence, I would add, is determined by the individual analyst's personal style. And there seem to be as many personal styles as psychoanalysts.

Whatever may have been Independent for one generation will not necessarily be so for the next. A legacy is there, but it is always open to being transformed into something new, for example, with regard to the vicissitudes of the concept of therapeutic regression through time, described by Hannah Browne in her 'Regression: Allowing the Future to be Re-imagined' (pp. 209–223 herein). The same could be said about the understanding of female sexuality, which was also historically transformed, as it can be observed in Megan Virtue's description in her chapter on the subject (pp. 263–274 herein).

At this point it is worth considering the question raised above, that of my writing being '*too French*'. I first published 'Reflections on Dora: The Case of Hysteria' (pp. 274–289 herein), in the *International Journal of Psychoanalysis* in 1984. It referred to a number of psychoanalytic authors from the French school as well as to the work of Oscar Masotta, who successfully introduced Jacques Lacan to intellectual and psychoanalytic audiences in Buenos Aires in the late 1960s. The main influence on my psychoanalytic education in Argentina was Kleinian, although, by the time I arrived in London in 1970, I was already acquainted with the works of Jacques Lacan and his French colleagues.

Lacan published his paper, 'Some Reflections on the Ego' in the *International Journal of Psychoanalysis* in 1953. Between 1953 and 1984, the same journal has a very limited number of references to the extensive number of papers and books published by Lacan – two of them by a British psychoanalyst, M. Masud R. Khan, who was particularly close to his French colleagues and knowledgeable about their writings (Khan, 1965, 1972a). There were significant introductions to Lacan's work in English: Anthony Wilden (1968), Anika Lemaire (1970), Maud Mannoni (1967), Stuart Schneiderman (1980), Cathérine Clément (1981), John Muller and William Richardson (1982), and Bice Benvenuto and Roger Kennedy (1986) all wrote important books on his work. A selection of Lacan's *Écrits* (1977) had been translated by Ann Sheridan. Two of the most important contributions to the understanding of Lacan's work were those by Juliet Mitchell: *Psychoanalysis and Feminism* (1974), published just before she became a candidate in training at the Institute of Psychoanalysis, and *Feminine Sexuality: Jacques Lacan and the école freudienne* (1982), edited with Jacqueline Rose, a few years after she qualified as a psychoanalyst.

The information about Lacan was 'out there', available to an English readership – but it had not permeated the psychoanalytic establishment. At the same time, there was a diversity of translations of the work of French psychoanalysts into English, including a remarkable volume edited by Serge Lebovici and Daniel Widlöcher, *Psychoanalysis in France* (1980), which included twenty-one chapters by different authors.

The ideas expressed in my 1984 paper, the Introduction written for the 1986 book and the bibliography included in those texts made evident the influence of Lacan and other French authors. Perhaps it is no surprise that they sounded 'too French' for some. Megan Virtue, in her 'The Centrality of Sexual Difference in Freud: the work of Juliet Mitchell and Gregorio Kohon' (pp. 263–273 herein), has accurately identified and described this influence in Juliet Mitchell's chapter as well as my own, both reprinted in this volume. In general terms, this was misunderstood and/or ignored by Independent colleagues, which only proved the point: the presence of the French influence made our ideas seem rather 'alien'. Mitchell has continued to develop her ideas in a number of publications (Mitchell, 2000, 2003, 2015); her latest work has been recently celebrated in *Juliet Mitchell and the Lateral Axis* (Duschinsky and Walker, 2015). For my part, I went on to publish further papers on sexuality, the latest addressing the question of bisexuality (Kohon, 1999b, 2005b, 2018).

Unsurprisingly, I heard similar comments concerning the French influence on my writings from colleagues fifteen years later, with the publication of *No Lost Certainties to Be Recovered* (1999b). It was always clear to me that there was no incompatibility between being an Independent analyst and my wish to reflect upon the French interpretations of Freud's theories on sexuality, transference and the like. In time, the mutual influence between two traditions has become evident in the work of British psychoanalysts like Dana Birksted-Breen, Roger Kennedy and, most notably, Michael Parsons, who has also become a member of the French Psychoanalytical Association (*APF*). In particular, this influence has been enriched during the last twenty-five years by the theoretical and clinical contributions of Rosine Jozef Perelberg. I am particularly grateful for her introductory chapter, 'A multi-dimensional frame of reference: The Independent tradition', in this volume (pp. 14–18 herein). Recently, I have written a paper on Green's concept of the negative, published in a book edited by Perelberg and Kohon, *The Greening of Psychoanalysis: André Green's New Paradigm in Contemporary Theory and Practice* (2017). Perelberg's book on bisexuality comprises a collection of papers by French and British authors (Perelberg, 2018).

There are new introductory chapters to the four different parts of the original book. The authors were invited to evaluate the new selection from the 1986 original papers and to reflect upon the relevance for each of them, *now* – no other instructions were given. The new texts have been written by psychoanalysts of a younger generation: Josh Cohen, Steven Groarke, Hannah Browne and Megan Virtue. Separately, they have each, in their individual contribution and in their own ways, identified links and similarities between the British analysts included in the 1986 edition, and the ideas and concepts developed by French psychoanalysts. Three of these colleagues identify themselves as belonging to the Independent tradition; a fourth is part of the Contemporary Freudian tradition. It is evident that the influence of French psychoanalysis on the British goes beyond one particular group. Perhaps, in the future, these correspondences, not yet fully recognized up to now, could and should be elaborated more fully. After all, the influence has been mutual and sustained over a considerable period of time.

In their General Introduction to *Reading French Psychoanalysis*, Dana Birksted-Breen and Sara Flanders included a section on the 'French–British reciprocal influences', where they referred to Lacan's reading of Melanie Klein's work, which he compared and contrasted with Anna Freud's contributions (Birksted-Breen and Flanders, 2010, p. 5). A series of discussions took place in 1994–95 between a number of prominent Kleinian and Lacanian psychoanalysts, brought together by Bernard Burgoyne and Mary Sullivan in a book, *The Klein–Lacan Dialogues* (1999). This was followed by *The New Klein–Lacan Dialogues*, this time edited by Julia Barossa, Catalina Bronstein and Claire Pajaczkowska (2015).

Birksted-Breen and Flanders also mentioned the connection between the work of Winnicott and the writings of André Green. In 1977, there was an issue of *Revue L'Arc No. 69*, a literary magazine published by Stéphane Cordier, dedicated to the work of Winnicott. It included articles by French authors (Bernard Pingaud, André Green, Octave Mannoni, J.-B. Pontalis, and Catherine Clément), British writers (Clare Winnicott, Marion Milner, M. Masud R. Khan, W. Clifford M. Scott, and Donald W. Winnicott himself), and Renata Gaddini, from Italy (Cordier, 1977). This was an early, important recognition of Winnicott's influence in France. In fact, Green's celebration and admiration of British psychoanalysis always included not just Winnicott, but also the contributions of Bion. The substantial and excellent review of current themes in French psychoanalysis, written by Rosine Perelberg for the *International Journal of Psychoanalysis* (2013), has delineated important connections between the two psychoanalytic cultures; she argues that 'The dialogue between French and British psychoanalysis is one of the most interesting in psychoanalysis today' (p. 616). Perelberg refers also to the Anglo-French dialogues organized by Anne-Marie Sandler and Haydée Faimberg, and the British–French ones, organized for the last two decades by Monique Cournut, Chantal Atlan, Danielle Kaswin and Rosine Perelberg.

In the newly written chapters included in the present book, a number of interconnections and mutual influences between the two cultures concern, for example, the notion of temporality and the concept of *Nachträglichkeit* (or *après-coup*); the unavailability of the infant psyche to direct inquiry; the concept of cumulative trauma; the importance of the Botellas' notion of psychic figurability and its connection to the idea of a trauma neither remembered nor experienced; the Independents' understanding of therapeutic regression; the function of silence and the importance of the process of free association; the fear of breakdown and the concept of absence; the unthought known and the lack of representation; different concepts concerning the theory of the psychosomatic; the work of the negative and a past that has never been lived; the complementary analytic perspectives of Laplanche and Winnicott; the inspiration taken by French analysts from Winnicott's ideas – and plenty more.

Looking back to the papers included in the 1986 edition, the dialogue between the two different traditions, the British and the French, was present in them – and yet 'unthought'. It has only become clear as an *après-coup* event, an appreciated and welcome discovery.

I hope that this book will help to promote that creative dialogue in the future.

2

A MULTI-DIMENSIONAL FRAME
OF REFERENCE
The Independent tradition
Rosine Jozef Perelberg

The British School of Psychoanalysis: The Independent Tradition, originally published three decades ago, has now become a classic. It contains key papers written by representatives of the Independent tradition of the British Psychoanalytical Society and is an important document in the history of the Society itself. The commentaries written by members of a younger generation of analysts that now introduce each section of the present book underline the continuity in time and the transmission of some of the key concepts of clinical and theoretical psychoanalysis elaborated by this tradition.

Gregorio Kohon defines the British School of Psychoanalysis as comprising analysts belonging to the British Psychoanalytical Society, within which three traditions have emerged and have been fostered: the Kleinians, the B Group (now designated as Contemporary Freudians), and the Middle Group, now called Independents. The Independents were native to this island prior to the arrival of both Melanie Klein and, later, Sigmund and Anna Freud and their Viennese colleagues. Britain was thus in a most privileged position by having given a home to these different traditions that have made unique contributions to the development of psychoanalysis, both in Britain and internationally. Kohon demonstrates in this Introduction that he is one of the few analysts in the British Psychoanalytical Society

14

capable of moving between these different schools and combine a solid grounding in Freudian metapsychology with the pillars of the Independent and other traditions, while at the same time pushing psychoanalytic thinking forward.

Historical and conceptual dimensions

The question of lay analysis was central from the early days of psychoanalysis onwards. Jones, Glover and Rickman supported it, leading the difficult negotiations with the British Medical Association. Although Jones himself was ambivalent about the need for medical training prior to psychoanalytic training, there was always a high proportion of lay analysts in the British Psychoanalytical Society – Melanie Klein, Anna Freud and Ella Sharpe, among many others. It is a commitment that the Society continues to uphold and one that has enabled the training of individuals coming from disciplines as diverse as anthropology, literature and philosophy, as well as from psychology. It is a rare commitment, as few societies in the international sphere have been able to take this step, which was strongly supported by the very founder of the discipline.

In his Introduction, Kohon underlines the relevance of the Controversial Discussions of 1943–44. He indicates the different notions of time that were present in the controversies: that of genetic continuity in Klein, in contrast to Freud's *Nachträglichkeit*, which emphasizes the notion that the history of an individual cannot be understood as being the result of a linear, deterministic development in which the past explains the present. These various notions illuminate the profound difference between the Oedipus complex as conceived by Sigmund Freud and by Melanie Klein. It is not only that Klein dated the Oedipus complex much earlier: for her, the relationship with the mother and the separation from the breast is primary and determines all future relationships. For Freud, it is castration that structures the differences between the sexes and the generations in the Oedipus complex and retrospectively illuminates the relationship with the pre-oedipal mother. There are fundamental structural differences in the conceptualizations of these two authors, which Kohon discusses and summarizes with great clarity; later, he would develop this further (Kohon, 1999b and 2005b; see his chapter and that of Juliet Mitchell in this volume; also Mitchell, 1986; and Perelberg, 2006).

15

It is worth pointing out that during the so-called Freud–Klein controversies Anna Freud left the discussions very early on, so that the antagonistic tone was carried on primarily in the exchanges between Edward Glover and Melitta Schmideberg on the one hand, and Melanie Klein on the other. Perhaps the battles were waged not only between Anna Freud and Klein, as is often suggested: the Independents themselves participated fiercely and made crucial contributions.

Kohon describes the various agreements reached at the political and administrative level in the British Psychoanalytical Society after the Gentlemen's Agreement, which continued to function until 2006 – that is, until two decades after this book was first published. In 2006, following discussions in Informal Joint Meetings in 2004 and 2005, the membership of the Society voted for the dissolution of the Gentlemen's Agreement. Equal representation of the three groups in the administrative sphere was no longer a rule, although a level of representation of each tradition continued to be present on the key Education Committees and subcommittees. Questions about *how plurality is going to be protected have emerged, and are currently being discussed in the Society.*

Countertransference and the role of absence in the analytic encounter

An important tenet of the Independent tradition is the requirement for the analyst to be attuned to the patient's *emotional response* and the need to monitor the impact this has on the analyst's counter-transference. Kohon warns against an overextension of the concept of projective identification and its current centrality in certain schools of thought. He suggests that Sandler, Holder, Kawenoka, Kennedy, and Neurath's (1969) description of transference as a 'multi-dimensional phenomenon' is equally applicable to counter-transference (p. 55 herein).

If, on the one hand, Limentani declares that 'any affect or feeling state exhibited by the analysand will have the analyst as the object' (p. 190 herein), Kohon, on the other, states that 'the belief that whatever happens in the psychoanalytic process is a result of some-thing emanating from the patient, which is then projected into the analyst, has contributed to the creation of a distinctively stagnant psychoanalytic product: the "you-mean-me" interpretations (Coltart, personal communication, 1977)' (p. 68 herein).

Kohon's discussion of the much-quoted paper by Strachey (1934) on the role of the analyst as an 'auxiliary superego' is lucid and inspiring. Kohon suggests that the idea of the analyst as a good object contributes to the idealization of the analyst. Kohon takes Enid Balint's notion of the analyst being just there (1968), together with Winnicott's formulation of the transitional object (1951) and proposes that, '. . . the analyst occupies that transitional space where the objects are not quite internal nor are they quite external. Like the transitional object, the analyst is and is not. This paradoxical quality of being and not being does not take away any reality from the psychoanalytic encounter' (p. 57 herein).

Kohon continues with the formulation that the analyst does not offer anything necessarily good or bad to the patient, but a *'progressive absence'* (a term taken from Pontalis, 1977), having as model the idea of the mother's progressive constitution as absence. The work of the transference makes the analyst excessively present. Kohon's thinking is in tune with Freud's concept that hallucinatory wish-fulfilment takes place in the absence of the mother. It is when she goes away that the baby can hallucinate the breast. These formulations are evocative of contemporary reflections on the (positive) work of the negative in the structuring of mental life, and the relevance of processes of mourning in an analysis. Green's notion of the framing structure and the negative hallucination of the mother is relevant here (Green, 1986; Perelberg, 2016). Most significantly, Green, according to his own declarations, found his inspiration in the work of both Bion and Winnicott.

Kohon is a psychoanalyst, a writer and a poet; his use of metaphors is powerful and evocative. He speaks of the 'monster of transference'; the silence of the analyst is what will 'give birth to that which needs to be named' (p. 60 herein). Our 'interpretations are like the swings, the slide, the climbing frame, the sandpit in the playground . . . in which analysand and analyst are playing . . . interpretations are formed by real words but they constitute imaginary stories' (p. 64 herein). 'All psychoanalytic theories, like the hysteric, suffer from reminiscences' (p. 71 herein). One could carry on . . .

These metaphors are ways of addressing what, by definition, is beyond words: they are the very expression of the mobility of the psyche. Freud himself consistently reminded us that the unconscious is not in the domain of the observable; it is reached only indirectly, through its derivatives in consciousness. Psychoanalysis takes place between domains, between the psychic and the somatic, between dreams and pain, to use Pontalis's felicitous expression (1977), between the capacity to represent and to enact, between the theory of the discipline and the unconscious phantasies of both patients and analysts. Kohon believes that psychoanalysis, as 'a literature of excess' (p. 71 herein), exceeds any attempt at systematization and classification, perhaps because of the imperious force of the unconscious that is always searching for new ways of expressing itself.

Kohon's Introduction to this book continues to be a testimony to the passion and inspiration of the writer.

18

PART II

INTRODUCTION

---------------------------------- 3 ----------------------------------

PREFATORY REMARKS

Gregorio Kohon

The British School of Psychoanalysis comprises all the psychoanalysts belonging to the British Psychoanalytical Society. Within this Society there are three groups, each with its own characteristics: the Kleinian group; the 'B' group (followers of Anna Freud); and the Independent group. The Independent British analysts include many eminent names: Edward Glover, James Strachey, Ernest Jones, Margaret Little, Donald Winnicott, Michael Balint, Paula Heimann, Ella Sharpe, Sylvia Payne, John Rickman, Ronald Fairbairn, Alix Strachey, James Glover, Barbara Low, Marjorie Brierley, Marion Milner, Charles Rycroft, Masud Khan. Most of these analysts were greatly influenced by both Melanie Klein and Anna Freud (in fact Heimann, Winnicott and Rickman were, at one point, regarded as followers of Melanie Klein). The same influence could be traced and described for most of the authors included in the present book.

'Independent', according to one of the definitions offered by *The Oxford English Dictionary*, means 'not depending upon the authority of another, not in a position of subordination or subjection; not subject to external control or rule; self-governing, autonomous, free.' 'Tradition', on the other hand, implies a dependency, a certain continuity in time, a body of experience, principles and/or laws, a complex of customs and beliefs that are rooted in the past and that link a certain group of people (e.g., professionals, artists) across generations. The contradiction between a true need for independence of thought and a fervent wish to respect the main teachings of Freud was at the very heart of the project carried out by the pioneers of the psychoanalytic movement in Great Britain.

The Independent British analysts created and developed the theory of object relations, a term that has now been overused. It denotes so many different theories, it includes so many varied authors, that it has become meaningless for some (see Greenberg and Mitchell, 1983). This is not my opinion. In the context of this book, the term 'object relations' designates 'the subject's mode of relation to his world; this relation is the entire complex outcome of a particular organization of the personality, of an apprehension of objects that is to some extent or other phantasied, and of a certain special type of defence' (Laplanche and Pontalis, 1967). It implies a way of relating that is considered as an interrelationship: the individual affects his objects as much as his objects affect him.

The term 'theory of object relations' is used here in a strict sense, as the theory developed by the authors mentioned above, and those included in this book. The theory concerns itself with the relation of the subject to his objects, *not* simply with the relationship between the subject and the object, which is an interpersonal relationship. This subtle (but complex) and fundamental differentiation has caused much confusion, sometimes even within the British psychoanalytic movement. It is not only the real relationship with others that determines the subject's individual life, but the specific way in which the subject apprehends his relationships with his objects (both internal and external). It always implies an unconscious relationship to these objects.

Object Relations writers concentrated their attention on the internal world of the subject, exploring further what Freud had initiated. It was a logical consequence of the increased interest in the issue of transference. But the development of the theory of object relations entailed a certain revision of Freud's theory of the instincts. This development was prompted by the difficulties encountered by analysts in the treatment of severely disturbed patients. All object relations theoreticians have been 'deeply rooted in clinical work' (Sutherland, 1980); their theory emerged from clinical practice, partly characterized by a strong refusal to adhere to a rigid method of treatment.

Sandor Ferenczi was perhaps the first analyst to acknowledge and recognize the importance of object relations, in the analysis of regressed patients and in the observation that the deepest analyses included regression to primitive object relations. He characterized the earliest relationship with the environment as a relationship to a 'passive object love', the wish to be totally loved by this object (embodied by the mother's breast). As the leader of the psychoanalytic movement in Hungary, he analysed Ernest Jones, Melanie Klein, and Michael Balint, all of whom later had great influence in England. Ferenczi's concept of 'early maternal deprivation', and his notion that object relations exist even in the deepest layers of the mind, were the theoretical background that allowed the ideas of Melanie Klein, Michael Balint, Ronald Fairbairn, Donald Winnicott, and others to develop. These authors concentrated their attention on the early development of the infant, rejecting the idea of an infant who does not relate to his objects from the very beginning. Michael Balint, for example, suggested that the physical and mental development of the child depended on the existence of object relations, the intense, complex libidinal involvement with the environment. When Michael and Alice Balint moved to England in 1939, they found that the ideas developed in London had progressed along similar lines.

Fairbairn, some of whose most important contributions date from the first half of the 1940s, gave great impetus to the theory of object relations. In his account of 'the origins and growth of object love', Fairbairn conceived the development of the personality as based on the actual experiences with objects from the very start of life. Fairbairn's underestimated contributions to British psychoanalysis could be summarized as follows: the instincts are not pleasure-seeking but object-seeking; the pleasure involved in object relations has a selective and formative function, it is not the primary aim of activity; since there are object relations from the beginning of life, this presupposes the existence of an early ego, or self; aggression is understood as a reaction to frustration in reality; the original anxiety is related to issues concerning the separation from the first, maternal object (see Sutherland, 1980). Most British analysts share these views.

The British object relations authors have been accurately characterized: '[They] do not constitute a "school" by virtue of subscribing to a set of shared beliefs but, like a school of painters, by virtue of a shared set of problems and sensibilities' (Greenberg and Mitchell, 1983). A common sensibility, a shared attitude or approach to similar clinical problems, do indeed distinguish the psychoanalysts of the British School of Object Relations beyond sometimes very serious theoretical differences.

This Introduction is not intended as a complete history of the psychoanalytical movement in Britain, nor is its aim to present a polished version of the theory of object relations, nor even to systematize the body of contributions from the Independent analysts. It offers an overview of some of the clinical and theoretical areas of interest, often derived from the work of Balint and Winnicott, of some of the contemporary analysts belonging to the Independent group.

First I consider the history of psychoanalysis in Britain, and focus my attention on three factors which have contributed to the distinctive characteristics of British psychoanalysis. These are: the acceptance of lay analysis; the development of the psychoanalysis of children; and the interaction with a specific cultural milieu.

These three factors grew out of particular historical contradictions. First, the acceptance, the protection, and the encouragement of lay analysts coexisted, and yet contrasted with a suspicious, distrustful attitude towards non-medical practitioners. Second, the flourishing of important schools of child analysis, which revolutionized attitudes and policies in British society, occurred in a culture that was characterized (at least, in its middle and upper classes) by a distinct distance between parents and their children. Finally, psychoanalysis developed in the context of a society where individuals were not supposed to ask for psychological help, psychotherapy was looked upon as an unnecessary indulgence, and psychoanalysis more or less ignored by the academic and professional institutions; nevertheless, the tolerance shown by that same society made the growth of the psychoanalytic movement possible.

Second, I concentrate on countertransference, an issue that has occupied British analysts from early on. The contributions to this subject made by Independent analysts are of singular importance; many other theoretical, clinical and technical issues crystallize around this particular notion.

I am expressing my own views, both in this Introduction and in the selection of papers. This book is not necessarily representative of the opinion and ideas of all Independent analysts; many will positively disagree with them. This is in the spirit of the Independent tradition.

4

NOTES ON THE HISTORY OF
THE PSYCHOANALYTIC
MOVEMENT IN GREAT BRITAIN
Gregorio Kohon

The beginnings

The history of the British Society is a history of failed beginnings, a history of individual and institutional crises, and of a successful struggle for survival through hard and complex times.

It is difficult to imagine that Freud would have accepted an invitation to emigrate to any other country but England. It was no easy task to convince him of the need to emigrate, in spite of the evident proofs at hand (A. Freud, 1979). In March 1938 German troops occupied Austria and Hitler entered Vienna. Freud's works had already been 'consigned to the flames', and the stock of books at the International Psycho-Analytical Press in Leipzig confiscated and destroyed. The entries in Freud's abbreviated diary for March 1938 read as follows: 'Sun 13/3 Anschluss with Germany – Mon 14/3 Hitler in Vienna – Tues 15/3 Inspection (by the Gestapo) of printing press and house – Wed 16/3 Jones (Ernest) – Thurs 17/3 Princess (Marie Bonaparte) – Tues 22/3 Anna with Gestapo' (E. Freud et al., 1978). Freud wished to remain in 'his Vienna', at 'his post', but he also wanted to protect Anna. Ernest Jones finally won the argument by telling him the story of the second officer of the *Titanic* who, when asked why he had left his ship, answered: 'I never left my ship – the ship left me' (Jones, 1957). From another point of view, Freud had

25

reasons to feel ambivalent towards England, and especially the psycho-analytic movement in London. As early as 1921, he had expressed strong criticisms of Jones as editor of the *International Journal of Psycho-Analysis*. This was followed by severe judgements about what he believed to be Jones's involvement with Joan Riviere (when she had been Jones's patient). Finally, Freud had been very annoyed at the British Society's positive reception of Melanie Klein and her ideas, while, at the same time, he was offended by the critical and personal attacks on his daughter (Brome, 1982; Steiner, 1985).

On the other hand, Freud had a very special regard for Britain from very early on in his life. He had visited close relatives in Manchester as a young man of 19, and had returned to England to discover London in 1908. Oliver Cromwell, William Shakespeare, and Charles Darwin always formed – for different reasons – part of his collection of highly admired figures. In 1880, he had translated what became the last (12th) volume of John Stuart Mill's collected works into German.

Right from the beginning, the publication of Freud's work in Britain produced a limited response. Frederic W.H. Myers gave an account of the 'Preliminary Communication' (Freud, 1893a) as early as three months after its publication. Michell Clarke praised the *Studies on Hysteria* (Freud, 1895d) in the well-known neurological journal *Brain* the year following its publication in German. (In fact, Freud had published a paper in *Brain* in 1884, originally written in English, 'A New Histological Method for the Study of Nerve-Tracts in Brain and Spinal Cords'.) *Brain* later published 'Freud's Conception of Hysteria', a paper by Bernard Hart, a psychiatrist working in an ado-lescent unit, who was to participate in the foundation of the first psychoanalytic society. Hart's bibliography is truly impressive, with references to papers by Freud, Abraham, Ferenczi, Jones, Jung, Stekel, and many other authors less well-known to us today (Hart, 1911).

Myers, Michell Clarke, Havelock Ellis, and Wilfred Trotter are the first names associated with the origins of the psychoanalytic movement in the British Isles (Jones, 1959). It was Trotter, a surgeon with strong views against the medical establishment and a close friend of Ernest Jones, who first mentioned the *Studies* to Jones. Together, the two friends studied the psychological works of William James, Frederic Myers and Milne Bramwell, as well as the French medical psycholo-gists, including Pierre Janet. Although at first impressed by Clarke's review, it was reading the 'Dora' case in the *Monatsschrift für Psychiatrie und Neurologie* that made a real impact on Jones. From then on, the history of psychoanalysis in England is completely entangled with the personal and professional history of Ernest Jones.

Jones met Freud for the first time in 1908, at the First Psycho-Analytical Congress in Salzburg. Jones presented a short paper, 'Rationalization in Everyday Life', in which he introduced the term 'rationalization' (Jones, 1908). Freud presented the case of the 'Rat Man', and in the history of the case, published the following year, Freud refers to Jones's concept, a 'typical occurrence in obsessional neuroses' (Freud, 1909d). The concept caught on and remained a very important one in common psychoanalytic usage.

'England seems definitely to be stirring,' Freud writes to Jung in a letter of 3 March 1911. 'In the next few days I am expecting our most exotic supporter, Lt.-Col. Sutherland from Suagor in India, who means to spend two days here on his way to London' (in McGuire, 1974, p. 400). W.D. Sutherland, a medical officer, was to participate two years later in the foundation of the first psychoanalytic society. Ernest Jones had meanwhile spent four years in Canada, where he had gone after troublesome times in London (for an account of this difficult period in Jones's life, see Brome, 1982; Jones, 1959). On his return to Europe in 1913, Jones spent some time in Budapest, where he had the opportunity to be briefly analysed by Sandor Ferenczi. The analysis took place twice a day, and lasted for two months. This was probably the first 'didactic analysis' (Gillespie, 1979), an analysis recommended by Freud to Jones specifically for training purposes. On his return to London Jones founded the London Psycho-Analytical Society, on 30 October 1913. It had fifteen initial members, only four of them practising psychoanalysis.[1]

The first organized psychoanalytic group survived for less than six years. David Eder, a disciple and former pupil of Ernest Jones, had presented the first case of a neurotic patient treated by psychoanalysis to the British public in 1911. Six years later he published a book called *War Shock – The Psycho-Neuroses in War Psychology and Treatment*. But, according to Jones, Eder was unable to understand and accept the differences, by then well established, between Freud's and Jung's theories. He made life difficult for Jones because he wanted to accept members into the society who had clear Jungian sympathies. After dissolving the London Society, Jones immediately proceeded to form a new British Psychoanalytical Society, on 20 February 1919. The group of founding members included Douglas Bryan, H. Devine, Barbara Low, Stanford Read, Eric Hiller, D. Forsyth, Robert M. Rigall, W.H.B. Stoddart, and J.C. Flügel.[2] In the next few years, the Society added to its membership people of the calibre of Joan Riviere, James and Edward Glover, Susan Isaacs, John Rickman, Sylvia Payne, James and Alix Strachey, Ella Sharpe; and David Eder who, after being analysed by Ferenczi, had returned to London to pursue a successful analytic career in the new Society.

From the day of its creation, the life of the Society developed very quickly indeed. Papers on diverse topics were presented at its Scientific Meetings, some of them predicting the subsequent interest particular to British analysts: 'The Psychology of the New-born Infant' by Forsyth was, according to the 'Minutes', the first paper discussed (15 May 1919). This was followed by 'Note-taking and Reporting of Psycho-Analytic cases', presented by Barbara Low, emphasizing the British preoccupation with the immediacy of the clinical situation (12 June 1919). The organization and publication of the *International Journal of Psycho-Analysis* (1920); the founding of the *British Journal of Medical Psychology* (through the influence of analysts participating in the British Psychological Society, in 1920); the creation of the International Psycho-Analytical Library (1921), and the association with Hogarth Press (1924); the foundation of the Institute of Psycho-Analysis (1924); the setting up of the London Clinic of Psycho-Analysis (1926); the organization of the Eleventh International Psycho-Analytical Congress in Oxford (1929), were all projects accomplished during the first ten years of the Society's life. It was a remarkable achievement.

This flourishing of psychoanalysis went hand-in-hand with a growing opposition. In Britain, as in many other countries, the new psychoanalytic science was strongly opposed by the general public, the Church, the medical and psychiatric establishment, and the press. Jones, in particular, spent a great deal of time trying to defend psychoanalysis against ignorant protests and unjust attacks. In a letter to Freud, he writes: 'The imbecility of discussing technical matters with ill-informed pseudo professors of psychology is too self-evident from their own wild ramblings about psychoanalysis' (quoted in Brome, 1982). Freud knew about the futility of such an attempt. Jones was now discovering the same from his own experience: 'a bunch of psychologically illiterate nincompoops', he says of his audience. Given the wild accusations that were developing against psychoanalysis and the public concern as expressed in the popular press, a Special Committee was appointed by the British Medical Association at the Annual Representative Meeting that took place in Nottingham in 1926. The Committee's purpose was 'to investigate the subject of Psycho-Analysis and report on the same'. The Committee met from March 1927 to May 1929, and included among its members H. Godwin Baynes, representing the 'Jungian School of Analytical Psychology', and Ernest Jones, representing the 'Freudian School of Psycho-Analysis'. Among others, J.C. Flügel and Edward Glover gave evidence to the Committee during its proceedings.

The professional opposition was as ignorant and 'psychologically illiterate' as the public opposition. The 'Minutes of the Psycho-Analytic Committee of the British Medical Association', a copy of which is kept in the Archives of the Institute of Psycho-Analysis, show with great clarity how confused and frightened Jones's colleagues were. The 'Minutes' in the Archives also include some letters exchanged between Jones and other members of the Committee. They make fascinating reading, and one gains a dramatic picture of what Jones had to deal with. When, towards the end of their meetings, the first drafts of the future report were under consideration, Jones wrote to Hawthorne, a physician colleague: 'I was rather in despair when I heard paeans of praise for a Report which to my mind was pretentious, tendentious and muddleheaded.' It would be better, he added, if the Committee 'refrains from adopting lofty attitudes' towards psychoanalysts (Letter, 7 February 1929). Jones must have felt quite desperate, but his chances of promoting a favourable report were improved by the Committee's decision to form a Sub-Committee of three members (including Jones) to prepare a final draft (Jones, 1957).

In its final 'Report' (published by the *British Medical Journal* in June 1929), the Committee declared that the investigation 'has enabled the Committee to get a clearer view of what psychoanalysis actually is, i.e., the technique and theory elaborated by Freud and his co-workers, and to approach some definition of the respects in which it differs from other methods of psychotherapy'. These other methods ought to be investigated as well, said the report, although at this particular time the Committee had contented itself with indicating their existence as different from the psychoanalytic method. In their Conclusions, the members of the Committee decided to respect 'the claims of Freud and his followers to the use and definition of the term' psychoanalysis, as applied to the theory (and the technique based upon it) devised by Freud, who was recognized as having been the first to use the term. The Committee also decided that 'psychoanalysis should not be held responsible for the opinions or actions of those who are not in the proper sense psychoanalysts'.

The disagreements among the members of the Committee were very extreme. A reference is included in their Conclusions about some members who 'do not even go as far as' accepting the existence of the unconscious as a reasonable hypothesis – even if it were called by a different name. The Committee, finally, declared itself to be incompetent to make a pronouncement on the criticisms of the theory and method of psychoanalysis, and to pass judgement on E. Jones's answer to their criticisms. The last paragraph reads: 'VI. From the nature of the case the Committee has had no opportunity of testing psychoanalysis as a therapeutic method. It is therefore not in a position to express any collective opinion either in favour of the practice or in opposition to it. The claims of the advocates and the criticisms of those who oppose it must, as in other disputed issues, be tested by time, and by discussion.'

The references in the literature concerning this report have mostly (the exception is Brome, 1982) held the view that it had drawn positive conclusions about psychoanalysis. Jones calls it 'satisfactory', and claims that it has been called 'the PsychoAnalytic Charter' (Jones, 1957); Gillespie speaks of it as the 'Magna Carta of psychoanalysis in Britain' (Gillespie, 1963); Pearl King sustains the view that it had given psychoanalysis its 'certificate of respectability' (King, 1979, 1981). The report produced very favourable *consequences* for the development of the psychoanalytic movement and for the establishment of a psychoanalytic community, but not for the reasons usually assumed. The report refused to approve, even appreciate, the claims sustained by psychoanalysis. Although it declared no opposition, it did not give psychoanalysis any credit. The Committee had declared itself ignorant to judge. It was only from this neutral point of view that its members recognized psychoanalysis as an independent science, outside their competence and their expertise. It was accepted as a method of treatment for the neuroses based on the discoveries of Freud about the unconscious. They agreed that the followers of Freud could use the term 'psychoanalysis' but this did not imply an acceptance of it. In any case, why should the acceptance of psychoanalysis as an independent discipline have been that important?

Jones acknowledged that the recognition of the British Medical Association could not make any special impression on Freud *because* it had been made by medical doctors (Jones, 1957).

The question of lay analysis

The question of whether psychoanalysis was creditable or not in the eyes of the medical establishment was interlocked with the question of lay analysis. I will extend myself on this particular question because I believe that it illustrates the conflict between an independent mind and the weight of tradition, leaving aside the rights and wrongs of both sides of the debate. Jones, then president of the British Society, was at the same time deeply involved in the work of the International Psychoanalytical Association. Freud had very recently published *The Question of Lay Analysis* (Freud, 1926e), whose sub-title, *Conversations with an Impartial Person,* referred to somebody who, in reality, could not finally be convinced. His work brought to the fore a serious difference of opinion that existed within the international psycho-analytic community, and that threatened to split up the international movement.

Given the importance of the issue, the British Society decided to appoint a Sub-Committee on Lay Analysis, on 2 February 1927. An 'Abbreviated Report', dated 26 May of the same year, was published (Jones *et al.*, 1927). The report ends on the following cautious note: '. . . *the British Psycho-Analytical Society is practically unanimously of the opinion that most analysts should be medical but that a proportion of lay analysts should be freely admitted provided that certain conditions are fulfilled'* (authors' italics). During that time, the American analysts, being very concerned with the proliferation of 'quacks', had managed to win State's approval in their fight against the lay analysts; in 1926 a law was passed in New York making the practice of psychoanalysis by lay practitioners illegal.[3] The question was going to be debated at the Innsbruck Congress and in preparation for it, a series of articles were pre-published in the *International Journal of Psycho-Analysis* (Jones, 1927a). Those articles reveal the intensity of the feelings aroused by the question under discussion, and the profound disagreements between the different authors. Clearly, the problem extended beyond the question of lay analysis to *what was psychoanalysis all about?*

There is a remarkable opposition to Freud's view, reminiscent of the opposition to psychoanalysis in general. Brill speaks scornfully of the 'master', only to show great pleasure in rejecting (for once) 'his brilliant expositions'. Another analyst from New York, Oberndorf, compares Freud's endorsement of lay analysis – at that point in time – to a doctor who had made a premature, unnecessary diagnosis (in other words, to a 'quack'). Among Freud's supporters, Hanns Sachs concentrated his attention on the difference between *analysis for therapeutic purposes* and *analysis for the purpose of training*. The papers presented by the British analysts, Jones, Glover and Rickman, are by far the most elaborate considerations of the subject (Jones, 1927a). It is useful to consider Ernest Jones's paper in some detail.

Jones speaks of the British Society being 'the most friendly towards lay analysis', its membership consisting of 40 per cent non-medical people, several of them being of 'first rank'. Nevertheless, after this opening, Jones comes down very much on the side of analysts being required to be qualified as medical doctors. When speaking of the need for some kinds of procedure to eliminate the 'less satisfactory types' of individuals, Jones states: 'It is in connection with *this essential process of preliminary selection* that the question urgently arises of the attitude to be adopted towards the would-be lay analyst' (my italics).

Why, indeed, this should be the case, he does not explain, except that his statement contains a belief in a preliminary selection done by a medical school, to which the aspiring lay analyst would not be subject. Furthermore, Jones sustains the view that psychoanalysis has the 'nearest and most promising point of contact' with medicine, more so than any other branch of science; most patients in need of help came through referrals made by medical practitioners. Medicine would be, according to Jones, the best 'education' against the temptations of the 'rarefaction of the mind into intellectualization, either through religion or philosophical methods'. After making a distinction between the *prescription* of treatment and the actual *carrying out* of treatment, he concludes that '. . . whether a lay person carries out an analysis or not, he should in no case prescribe it, i.e., he should not engage in practice independently of the medical profession'. This rule, Jones says, should be *'an absolute one'* (my italics). A physician should decide on the suitability of patients and their need for treatment at the hands of lay analysts. In Jones's understanding, this was assumed to be a strict rule in the British Society. Among his papers, held at the Institute of Psycho-Analysis in London, is a copy of the following letter sent to lay members on 29 November 1929, signed by Jones and Edward Glover:

> The closer knitting of the relationship between medical and lay analysts in the reorganization of the Institute would seem a suitable occasion to clear up some misunderstandings which evidently exist in the minds of some of the latter in regard to the professional obligations they have undertaken. While on their side medical

analysts have undertaken to cover legally and to support in every way the therapeutic practice of their lay colleagues, the latter have equally undertaken *to refrain from independent practice*. This means that if a prospective patient wishes to consult them, to obtain their opinion, diagnosis, etc., *they explain to such a patient that they are not engaged in independent practice, have no intention of usurping the duties of the medical profession, and cannot see any such patient till he has first consulted a physician*. To get such a patient formally inspected by a physician after holding a consultation with him is contrary to the whole spirit of the undertaking. This principle, that *consultation and diagnosis are the province of the physician only, which he cannot share with anyone else,* a principle incorporated into the laws of every country, is accepted so completely by every medical analyst that we wish to convey our sense of its importance so as to leave no opening for possible misunderstandings in respect of it. (my italics)

This angry, unfriendly letter was sent to colleagues who were not medically qualified, only six months after the excruciating and painful negotiations with the British Medical Association had ended. The pressure on Jones must have been very great, and his wish to keep psychoanalysis free from any risk of being slandered might have been one of the motives for this letter.[4]

In his 'Discussion on Lay Analysis' Jones expresses the opinion that 'it is desirable that most analysts be medically qualified, but there is no good reason why selected lay persons should not conduct analyses under certain definite conditions' (Jones, 1927a). One should notice again that he speaks of selection for lay analysts, not for medical people. He goes on to state, against Freud's opinion and wishes, that psychoanalysis should be considered a special branch of medicine, not an independent profession. Jones also supported the idea that a medical education should be recommended to any non-medical candidates, and he hoped that the International Association would make this an official rule. Should this advice prove to be inexpedient (impossible, for example, for financial reasons), then a candidate could be exempted. In line with this opinion, Jones suggested to anyone who approached him for training that they take up medical studies: Karin and Adrian Stephen were two of those who followed his advice. James Strachey, on the other hand, lasted about one week in medical school. He then decided to forget Jones's advice, and wrote 'out of the blue' directly to Freud, who immediately invited him over to Vienna.

33

The future that Jones imagined for psychoanalysis is very relevant:

> The majority of analysts, however, would be, as now, medically qualified, so that direct continuity would exist between the psychological and physiological points of view. Psychoanalysis would be regarded as essentially a branch of clinical medicine. ... It would only be a question of time when psychiatrists also would make a regular practice of being trained in psychoanalysis, for I do not regard this expectation as in the least chimerical; the process is indeed already beginning. Once psychoanalysis had obtained a secure foothold in the more psychological departments of medicine, the rest would automatically follow: that is to say, the gradual penetration of psychoanalytical doctrine among the ranks of the profession, and the incorporation of truly psychological, i.e., psychoanalytical, points of view into general medical education. The naturalistic and biological outlook characteristic of both disciplines could only result in their reinforcing and supplementing each other to their mutual benefit.
>
> (Jones, 1927a)

Jones is well aware of Freud's position throughout his exposition. Jones insists that the medical qualification would protect the public. He claims that lay analysts have been spared the time, labour and money involved in medical training, and considers the suggestion made by some people that, because lay analysts have invested far less in training, they could afford to charge lower fees to their patients. Finally, he refers to lay analysts' 'disadvantages' and 'inferior position', which motivate them to look for compensatory behaviour (i.e., 'to have resort to artificial devices for maintaining self-respect').

Let us compare Freud's vision with that of Jones. Freud says to his imaginary interlocutor:

> Permit me to give the word 'quack' the meaning it ought to have instead of the legal one. According to the law, a quack is anyone who treats patients without possessing a state diploma to prove he is a doctor. I should prefer another definition: a quack is anyone who undertakes a treatment without possessing the knowledge and capacities necessary for it.
>
> (Freud, 1926e)

Not only was the situation very complicated then, as it is in many ways even more complex today, but one has to allow for differences in the social and cultural contexts between New York, Vienna, and London. Jones was concerned with the activities of the 'wild analysts', whose number – he believed – was greater in London than in any other place at the time. But this is not the whole story. There is a more fundamental disagreement between Freud and Jones. While the latter recommends that candidates obtain medical qualifications, the former states: '. . . in his medical school a doctor receives a training which is more or less the opposite of what he would need as a preparation for psychoanalysis.' And later on: 'It would be tolerable if medical education merely failed to give doctors any orientation in the field of the neuroses. But it does more: it gives them a false and detrimental attitude.' Freud's position is clear: '. . . I lay stress on the demand that *no-one should practise analysis who has not acquired the right to do so by a particular training*. Whether such a person is a doctor or not seems to me immaterial' (Freud's italics).

A year later, Freud is even less prepared to compromise. In his 'Postscript' (Freud, 1927a) to *The Question of Lay Analysis* he writes: 'I cannot see how it is possible to dispute this. Psychoanalysis is a part of psychology,' not a specialized branch of medicine. He continues angrily: '. . . I still feel some doubts as to whether the present wooing of psychoanalysis by the doctors is based, from the point of view of the libido theory, upon the first or upon the second of Abraham's sub-stages whether they wish to take possession of their object for the purpose of destroying or of preserving it.' Finally he adds his ironic, personal touch to the discussion:

> I became a doctor through being compelled to deviate from my original purpose; and the triumph of my life lies in my having, after a long and roundabout journey, found my way back to my earliest path. I have no knowledge of having had any craving in my early childhood to help suffering humanity. My innate sadistic disposition was not a very strong one, so that I had no need to develop this one of its derivatives.
>
> (Freud, 1927)

Jones was torn between his conviction on the need for medical training for future analysts and the convenience of the medical outlook, characterized as 'naturalistic and biological'; and Freud's ideas about the same issue, which he took seriously. More tellingly, Jones admired and respected the work of lay analysts of the stature of Melanie Klein, who had, in September 1926, started a successful treatment of Jones's children.

In those days, lay analysis was associated and confused with 'wild analysis' by the public and by the medical profession. In English, the word lay can mean *non-professional, not learned*, although Freud intended it to mean *non-doctor*. This connotation attracted a lot of prejudice and, in some quarters, it still does. The question was further complicated by the fact that lay analysis was also associated with child analysis, which in those days was considered 'easier' to do than to practise 'proper', adult psychoanalysis. Jones was indeed concerned with the possibility of jeopardizing the growth and development of psychoanalysis in Britain, and wanted to protect the new science as much as possible. It is likely that he genuinely believed he was doing so, by wanting to turn psychoanalysis into a medical specialty.[5]

It was hard to be a creative disciple and to remain faithful to the teacher. While Jones opposed Freud's ideas, he fulfilled his teacher's wishes of keeping the doors open to lay analysts in the British Society. He had committed himself to this when, in 1926, he wrote to Freud: 'The thing I think you have settled beyond all doubt is that it would be very injurious to our movement to forbid lay analysis. There will be lay analysts, and there must be because we need them' (Letter, 23 September 1926, quoted in Jones, 1957). Jones and his early colleagues rejected the easier option of satisfying the demands of the medical establishment and the general public. Whatever he might really have thought about lay analysis, he supported and protected his lay colleagues. The maintenance of a high proportion of lay analysts in the British Society has been one of the most consistent and courageous achievements on the part of the British psychoanalysts. It has also been one of the most important factors forming the specific character of British psychoanalysis, both within and outside the British Psychoanalytical Society. Twenty years later, the question seemed to be definitely settled. Ella Sharpe wrote, before her death:

> If psychoanalysis is a science that concerns the whole field of mental and emotional development then it follows that every psycho-analytically trained observer can be of value. Since all human problems are ultimately psycho-physical the science imperatively needs the services of the trained medical man. It needs the biologist, physiologist, neurologist. Equally it needs the chemist and the physicist. But likewise, the historian, the anthropologist, the sociologist, the educationalist, the trained observer of infants,

children, delinquents, all are indispensable for the building up of an unassailable body of truth concerning psychological development.

(Sharpe, 1947)

The psychoanalysis of children

Melanie Klein, who was then living in Budapest and being analysed by Ferenczi, read her first paper, 'The Development of the Child' to the Hungarian Society in 1919. In 1921 she moved to Berlin, entered into further analysis with Abraham, and read 'The Child's Resistance to Enlightenment' to the Berlin Psycho-Analytic Society. The papers, published as one in 1921 in the journal *Imago*, give an account of her treatment of a boy named Fritz. Later, Melanie Klein came to see this case as the start of her psychoanalytic play technique (Klein, 1921).

About the same time another school of thought concerning child analysis was emerging, developed independently by Anna Freud in Vienna. By the middle of the 1920s, it had become clear that the two leading figures of child analysis, Klein and Anna Freud, had taken different paths and opposed each other in more than one way. Melanie Klein thought of her play technique as a comparable replacement for the basic rule of free association in adult analysis. Anna Freud saw the interpretation of the play of a child as mere interpretation of symbols, similar to a purely symbolic dream interpretation, and therefore inadequate and unsatisfactory. The differences in technique were the logical consequence of fundamental disagreements in their theoretical beliefs. These covered, among other things, the dating of the Oedipus complex, the emergence of the ego and of the superego, the question of the possibility of transference neurosis in children, the role of early anxieties, and indications for treatment.

Melanie Klein worked in Berlin until 1926. During that time people like James and Edward Glover, Alix Strachey, Barbara Low, Mary Chadwick, Ella Sharpe and Sylvia Payne left London to have training analyses in Berlin. James and Edward Glover reported Klein's paper 'Early Analysis' (translated first as 'Infant Analysis', 1923) to the British Society. The first child analyst in England was Mary Chadwick, who started seeing children in therapy in 1922 (Glover, 1949). There were also other women analysts interested in child analysis in London, including Nina Searl (later to become a colleague of Klein's), and Sylvia Payne, who, although she was not seeing child patients, read a paper to the Society on child analysis. Alix Strachey – who was having her analysis with Abraham – sent a report from Berlin in 1924 on the treatment of children as developed by Melanie Klein. In July 1925 Melanie Klein, on her own initiative and suggestion, gave a series of six lectures to the members of the British Society. Soon afterwards, deprived by Karl Abraham's death of her main supporter in Berlin, Klein accepted Jones's invitation to move to London, where she quickly became involved in the scientific life of the Society. She stayed in London until her death in 1960, having become one of the most influential figures in the development of psychoanalytic theory.

Anna Freud published her book on child analysis in German in 1927 (A. Freud, 1929), and it was summarized by Barbara Low for the British Society. This was followed by a 'Symposium on Child Analysis' held on 4 and 18 May 1927 (Klein *et al.*, 1927). Melanie Klein opened the symposium with a detailed critique of Anna Freud's book, followed by presentations by Joan Riviere, Nina Searl, Ella Sharpe, Edward Glover and, finally, Ernest Jones. This provoked a true polarization between London and Vienna, as well as between London and Berlin. Freud immediately expressed his disagreements with Melanie Klein's position, and his annoyance at Jones's approval of it (Steiner, 1985). But whatever Freud thought about it, the fact remains that Melanie Klein had arrived at a terrain already fertile and receptive to her ideas. Pearl King rightly points out:

> Some of the points of view and theoretical formulations put forward by Ernest Jones, and which were generally accepted in the British Society, were parallel to some of those held by Melanie Klein. Among these were the importance of pregenital and innate determinants over and above the influence of external and environmental stress, and their vital role in determining beliefs and perceptions of reality; the role of hate and aggression and their relation to morbid anxiety and guilt; and the early development of female sexuality.
>
> (King, 1983, p. 252)

It was only natural that London became influenced by her teachings.

There was an initial period of harmonious honeymoon between Melanie Klein, her supporters, and the rest of the psychoanalysts of the British Society (King, 1983; Segal, 1979). The romance lasted until about 1935, when Klein presented her paper 'A Contribution

to the Psychogenesis of Manic-Depressive States', in which she introduced the concept of the depressive position (Klein, 1935). Some of
her followers claim that this marked the constitution of a Kleinian
school of psychoanalysis, as distinct from the British (or English)
school (Segal, 1979). At this time an exchange of lectures between
Vienna and London was arranged, aimed at producing a better understanding between the two psychoanalytic centres. Jones went to
Vienna in 1935, and Robert Waelder returned his visit. Joan Riviere
followed Jones in 1936. During this same period the opposition to
Melanie Klein's ideas within the British Society began to take shape,
and included people like Barbara Low, Edward Glover, Melitta
Schmideberg (Melanie Klein's daughter), Barbara Lantos, and Kate
Friedlander. These last three were among a group of analysts who
had emigrated because of the growing Nazi threat; by 1936, the
British Society had opened its doors to about 36 analysts from
Germany. (This generous reception was not, of course, exempt from
ambivalence. Many of them were merely seen as 'old-fashioned
Continental analysts' [Lantos, 1966].) The opposition to Klein was
further reinforced with the arrival of the Freud family and colleagues
from Vienna. Most of the parties in conflict now came together under
one roof, that of the British Psychoanalytical Society.

Members of the Society began to express their unease at the way
things were developing. There were two main manifest sources of
discontent: in the first place, the atmosphere of the Scientific Meetings
was made 'increasingly unpleasant' by the disagreements between the
different parties (King, 1979); the conflicts created a house divided
against itself. At the same time, the 'monarchical' (Strachey, 1963b),
undemocratic management of the institution, concentrating power
in the hands of a few, created the second source of unrest. Although
the Society was clearly going through a period of *Sturm und Drang*,
it had by then developed enough for the rules to be changed. A new
constitution set a maximum of three consecutive years for most of
the high offices and, under this new rule, Sylvia Payne became the
first president, elected in 1944.

The Controversial Discussions

As far as the theoretical disagreements were concerned, a series of
meetings was arranged which is now known as the 'Controversial
Discussions'. They took place between January 1943 and May 1944

during the Scientific Meetings of the Society, and consisted of a debate on four papers that had been previously circulated to all members. Three of the papers were later published as 'The Nature and Function of Phantasy' by Susan Isaacs; 'Certain Functions of Introjection and Projection in Early Infancy' by Paula Heimann; and 'Regression' by Paula Heimann and Susan Isaacs (all included in Riviere, 1952). There was also a paper by Melanie Klein, 'The Emotional Life and Ego Development of the Infant with Special Reference to the Depressive Position', which remains unpublished.

The Controversial Discussions constitute the most important period in the history of the British Psychoanalytical Society. The complexities of the arguments involved can be grasped by reading the limited literature available on the subject (Brome, 1982; Gillespie, 1963; Glover, 1949, 1966; King, 1979, 1981, 1983; Schmideberg, 1971; Segal, 1979; Steiner, 1985), as well as the official records of the discussions reproduced in the 'Scientific Bulletin' of the British Psychoanalytical Society (1967). A considerable amount of material – letters, biographical accounts, etc. – remains unpublished. It goes well beyond the scope of this Introduction to give an account of the arguments that took place and of the issues at stake during the Discussions. Here I will make only a few points.

The purpose of the Discussions was to clarify Klein's position *vis-à-vis* the metapsychology of Sigmund Freud. The quarrelling parties in this supposed Armageddon have been presented as participating in a grave marital conflict between 'mamma', Melanie Klein, and 'papa', Sigmund Freud (see Strachey, 1963b). This row seriously threatened the unity of the psychoanalytic family, while the children were the witnesses to this war between the sexes. The fact is that the hostilities were fought out by two women – Melanie Klein and Anna Freud – not by a man and a woman (which prompted Glover to call it a 'bisexual controversy', 1966).

Anna Freud and her colleagues had developed their own specific version of Freud, quoted as much as the Kleinians quoted theirs. One aspect of their interpretation of Freud's contributions was the emphasis on the genetic aspects of the libido. Melanie Klein was not interested in the different stages of psychosexual development; she was more concerned with describing different *positions*, present throughout the life of an individual and denoting specific forms of object relations, with particular anxieties and corresponding defences.

In contrast to Melanie Klein, Anna Freud focused on the developmental view of the libido in the manner of Abraham. It must be said that Freud, who had first described the different stages of libidinal development in the *Three Essays* (1905d), was not really concerned with a genetic point of view. He constantly makes use of the concept of *Nachträglichkeit* and of *nachträglich*, translated in the *Standard Edition* as 'deferred action' and 'deferred' respectively. Laplanche and Pontalis define 'deferred action' in the following way:

> Term frequently used by Freud in connection with his view of psychical temporality and causality; experiences, impressions and memory traces may be revised at a later date to fit in with fresh experiences or with the attainment of a new stage of development. They may in that event be endowed not only with a new meaning but also with psychical effectiveness.
>
> (1967)

In Anna Freud's interpretation of Freud, the concept of developmental lines is fundamental for the rest of her theories. Nevertheless, the notion of *Nachträglichkeit* (which is not really fully conveyed by the English translation) makes it impossible to interpret the history of an individual as merely the result of a linear, deterministic development, in which the present is explained by the past.

At the same time, Melanie Klein's lack of interest in the stages of libidinal development did not stop her from having a genetic point of view, as could be gathered from the question of the early Oedipus complex. It was not just a matter of the dating of the Oedipus complex. In Freud, the relationship to the father *retrospectively* determines the relationship with the pre-Oedipal mother; in Melanie Klein, however, the relationship with the mother determines the relationship with the father following a linear cause-and-effect movement. For Freud, the position of the subject in relation to the castration complex determines his relationship to the first object. For Melanie Klein, the experience of separation from the first object, the breast, determines all later experiences.

Melanie Klein refuted what her opponents always maintained: that she had departed from the main body of Freudian psychoanalytic theories. Klein and her followers wanted to prove that their contributions continued the theoretical lines suggested by Freud. With hindsight, it is no surprise that a theoretical accord between the two warring factions was never reached. Melanie Klein was creating a different metapsychology, a different model of the mind, based on different hypotheses from those that Freud had developed. For

41

example, the Kleinians kept the Freudian terminology but formulated a completely different concept of the death instinct. In changing the death instinct, they changed the rest of the theoretical construct, not just that one concept. Further changes were related to notions such as the unconscious phantasy life of the child at a pre-verbal stage; the archaic structure and sadism of the superego; the belief in the existence of object relations right from birth; the dating of the emergence of the ego; the different conception of female sexual development; the elimination of primary narcissism; the role of early anxieties; and so on. These interconnected changes formed a new body of metapsychological ideas (see Bianchedi *et al.*, 1984; Mitchell, 1986).

These brief considerations give a rough idea of the intricate, complex problems involved in the Discussions. There were great differences in theoretical beliefs, in what each party saw as the aims of psychoanalytic treatment, in the relationship between theory and practice. There were profound disagreements over the question of formulating and giving transference interpretations to the patient. One should also remember the personal likes and dislikes, the loyalties and allegiances provoked by the situation of training, the weight of contrasting cultural traditions, the tendencies to political confrontations present in any institution, etc. At the end of it all, the gaps that had existed before the confrontations became greater and nastier.

The two sources of discontent mentioned above – the scientific disagreements and the structure of power – were closely interconnected. The crucial crossroads where all the interested parties met (or, with less luck, could have collided) was at the point of the training of candidates. Since the Controversial Discussions had done very little to resolve the splits, the only solution was to devise ways of allowing the rival groups to coexist. What had started as a war between two women ended up with a 'gentlemen's agreement' signed by three women: Melanie Klein, Anna Freud, and Sylvia Payne (Pearl King calls it a 'ladies' agreement', 1983). The compromise in the sphere of training was agreed by the Society in 1946, by which two parallel courses – A and B – were introduced. Both courses were the responsibility of one Training Committee, which was also in charge of the selection and qualification of students. While the leaders of the seminars in Course A were drawn from the Society at large, Miss Freud and her followers would teach the seminars and lectures on psychoanalytic technique for the students of Course B. The supervisor for the students' first training case was chosen from their own group, the second was to be elected from the group of analysts who did not identify themselves as either Kleinian or Anna Freudian. In this way, a Middle Group was created: the Society remained one, but divided into three separate groups with two training courses. This arrangement was complemented by a political compromise by which all three groups were to have representatives on the main committees of the Society. While the training has greatly changed since 1946, the political side of the agreement has been maintained to the present day.

It was another characteristic achievement of the British psychoanalysts, accomplished through their remarkable capacity for compromise. Unfortunately, the system did not quite fulfil its promise; new discontents soon emerged. After several changes, a new organization of the training was finally established. In 1973 it was decided that each candidate would be free to select his own programme of lectures and study groups from the curriculum, with the help of a senior analyst.

Although there has been peaceful coexistence between the three groups, they have remained separate. In spite of the restoration of good relations, a subtle, unorthodox individuality remains within each of them. The identity of the groups is more or less maintained by the expectation that a student will belong to the same group as his analyst. While in the Kleinian group the students are expected to be supervised by people of that same group, the students training with an Independent, or a B group analyst, have more freedom to choose. Nevertheless, it is in theoretical work that the separations are – for some analysts – tightly maintained: they would never be found quoting from colleagues of any of the rival groups.

The cultural milieu

One specific thing made possible the successful development of psychoanalysis in England. The interest and the direct or indirect support that psychoanalysis received from 'lay cultural sources' (Glover, 1949) cannot be dismissed, and although it was coloured by intense ambivalence, it was nonetheless there. Psychoanalysis drew a large number of active participants from this lay cultural establishment. This was not exclusive to England; Freud, when referring to the kind of people who had become analysts, spoke of 'people of academic education, doctors of philosophy, educationalists, together with women of great experience in life and outstanding personalities'

43

(Freud, 1926e). There were also anthropologists, psychologists, professors of literature.

In England, some of the early psychoanalysts came from a powerful intellectual elite, sometimes connected to what has been called, in a vague, journalistic way, the 'Bloomsbury group'. This same sort of intellectual elite also contributed to formal groups, like the 17 Club, the Fabian Society, and the Labour Party. Bloomsbury itself was basically a group of friends, with a complex relationship with the psychoanalytic movement. Adrian Stephen, the brother of Virginia Woolf and Vanessa Bell, approached psychoanalysis from this lay intellectual background. The same applies to his wife, Karin Costelloe, who had been a pupil of Bertrand Russell's, had written papers on philosophical issues, and been accepted as a member of the Aristotelian Society in 1912, the same year that she married Adrian. Joan Riviere was another analyst who came from a similar background: she belonged to the Verrall family, her uncle being Arthur Verrall, a Cambridge classical scholar. The Verralls were very involved with the Society for Psychical Research, which had been started in Cambridge by F. Myers and Henry Sidgwick. This Society itself had a great impact on numerous people, and it was the only place where there was access to psychological literature. Freud himself read a paper at one of its meetings. James Strachey acknowledged in Riviere's obituary: 'We came from the same middle-class, professional, cultured, later Victorian, box' (Strachey, 1963a). John Rickman and, more recently, Charles Rycroft, came from similar stock. In the books written by, or about, the members of the Bloomsbury group, the references to Alix Sargant Florence (later to become James's wife) are numerous.

The fact that so many psychoanalysts came from this particular background led to the acceptance of people with a certain degree of psychological disturbance, but who could be of 'outstanding personality'. In his speech at the celebration of the 50th Anniversary of the British Society, referring to the changes in the regulations qualifying a candidate for membership, and especially referring to their curriculum vitae, Strachey says:

> Documents of this kind fill me with bloodcurdling feelings of anxiety and remorse. How on earth could I fill up one of them? A discreditable academic career with the barest of B.A. degrees, no medical qualifications, no knowledge of the physical sciences,

no experience of anything except third-rate journalism. The only thing in my favour was that, at the age of 30, I wrote a letter out of the blue to Freud, asking him if he would take me on as a student. For some reason he replied, almost by return of post, that he would . . .

(Strachey, 1963b)

He then goes on to explain that, back in London a couple of years later, he was made an associate member: 'I can only suppose that Ernest Jones had received instructions from an even higher authority.' He ends with the following remarks: '. . . there I was, launched on the treatment of patients, with no experience, with no supervision, with nothing to help me but some two years of analysis with Freud.' He agrees with the need for 'the gradual development of systematic machinery for training candidates', but finally asks: 'Whether it is possible for it to become over-institutionalized is an open question. Is it worthwhile to leave a loophole for an occasional maverick? I don't know . . .' (Strachey, 1963b). I suspect that he did know. He uses 'maverick', a word which means someone who does not have masters, somebody who is independent. Its origin derives from a Texan rancher who neglected to brand his calves.[6]

However, within the same cultural group there was also strong opposition to psychoanalysis. Lytton Strachey, for example, wrote a comic parody of Freud's discoveries in 1914 in an article called 'According to Freud'. Later on he apparently changed his mind, influenced by his brother James (Sherman, 1983). Leonard Woolf, who never dreamt of taking Virginia to a psychoanalyst, was publishing Freud's work at Hogarth Press. Whether Virginia Woolf was mad or not, the fact remains that she was always treated by highly incompetent psychiatrists who were, nevertheless, successful in their profession in those days.[7] It is doubtful whether Virginia would have accepted a recommendation for analytic treatment, or even whether it might have helped her. Her prejudices at the time (1924) about psychoanalysis were clear:

I shall be plunged in publishing affairs at once; we are publishing all Dr Freud, and I glance at the proof and read how Mr A.B. threw a bottle of red ink on the sheets of his marriage bed to excuse his impotence to the housemaid, but threw it in the wrong place, which unhinged his wife's mind – and to this day she pours claret on the dinner table. We could all go on like that for hours; and yet these Germans think it proves something – besides their own gull-like imbecility.

(Letter to Molly MacCarthy; see text)

The early pioneers of psychoanalysis shared three basic characteristics with the members of the intellectual elite. Whether these were for or against the new science, many of them had a certain degree of psychological disturbance, which still seems to be an important element in creative thinking; they all shared an immense, greedy intellectual curiosity, without which psychoanalysis could not, and cannot, survive; and, lastly, they lacked moralistic judgements, which did not in any way exclude an ethical commitment to professional standards.[8]

Psychoanalysis was very lucky not to be accepted by the medical establishment in Great Britain, and to find that the academic psychologists, the university professors, the philosophers, had very little time for its theories. It was perceived as belonging to a different realm. Psychoanalysts and their patients were tolerated as part of a wild but harmless bunch of eccentrics in a land of eccentrics. In 1951, Rickman could still say that 'A group of people reckoned as eccentric is never given professional status, they are thought of as outsiders' (Rickman, 1951b).

The Independent Group

Let us return to the history of the Society. As a result of the complicated political process that took place after the Controversial Discussions, the 'Middle' group was created. In fact, at the beginning this was not a group at all; the analysts who found themselves belonging to it had merely refused to belong to either of the sectarian groups that had been formed. This was then, and still continues to be today, the attraction for many analysts. Most of its members refuse to be politically organized, or to have any one leader, or to proselytize. This, in a tough world of political life, might in the end make it disappear. In any case, the creation of the group was the result of a process of elimination: if one was neither 'Kleinian' nor 'Freudian', one was 'Middle' group. The analysts of the Middle group became a political force without wanting to be one: ironically, since they were the majority, they held the political balance in the British Society. Depending on what one thought of it, the group was seen as rather 'timid' and 'uneasy' (Glover, 1949); or as a bunch of peace-loving people who rejected participation in the intrigues conducted by extremists (Schmideberg, 1971); or, more recently, as the group of the 'non-aligned analysts' who sometimes fall into 'the special dogmatism of the self-professed eclectic' (Steiner, 1985); or, in rather less generous fashion, as the group of 'uncommitted analysts' (Segal, 1979). In the 1960s the Middle group was finally constituted as a Group and, after the reorganization of the training programme, was officially known from 1973 as the 'Independent Group'.

For all 'official' purposes, those analysts who do not belong to the B Group or to the Kleinian Group are considered as Independent. Some analysts, like Michael Balint or Donald Winnicott, always refused to be identified as belonging to any one sectarian faction. The Independent analysts only agree to constitute a group for the specific purpose of participating in the political and institutional life of the Society. The Independent position is characterized by a reluctance to be restricted by theoretical or hierarchical constraints. Some others expressed their wish to remain independent by moving away from the Society, although I am sure this was never the only reason. Still others, while participating in the life of the institution, refused to become training analysts, thus excluding themselves from the corridors of political–institutional power. At the same time, many analysts – while belonging to the Independent group – are, in their theoretical outlook as much as in their practice, more Kleinian or more Anna-Freudian than anything else.

The authors in this book are all Independent analysts; some refused to belong to any group; some others became Independent after having been trained in other groups; and one of them resigned from the Society a few years ago.

Notes

1   Brome quotes a letter from Jones to Freud, 29 November 1913, where he speaks of 'a membership of nine'. The figure stated by Jones (1959) and in all later accounts (including Brome's) is fifteen. The original list of members as published in the *Internationale Zeitschrift für Psychoanalyse* (1914), 2: 411, included fifteen names, six of them with addresses outside London: in Scotland, Ireland, Canada, India and Syria. It is this fact that probably accounts for the difference.
2   Bryan, Devine and Forsyth had participated in the foundation of the London Psycho-Analytical Society together with Jones. Owen

Berkeley- Hill and Lt.-Col. Sutherland had been members of the previously dissolved Society and were soon to become members of the new one.

3   Half a century later, the American analysts, concerned with the sterility of their productions and their creativity, are beginning to reconsider opening the doors of their Institutes to non-medical candidates (see Joseph and Widlöcher, 1983). It is clear, in any case, that the 'law of the country' in the USA does not seem to prohibit the practice of psychoanalysis by non-medical practitioners (see Eissler, 1965).

4   In 1986, at the time of the publication of the first edition of *The British School of Psychoanalysis: The Independent Tradition*, there was still a rule concerning practice by lay psychoanalysts of the British Psychoanalytical Society, which established that a medical practitioner should take medical responsibility for the treatment of a patient. This implied that a patient should have been seen by a medical practitioner before treatment was begun.

5   I would like to make another more complex point concerning the issue of lay analysis. Through the considerations presented by Jones on the practical question of lay analysis, one can see how his 'naturalistic and biological outlook' also determined his theoretical conceptions. His paper 'The Early Development of Female Sexuality' was published in 1927 (Jones, 1927b), at the same time that lay analysis was being discussed. In presenting his ideas about female sexuality, Jones adopts a biological, naturalistic perspective (Kohon, 1984 [pp. 274–289 herein (ed.)]; Mitchell, 1982). His support for psychoanalysis is perfectly concordant with his theoretical conclusions: the body he has in mind when he writes about female sexuality is the same body that belongs to the medical sciences. The body implicit in Freud's practical and theoretical positions is not a biological body but a sexualized one; it is a body where sexual desire lives, or, better still, where it hides, only betraying its existence through symptoms. Jones's body can be investigated, can be known, can be cured. The only thing that we know for sure about Freud's body is its fundamental fragmentation, its basic split. Being a sexualized body, we can only suspect that we are all afraid of its desires. Freud always saw the movement against lay analysis as another form of resistance. I believe that it was the biological implication of his theories that made Jones, right from the beginning and throughout the years, feel closer to Melanie Klein, with whom he agreed on a number of theoretical issues. The development of female sexuality, for example, was one; another was the importance of innate determinants in the development of the individual. Melanie Klein, by the same token, found affinities in Jones's ideas, and this must have helped her to make the decision to leave Berlin – where she was opposed and disliked, except by her own analyst, Abraham, and a few of her other colleagues.

6   In their procedures of selection, psychoanalysts have been aware of this
     'need for a maverick', but I suspect that even this aspect is now under
     threat of becoming institutionalized: candidates *must show* a certain
     amount of neurosis to be accepted. Revolutionary movements seem to
     share similar destinies. The psychoanalytic movement, since its creation,
     has been under a particular threat: instead of being a challenging
     institution, where the aim is to further new studies, debate new ideas
     and provide intellectual stimulus for its members, it is in danger of being
     just an institution aimed at forming professionals, to protect their
     careers.

7   Henry Head, who held 'enlightened and sympathetic views', was per-
     haps the only exception, but Virginia only met him once, and treatment
     was never pursued (Trombley, 1981).

8   This lack of moralistic implications has probably changed. It has been
     most noticeable in the changes concerning the view of sexuality, the
     latter being greatly influenced by a particular reading of the implications
     of the depressive position, introduced by Melanie Klein: that which in
     Freud was an ethical concern (between a person and his own self) became
     a moral concern (between him and others).

COUNTERTRANSFERENCE
An Independent view
Gregorio Kohon

The concept of countertransference

For psychoanalysis, according to Laplanche and Pontalis (1967), transference is

> a process of actualization of unconscious wishes. Transference uses specific objects and operates in the framework of a specific relationship established with these objects ... As a rule what psychoanalysts mean by the unqualified use of the term 'transference' is *transference during treatment*. (authors' italics)

Countertransference, on the other hand, for the same authors is 'The whole of the analyst's unconscious reactions to the individual analysand – especially to the analysand's own transference' (Laplanche and Pontalis, 1967). From the very beginning the concept of countertransference has had a double connotation: on the one hand, countertransference was to be seen as the awakening of the neurotic conflicts of the analyst through an unconscious reaction to the patient's influence on the analyst. This is the way that Freud referred to it in the first instance, in 'The Future Prospects of Psycho-Analytic Therapy', stating that 'no psychoanalyst goes further than his own complexes and internal resistances permit' (Freud, 1910d). Thus he recommends adequate and continuous self-analysis. Later on, he advocates the need for a 'training analysis' ('The Dynamics of

Transference', 1912b). Some 25 years later, in 'Analysis Terminable and Interminable', his recommendation becomes a suggestion that the analyst returns to analysis from time to time, specifically to deal with problems that he might eventually find in himself.

In the analysis of his patients (Freud, 1937c), countertransference, simply put, was considered at this stage a resistance on the part of the analyst. In this line of thinking we can include later authors like Fliess (1953), A. Reich (1951), Hoffer (1956), and Tower (1956); and Winnicott, who described countertransference as the analyst's neurosis spoiling his capacity to sustain a professional attitude (1960a).

On the other hand, Freud also suggested that the analyst's unconscious should be like a 'receptive organ', a 'telephone receiver'. It is through his own unconscious that the analyst will be able to reconstruct the unconscious of the patient ('Recommendations to Physicians Practising Psycho-Analysis', 1912e). Freud was not referring here to countertransference, and although he never came to see countertransference as an important tool for the analyst, his considerations opened up the possibility of turning countertransference into something that could be used to gain insight into the patient's predicament.

This double quality of the countertransference, as resistance and as a useful tool, has marked two different technical approaches that Kernberg has described in a rather simplified way as the 'classical' and the 'totalistic' (Kernberg, 1965). They are not only different views of the countertransference, of *what* and *when* the analyst should interpret, but also different views of the position of the analyst in the treatment, and of treatment itself.

Countertransference is a concept that members of the British School should, and probably do, feel proud of having developed. The influence of Melanie Klein has been decisive in this respect. It was through her inspiration that Paula Heimann came to write the paper on countertransference which became a turning point in the history of psychoanalytic technique (Heimann, 1950). The time was obviously ripe for such a contribution. Winnicott had, for example, originally written his paper 'Hate in the Countertransference' (1949b) in 1947. It has been through contributions from Ella Sharpe (1930, 1947), James Strachey (1934), Barbara Low (1935), Michael Balint (1933, 1949), Alice and Michael Balint (1939), Donald Winnicott (1949b), Margaret Little (1951, 1957), Charles Rycroft (1956a), and again Paula Heimann (1960), that the Independent analysts' work and thoughts on countertransference were developed and expanded.

The Object Relations view is that the psychoanalytic situation is always created and developed from the specific and unique interaction between the patient and the analyst. The analyst is never an 'outsider'; he is part and parcel of the transference situation. In fact, one could argue that the transference is as much a function of the counter-transference as the countertransference is a result of the transference. Klauber, in the paper included in this book, stresses what he considers to be the most neglected aspect of the psychoanalytic encounter: that it is a relationship. Almost provocatively, he states that 'Patient and analyst need one another.' They form a private, intimate, secret relationship. Klauber acknowledges that there is always 'an element of a tease in psychoanalytic therapy since emotions are constantly aroused which the analyst will never satisfy.' Hopefully, the analyst will be more interested in analysing his patient than in satisfying his own, or his patient's, instinctual needs. But Klauber reminds us of something that psychoanalysts have sometimes tried to forget: the recognition by Freud that some aspects of the patient's love for the analyst are 'genuine'. What about the analyst's feelings for his patients?

One thing is certain: it is impossible for the analyst to share the experience of this peculiar relationship with anybody else. The analyst, I believe, is always betraying or being unfaithful to somebody else in his involvement with his patients. Love and hate will develop in the context of the analytic encounter, and this will put a certain amount of strain on the relationship. Klauber does not play down its consequences, and he asks: 'What elements of the transference can reasonably be expected to be resolved?'

Limentani, in his paper, refers to the *unique atmosphere* an analyst will create for his patients, and describes some of the ambiguities present in the analytic situation in the following manner:

> . . . at the outset, we invite the patient to enter into a relationship which offers a mixture of satisfaction and frustrations, and with a demand for utter trust which he can hardly experience towards a total stranger. We stipulate that words shall be the method of communication, knowing full well that most affects cannot be adequately described in words. We assure the analysand that both of us will be able to work better if we are not to stare at each other, yet we know how difficult it is for an infant in the first months of life to take his eyes off his mother . . . It should cause little surprise if certain patients may wish from time to time to use every means at their disposal to express their feelings and to create unforeseen

situations which can exercise the analyst's emotional responses as well as his technical skills.

One characteristic of the British Independent analysts has been the importance they have always given to 'the analyst's emotional responses', not only to 'his technical skills'. Given the emphasis on this interrelation between patient and analyst, countertransference has developed as the source of the most important clues for the formulation of transference interpretations. But this, to my mind, has become a mixed blessing. Nowadays, the concept of countertransference is sometimes used and misused to hide the prejudices, at other times the mistakes, very frequently the lack of information, the ignorance, even the simple stupidity on the part of the analyst (a point made by Jacques Lacan) in his relationship to his patients.

Not all Independent analysts would agree, I suspect, with Michael Balint's notion of the countertransference as comprising the totality of the analyst's attitudes, feelings and behaviour towards his patients. Most would probably agree, however, that it is the quality of the analytic relationship that matters for the outcome of the analysis. Although the only thing that the analyst is supposed to do, and does do most of the time, is to interpret, it is the nature of the relationship, formed through the interpretative work, that really matters for the end result. Masud Khan (1960b), Pearl King (1962, 1978), Enid Balint (1968), John Klauber (1972), Dennis G. Brown (1977), and Christopher Bollas (1982, 1983) are all British Independent analysts who have made direct or indirect contributions to the theory and the clinical uses of countertransference. One should also add to this list the papers included in this book by Adam Limentani, Harold Stewart, Christopher Bollas, Patrick Casement, Nina Coltart, and Neville Symington.

In her 1950 paper Paula Heimann uses the term countertransference to cover all the feelings that the analyst experiences towards the patient; these feelings, she says, represent 'one of the most important tools for his work. The analyst's countertransference is an instrument of research into the patient's unconscious.' She specifically emphasized the fact that the analytic situation is a relationship between two people. 'Our basic assumption,' she says, 'is that the analyst's unconscious understands that of his patient. This rapport on a deep level comes to the surface in the form of feelings which the analyst notices in response to his patient, in his "countertransference"' (Heimann, 1950).

This view, which was revolutionary at the time, became extremely influential, and is today part of our common psychoanalytic heritage. But I think, in the same way that there has been an 'overextension' of the concept of transference (Sandler *et al.*, 1969), that something similar has occurred with the concept of countertransference. This 'overextension' has resulted from the very same ideas emanating from Heimann's paper. At the end of the paper she says that the analyst's countertransference is 'the patient's *creation*, it is part of the patient's personality'. Thus in the same way that it came to be believed that everything created or produced by the patient was 'transference', everything created or produced in the analyst came to be considered 'countertransference'. I believe these two 'overextensions' of the terms in fact go together, and are the result of an overemphasis on, and a certain abuse of, the concept of projective identification.

For many colleagues, especially Kleinians, projective identification has become the most important mechanism in the analytic situation. For example, Brenman Pick, in a recently published good paper, writes that 'Constant projecting by the patient into the analyst is the essence of analysis . . .' (Brenman Pick, 1985). Another Kleinian analyst states:

> What should be at the centre of the interpretation . . . is the immediate relationship between analyst and patient, with its verbal and non-verbal expressions. This means that the knowledge of 'projective identification' is central to the understanding of the analytical material. Projective identification is an unconscious fantasy through which the person projects parts of himself into his object, which is then perceived as affected by that which was projected.
>
> (Riesenberg–Malcom, 1985)

The assumption contained in both of these views is that all aspects of the patient's relationship to the analyst are exclusively repetitions of past relationships, and they were in fact described as such by Melanie Klein (Klein, 1932). The task of the analyst would then be to decode these projections that have been put into him, which is where the value of the countertransference is seen to reside. We all know that this does happen in any psychoanalytic treatment; the question remains as to whether this is the *only* thing that happens. Basing all interpretations on countertransference feelings, understood

54

only as a result of projective identification, denies what the patient has to say. The analysis is now based more on the discourse of the analyst, not on that of the patient.

The theory of the countertransference has come to be used as a defence against the impact of the analytic relationship, a defence that belongs to the analyst, not to the patient. I agree with the way Sandler *et al.* pose the question of transference (and I would extend it here to include countertransference). They argue that transference – and countertransference – are multi-dimensional phenomena. They are clinical rather than metapsychological concepts, and include a whole variety of different elements that enter into object relations. These elements are facilitated in the special conditions of the analytic situation. Thus the important question, they say, is 'not what is and what is not transference' (and, I would add, countertransference) 'in the analytic situation, but rather *what dimension of relationships enters into the special and artificial analytic situation, and how are these involved in the process of treatment?*' (Sandler *et al.*, 1969, authors' italics).

Contributions by Independent analysts to the theory of countertransference

I would now like to refer in some detail to four papers by members of the Independent Group of the British Psychoanalytical Society which I see as important contributions to the theory of countertransference. (Two of these papers are included in the present book.) I will start with Enid Balint's paper on the analyst as a mirror or receiver (E. Balint, 1968), which followed another excellent paper, 'On Being Empty of Oneself' (E. Balint, 1963). The opaque mirror technique suggested by Freud (1912e) – by which the analyst should show to his patients only what is shown to him – is understood by Balint as: 'a biphasic attitude in which the analyst first identifies with the patient and then, by his interpretation, shows what the patient's thoughts and ideas "look like" to him . . . This assumes a high degree of identification by the analyst and a minimum of projection.' This metaphor of Freud's has been widely criticized (not least by some of the authors represented in this book), but Balint's re-evaluation of it is a very refreshing one. She retranslates Freud's position as follows: 'Freud's intention was to make it clear that the analyst's personality and opinions should not be shown to the patient, nor should he give advice, sympathy or consolation. *His job was just to reflect back to the patient what he was able to understand*' (my italics).

55

Gregorio Kohon

Although acknowledging, as Freud himself did, that the analyst responds with his total being, Enid Balint – disagreeing here with quite a number of colleagues – argues that the patient will not perceive the analyst as he really is. 'We will be seen,' she says, 'in at least as many different ways as we have patients.' This would seem to confirm the view, quoted above, of the analysis as a constant process of projection by the patient into the analyst. But Enid Balint takes this further, into another problem. She questions an overemphasis that had been put on the personality of the analyst, and of its effect on the treatment. This point is a fundamental one. It somehow put right something that had formed the basis for a misunderstanding dating back to James Strachey's classical paper on the function of interpretation (Strachey, 1934).

Strachey's paper is still a source of ideas and inspirations. His concept of the function of mutative interpretations, his view of the therapeutic action of analysis as a process affecting analyst as much as patient, have been crucial in our understanding of psychoanalytic treatment. But the misunderstanding is related to his statement about the patient's internalization of the analyst as a substitute, 'auxiliary' superego. When Strachey makes this proposition he is trying to criticize Sandor Radó's concept of a 'parasitic superego', the internalization of the superego of the hypnotizer by the person being hypnotized. Although Strachey argues that in psychoanalysis this process is different, in that there is an internal change in the nature of the patient's superego itself, I do not find the distinction convincing. We are still talking here about a process of suggestion: the substitution of the superego of the analyst for the superego of the patient.

It is ironic that that which was put forward by Freud as a psychoanalytic explanation for hypnosis ends up being used as an explanation for psychoanalysis (Miller, 1979). This conception has supported the idea of 'the goal of analysis' in terms of a successful internalization of the analyst as a 'good object', or a 'benign figure'. It has contributed to the idealization of the analyst as an object.

Enid Balint has something different in mind, and her position makes the outcome of analysis a more problematic, uncertain process. She suggests that our patients might be quite grateful to us for our adhering to the mirror model: it is, she says, the analyst who more frequently wishes to deviate from that model. Consequently, she also claims, she has not found that 'an analyst needs to express sympathy

except when things go wrong in the conduct of the analysis itself.'
At this point Enid Balint introduces a very simple but fruitful idea:
she refers to the *distance* of the analyst from the patient. She states:
'In my opinion, the mirror model enables the analyst to be neither
distant nor close, but just there . . .'

I would like to link this notion of being *just there* to the concept
of the transitional object, in order to understand the dynamics of the
transference–countertransference process. What is transitional is not
the object, says Winnicott, but the use that one makes of it. The
analyst occupies that transitional space where the objects are not quite
internal, nor are they quite external. Like a transitional object, the
analyst *is* and *is not*. This paradoxical quality of *being* and *not being*
does not take away any reality from the psychoanalytic encounter.
We are, as analysts, as important to our patients as teddy bears are to
children. As objects, we have been created by the patient, very much
like the teddy bear is created by the child. Patients do not get better
by internalizing the good images that we can offer them. We do not,
in fact, 'offer' anything 'good' or 'bad'; what we offer them is very
little, and as Enid Balint suggested, patients know very little about
the reality of our 'goodness' or 'badness'. Hopefully, what they get
from us is what I would call our *progressive absence*. (The idea for this
is taken from Pontalis (1977), who talks of the mother's progressive
constitution as *absence*.) We are just there, although the situation of
the transference makes us excessively 'present'. The working through
of the transference should make us become more and more absent,
and not more and more present.

This idea of a progressive absence is just the opposite of what
Strachey's notions suggested. The success of the analysis is not
achieved through the identification with, or the incorporation of, the
analyst into the patient's inner world. The dissolution of the transference is, to my mind, one and the same thing as the dissolution of
the figure of the analyst, whether as 'good' or 'bad'. A good-enough
mother is also somebody who becomes more and more absent: she
is not the one who loves us alone, but the one who has somebody
else to love and be loved by. Her narcissism does not depend entirely
on the child; or to be more precise, her narcissism depends pro-
gressively less and less on the child. In this sense, she will turn
more and more into an absence. The same applies to the analyst.
Our health could be said to be based on the possibility of having a
good relationship inside ourselves with that absence, which will

form, in the way described by Winnicott, the basis of our capacity to be alone.

This is what is created and re-created in the process of an analysis: the fact that the analyst is *just there* confronts the analysand with the fact that the space occupied by the analyst will always be defined as absence. It is in this contradiction – that the analyst is there to announce an absence – that the status of the primary object resides. The analysand will have to reconcile himself with the fact that the primary object will never be found again. It is not an object, in the sense that our keys are objects: one loses the keys to one's house only to discover later on that one's children have been playing with them. The primary object is an object which will never be found again. The misfortunes of the subject did not start 'the day the breast was withdrawn from his lips' (Masotta, 1976); it is the very process of being lost forever that counts. A cure conceived along the lines of a replacement of 'bad' by 'good' by definition maintains the illusory implications of the patient's transference. The notion that Enid Balint proposes, that of *just being there*, is not the same as suggesting that 'good' should replace 'bad'. If it were, we would be confirming the analysand's hopes that he could – if only he tried hard enough – find a 'better' mother than his own, 'real', 'bad' mother.

I will leave this question here, and move on to Nina Coltart's paper presented to the English-Speaking Conference of Psychoanalysts in 1982 (this volume). '"Slouching Towards Bethlehem . . ." or Thinking the Unthinkable in Psychoanalysis' provoked a certain amount of hostility among members of the British Society who were in the audience: not only did the then director of the London Clinic of PsychoAnalysis shout at one of her patients, but she was transforming her ignorance into a virtue, into an ideology. I found the paper an important contribution: it brought to everybody's attention characteristics of the psychoanalytic stance that belong to the best of the Independent tradition. 'It is of the essence of our impossible profession,' Coltart says, 'that in a very singular way we do not know what we are doing.' In spite of our training, our literature, our experience, however much we gain confidence, or refine our technique, each hour spent with a patient, claims Coltart, is an act of faith. This faith is mainly concerned with what she calls 'the sheer *unconsciousness* of the unconscious'.

This declaration of belief in the power of the unconscious results in a clear attempt to cut the supposed power of the analyst down to size. What Coltart reaffirms for us is the unconditional trust that we, as analysts, need to have in order to believe that whatever else happens in the analysis, IT will continue working ... We do not always know what is going on with the patient, we rarely know what is going on *inside* the patient, and this limitation of our knowledge makes reference to the vicissitudes of the transference. What Nina Coltart adds to this is that we do not always know what is going on with the analyst; in fact we know very little of what is going on *inside* the analyst, and this is a reference to the vicissitudes of the counter-transference.

A patient tells me of his objections to circumcision, and the barbarism of its practice; he then follows this with his complaints about baptism in the Christian religion, or how – he says – this religious ritual puts a limit, right from birth, on the freedom of the individual. He then moves on to the practice of medicine in the USA, the lack of clear political definitions about the problem of nuclear disarmament in a certain political party, his dissatisfaction with a professor in the postgraduate course that he is attending. We are now getting closer and closer to the *here-and-now*, and I can see the monster of the transference emerging, moving slowly, growing faster, getting to the target. Far from being psychotic, this patient is in fact a pervert, fighting, struggling with himself in a battle I have no certainty he is going to win.

A few hours later another patient, this time a fairly disturbed one, tells me about his aspirations to belong to the upper classes, to have lots and lots of money, his wish to be a millionaire so he could have his shoes handmade to order by some famous shoemaker who is becoming old and is in the process of retiring. In the middle of this, he says: 'Suddenly, this song came to my head: "*I fought against the Law, and the Law defeated me* ..."'

There is not much to these stories. While the first patient awakens in me a certain impatience, which nevertheless does not exclude my sympathy and the possibility of working together, the second patient forces me to smile. With the first one I would like to argue, although all I will do is interpret; with the second one I would like to know more about the song, and although I feel free to ask, I decide to remain silent. To speak of 'a decision' here is mystifying: IT decides, I would say. Our own analysis and our own training, plus our experiences, our reading, our learning, have taught us to accept certain rules. They are fairly rigid rules, which in our daily practice become habits: we

59

greet our patients in a certain manner, we state our interpretations in a certain way. Once habits, they come to form a style, and this style, instead of putting rigid limits to our work, forms the background to our spontaneous acts. Interpretations will come to us, against this background, as a novelty. They will impose themselves on us, will burst into light coming from an area within ourselves that we know little about.

Israel (1972) refers to a painting of Rene Magritte's entitled *The Therapist*, in which a man is sitting on a sand dune with a leather bag by his side. The upper part of his body is made like an open cage; there is a pigeon in the cage, and another one outside the cage. The cage is partially covered by a blanket, and on top of it there is a hat. Interpretations must have been made of this painting; it is too tempting not to do so, but part of the attraction of this wonderful picture is the mystery in it, a certain obscurity present in most Surrealist paintings: something is being suggested, but not quite said. In fact, it is not clear that anything could be said. We live with this contradiction most of the time: the feeling that what I say to the patient is completely useless and has no meaning, together with the knowledge, the conviction, the belief that for the patient there is nothing more serious in the world. The therapist in that picture is a surrealistic object himself: like the patient, the analyst also escapes a certain objective understanding.

This is different from 'encouraging ignorance as a virtue'. We are faced every day, in our work with our patients, with the true limits of our knowledge: the question is not how much we are learning, but how little we know. In her paper, Coltart is far from supporting a mystical or religious attitude, where the 'Beyond Words' (the title of the conference at which the paper was presented) would form the realm of reality. Just the opposite: language is the only possible realm of psychoanalysis. One can only be preoccupied with silence, as Coltart is, if one believes at the same time that words restore a certain existence, they give birth to that which needs to be named. What makes our profession impossible is that, however much we name it, IT is never finished; however much we think we know it, IT remains obscure; however much we can grasp it, IT escapes us.

Coltart reacted with passion to her patient. There is always this sneaky feeling that when we talk of countertransference, we are putting ourselves above the confusing world of passions. Eric Brenman, a Kleinian analyst, referred to this in a paper read to the

Society: 'To eat from the Tree of Knowledge,' he said, 'carries with it the danger of attempting to become God' (Brenman, 1978). Not that we take ourselves to be God – since we are too clever to do that – but more that, like him, we are *beyond passions* (Leclaire, 1975). If passion were not present in the analyst's life, why would we need so many measures to deal with our own feelings? Why otherwise would 'supervision' be called 'control'?

Lévi-Strauss has demonstrated how belief systems, myths and mythical stories are in fact preoccupied with the problems of boundaries. Our own psychoanalytical mythologies fulfil the same purpose. The idealization of a possible 'right' kind of technique that is proposed by some colleagues, the idealization of a particular theory, like the negative of a photograph, show that which is being repressed. Freud said that 'the formation of an ideal heightens the demands of the ego and is the most powerful factor favouring repression' (1914c). Coltart's reaction to her patient is not an act of repression but a creative act: her faith in the unconscious gives meaning to the patient's desolation, despair, and loneliness.

The third paper I will make reference to is Neville Symington's 'The Analyst's Act of Freedom as Agent of Therapeutic Change' (1983, this volume). In it, Symington describes what he calls an 'x-phenomenon'. The very fact that he calls it by this name suggests how little we might know about it. Symington's basic assumption is that at one level the analyst and patient together make a single system. Together they form an entity which we might call a corporate personality. From the moment that patient and analyst engage in what we call an analysis the two are together part of an illusory system. Both are caught into it . . . The analyst is lassoed into the patient's illusory world. He is more involved in it, more victim to it than the average social contact. As the analytical work proceeds the analyst slowly disengages himself from it. In this way, transference and countertransference are two parts of a single system; together they form a unity. They are the shared illusions which the work of analysis slowly undoes.

The illusions or delusions are shared; they belong to both patient and analyst. This implies a radical change of view as regards resistance: the resistances that we traditionally place on the side of the patient belong to the analyst as well. It might happen that sometimes they belong more to the analyst than to the patient. But the main point put forward by Symington is that the resistances belong to the process. Patient and analyst are locked into it, and both of them need to be freed from it. The 'x-phenomenon' is then that inner act of freedom on the part of the analyst by which he frees himself from some of the illusion, and it is this which causes a shift, a therapeutic change in both participants of the analytic interaction.

Symington takes good care to distinguish the process of mutual involvement between analysand and analyst from the process of projective identification, by which the patient ends up being blamed for what the analyst feels: 'The analyst's feelings are *his* feelings even though they may have been stirred up by the patient.' The psychoanalytic process, in this view, as in Enid Balint's and Coltart's views, is a humble process. The limitations intrinsic to the interaction between analysand and analyst do not make it any less painful, less powerful, or I dare say less mysterious.

Symington argues that the shared illusions are located in the superego. I would like to add that the illusions relate to the ego-ideal, perhaps as a specific structure within the superego. These two concepts are sometimes considered synonymous but I find it useful to differentiate between them. Lagache (1966) introduced a distinction whereby the superego corresponds to *authority*, while the ego-ideal corresponds to *the way the subject should behave* in order to respond to the authority's expectations. The distinction is subtle but relevant to the work of the analyst, whose individual ego-ideal might interfere with his work by its adherence to the institutional superego. (For a thoughtful consideration of the concept of the ego-ideal, see Chasseguet-Smirgel, 1975.)

The fact that the 'x-phenomenon' is defined as an act of freedom goes against any notion that there is a 'right' kind of technique, or a 'right' kind of interpretation. Cookery books never made good cooks. Of course we need cookery books and recipes, but we also need a certain amount of creativity when the sauce is being made: it is then that one sees the real skill of the cook. The notion that there is only one 'right' kind of technique, or recipe for deciphering the unconscious of the patient, might account for a certain sterility in the productions of psychoanalytic writers; something that has been justly acknowledged both inside and outside psychoanalytical societies.

I see the 'x-phenomenon', the act of freedom on the part of the analyst as described by Symington, as an act of commitment. Whether I make a mistake or not, an interpretation – in fact any intervention on my part – is always something that will come from a personal, though hopefully, professional stance: it is never 'impersonal', out of the boundaries of my responsibility, something for which I could blame the patient. The very fact that it is a matter of freedom on the part of the analyst makes it clear that it is an ethical concern: not so much related to what we 'should' do according to some absolute knowledge, but simply to do what we can in the best possible way.

The fourth and last paper by an Independent analyst that I shall mention is Christopher Bollas's 'Expressive Uses of the Counter-transference – Notes to the Patient from Oneself' (Bollas, 1983). The titles of the different sections of this paper give a fair flavour of its content: 'Countertransference readiness', 'Analyst as patient to himself', 'The analyst's use of the subjective', 'Self relating in the analyst', 'Sensing', 'From indirect to direct use of the counter-transference'. Like others, Bollas's assumption is that the analytic situation involves two subjectivities in mutual interrelating and experiencing. He speaks of the establishment by the patient of an *environment* through which the patient's internal world is conveyed, and in which both patient and analyst live a 'life' together. The analyst becomes what Bollas had called in a previous paper a *transformational object*, not so much an object in fact as a process of alteration of self experience (Bollas, this volume). Bollas believes that it is possible for the analyst:

> to report selected subjective states to his patients for mutual observation and analysis. By disclosing certain subjective states of mind the analyst makes available to the patient certain freely associated states within himself, feelings or positions that he knows to be sponsored by some part of the patient.

The analyst might find himself in the position of not quite knowing what the meaning of his subjective state of mind could be, but he can share this with his patient 'as long as it is clear to the analysand that such disclosures are in the nature of reports from within the analyst, in the overall interests of the psychoanalysis.'

Bollas distinguishes between indirect and direct uses of the countertransference. By indirect use he means 'those occasions when the analyst becomes witness to his own feeling state and may in the presence of the patient offer this feeling state for consideration.' By doing so, Bollas clearly redefines the subjectivity of the analyst, establishing it as a 'useful and consistent source of material in the psychoanalytic situation'. By direct use of the countertransference, Bollas is referring to 'that quite rare occasion, but one which may be of exceptional value to the effectiveness of the analysis, when the analyst describes his experience as the object.' The analyst could, let us say, sense something about the patient; the use of this 'sensing' would be an indirect use of the countertransference. When the analyst describes to the patient how he feels in terms of being the patient's object, the analyst would be using the countertransference in a direct way.

As Symington does, and as Balint and Coltart imply in their respective papers, Bollas also objects to the characterization of the countertransference as based solely on the process of projective identification. (I gather that most Independent analysts would agree that the concept of projective identification is an extremely useful one: a certain tendency on our part to make jokes about it admittedly represents a caricature parallel to a caricatured version of its use.) If the freedom postulated by Symington confronts us with our need for commitment, Bollas's conception restores a certain responsibility to the position occupied by the analyst. The place of the analyst is a very privileged one but his experiences, his feelings, his ideas are certainly not: they do not constitute, for example, the 'official' version of what the truth about the patient's unconscious could be. Everything the analyst puts forward can only be considered as interpretation, that is to say as hypotheses to be investigated by patient and analyst. These hypotheses can no doubt be changed, turned around, turned upside down, can frequently contradict each other, be confirmed, disproved, or, as Bollas himself says: 'kicked around, mulled over, torn to pieces'. What we create in one interpretation might be destroyed by the next, and reappear again in the following one.

This is not to say that we have a careless attitude as regards the interpretations we make. Interpretations are like the swings, the slide, the climbing frame, the sandpit in the playground – a word used by Freud to refer to the transference situation – in which analysand and analyst are playing. Interpretations are not the dice in a game, but at the same time they cannot be considered statements of fact. Interpretations are formed by real words but they constitute an imaginary story. The story is a fiction that takes place in a world created by the mutual working influence of analyst and analysand, with characters borrowed from reality. When we interpret we try to explain, we attempt to elucidate, we would like to make something clear; but we also give our own interpretation, as one does in interpreting a composition in music, a landscape in painting, or a drama in the theatre. In our daily work we give our own interpretations of the melody we hear coming from the couch, but we are not the creators of that melody. We interpret but that does not give us the right to believe we have understood: the proof of this is that probably any other analyst playing the same melody coming from the couch would give it a different interpretation. Not all the Independent analysts would agree with the choice of words that Bollas uses with his patients, but the description given by Bollas of this 'open struggle' to put into words something 'beyond words' validates a way of working that most Independent analysts do share. The analyst is not the spokesman of some hidden truth about the patient. Such a way of working embodies an attitude which is the opposite of one that could be characterized as interpretative fervour, or 'militant interpreting' (Bollas, personal communication, 1984). The attitude of militant interpreting assumes that the analyst not only should understand everything, but should also interpret everything he thinks he has understood. For those analysts who think they have understood it is very difficult to admit the possibility that something *different*, something *new* might be happening.

The work of the analyst as described by Bollas echoes Winnicott's provocative statement that one of the reasons for making interpretations in a session, paradoxically, is 'not to give the impression to the patient that he, the analyst, understands everything' (Winnicott, 1962). The analyst in this picture does not occupy the place of an omnipotent superego demanding obedience, forcing the patient to identify himself with the superego of the analyst; does not submerge or drown the words of the patient in the discourse of the analyst. There are no early, premature interpretations, no room for quick, sharp understanding of the patient's predicament, no overdoses of symbolic meaning.

★   ★   ★

This analyst I go to suddenly went deaf. He diagnoses hysteria and is working on it but it's a blow to his purse as well as his pride. Meanwhile, those of his patients who don't feel defrauded by the thought of a deaf psychoanalyst are trying to adjust to his altered patterns of behaviour. There's about a dozen of us left – the hardcore sons of his fatherfigure-hood.

. . . He still thinks he's going to get his hearing back but I'm far from encouraging.

65

'Mac', I say to him, 'the only way to get back your hearing is give up being an analyst. It's your drums rejecting all this garbage you provoke – a defence mechanism!' He smiles benignly and shakes his head. He can't hear me . . .

Anthony Edkins, 'Why I Like Ess' (1979)

I believe, with Masotta, that the only serious thing about human beings is that we are structured like a joke (Masotta, 1976). Like dreams, like symptoms, like artistic creations, like slips of the tongue, we also are the products of condensation and displacement. One of the most wonderful jokes in psychoanalysis is that Freud discovered psychoanalysis through his relationship with Fliess. We all consider that remarkable relationship between Freud and Fliess as the first transference situation, the first, original analysis. Now, this man Fliess was a very tense, mad scientist, with a mad and delirious scientific mind. Freud makes him the object of his idealizations, turns him into the father figure of his preoccupations, his master and friend. Freud could have chosen other, more important figures of his time: Brücke, von Fleischl-Marxow, Helmholtz, Charcot, Breuer, etc. In fact they all became his heroes but Freud, nevertheless, follows what his transference dictates, and the great surprise is that it gets him somewhere. To use an image offered by Freud himself: Fliess made him 'summon up a spirit from the underworld by cunning spells'. We have been lucky enough that Freud did not 'send him down again without having asked him a single question' (Freud, 1914d). What a misunderstanding! Fliess expected something from Freud, and Freud expected to find knowledge in Fliess. Is this what happens between patient and analyst? What kind of knowledge is this psychoanalytic knowledge?

Transference is an illusion. In this sense, though, it is no more or less of an illusion than any other relationship. As soon as love and hate develop in a relationship, illusions, and sometimes delusions, take shape and develop. In the *commedia dell'arte* all characters wore masks, except for the lovers: not because love shows the truth but because it is in itself enough to hide the lovers' gestures (García, 1980). In a Valentine's Day postcard by the cartoonist Mel Calman all we can see is a blind man with his walking stick and a pair of sunglasses: he does not look particularly happy or unhappy; the only thing that makes him so distinguishable – and yet so universal – is the shape of the frames of his glasses: that of two small hearts. Love is blind, yet very real. Breuer escaped from the consequences of the transference, but then he did not discover the Oedipus complex. The analysand knows very well who we are; we do not need to tell him that we are not his father, mother, brother, or sister, although this is what we try to show him a lot of the time during an analysis.

The very notion of a psychoanalytic type of knowledge implies the recognition that there is a certain part of ourselves that will never be reachable, never become clear. If we continue with our self-analysis, and sometimes with further analysis, it is not only because there are parts of ourselves that remain obscure to our knowledge, but also because there are parts of ourselves that will always be in the process of being re-created. This accounts, in part, for the fact that the same person can have such different analyses when he happens to have more than one. For that process of re-creation, what the patient has to learn is not something about the unconscious – it is more than that: it is something about love and hate, in which the unconscious has a place, and fulfils a function (Mannoni, 1980).

A patient comes in a very damaged state to the analysis; one could say that the task of the analysis is to help him to repair his damaged internal objects. This is part of the process, and in fact we all refer to it more or less in those terms. But at the same time a patient does not come to us in the way that a car goes to the garage to be repaired after a crash. In a sense, for the patient nothing can be repaired. What he will have to be faced with, in the end, is not the damage, or the lost happiness, or the lack of happiness in the past, but rather the sheer narcissistic hurt that forces him to accept the impossibility of that happiness. In other words, the primary object is not some object that was lost somewhere along the line of development but an object that is structured by its own loss. There is something about the nature of the object itself that makes it not-available. I think this is the real meaning of the depression that Melanie Klein refers to as happening at the end of every analysis. Or, in Freud's terms, the real bedrock of castration that the subject will have to face.

The same applies to the analyst. What gives me my status as a psychoanalyst is not my having become a member of the Institute of Psycho-Analysis. What turns me into an analyst is that precise moment in which a patient shows signs that I have become an object in his imaginary world: he is now interested in me, he attributes to me a knowledge, expects something special from me. My work as an analyst can now start, it is the time when the analysis can begin. It will entail, will imply a narcissistic hurt for me as much as for the patient, in the sense that I will also be faced with the impossibility of being either close to or distant from him. I will be *just there*, not in a state of inactivity or passivity, but the opposite, usually working quite hard, and perhaps sharing, with some luck, the impossibility of our relationship.

Independent analysts question any notion of the psychoanalytic process as exclusively one of projection and projective identification. This does not mean that they do not use these concepts for the understanding of the psychoanalytic situation (see, for example, the careful consideration of his patient's projective process that Patrick Casement makes in the paper included here). The belief that whatever happens in the psychoanalytic process is a result of something emanating from the patient, which is then projected into the analyst, has contributed to the creation of a distinctively stagnant psychoanalytic product: the 'you-mean-me' interpretations (Coltart, personal communication, 1977). 'You-mean-me' interpretations automatically refer everything that the patient says to a comment about the analyst. Such comments are then said to be 'transference' interpretations. In fact they represent a certain paranoid position on the part of the analyst, systematized and presented under the useful disguise of good, 'depressive', 'maternal' work.

Independent analysts put forward a different conception of what they understand psychoanalysis, and the place of the analyst, to be. One hears sometimes that the Independent Group is not a 'middle' group but a 'muddled' group. There is some truth in this. The Independent analysts are 'muddled', in one sense, for example, since they start from a point of *theoretical* uncertainty with their patients. But what other people might see as their handicap is in fact the Independents' strength. What they have to offer is primarily but not exclusively a professional stance, a *professional attitude* (this term comes from Sandler *et al.*, 1973): this is what allows the necessary distance of the analyst from the patient.

Attitude is for some a bland word but I think it is the adequate term. The word originated in the arts, with which I think we have a lot in common. It refers to a position of the body as much as to a frame of mind; it describes a kind of habitual behaviour as well as a certain readiness, fitness, and disposition. Charles Rycroft (1958) defines the analyst's attitudes as a *sentiment*, 'an organized, enduring disposition of emotional tendencies, which is maintained more or less consistently'. Our psychoanalytic attitude could be defined by the respect that our theory shows for the complications, subtleties, and variations of human relationships, evident on the patient's side as much as on the analyst's. 'To say that the analyst,' says Ella Sharpe, 'will still have complexes, blind spots, limitations is only to say that he remains a human being. When he ceases to be an ordinary human being he ceases to be a good analyst' (Sharpe, 1947).

The patient comes to analysis, and all he wants at the beginning is for a lullaby to be sung to him. It is a very vulnerable, though understandable, position to be in. Sometimes we hear of some truly mad lullabies being sung to patients. What can the patient do? A lullaby, however mad, is after all better than none; and all the more so if it is sung with an 'air of undue certainty' (Kernberg, 1965), and the analyst singing it does not seem to present any doubts. By contrast, the Independent authors referred to in this Introduction, and those included in this book, show great care in describing how the analyst should avoid putting alien feelings into the analysand's heart, and foreign words into the analysand's mouth.

6

CONCLUDING REMARKS

Gregorio Kohon

Most of the authors of the object relations school have certainly moved away from the classical, Freudian frame of reference, but this does not make them non-Freudians. I believe that what characterizes British psychoanalysts above anything else is an extremely astute clinical sense, which surpasses a simple opposition between theoretical and clinical practice. The British insistence on the clinical aspects of psychoanalytic practice does not exclude a capacity to use and create theory, or to exercise speculative abilities: without these abilities the writings of Fairbairn, Michael Balint, Winnicott would not have been possible.

What brings the authors of this 'school of painters' together, and what so far has kept them together, is their firm belief in the Freudian unconscious, and in the essential need to listen to the patient. It was from his patients that Freud learned psychoanalysis.

Psychoanalysis itself militates against any possibility of a single theory that would be definitive, unitary, free from contradictions. This tendency helps to explain the theoretical differences between the diverse authors who belong to the British school. Freud opposed the illusion of religion (to believe in something through ignorance), and the illusion of philosophy (the search for systems that develop into a need for some kind of final unity). He only kept his sympathy for the illusion of the aesthetic experience. We can study the works of the 'painters' of the British school, but we could never codify or systematize them. Any attempt to do so deforms and changes their creations. Their writings constitute what I would call a 'literature of excess'. Psychoanalysis has always been a literature of excess: it exceeded custom and reason, it overstepped acceptable scientific limits, it courageously explored beyond the prescribed authorities of modern thought. The excesses of an immigrant new science flourished and did very well in a country of moderation and restraint, which was able to contain other creative and cultural forms of excess. If one removes excess from psychoanalysis, we have no work of art left.

The contributions made by the Independent analysts emphasized the interrelations between the analysand's and the analyst's subjective experience. This emphasis on subjectivity caused the creation, development, and re-evaluation of theoretical concepts and clinical notions like: *countertransference*, as something of clinical relevance, not just a psychopathological interference; *acting out*, as a means of communicating something significant emerging from the history of the individual; the revision of the *criteria for the selection of cases*, enlarging the spectrum of patients considered suitable for analysis; a demand for *modifications in technique*, in order to adapt the technique to the patient, not the patient to the technique; and the positive *uses of regression*, and the creation of a *facilitating environment* in the context of the psychoanalytic treatment (James, 1980).

I believe that only people properly trained as psychoanalysts should practise psychoanalysis. Nevertheless, we also need the development of a psychoanalytic theory as much as we need our practice. No amount of clinical experience, by itself, is going to solve our theoretical problems. All psychoanalytic theories, like the hysteric, suffer from reminiscences. There is no possibility of a psychoanalytic theory that is not created by the desire of the theoretician. The conditions for the existence of a theory, like those for a work of art, are that it should be different from a symptom; we could compare the creation of a symptom to the creation of a work of art or a theory, but they are not the same.

Like art, psychoanalysis is a discipline of contradictions: the task of the analyst, as much as of the patient, is to accept them. The revolution provoked by psychoanalysis has to do with the way in which it turned our own relationship to knowledge upside down, by revealing our libidinal involvement with knowledge. Given the proliferation of other psychotherapies, the variety of trainings now offered in the market, and the watering-down of psychoanalytic findings, I suspect that we are, ironically, back to the early days of the psychoanalytic pioneers. In spite of the apparent acceptance of psychoanalysis, we are again in a position of having to show real courage to believe in psychoanalysis.

Psychoanalysis continues to be full of contradictions and ambiguities. In the end, these only reflect our human condition.

72

PART III

EARLY ENVIRONMENT
Success and failure

7

PSYCHIC LIFE

A new focus on earliest infancy

Josh Cohen

Historians of psychoanalysis have long and rightly distinguished the Independent tradition by its concern with the impact of the infant's environment, and especially of the earliest environment of maternal care, on his psychic development. Eric Rayner (1990) and John Keene (2012), as well as Gregorio Kohon in his Introduction (pp. 21–72 herein), have traced the emergence of this concern from the various professional, intellectual and cultural milieus in which the first generations of British psychoanalysts were embedded.

The same writers have drawn out, each in their particular ways, some of the key theoretical implications of this new emphasis on the early environment. For example, Keene argued that the conviction in the formative force of the early environment in psychic development brought some contemporary Independents to seek coherence with attachment theory (Bowlby, 1969), on the one hand, and the American tradition of observational developmental psychology, on the other (Mahler *et* al., 1975; Stern, 1985). This rapprochement between psychoanalysis and psychology implies above all a privilege of external reality over unconscious fantasy, both in the understanding of psychic life and in the formulation of clinical technique.[1] In this view, evident in at least one strand of Independent authors, the competing claims of a verifiable external and a concealed psychic reality, famously left unresolved and open by Freud,[2] are settled firmly in favour of the former.

The often explicit corollary of this resolution is the suggestion that inferences about early infancy from the adult psychoanalytic setup are poor in reliability relative to the findings of observation in situ of the mother–infant set-up. While this introduction is not the place for a detailed rehearsal of these debates,[3] the three papers gathered by Kohon in this section convincingly trouble the premise that the psychic reality of the infant could be available to direct observation. While fully consistent with the Independent tradition of inquiry into the shaping of the infant's emerging psyche by its environment of care, they also show that, as an object of knowledge, the infant psyche can be discerned only *nachträglich* – that is, only through its retrospective processing and resignification in later life. I hope to draw out some of the implications of this *nachträglich* temporality for our understanding of Independent thinking and the place of early infancy within it.

As Freud noted at the outset of the Wolf Man case, the 'deepest strata' of the infant psyche are 'impenetrable to consciousness', for the infant possesses neither the language nor the psychic structure that would render these strata intelligible, either to herself or to her adult carer. *This unavailability of the infant psyche to direct inquiry is an integral premise of each of these papers.* Their descriptions of the processes at work in the early environment derive from clinical inference and meta-psychological speculation rather than from empirical observation. The *Nachträglichkeit* or 'afterwardsness'[4] of infancy is not an obstacle to be overcome, but the necessary and paradoxically productive condition of psychoanalytic thinking.

Appearing first in the *International Journal of Psychoanalysis* in 1979, Christopher Bollas' paper was the last of the three papers to be published. It is also, as the opening chapter of Bollas' first book, the first of them I read. *The Shadow of the Object* (1987) was on a reading list I had compiled soon after I began to contemplate psychoanalytic training, for a hastily cobbled, self-taught course in contemporary British thinking. I had come to the idea of training from a background in the academic humanities, where, in the secondary medium of cultural theory and criticism as well as in their own words, I had read Freud, Lacan, Kristeva and others. The possibility of training in this country alerted me to how little I knew of British psychoanalysis, and of how unthinkingly I had absorbed a prejudice against its supposed naive empiricism and aversion to rigorous theoretical speculation.

Bollas' book was a revelation in this context, its vivid and layered portrait of the earliest forms of psychic life and the mother–infant

relation rooted in a dense and psychoanalytically specific concep-
tuality. Within each chapter, familial and clinical histories shaded
imperceptibly into substantial contributions to some of the most
enduring and recondite problems of psychoanalytic theory. *The
Shadow of the Object* showed me that bold theoretical speculation was
properly the companion rather than the contrary of exact and
immersive description. As such, it provided me with a way into the
broader Independent tradition and, more particularly, its presiding
spirit, D.W. Winnicott, in whom speculation and description, the
theoretical and the empirical, also converged in complex and
enigmatic ways. The papers included in this section and their authors
have continued to serve as a model for my own understanding of
the fluid and creative interplay of theory and practice in psychoanalysis.

In these three papers, the characteristic emphasis of British
psychoanalysis on the vicissitudes of early life becomes an occasion
for the cultivation of new perspectives on unresolved tensions in
Freudian metapsychology. The first of these tensions turns on nothing
less than Freud's conception of the unconscious. In the early Freud,
the Unconscious is a repository of representations engendered by the
dynamic conflict between the sexual drive and its repression. This,
the ongoing accretion of displaced and distorted wishes and impulses
inadmissible to consciousness, is the excessive and transgressive
Unconscious of popular imagination.

The later Freud's famous revision of the topography of the psyche,
laid out systematically in *The Ego and the Id* (1923b), complicates this
version of the unconscious. In that book, Freud would aver that:

> We recognize that the *Ucs.* does not coincide with the repressed;
> it is still true that all that is repressed is *Ucs.*, but not all that is *Ucs.*
> is repressed. A part of the ego too – and Heaven knows how
> important a part – may be *Ucs.*, undoubtedly is *Ucs.*
>
> (Freud, 1923b, p. 18)

In expanding the Unconscious to include a region of the ego,
Freud opens the territory into which the papers that follow Kohon's
Introduction in the present book will venture: it is the territory of
the infant's early experience. The unconscious ego is first of all
identified by Freud as the agency of resistance, repression and
censorship. 'There is no such thing as an unconscious "No"', the early

Freud had stated repeatedly, speaking of the repressed unconscious of wishful impulses. But if for the repressed unconscious every 'no' is an intolerable denial of its gratification, for the unconscious ego every 'yes' is a potentially dangerous destabilization of its boundaries.

The common denominator of resistance, repression and censorship is, of course, defence. The unconscious ego is invested above all in protecting itself from breaches of its own integrity and equilibrium. In his 'Introduction' to *The Shadow of the Object*, Bollas writes that 'the unconscious ego differs from the repressed unconscious in that the former refers to an unconscious form and the latter to unconscious contents' (Bollas, 1987, p. 8). The unconscious ego is the agency through which the self maintains its precarious coherence and continuity; until it is established, there can be no repressed unconscious – that is, no protected psychic preserve of sexual and destructive wishes. Put more succinctly, there can be no repressed before there is a mechanism of repression.

This is why developmental and metapsychological perspectives in these papers are so closely bound up with one another as to be near-indistinguishable. Bollas, Khan and Winnicott each describe how the everyday vicissitudes of the early environment give birth to a specific region of our psychic topography.

The convergence of these perspectives is nicely concentrated in a key formulation of Masud Khan's 'Cumulative Trauma' paper:[5] 'the mother as protective shield'. In its original incarnation in Freud's *Beyond the Pleasure Principle* (1920g), the protective shield designates not a person but a basic psychic mechanism. Freud describes a rudimentary 'living organism', whose outward-facing surface serves as an organ mediating between the organism and the external world. In so doing, it acquires a 'crust' or 'protective shield', defending the organism from the dangerously destabilizing and debilitating effects of external stimuli. 'Trauma' is then defined as the force of excitations 'powerful enough to break through the protective shield' (Freud, 1920g, p. 31).

This shield is, of course, the foundation of the psychic defences, tasked both with preventing breaches of their own boundaries and with mastering or 'binding' those excitations that inevitably do 'break in'. In speaking of her as 'protective shield', Khan identifies this structural function with the mother. Khan, I suggest, is developing, rather than challenging, Freud's metapsychological premise, pointing to the ways in which psychic structure is shaped by the forms of maternal care.

From infancy to adolescence, the mother serves the child as 'an auxiliary ego to support his immature and unstable ego-functions' (p. 108 herein). This function fleshes out the distinction between the repressed unconscious and the unconscious ego. For the former, the mother is an erotically cathected object, the source and focus of prohibited oedipal wishes. For the unconscious ego, however, the mother is less the impossible object of its desire than the support of its psycho-biological helplessness. By ministering to her infant's biological needs and containing the disruptive effects of both internal and external excitations, the mother underwrites the growth and development of his psychic structure.

But, as Freud had shown in *Beyond the Pleasure Principle* (1920g), it is in the very nature of the protective shield that it is regularly breached. In the first section of his paper, Khan outlines five stages in the history of the concept of trauma in psychoanalysis. The first stage involved the environmental traumas revealed in the reminis- cences suffered by hysterics and obsessional-neurotics, while the second and third comprise sexuality and the repetition compulsion, the two fundamental contents of the repressed unconscious. It is with the fourth stage that we enter into the territory of Khan's concerns.

This stage covers the last thirteen years of Freud's life, beginning with the publication in 1926 of *Inhibitions, Symptoms and Anxiety* (1926d), in which he conceptualizes the 'helplessness' (*Hilflosigkeit*) of the infant: his constitutional inadequacy to his own needs and his consignment to and dependence on the care of adults, a condition ameliorated only by the gradual development of the ego as facilitated by the 'extraneous help' of the mother. The fifth and final stage in the history set out by Khan emerges from this one and encompasses the post-Freudian development of ego psychology (Hans Hartmann and Anna Freud are named here) and the new significance given to the infant–mother relationship. It is to this stage that Khan's own paper is intended as a contribution.

Over the preceding two decades, Winnicott, Khan's own analyst, had described the processes by which the mother shields her baby from the traumatic realization of his fundamental biological and psychic unpreparedness for worldly life by nurturing the baby's illusion of omnipotence. Khan shows much more explicitly and systematically than Winnicott the metapsychological implications of this account of the mother–infant set-up.

Winnicott had posited the mother's fostering of psychic omni- potence in the baby's early life as preliminary to a gradual disillusionment engendered by ordinary and inevitable failures in the mother's provision of care. Repeated, though not excessive, time-lags in responding to the baby's hunger cries, for example, will mean that the breast's appearance is not magically coincident with his need, facilitating his acknowledgment of a separate or 'not-me' source of satisfaction.

This fraying of the fabric of omnipotence has the effect of a breach, insofar as it exposes the baby increasingly to the truth of his own helplessness and so intensifies the unpleasurable excitations felt from within and without. But the importance of Khan's contribution consists in more than simply translating Winnicott's ideas into a more strictly Freudian metapsychological vocabulary. Its originality lies in the way it frames the relationship between early and adult life. The idea of cumulative trauma is one of the few explicit attempts in British psychoanalysis to address the question, so central in French psychoanalysis of the same period, of the temporality of psychic experience.

Ordinary breaches in the maternal protective shield do not unduly distort the ego's development so much as '*bias* it', suggests Khan. Rather than being felt by the infant *in statu nascendi*, they 'cumulate silently and invisibly'. While one can understand this silent and invisible process at the level of developmental description, I would argue that its real significance is theoretical: if trauma is experienced cumulatively and imperceptibly rather than immediately and directly, it assumes the logic of *Nachträglichkeit*. As Khan writes, 'I would like to restrict myself merely to stating that the use of the word trauma in the concept of cumulative trauma should not mislead us into considering such breaches in the mother's role as protective shield as traumatic at the time or in the context in which they happen. They achieve the value of trauma *only cumulatively and in retrospect* (p. 109 herein, italics added).

With this rather understated qualification, Khan offers an understanding of trauma as produced in and by the time-lag between infancy and later life, as distinguished from those discrete traumas arising from isolated events. Its adaptation of the 'protective shield' metaphor is more than impressionistic, for it follows Freud in employing the metaphor to delineate a traumatic dimension at the heart of normal psychic development. For both writers (as well as for Winnicott), breaches of the shield, far from being exceptional, are necessary vicissitudes of the infant's care.[6]

All three papers, in fact, take us into the region of life prior to the formation of an organized ego whose bodily integrity, motor coordination and differentiated perception will eventually mitigate the original helplessness of the infant. They – but especially Khan's and Bollas' papers – explore the unperceived psychic work of the mother in transmitting and cultivating these ego-functions, as well as the various ways in which these processes are inevitably distorted.

The imperceptibility of these processes, moreover, is intrinsic to their disjointed temporality. We might take as illustrative the everyday experience of discerning the uncanny presence of a parent in their child's facial expressions, gestures or laughter. We are witness here to the unconscious – or, as Bollas would have it, 'unthought' – transmission of unconscious ego-functions to the infant, but only *nachträglich*, in the light of the child's incremental cumulation of the forms (and failures) of care by his environment.

Given its expansion of psychoanalytic inquiry into the field of early infancy, whose forms and contents are perceptible only in such retrospective expressions, it is surprising that British psychoanalysis has, at least until recently, tended largely to neglect the question of psychic time.[7] Winnicott's 'Fear of Breakdown', however, is a major exception to this tendency.

Winnicott's fragmentary yet seminal paper differs from Khan's in its focus on gross (rather than ordinary) environmental failure. Its concern is with the effects of such failure on a psyche whose ego is not yet established. Like Khan's paper, it describes the development of ego-functions by means of the mother's management of her infant's basic needs.

During the phase of unintegration, characterized by a kind of aimless diffusion of the baby's body and psyche, the mother's task is one of holding, the provision of a rudimentary form for the formlessness of his experience. The more threadbare this form, the more ordinary unintegration is likely to shade fatefully into primitive agonies: disintegration, precocious self-holding, depersonalization, and retreat into autistic states. Winnicott locates the sources of psychotic illness in these early disturbances of the undeveloped and precarious ego. The insight here is both simple and startling: in the absence of an established ego, there can be no *experience*, at least as we ordinarily understand the word. Experience requires a subject to whom the experience can happen, and by whom it can be rendered intelligible.

The breakdown feared by a certain type of patient is one that '*has already been*' – but it has occurred in the absence of a subject who could undergo it. A breach of psychosomatic boundaries occurs which the infant has no ego-resources to metabolize or defend against. The unconscious residue of this breach remains in the psyche without being claimed for memory or cognition. Moreover, as Winnicott points out, when we speak of the unconscious in this context, we do not have in mind the repressed Freudian unconscious of psychoneurosis, nor the mythic Jungian unconscious: 'In this special context, the unconscious means that the ego integration is not able to encompass something. The ego is too immature to gather all the phenomena into the area of personal omnipotence' (p. 124 herein).

This region of the unconscious, opened up by the earliest experience of the infant, cannot by definition manifest itself in the present, for the immature ego has no means to represent it to itself. It manifests itself, rather, in the *après-coup* of the adult psychoanalytic encounter. 'The patient', suggests Winnicott, 'needs to "remember" . . . something . . . that has not yet happened . . . [insofar as he] was not there for it to happen to' (p. 126 herein). This something thus cannot be the object of memory; to become such, it must be 'experienced by the patient for the first time' (p. 126 herein), in the here-and-now of the transference.

It is no surprise that the paper has been especially influential in France, where psychoanalysis came, via Lacan, to place the *après-coup* at the centre of its theoretical edifice. Haydée Faimberg, for example, takes up the motif of the experience not yet undergone to describe the spectral transmission of the unprocessed traumas of past to successive generations.[8] One also finds palpable resonances of this idea in César and Sandra Botella's seminal work on psychic figurability, which adumbrates a mode of analytic receptivity beyond the standard frame of the transference–countertransference, alerting the analyst to the presence in the patient of trauma neither remembered nor experienced.[9]

But the impact of the paper is certainly not confined to France. The perspectives it opens up on early infantile trauma have been developed by a range of Anglophone analysts. In the United States, for example, it has deeply informed Michael Eigen's work on psychotic mechanisms, as well as Thomas Ogden's on the most rudimentary levels of psychic functioning[10]. Recent British Independent writers have also made use of the paper to develop clinical insight into the persistent traces of early trauma in areas as diverse as adult pathology and aesthetic experience.[11] It is in Bollas' work, however, that we find perhaps the most systematic and expansive elaboration of Winnicott's ideas on early psychic function.

Bollas' transformational object alludes explicitly to the best known and most celebrated of the earlier thinker's concepts: the transitional object. The transitional object is one that mediates between the worlds within and outside the infant, and as such assumes the possession of a self with at least a basic sense of its own psycho-physical boundaries. The transformational object, in contrast, is an elaboration of Winnicott's environment-mother, the mother intuited by the infant whose ego-function is yet to emerge. This is the mother as process rather than object, a figure of 'existential as opposed to representational knowing' (p. 89 herein).

Where a representational knowing implies the accumulation of discrete and integral objects of knowledge, an existential knowing is one absorbed without such subjective mediation and organization. It is the realm of the unthought known, of a processual, non-cognitive knowledge manifest in an individual's very style of being – her bodily bearing, vocal patterns, facial tics and all the other marks of a personal 'idiom'[12] – that we experience as existentially given rather than consciously learned.

Therefore, the transformational object of Bollas' thinking incorporates, but also significantly enriches, Khan's concept of mother as protective shield. Where the latter is conceived largely in terms of defensive ego-functions, the former has a more variegated and complex structure. More than the hard skeletal structure of the ego, it is the fluid, imperceptible psychic matter that will eventually congeal into the elusive entity we call 'character'.

But the unthought known is a region expansive enough to encompass traumatic as well as ego-supportive experiences of the transformational object and, as such, adds significantly to the discussion initiated by Winnicott in 'Fear of Breakdown'. The clinical case of Peter, for example, is a usefully compressed study of cumulative trauma, in which Peter's adult character structure bears the traces of his impoverished experience of care as an infant.

There is, as far as the clinical evidence suggests to Bollas, no one infantile experience that can be identified as the source of the adult Peter's emptiness and 'inexorable sadness'. This interior life has instead been built up imperceptibly over time by the effective absence of a reliable environment-mother. Because Peter existed psychically for his mother only as the mythical object who would relieve her humdrum misery, not as 'an actual infant', his unthought known, the structure of his personality, is founded on his mother's lifeless projections, which have blocked his capacity to 'experience his internal psychic space as his own' (p. 94 herein). This absent capacity can be belatedly realized, as both Winnicott and Bollas argue, through the analyst's provision of the environmental care and attentiveness the patient has not yet known.

Bollas' unthought known also opens onto a theory of aesthetic experience that will be a key dimension both of the remaining chapters of *The Shadow of the Object* and of his consequent work, over the more than three decades since. This is rather more than an application of the concept. Art is not simply the expression of the unconscious idiom of a given artist, but the way in which the artist's ongoing search after the transformational object relation comes to enact itself. From this perspective, art – and culture more generally – can be understood as a primary attestation to the force of the *après-coup*.

I have tried to show the major contribution these papers make to key theoretical and technical problems in psychoanalysis, arising from the new focus in the British tradition on earliest infancy in the formation of the ego. They offer an important corrective to the temptation to frame the effects of the early environment in the linear causal terms implied in Strachey's elegant but misleading translation of *Nachträglichkeit* as deferred action, whereby earlier events can be seen to impact and shape later ones.

This is not merely a matter of specialized theoretical interest, for this implicit conception of psychic time has palpable effects on the terms and culture of, in particular, clinical discussion in contemporary British psychoanalysis, whether in formal papers or informal professional groups. Thought of as 'deferred action', Peter's lifelessness becomes the consequence of his mother's impoverished emotional communication in infancy. But to posit the earlier as the cause of the later in this way is to miss the intricate relay between past and present, and the strange temporal inversion whereby the later can give birth to the earlier. Just as the Wolf Man's primal scene comes into being only via the analysis of the dreams, fantasies and relationships of his later life, so it is the unprecedented later experience of the analyst's attentiveness to Peter's feelings, especially as registered in the inarticulate, infantile forms of bodily discomfort and dispersion, that allows the absence of such receptivity in the original situation of care to emerge.

To recast psychic time in this way means more than refining and complicating the ways in which we speak of the interplay between early and later life. Against the automatic assumption of the causal priority of the earliest event, it enables us to appreciate the crucial role of later experiences in shaping, intensifying, diminishing and changing the effects and meanings of earlier ones.

Each of these papers alerts us to the clinical as well as theoretical difficulties arising from the incorporation of the patient's earliest environment into psychoanalytic thinking. But related to this, and equally central, is their development of Freud's basic lineaments of the unconscious ego. An important question arises from the sub-division of the unconscious into the domains of the repressed un-conscious and the unconscious ego (or unthought known) – namely, how we should conceive the relationship between them. For if we cannot doubt that the Unconscious does not just coincide with the repressed, and that there is a part of the ego that is also unconscious, this then leaves unresolved the ways in which the two interact with and intrude upon one another.

Khan's response to this question reveals the influence on his thinking of American ego-psychology as well as Anna Freud. In the work of Hans Hartmann, Ernst Kris and Phyllis Greenacre, among others, psychoanalytic theory and technique were framed in terms of the cultivation in the subject of an autonomous and conflict-free region of the mind. For Khan, the maternal protective shield would be the transmission of the adaptive and organizing capacities of this area of the unconscious ego of the infant: 'The protective-shield role is the result of conflict-free autonomous ego-functions in the mother' (p. 112 herein).

Psychoanalytic theorists of varying stripes have since cast in doubt the notion of a conflict-free and autonomous psychic agency that could be discretely isolated from the vicissitudes of the drives. But read in the context of the paper as a whole, Khan's use of the concept seems more complex. The fact that there will inevitably be breaches in the protective-shield function means that a conflict-free region can exist only as a theoretical heuristic. In the psychic reality of the mother, ego-function will always have been shaped and distorted by her own unconscious investments, and indeed by the ways in which ego-function was transmitted in her infancy by her own adult carers.

Bollas' idea of the transmission of a maternal idiom is particularly helpful here, for an idiom or an individual style of being is the particular expression that unconscious ego-functions assume in a

85

singular self. We have a distinct and unrepeatable character, we might say, in large part because the form of the unconscious ego transmitted to us will necessarily have been stamped by the content of the repressed unconscious. Peter's lifelessness, for example, revives and remakes that of the ego-function he received from his mother; but the form of her own ego was undoubtedly affected, and profoundly so, by her own investments of love and hate.

What we see in these papers' inquiries into the forms of the unconscious ego is not then a reorientation of psychoanalysis away from repressed unconscious, but a deepening and expansion of the entire territory of psychic life.

Notes

1 For a useful and comprehensive synthesis of the developmental psychological perspective in Independent psychoanalytic thinking, see Rayner *et al.* (2005). The work of Peter Fonagy and Mary Target (Fonagy and Target, 2003; Mayes, Fonagy, and Target, 2007) has been especially influential in the effort to articulate psychoanalysis and developmental psychology.
2 See the famous discussion of the Wolf Man's primal scene, in which the status of the primal scene as fantasy or reality is judged undecidable or '*non liquet*' (Freud, 1918b, pp. 57–60).
3 See the dialogue between André Green and Daniel Stern over the competing claims of observation and clinical inference in Sandler, Sandler, and Davies (2000).
4 This is the translation of the term proposed by Jean Laplanche in his 'Notes on Afterwardsness' (1999).
5 Khan's seminal paper cannot escape the shadow cast on his work by a former patient's revelations of serious and consistent boundary violations in his clinical practice, and by his expulsion from the British Psychoanalytical Society following the inclusion of an anti-Semitic tirade against a Jewish patient in *When Spring Comes* (1988). These revelations mime uncannily the traumatic breach of the protective shield Khan describes in his most influential paper (1963) – in this case, the shield protecting the psychoanalytic setting itself. The impression is amplified by the paucity of specifically psychoanalytic discussion of the complaints against him as well as by the relative obscurity into which Khan's work has since fallen – although, since those revelations, his psychoanalytic contributions have been referred to, commented upon, and quoted by Independent analysts like Christopher Bollas, Roger Kennedy, Gregorio Kohon, Michael Parsons, Jonathan Sklar, Paul Williams, and others.

6 Bion also used the concept of a contact-barrier (1962a, p. 17). Cf. the important link, elaborated by Sebastián Kohon (2014), between Bion's notion and Freud's, and his drive theory and the economic point of view in psychoanalysis. In comparing Bion's concept to Freud's description of the contact-barrier in the 'Project for a Scientific Psychology' (1950 [1895]), Kohon illustrates the clinical relevance of such concepts; furthermore, he also clearly shows Freud's influence on Bion's ideas.

7 For recent contributions to the question of temporality by British psychoanalytic writers, see Gregorio Kohon (1999b, especially Chapters 1 and 7; 2016); Rosine Perelberg (2008), Dana Birksted-Breen (2003), and Michael Parsons (2014). Sodré (2005) offers a valuable account of the apparent absence of a concept of *après-coup* in the Kleinian theoretical tradition.

8 See Faimberg (2005, especially Chapter 10), as well as her reading of Winnicott's 'Fear of Breakdown' paper (Faimberg, 2013).

9 See Botella and Botella (2005).

10 See Eigen (1999, especially Chapter 10), and Ogden (1992, 2005).

11 See, for example, the chapters by Paul Williams (2012) and Roger Kennedy (2012) and Michael Parsons (2014, especially Chapter 8).

12 Bollas develops the idea of the personal 'idiom' in his second book, *Forces of Destiny* (1989).

8

THE TRANSFORMATIONAL
OBJECT

Christopher Bollas

We know that because of the considerable prematurity of human
birth the infant depends on the mother for survival. By serving as a
supplementary ego (Heimann, 1956) or a facilitating environment
(Winnicott, 1963c) she both sustains the baby's life and transmits to
the infant, through her own particular idiom of mothering, an
aesthetic of being that becomes a feature of the infant's self. The
mother's way of holding the infant, of responding, of selecting
objects, of perceiving the infant's internal needs, constitutes the
'culture' she creates for herself and her baby, a private culture that
can only be inhabited by the two – mother and child – composed of
a language of highly idiomatic syntaxes of gestures, sound, pattern
and mood that ensures its privacy, and emphasizes the sequestered
ambience of this first relation. In his unparalleled work on the
mother–child relation, Winnicott (1960c) stresses what we might call
its stillness: the mother provides a continuity of being, she 'holds' the
infant in an environment of her making that facilitates his growth.
And yet, against this reciprocally enhancing stillness, there is an active
exchange between mother and child, a constant process of negoti-
ated moments that cohere around the rituals of psychosomatic needs:
i.e., feeding, diapering, sleeping, holding. It is undeniable, I think,
that as the infant's 'other' self, the mother continually *transforms* the
infant's internal and external environment. Writes Edith Jacobson:

when a mother turns the infant on his belly, takes him out of his crib, diapers him, sits him up in her arms and on her lap, rocks him, strokes him, kisses him, feeds him, smiles at him, talks and sings to him, she offers him not only all kinds of libidinal gratifications but simultaneously stimulates and prepares the child's sitting, standing, crawling, walking, talking, and on and on, i.e., the development of functional ego activity.

(1965, p. 37)

Winnicott (1963a) terms this comprehensive function of the mother, the 'environment' mother, because he wants to acknowledge that, for the infant, the mother is not yet another; far more, she is the total environment. To this I would add that the mother is less identifiable as an object than as a *process* that is identified with cumulative internal and external gratifications. Because my paper will be about the *trace* in adult life of this early object relation, I want to identify the first object as a *transformational object*. By that I mean an object that is experientially identified by the infant with the process of the alteration of self experience; an identification that emerges from symbiotic relating, where the first object is 'known' not by cognizing it into an object representation, but known as a recurrent experience of being – a kind of existential, as opposed to representational, knowing. As the mother integrates the infant's being (instinctual, cognitive, affective, environmental) the rhythms of this process, from unintegration(s) to integration(s), informs the nature of this 'object' relation rather than the qualities of the object *qua* object. The mother is not yet identified as an object but is experienced as a process of transformation, and this feature remains in the trace of this object-seeking in adult life, where I believe the object is sought for its function as signifier of the process of transformation of being. Thus, in adult life, the quest is not to possess the object; it is sought in order to surrender to it as a process that alters the self, where the subject-as-supplicant now feels himself to be the recipient of enviro-somatic caring, identified with metamorphoses of the self. As it is an identification that begins before the mother is cognized as an object, it is not an object relation that emerges from desire, but from a kind of proto-perceptual identification of the object with its active feature – the object as enviro-somatic transformer of the subject – and manifests itself in the person's search for an object (a person, place, event, ideology) that promises to transform the self. I shall outline

89

the features of this early object tie, provide a clinical example that hyperbolizes one pathological variant of it, and finally, argue that this relation not only emerges in the transference of many patients, but is unconsciously acted out by psychoanalysts, as, I will argue, the analytic ecology enacts what Freud excluded: the early object relation of mother and child.

The experience of the mother as transformation is supported from several directions. In the first place, the mother assumes the function of the transformational object; she constantly alters the infant's environment to meet his needs. That the infant identifies the mother with transformation of being, through his symbiotic knowing, is not a delusion, but a fact, the mother actually transforms the infant's world. In the second place, the infant's own emergent ego capacities – of perception, motility, integration – also transform his world. The acquisition of language is perhaps the most obvious such transform-ation, but learning to handle an object, to differentiate objects, to remember objects that are not present, are transformative achieve-ments: they result in ego change that alters the nature of the infant's object world. It is not surprising that the infant identifies these ego achievements with the presence of an object, as the failure of the mother to maintain provision of the facilitating environment, through prolonged absence or bad handling, can bring about ego collapse and psychic pain. With the infant's creation of the transitional object, the transformational process is displaced from the mother-environment (where it originated) into countless subjective-objects, so that this transitional phase is heir to the transformational phase, as the infant evolves from experience of the process to articulation of the experi-ence. With the transitional object, the infant can play with the illusion of his own omnipotence (lessening the loss of the environ-ment-mother with generative and phasic delusions of self and other creation), he can entertain the idea of the object being got rid of, yet surviving his ruthlessness; he can find in this transitional experience the freedom of metaphor: what was an actual process can be displaced into symbolic equations that, if supported by the mother, mitigate the loss of the original environment-mother. In a sense, the use of a transitional object is the infant's first creative act, an event that does not just display an ego capacity – such as grasping – but which indicates the infant's first proto-subjective experience of such capacities.

The search for the transformational object in adult life

It is in adult life that I think we have failed to take notice of the wide-ranging collective search for an object that is identified with the metamorphosis of the self. In many religious faiths, for example, the subject believes in the deity's actual potential to transform the total environment, thus sustaining the terms of the earliest object tie within a mythic structure – where knowledge remains symbiotic (i.e., the wisdom of faith) – that coexists alongside other forms of knowing. In secular worlds, we can see how the hope invested in many objects (a new job, a move to another country, a vacation, a change of relationship) may be both a request for a transformational experience, and, at the same time, a continual 'relationship' to an object that signifies the experience of transformation. We know that the advertising world makes its living on the *trace* of this object; as the advertised product usually promises to alter the subject's external environment and thus change internal mood.

In adult life, the search for such an experience may generate hope, even a sense of confidence and vision, but though it seems to be grounded in the future tense, in finding something in the future to transform the present, it is an object-seeking that recurrently enacts a pre-verbal ego memory. It is usually on the occasion of the aesthetic moment (Bollas, 1978) that an individual feels a deep subjective rapport with an object – a painting, a poem, during an opera or symphony, before a landscape when the person experiences an uncanny fusion with the object, an event that recalls the kind of ego experience which constituted his earliest experiences. But such occasions, as meaningful as they might be, are less noteworthy as transformational accomplishments than they are for their uncanny quality: the sense of being reminded of something never cognitively apprehended, but existentially known, the memory of the ontogenetic process, rather than thought or fantasies that occur once the self is established. That is, such aesthetic moments do not sponsor memories of a specific event or relationship, they evoke a total psychosomatic sense of fusion – an ego experience – that is the subject's recollection of the transformational object. This anticipation of being transformed by an object – itself an ego memory of the ontogenetic process – inspires the subject with a reverential attitude toward the object, so that, even as the transformation of the self will not take place on the scale it did during early life, the adult subject tends to nominate the objects as sacred.

91

In adult life, therefore, to seek the transformational object is really to recollect an early object experience, to remember not cognitively, but existentially through intense affective experience, a relationship that was identified with cumulative transformational experiences of the self. Its intensity as an object relation is not due to the fact that the object was desired, but because the object is identified with such considerable metamorphoses of being. In the aesthetic moment, the subject briefly re-experiences through ego fusion with the aesthetic object, the sense of the subjective attitude towards the trans-formational object, but such experiences are only memories, not actual recreations. The search, however, for such symbolic equations of the transformational object and the experience with which it is identified continues in adult life. Man develops faith in a deity whose absence, ironically, is held to be as important a test of man's being as his presence. We go to the theatre, to the museum, to the landscapes of our choice, where we search for aesthetic experiences. We may *imagine* the self as the transformational facilitator, and we may invest ourselves with capacities to alter the environment that are not only impossible but downright embarrassing on reflection. In such daydreams the self as transformational object lies somewhere in the future tense, and even ruminative planning about the future (what to do, where to go, etc.) however it may yield practical plans, is often a kind of psychic prayer for the arrival of the transformational object: a secular second coming of an object relation experienced in the earliest life.

It should not be surprising that varied psychopathologies emerge from failure, as Winnicott put it, to be disillusioned from this relationship. The gambler, who invests his game with the certainty of a transformational object that is only just about to metamorphose his entire internal and external world, is one example. This goes for much criminality, for, again as Winnicott (1956a) has pointed out, the delinquent is adamant that the environment must make something up to him. In my concept, he relates to the environment as if he can through the perfect crime discover the perfect object, a crime that will transform the self, internally (repairing ego defects and fulfilling id needs) and externally (bringing wealth and happiness). Indeed, different forms of erotomania may be efforts to establish the other as the transformational object. I do not think that the search for the perfect crime or the perfect woman is only an idealized split; it is also some recognition in the subject of a deficiency in ego experience and a recurrent reliving of the area of what Michael Balint (1968) called the 'basic fault'. The search to commit the complete crime, the planned seduction of the perfect woman, however they serve to split the bad self experience away from the subject's cognitive knowledge, are nonetheless semiological acts that signify the person's search for a particular object relation that is associated with ego transformation and repair.

Clinical example

I think that one of the most common psychopathologies of the transformational object relation occurs with what we have called the schizoid self: the patient who may have a wealth of ego strengths (intelligence, talent, accomplishment, success) but who is personally bereft and sad without being clinically depressed. I have written about Peter before in another paper (Bollas, 1976).

Peter is a 28-year-old single male whose sad expressions, dishevelled appearance, and colourless apparel are only mildly relieved by a sardonic sense of humour which brings him no relief, and an intelligence and education which he uses for the sake of others, but never for himself. He was referred by his general practitioner for depression, but his problem was more of an inexorable sadness and personal loneliness. Since his break-up with a girlfriend he had lived alone in a flat, dispersing himself during the day into multiple odd jobs. Though his days were a flurry of arranged activity he went through them in a style of agitated passivity as if he were being aggressively handled by his own work arrangement. Once home he would collapse into the slovenly comfort of his flat where he would prop himself before the TV, eat a scanty meal of packaged food, masturbate and, above all, ruminate obsessively about the future and bemoan his current 'bad luck'.

Every week, without failure, he would go home to see his mother. He felt she lived in order to talk about him and thus he must be seen by her in order to keep her content.

Reconstruction of the earliest years of Peter's life yielded the following. Peter was born in a working-class home during the war. While father was defending the country the home was occupied by numerous in-laws, all middle-European who were holding on to their lost culture by speaking constantly about local folklore and disclosing regional and familial curses, hexes and signs. Peter was the first child born in the family and he was lavishly idolized, particularly by his mother who spoke constantly to her relatives about how Peter would undo their misery through great deeds. An inveterate dreamer about golden days to come, mother's true depression showed up in the lifeless manner in which she cared for Peter, investing all her liveliness towards him as mythical object rather than actual infant. Soon after Peter's therapy began it became clear to me that he knew himself to be primarily inside a myth he shared with mother; indeed, he knew that she did not actually attend to the real him but to the object of her dreams which happened to be him. As *her* mythical object he felt his life to be suspended and, indeed, this was the way he lived. He seemed to be preserving himself, attending to somatic needs, waiting for the day when he would fulfil mother's dream. But because it was mother's myth, he could do nothing, only wait for something to happen. He seemed compulsively to empty himself of his true self needs in order to create an internal empty space to receive mother's dream thoughts. Each visit to the home was curiously like a mother giving her son a narrative feeding. So he would empty himself of personal desire and need in order to fulfil mother's desire and he would preserve himself in a state of suspension from life, waiting for the myth to call him into a transformed reality. Because mother has transmitted to him his crucial function as her mythic object, Peter does not experience his internal psychic space as his own. Inner space exists for the other, so that in reporting inner states of being Peter does so through a depersonalized narrative as this region is not the 'from me' but the 'for her'. There is a notable absence in Peter of any sense of self, no quality of an 'I', nor even of a 'me'. Instead his self representation bears more the nature of an 'it' on an existential plane. Being an 'it' means for him being dormant, suspended, inert. Free associations with Peter are more like *logs* of 'it' states: ruminative reports on the happenings of his body as depersonalized object. As mother's primary concern was for him to remain in good health in order to fulfil her dreams for him, he was consequently obsessed with any somatic problem, which he reported with almost clinical detachment.

Gradually I recognized that the mythic structure (existing in a narrative rather than existential reality) masked the secret discourse of the lost culture of Peter's earliest relation to his mother. His ego-states were an utterance to mother who used them as the vocabulary of myth. If he was feeling like a casualty because of ego defects and the failure of id needs, it was because he was her knight errant who had fought battles for her and must rest for future missions. If he felt depleted by his personal relations it was because he was a cherished god who could not expect to mix successfully with the masses. If he spoke to his mother with a sigh she responded not by discovering the source of the sigh, but by telling him not to worry, that soon he would make money, become famous, go on TV, and bring to the family all the wealth that they deserved. His existential despair was continually flung into mythic narrative: a symbolic order where the real is used to populate the fantastic. On the few occasions when he tried to elicit from his mother some actual attendance to his internal life she flew into a rage and yelled that his misery threatened their lives, as only he could deliver them. He must remain the golden larva, the unborn hero, who, if he does not shatter mythic function with personal needs, will soon be delivered into a world of riches and fame beyond his imagination.

In the transference Peter spoke of himself as an object in need of care: 'my stomach hurts', 'I have a pain in my neck', 'I have a cold', 'I don't feel well'. He spoke to me in the language of sighs, groans, and a haunting laughter which served his need to empty out agitated desire and to elicit my acute attention. He rubbed his hands, looked at his fingers, flopped his body around as if it were a sack. As I came to realize that this was not obsessive rumination which served as a resistance, but was, in fact, a secret discourse recalled from the culture of his earliest relations to mother, he found my attention to his discourse an immense relief. I felt that he was trying to share a secret with me, within the transference, but it was a secret utterance that was prior to language and masked by its enigmatic quality. I could only enter this sequestered culture by speaking to him in its language: to be attentive to all groans, sighs, remarks about his body, etc. Above all, I was to learn that what he wanted from me was the sound of my voice which I gradually understood to be the need for a good maternal sound which framed his experience with me and eventually transformed our relationship. My interpretations were appreciated less for their content, and more for their function as structuring experiences. He rarely recalled the content of an interpretation. What he appreciated was the sense of relief brought to him through my words.

Peter's sense of fatedness, as a potential transformational object to the other, suggests that not only does the infant require separation and disillusion from the mother's apparent function as the sole agent of transformation, but equally, the mother must suffer some generative depressive experience after the birth of her infant, a 'let-down', brought on by the real needs of the infant, which mitigates the mother's unconscious wish for an infant to be her transformational object. Peter's mother continually refused to recognize and attend to him as a real person, though admittedly, there was a quality of what we might call covetous mothering about her care: she possessed him as if she was an alchemist guarding dross that was her potential treasure. His real needs went unmet, as mother insisted that Peter fulfil her sense that destiny would bring her a deliverer-child.

Discussion

Now this is an obvious example of the psychopathology of the transformational object relation, and our work with narcissistic patients (who function with the illusion of self as transformational object, but who exhibit the forlorn depressive features of one who is forever failed in self-provision), and with schizoid persons, hyperbolizes the features of this particular object situation. I believe, however, that the search for the transformational object, in both the narcissistic and schizoid character, is in fact an internal recognition of the need for ego repair and, as such, is a somewhat manic search for health. To be sure, one of the features of such patients is their comparative unavailability for relating to the actual other – their obtuseness or excessive withdrawnness – but I think such characteristics, reflective of psychodevelopmental arrests, also point towards the patient's need to assert the region of illness as a plea for the arrival of the regressive object relation that is identified with basic ego repair. In analysis this can result in the patient's almost total inability to relate to the analyst as a real person, while at the same time maintaining an intense relation to the analyst as a transformational object. What is the patient trying to establish? It seems to me, as I have written about Peter, and as other authors have pointed out (Smith, 1977), that such patients seek to live within a special ambience with the analyst, where the analyst's interpretations are far less important for their content, and more significant for what is experienced as a maternal sound – a kind of verbal humming. Indeed, so-called analytic neutrality of expression – ostensibly to mitigate the hysterical or obsessional patient's dread of feeling criticized and to facilitate the analysand's freedom of association – actually works in a different way for narcissistic or schizoid patients; they become *enchanted* by it, and can appear oblivious to the actual content of the interpretation so long as the song of the analytic voice remains constant. Now, we may look upon this as a complication in the path of analysability, or we may recognize that the analytic space (the provision of the holding environment) facilitates a process in such patients that leads to the evocation of a deeply regressed state which may be a part of this patient's necessary path to cure. Indeed, my experience with such patients is that a regression to this form of object-relating takes place often in the *first* session of therapy, and that the ecology of the analytic room (analyst, analyst's interpretations, couch, the rest) becomes a kind of sacred space for the patient. As I view it, the patient is regressed to what Balint has called the level of the basic fault, but as each regression points to the region of illness within the person, it also suggests the requirement of a cure, and in such patients I believe what is needed is a prolonged experience of successive ego transformations that are identified with the analyst and the analytic ecology. In such moments, the patient experiences interpretations primarily for their capacity to *match* his internal mood, or feeling, or thought, and such moments of rapport lead the patient to 're-experience' the transformational object relation. Such patients appreciate the analyst's fundamental unintrusiveness (particularly the analyst's not demanding compliance) not because it leads to freedom of association, but because it feels like the kind of relating that is needed to become well. Now some analysts might regard this perception of the patient only as a resistance, but if so, I think we overlook the undeniably unique atmosphere we create for relating. We know that the very offer of treatment invites regressive longings in many patients. We know that placing the patient on the couch induces a sense of anxious expectation and dependency. Our reliability, our unintrusiveness, our use of empathic thought to meet the requirements of the patient, is often far more of a maternal ambience for the patient than the actual mother provided. And in such moments, the patient's identification with the analyst as the transformational object is not dissimilar to the infant's identification of the mother with such processes. Indeed, just as the infant's identification of ego transformations with the mother is a perceptual identification – and not a desire – so, too, the patient's identification does not seem to reflect the patient's desire for us to be transformational, but his adamant perceptual identification of the analyst as transformational object. In the treatment of the narcissistic, borderline and schizoid characters, this phase of the analysis is both necessary and inevitable.

This stage of treatment is very difficult for the therapist, as in a sense there is as yet no *analysis* of the patient taking place, and interpretive remarks made may be met with a gamut of refusals: from polite contempt to rage. One such patient would often nod politely, say that yes he did see what I meant, indeed was impressed with how accurate my remark was, but invariably he would end by saying: 'But of course, you know what you have said is only technically correct. It doesn't help me with life experiences, so, as such, as correct as it is I don't see what you think I can do with such a remark.' He was convinced I knew how to take care of him, and even if it was only for an hour a day, he wanted me to soothe him. Analysis proper was regarded as an intellectual intrusion into his tranquil experience of me, and I was for him a kind of advanced computer storing his information, processing his needs into my memory banks, all this towards an eventual session when I would suddenly emerge with the proper solution for him and in an instant remedy his life. I have come to regard this part of his analysis as that kind of regression which is a re-enactment of the earliest object experience, and I think it is folly for a therapist to deny that the culture of the analytic space does indeed facilitate such recollections. If such regressions are a resistance to the analysis of the self, they are resistances only in the sense that the patient *must* resist analytic investigation *as it is experienced as a precocious overachievement of the patient's psychic position*, and in the transference – which is as much to the analytic space and process as it is to the person of the analyst – the patient's regression is to the level of relating to the transformational object, that is, experiencing the analyst as the environment-mother, a pre-verbal memory that cannot be cognized into speech that recalls the experience, but only speech that demands its terms be met: unintrusiveness, 'holding', 'provision', insistence on a kind of symbiotic or telepathic knowing, facilitation from thought to thought, or from affect to thought, that means many of these sessions are in the form of *clarifications* which the patient experiences as transformative events. Interpretations which require reflective thought, or which analyse the self, are felt to be precocious demands on the patient's psychic capacity, and such patients may react with acute rage or express a sudden sense of futility.

Perhaps because so much of psychoanalytic theory evolved from work with the hysterical patient (who interpreted the analytic ecology as a seduction) or the obsessional patient (who adopted it willingly as another personal ritual) we have tended to regard regressive reactions to the analytic space as resistances to the working alliance or the analytic process. And yet, perhaps the hysteric's sexualization of the transference, and the obsessional's ritualization of the analytic process (free dissociation?) were themselves defences against the very 'invitation' of the analytic space and process towards regression. Thus, in the analyses of such patients, psychic material was readily forthcoming and one could be relatively pleased that there was considerable grist for the analytic mill, but treatment often continued endlessly with no apparent character change, or was suddenly intruded upon by archaic or primitive material. In such cases I believe the analyst was unaware that the failure of the patient to experience the analytic situation as a regressive invitation was − if we will − a resistance; indeed, the analytic process, with premium on the mechanics of free association and interpretation of the patient's defences, could often result in denial of the very object relation that was 'offered' to the patient. If the analyst cannot acknowledge that in fact he is offering a regressive space to the patient (that is, a space that encourages the patient to relive his infantile life in the transference), if he insists that in the face of the 'invitation' *work* must be carried out, it is not surprising that in such analyses patient and analyst may either carry on in a kind of mutual dissociation that leads nowhere (obsessional collusion), or in a sudden blow-up on the part of the patient, often termed 'acting out'.

As I view it, then, the analyst functions as an evocative mnemic trace of the transformational object, as the situation will either induce a patient's regressive recollection of this early object relation, or the variations of resistance to it: i.e., either denial by sexualization, or obsessional ritualization. Indeed, the transference, from this point of view, is first and foremost a transference reaction to this primary object relation and will help us to see how the patient remembers his own experience of this early object situation. There may be a deep regression to a demand that the analyst fulfil the promise of the invitation and function in a magically transformative manner, or the patient may have enough health to be able to report his experience of the situation, and to have enough insight into regressive recollections, to carry on with subsequent work in the analysis, and yet do so while remaining in touch with more archaic aspects of the self. Indeed, I believe that much of the time a patient's passivity, or wordlessness, or expectation that the analyst either knows what to do or should do something is not a resistance to any particular conscious or preconscious thought, but is a recollection of the early pre-verbal world of the infant being with mother. Unless we recognize that psychoanalysts share in the construction of this pre-verbal world, through the analyst's silence, the total absence of didactic instruction and empathic thought, we are being unfair to the patient and he may have reason to be perplexed and irritated.

I have taken this diversion into (hopefully) excusable oversimplification of clinical issues, in order to clarify my belief that the transference relation rests on the paradigm of the first-transformational-object relation. Freud tacitly recognized this when he set up the analytic space and process and, though there is comparatively little about the mother–child relation within Freud's theory, we might say that Freud acted out his non-verbal and unconscious recognition of it in the creation of the analytic ecology. Indeed, the construction of the psychoanalytic process rests itself on the memory of this primary relation, and the psychoanalyst's collective unconscious re-enactment (a professional countertransference) is to recollect by enactment the transformational object situation. What Freud could not analyse in himself – his relation to his own mother – was acted out in his choice of the ecology of psychoanalytic technique. And unless we can grasp that as psychoanalysts we *are* enacting this early paradigm, we continue to act out in the countertransference Freud's one, and eminently excusable, area of blindness.

Though the search for transformations and for the transformational objects is perhaps the most pervasive archaic object relation, it bears restressing that the search is not out of desire for the object *per se*, nor *primarily* out of craving or longing, but derives from an insistent perceptual identification with the object of transformations of the self. To be sure, the entire range of human feeling may be elicited in the search for the object – euphoria if felt to be found, despondency if felt to be non-existent – but the search for the object is out of certainty that it will transform the subject. Of course this may lead to the object's achieving a secondary idealization – as in the legend of Christ – but making the object sacred occurs only after the object's transformational potential has been declared. In each instance, I believe, the reason for the isolated affect of adamant certainty that the object will deliver transformation is based on the object's nominated capacity to resuscitate the memory of early ego transformation. In arguing this, I am maintaining that though no cognitive memory of the infant's experience of the mother is available, the search for the transformational object, its nomination as the deliverer of environmental transformation, is an ego memory. In a curious way, it is solely the ego's object, and may, indeed, be to the utter shock or indifference of the person's subjective experience of their own desire. A gambler is compelled to gamble: subjectively, he may wish he did not gamble, and this internal identification with the perfect moment may indeed cause personal misery. In Melville's novel *Moby-Dick* Ahab feels compelled to seek the whale, even though he feels alienated from the source of his own internal compulsion. He says:

> 'What is it, what nameless, inscrutable, unearthly thing is it; what cozening, hidden lord and master, and cruel, remorseless emperor commands me; then against all natural lovings and longings, I so keep pushing, and crowding, and jamming myself on all the time; recklessly making me ready to do what in my own proper, natural heart, I durst not so much as dare? Is Ahab, Ahab? Is it I, God, or who, that lifts this arm?'
>
> (1851, pp. 444–5)

There is something *impersonal and ruthless* about the search for the whale, and all objects nominated as transformational. Once early ego memories are identified with an object that is contemporary, the subject's relation to the object can become fanatical, and I think many extremist political movements indicate a collective certainty that their revolutionary ideology will effect a total environmental transformation that will deliver everyone from the gamut of basic faults: personal, familial, economic, social, and moral. Again, it is not the revolutionary's desire for change, or the extremist's longing for change, but his *certainty* that the object (in this case the revolutionary ideology) will bring about change that is striking to the observer.

Conclusions

In work with certain kinds of patients (schizoid and narcissistic) who hyperbolize a particular object-seeking, and in our analysis of certain features of culture, I think we can isolate the *trace* in the adult of the earliest experience of the object: the experience of an object that transforms the subject's internal and external world. I have called this first object the transformational object, as I want to identify it with *the object as process*, thus linking the first object with the infant's experience of it. Before the mother is' personalized to the infant as a whole object, she has functioned as a region or source of transformation, and as the infant's own nascent subjectivity is almost completely the experience of the ego's integrations (cognitive, libidinal, affective) the first object is identified with the alterations of

101

the ego's state. With the infant's growth and increasing self-reliance, the relation to the mother changes from the mother as the other who alters the self, to a *person* who has her own life and her own needs. As Winnicott says, the mother disillusions the infant from the experience of mother as the sole preserver of his world, a process that occurs as the infant is increasingly able to meet his own needs and requirements; but the ego experience of being transformed by the other remains as a memory that may be re-enacted either in the subject's search for aesthetic experiences, in a wide range of culturally-dreamed-of transformational objects, such as new cars, homes, jobs, vacations, that promise total change of internal and external environment, or in the varied psychopathological manifestations of this memory: in the gambler's relation to his object, in the extremist's relation to his ideological object. I have argued that the ecology of the psychoanalytic space, outfitted with a silent and empathic analyst, a couch to 'hold' the patient, the release from socialization, and the emphasis on fantasizing to the analyst, etc., often leads to the identification of the analyst with the transformational object. This occurs *because* the analytic ecology sponsors such a regressive relating, and because the idiom of the analytic relation bears considerable psychic resemblance to the mother's attendance to the infant. As such, the patient's insistence that the analyst is the transformational object is not necessarily a resistance to the work of analysis, but is a memory resuscitated by the analytic process itself, and it behoves the analytic profession to analyse more thoroughly the unconscious communication of the analytic ecology. I have argued that we continue to *act out* in what is now the ritual idiom of the analytic technique a lacuna in Freud's self-analysis: his own relation to his mother. Recollected aspects of this relation, I suggest, are reproduced in the analytic technique, though psychoanalysts, having inherited Freud's insights, have also inherited his blindness in not recognizing how psychoanalytic technique both enacts and elicits memories of the earliest object relation. We might call this a professional unconscious countertransference, as we offer a patient one kind of relationship (the regressive re-experience of infant to mother) which still revives not only ego memories but expectations and, on the other hand, we insist, at least in more classical formulations, on proceeding to analytic 'work'. Such work cannot take place, I maintain, until the analyst has a thorough understanding of his own profession as a countertransference enactment of an early object setting and relation. Until we cognize this non-verbal enactment of our own, we cannot successfully facilitate our patients through their own recognition of it. Finally, we can see, perhaps, how in the aesthetic moment, when the person engages in deep subjective rapport with an object, the culture finds in the arts varied symbolic equivalents of the search for transformation, as in the *quest* for a deep subjective experience of an object, the artist both remembers for us and provides us with occasions for the experience of ego memories of transformation. In a way, the experience of the aesthetic moment is neither social nor moral; it is curiously impersonal and in a way ruthless, as the object is sought for only as a deliverer of an experience. The aesthetic space allows for an appropriate enactment of the search for this object relation, and we might say the culture engages in memories of ego experiences that are now profoundly radical experiences, as the culture cannot possibly meet the needs of the subject as the mother met the needs of the infant, but in the arts we have a location for such occasional recollections, intense ego memories of the process of self-transformation.

9

THE CONCEPT OF CUMULATIVE TRAUMA

M. Masud R. Khan

Every phase of theory-making in psychoanalysis has influenced the current concept of trauma and its clinical evaluation (Fenichel, 1937). I shall, somewhat arbitrarily, divide the total span of analytic researches into five stages. This is an artificial division to show what new ideas emerge at which stage. One stage does not cancel out the other. They run parallel, reinforcing and partially correcting each other, and each time a new strand is added to the growing complexity of psycho-analytic metapsychology.

In the first phase, 1885 to 1905, while Freud was postulating the basic concepts for the understanding of the unconscious – dream work, primary and secondary processes, the psychic apparatus, symptom formation, and the aetiology of hysteria and obsessional neurosis – the concept of trauma played a very vital and significant role (Freud, 1893a, 1895b). Trauma was conceived of essentially as (a) an environmental factor that intrudes upon the ego and which the ego cannot deal with through abreaction or associative elaboration: 'hysterical patients suffer from incompletely abreacted psychical trauma' (Freud, 1893a); and (b) as a stage of strangulated libidinal energy which the ego can-not discharge. The paradigm of this traumatic situation is sexual seduction. We have a vivid account by Freud himself (1954, Letter 69; also 1914d) and by Jones describing (1953) how frustrated and demoralized Freud felt when he discovered that these traumatic events of seduction had never actually happened. During this phase the corresponding theory of anxiety is: 'Neurotic anxiety is transformed sexual libido' (Freud, 1897b). The chief defence mechanism discussed is repression.

The second phase, 1905 to 1917, is characterized by systematic attempts at working out infantile sexual development (Freud, 1905d) and psychoanalytic metapsychology (Freud, 1914c, 1915c, 1915d, 1915e, 1917e). In terms of infantile sexual development and libido theory the paradigmatic traumatic situations are (a) castration anxiety, (b) separation anxiety, (c) primal scene, and (d) Oedipus complex. Trauma pertains to the strength and urgency of sexual instincts and the ego's fight against them. It is in terms of unconscious fantasy and inner psychic reality that all conflicts and hence traumatic situations are envisaged. During the latter half of this phase Freud worked out his first systematic statement of metapsychology, and we have the concept of ego-libido, primary narcissism, and ego-ideal on the one hand, and a detailed examination of the mechanisms of introjection, identification, and projection on the other. The paper on 'Mourning and Melancholia' (2017e) marks the end of this phase, and by opening up the discussion of aggression and guilt starts the next.

The period of 1917 to 1926, the third phase, gives us the 'final phase' of Freud's metapsychological thinking. In *Beyond the Pleasure Principle* (1920g) we have the first statement of the repetition compulsion as a principle of psychic functioning and its relation to the death instinct (principle of inertia in organic life). Here, Freud arrived at his dualistic theory of instincts, and from his earlier distinction between sexual instincts and ego instincts moves on to the duality of life versus death instincts. With the hypothesis of dual instincts and repetition compulsion, and the definition of psychic structures in terms of ego, id, and superego (Freud, 1923b), the concept of trauma took on an exclusively intersystemic and instinctual frame of reference. The vast literature on guilt, masochism, melancholia, depression, and internal anxiety situations documents at great length such traumata and the ego's mode of handling them. The extreme and most detailed discussion of such intersystemic and instinctual traumata is perhaps by Melanie Klein (1932) in her description of paranoid and depressive positions. This phase in Freud's own researches achieves its culmination in his revision of the concept of anxiety in *Inhibitions, Symptoms and Anxiety* (1926d).

105

The fourth phase, 1926 to 1939, is launched by the revision of the concept of anxiety and inaugurates the beginnings of ego-psychology proper. Strachey (1959, pp. 77–86) has given us a masterly summary of the evolution of Freud's concept of anxiety. I shall single out for comment only the fact that in *Inhibitions, Symptoms and Anxiety* Freud clearly distinguished between traumatic situations and situations of danger, corresponding to which are the two types of anxiety: automatic anxiety and anxiety as a signal of the approach of such a trauma. 'The fundamental determinant of automatic anxiety is the occurrence of a traumatic situation; and the essence of this is an experience of helplessness on the part of the ego in the face of an accumulation of excitation . . . the various specific dangers which are liable to precipitate a traumatic situation at different times of life. These are briefly: birth, loss of the mother as an object, loss of the penis, loss of the object's love, loss of the superego's love' (Strachey, 1959, pp. 81–2).

With the revised concept of anxiety and traumatic situations the role of environment (mother) and the need for 'extraneous help' in situations of helplessness comes into the very centre of the concept of trauma. Thus the intrapsychic, intersystemic, and environmental sources of trauma are integrated into a unitary frame of reference. Toward the end of this phase in his two papers 'Analysis Terminable and Interminable' (1937c) and 'Splitting of the Ego in the Process of Defence' (1940e) Freud focused his attention on the ego in terms of the modifications acquired during the defensive conflicts of early childhood, as well as through primary congenital variations and the disturbances of the synthetic function of the ego. This is why I have characterized this phase as inaugurating ego-psychology proper. These new formulations have far-reaching implications for the evaluation of the source and function of trauma.

The last phase is from 1939 to today. In this the developments of ego-psychology through the researches of Anna Freud (1936 onwards), Hartmann (1939, 1950b, 1952) and others, and the whole new emphasis on infant–mother relationship, have changed our very frame of reference for the discussion of the nature and role of trauma.

Function of mother as protective shield

In *Beyond the Pleasure Principle* (1920g) Freud set up a conceptual model to discuss the fate of a living organism in an open environment.

'Let us picture [he said] a living organism in its most simplified possible form as an undifferentiated vesicle of a substance that is susceptible to stimulation.' Freud next proceeds to point out that the two sources of stimuli possible are the external and the internal ones. He continues: 'Then the surface turned towards the external world will from its very situation be differentiated and will serve as an organ for receiving stimuli' (p. 26). This gradually develops into a 'crust' and eventually into a 'protective shield'. Freud postulated that '*Protection against* stimuli is an almost more important function for the living organism than *reception* of stimuli. The protective shield is supplied with its own store of energy and must above all endeavour to preserve the special modes of transformation of energy operating in it against the effects threatened by the enormous energies at work in the external world' (p. 27).

Continuing his argument Freud postulated that this sensitive cortex, which later becomes the system *Cs.*, also receives excitations from within. It is, however, less effective against inner stimuli, and one way the organism protects itself against the unpleasure from inner stimuli is to project them to the outer environment and treat them as 'though they were acting, not from the inside, but from the outside, so that it may be possible to bring the shield against stimuli into operation as a means of defence against them'. In this context Freud described as 'traumatic' any

> . . . excitations from outside which are powerful enough to break through the protective shield. It seems to me that the concept of trauma necessarily implies a connection of this kind with a breach in an otherwise efficacious barrier against stimuli. Such an event as an external trauma is bound to provoke a disturbance on a large scale in the functioning of the organism's energy and to set in motion every possible defensive measure. At the same time, the pleasure principle is for the moment put out of action. There is no longer any possibility of preventing the mental apparatus from being flooded with large amounts of stimulus, and another problem arises instead – the problem of mastering the amounts of stimulus which have broken in and of binding them, in the psychical sense, so that they can then be disposed of (pp. 29f.). [Developing his argument further, Freud concluded:] what *we* seek to understand are the effects produced on the organ of the mind by the breach in the shield against stimuli and by the problems that follow in its

107

train. And we will attribute importance to the element of fright.
It is caused by lack of any preparedness for anxiety, including lack
of hypercathexis of the systems that would be the first to receive
the stimulus. Owing to their low cathexis those systems are not in
a good position for binding the inflowing amounts of excitation
and the consequences of the breach in the protective shield follow
all the more easily. It will be seen, then, that preparedness for
anxiety and the hypercathexis of the receptive systems constitute
the last line of defence of the shield against stimuli. In the case of
quite a number of traumas, the difference between systems that are
unprepared and systems that are well prepared through being
hypercathected may be a decisive factor in determining the outcome; though where the strength of a trauma exceeds a certain
limit this factor will no doubt cease to carry weight.

(pp. 31f.)

The total context of Freud's discussion is the observation of an
infant's play with a reel that related to 'disappearance and return' (of
the mother) and the traumatic dreams in general. If we replace
in Freud's model 'the undifferentiated vesicle of a substance that is
susceptible to stimulation' by a live human infant, then we get what
Winnicott (1960c) has described as 'an infant in care'. The infant in
care has for his protective shield the caretaking mother. This is the
uniquely human situation, in so far as this dependency in the infant
lasts much longer than in any other species that we know of
(Hartmann, 1939); and from this prolonged period of dependency,
the human infant emerges as a more highly differentiated and
independent organism *vis-à-vis* his environment.

My aim here is to discuss the function of the mother in her role
as a protective shield. This role as a protective shield constitutes 'the
average expectable environment' (Hartmann, 1939) for the anaclitic
needs of the infant. My argument is that cumulative trauma is the
result of the breaches in the mother's role as a protective shield over
the whole course of the child's development, from infancy to
adolescence – that is to say, in all those areas of experience where
the child continues to need the mother as an auxiliary ego to support
his immature and unstable ego-functions. It is important to distinguish
this ego-dependency of the child on the mother from his cathexis of
her as an object. (Ramzy and Wallerstein, 1958 have discussed this
aspect in terms of *environmental reinforcement*.) Cumulative trauma thus
derives from the strains and stresses that an infant–child experiences

in the context of his ego-dependence on the mother as his protective shield and auxiliary ego (cf. Khan, 1963a, 1963b, 1963c).

I want to stress the point that what I am describing as breaches in the mother's role as protective shield are qualitatively and quantitatively different from those gross intrusions by the mother's acute psychopathology which have been often discussed in our literature in relation to schizophrenic children or overtly hostile and destructive patterns of behaviour in delinquent children (e.g., Beres, 1956; Lidz and Fleck, 1959; Mahler, 1952; Searles, 1959, 1962; Shields, 1962; etc.). The breaches I have in mind are in the nature of maladaptation to the infant's anaclitic needs (Winnicott, 1956a).

The mother's role as a protective shield is a theoretical construct. It should include the mother's personal role *vis-à-vis* the infant as well as her management of the non-human environment (the nursery, the cot, etc.) on which the infant is dependent for his total well-being (cf. Searles, 1960). I should emphasize also that the breaches in this protective-shield role, as I envisage them, are not traumatic singly. To borrow the apt phrase from Kris (1956b), they have the quality of a 'strain', and do not so much distort ego-development or psycho-sexual evolution as *bias* it. In this context it would be more accurate to say that these breaches over the course of time and through the developmental process cumulate silently and invisibly. Hence the difficulty in detecting them clinically in childhood. They gradually get embedded in the specific traits of a given character structure (cf. Greenacre, 1958). I would like to restrict myself merely to stating that the use of the word trauma in the concept of cumulative trauma should not mislead us into considering such breaches in the mother's role as protective shield as traumatic at the time or in the context in which they happen. They achieve the value of trauma only cumulatively and in retrospect. If the concept of cumulative trauma has value and validity, then it should help us to identify more accurately what sort of ego distortion and disturbance of psychosexual development can be related to what type of failure of environmental provisions, in relation to anaclitic needs in the infant and the child. It should help in replacing such incriminating reconstructions as bad, rejecting, or seducing mothers, as well as such anthropomorphic part-object constructs as 'good' and 'bad' breast. Its place could be taken by a more meaningful examination of the pathogenic interplay of specific variables in the total relationship of an infant-child's psychic and physical equipment and how the environment meets it. This in turn would sponsor the clinical search for effective therapeutic measures rather than merely prescriptive ones. I have given a detailed account elsewhere, from the treatment of a female patient, to show how an early disturbed relation between mother and daughter led to homosexual episodes in her adult life (Khan, 1963b).

In the past two decades, research in ego-psychology and infant-care techniques have gained in complexity and depth. From these researches it is possible to distinguish theoretically between four aspects of a human infant's total experience:

1   The role of the caretaking environment and its contribution toward the release and stabilization of the intrapsychic poten-tialities and functions (cf. Freud, 1911b, p. 220).
2   The special sensitivity of an infant making demands on the primary environment, which I am designating here as a mother's role of protective shield (cf. Escalona, 1953).
3   The unfolding of the maturational processes, autonomous ego-functions, and libido development.
4   The gradual emergence of the inner world and psychic reality, with all the complexity of instinctual needs and tensions, and their interplay with inner psychic structures and object-relationships.

In our literature, perhaps, one of the most sensitive and elaborate descriptions of the caretaking role of the mother is in Winnicott's writings. According to Winnicott (1956b), what motivates the mother for her role as a protective shield for the infant is her 'primary maternal preoccupation'. The incentive for the mother's role is her libidinal investment in the infant and the infant's dependence on it for survival (cf. Benedek, 1952). From the infant's subjective point of view there is at the beginning little perception of this dependence or of the need for survival.

What the mother's caretaking role achieves in optimal circum-stances is:

1   Through making herself available as a protective shield the mother enables the growth of the maturational processes both of autonomous ego-functions and instinctual processes. The mother's role as a protective shield defends the infant against the mother's subjective and unconscious love and hate, and thus allows her empathy to be maximally receptive to the infant's needs (cf. Spitz, 1959).

2   If her adaptation is good enough, then the infant does not become precociously aware of this dependence on the mother – hence does not have to exploit whatever mental functions are emergent and available toward self-defence (cf. Freud, 1920g; James, 1960).

3   The protective shield of the mother enables the infant to project all the unpleasurable inner stimuli on to her, so that she can deal with them and thus sustain the illusion of omnipotence of well-being in the infant. Erikson (1950) has defined this sense of well-being as 'trust', Benedek (1952) as 'confidence', and Kris (1962) as 'comfort' (see also Searles, 1962).

4   Through functioning as a protective shield, and so providing a model, the mother enables the infant's psyche to integrate what J. Sandler (1960) has called a 'qualitative organizing component'. In later ego-development and functioning we can identify this as guiding the synthetic function of the ego on its discriminating role, both in relation to inner instinctual reality and to the demands of the external environment.

5   By providing the right dosage of life experience (Fries, 1946) and need satisfactions through her body care, she enables the infant's inner world to differentiate into id and ego as well as gradually to demarcate inner from outer reality (cf. Hoffer, 1952; Ramzy and Wallerstein, 1958).

6   By lending her own ego-functions as well as her libidinal and aggressive cathexes (through her role as a protective shield) she helps the infant to build up supplies of primary narcissism, neutralized energy, and the beginnings of the capacity and wish for object cathexes (cf. Hoffer, 1952; Kris, 1951). Both what she provides and what emerges through the infant's maturation interact and supplement each other (Erikson, 1946; Freud, 1911b; Hoffer, 1949; Winnicott, 1951).

7   If these tasks are accomplished successfully, then the shift from primary dependence[1] to relative dependence can take place (Winnicott, 1960c). In this stage the function of her role as a protective shield becomes more complex; it takes on an essentially psychological aspect. She has now to help the infant with his first experiences of inner instinctual conflicts on the one hand, and yet sustain for him that flux from primary identification to realization of separateness which is the essence of disillusionment (Winnicott, 1948a) and a precondition for a true capacity for object cathexes (cf. A. Freud, 1958; Milner, 1952).

111

8   If she is successful in these achievements, then the infant gradually becomes aware of the mother as a love object and of his need for her love. This is now an object cathexis which employs instinctual (id) cathexes that have become available in the meantime (A. Freud, 1951).

9   By providing phase-adequate frustrations she sponsors the capacity for toleration of tension and unpleasure, thus promoting structural development (cf. Kris, 1962). Rubinfine (1962), in his valuable discussion of this aspect of maternal care, concludes:

> . . . where need satisfaction is always and immediately available (i.e., deanimated), there should be a relative absence of tension. Without appropriately timed experiences of frustration and delay, there may result retardation in the development of various ego-functions, among them the capacity to distinguish between self and nonself. Such failure of differentiation of self from object, and the consequent failure of defusion of self- and object-representations, leads to interference with the development of the capacity to discharge aggressive drives toward an external object, and results in the turn of aggression against the self.

Winnicott (1952) has stressed the point that a mother should and indeed must fail the id, but never the ego of the infant.

The vehicle of all these transactions between mother and infant is dependency. This dependency is to a large extent not sensed by the infant. Similarly, it is important to keep in mind that the mother's role as a protective shield is a limited function in her total life experience. In the beginning it is an all-engrossing one for her. Still, theoretically it is significant for us to be able to see it as a special instance of her personality and emotional functioning. Spitz's (1962) distinction between the totality of the infant's anaclitic needs and the implementation of the mother's diatrophic attitude in response to these needs is pertinent to remember in this context. Unless we can do this we cannot identify how this role as a protective shield can be and does become invaded by her personal needs and conflicts. It is the intrusion of her personal needs and conflicts that I characterize as her failure in respect of her role as a protective shield. The mother's role as protective shield is not a passive one but an alert, adaptive, and organizing one. The protective-shield role is the result of conflict-free, autonomous ego-functions in the mother. If personal conflicts intrude here, the result is a shift from the protective-shield role to that of symbiosis or rejective withdrawal. How an infant will react to these failures depends upon the nature, intensity, duration, and repetitiveness of the trauma.

In our literature three typical instances of this type of failure of the mother as a protective shield have been thoroughly discussed:

1   The most extreme and pathogenic is through the excessive intrusion of the mother's psychopathology. Winnicott (1949c, 1952) has discussed it as failure of the good-enough holding environment leading to psychosis or mental defect. Mahler (1952, 1961) has coined the phrase of symbiotic relationship between mother and child that leads to schizophrenic illnesses. In this context I would like also to mention, among others, the researches of Beres (1956), Geleerd (1956, 1958), Lidz and Fleck (1959) and Searles (1959).

2   The breakdown of mother's role of protective shield has also been discussed in terms of loss of or separation from her. Here again the pioneer researches of Anna Freud and Burlingham (1942, 1944) and Winnicott (1940, 1945a), and the later exhaustive investigations of Bowlby (1960), Spitz (1945, 1951), and Provence and Lipton (1962) stand out as particularly important (also cf. Hellmann, 1962).

3   The third instance of breakdown of mother's role as protective shield occurs when either some constitutional sensitivity (Escalona, 1953) or physical handicap (Burlingham, 1961; Sandler, A.-M., 1963) impose an impossible task on the mother, or when a severe physical illness in the infant or child creates a special demand which no human adult could possibly meet (cf. Frankl, 1961; A. Freud, 1952).

Aetiology of cumulative trauma

I am here tentatively trying to conceptualize a fourth type of partial breakdown of the mother's role as a protective shield, which becomes visible only in retrospect as a disturbance and can be designated as cumulative trauma. I have been specifically guided and helped in arriving at this hypothesis through the researches of Winnicott, Kris, and Greenacre.

Over the past twenty years Winnicott has been persistently drawing our attention to the importance of the mother's caretaking function, the vital role of dependence for the infant's emergence into self-status, etc. James (1962) has recently given us a valuable critique

113

of Winnicott's researches. What is pertinent for my purposes in Winnicott's hypotheses is his elucidation of the role of regression to dependency needs in the therapeutic process (1949a), his researches into the antisocial tendency (1956a), and his careful delineation of the early psychic and affective processes of integration in the child (1945b).

It is Winnicott's basic hypothesis (1952) that all relative failures in infancy of the good-enough holding environment (mother's role as a protective shield) set up a compulsion in the relatively matured child and the grown adult to correct the imbalances and dissociations in ego–integration. This is achieved through regression to dependency needs. In Winnicott's idiom, establishment of 'the false self' is one result of such caretaking environment's failure to adapt through good-enough holding (1949c). What Winnicott calls 'the false self' is a characterological consequence of the disruption and distortion of ego–autonomy. What Winnicott calls 'impingements' are the failure of the mother in infancy to dose and regulate stimuli – both external and internal. Winnicott believes that these impingements are disruptive of true ego–integration, and lead to premature defensive organization and functioning (1948a). What Kris (1962) has described as 'a specific kind of provocative overstimulation which was bound to produce mounting tension in the child without offering appropriate avenues of discharge' and also as 'tantalizing', Winnicott designates as 'impingements'. I am here considering these as some of the most pathogenic genetic elements in cumulative trauma (cf. Erikson, 1950).

Kris in his paper 'The Recovery of Childhood Memories in Psychoanalysis' (1956b) has distinguished between 'shock trauma' and 'the strain trauma'. The latter he has defined as the 'effect of long-lasting situations, which may cause traumatic effects by accumulation of frustrating tensions'. The clinical examples that Kris offers here and in his contemporary paper on 'The Personal Myth' (1956a) leave me in no doubt that 'the strain trauma' and the screen memories or precocious early memories that the patients recount are derivatives of the partial breakdown of the protective-shield function of the mother and an attempt to symbolize its effects (cf. A. Freud, 1958). Kris's sensitive and consummate account of the predicament of the infant Anne in his paper 'Decline and Recovery in a Three-Year-Old' (1962) is the most apposite material in relation to my concept of cumulative trauma. It is interesting to note in Kris's account that

114

even though the mother and infant were observed from the start, it was only later, i.e., in relative retrospect at 34 weeks, that the fact of disturbed maternal handling constituting a 'tantalizing' situation for the infant Anne could be definitely established.

Greenacre's studies (1954, 1960a, 1960c) have been largely concerned with the vicissitudes of the maturational factor in infancy and its effect on ego and instinctual development. In 1959 she introduced the concept of *focal symbiosis* to identify a specific variant of what Mahler has described as symbiotic relationships. Greenacre defines focal symbiosis as 'an intensely strong interdependence (usually between mother and child, but sometimes, as in my cases, with people other than the mother) which is limited to a special and rather circumscribed relationship rather than a nearly total enveloping one . . . In limited or focal symbiotic relationships, there is often a peculiar union of the child's special need with the parent's special sensitivity, and . . . the total personality of either parent or child may not be as much involved as in the severe case of symbiotic psychoses described by Mahler' (pp. 244, 245). Greenacre (1959, 1960b, 1960c) furthermore relates a great deal of the psychopathology of perversions, borderline cases, and body-ego development to focal symbiosis. In her concept of focal symbiosis she has fruitfully extended the range in time and developmental process through which the child and his human environment can involve each other in terms of the archaic dependency relationship.

In the context of these formulations I shall now examine the nature and function of the cumulative trauma. Cumulative trauma has its beginnings in the period of development when the infant needs and uses the mother as his protective shield. The inevitable temporary failures of the mother as protective shield are corrected and recovered from the evolving complexity and rhythm of the maturational processes. Where these failures of the mother in her role as protective shield are significantly frequent and lead to impingement on the infant's psyche-soma, impingements which he has no means of eliminating, they set up a nucleus of pathogenic reaction. These in turn start a process of interplay with the mother which is distinct from her adaptation to the infant's needs. This interplay between mother and infant can have any or all of the effects described below.

1   It leads to premature and selective ego-development. Some of the emergent autonomous functions are accelerated in growth and

used in defensive action to deal with the impingements that are unpleasurable (James, 1960; Winnicott, 1949a).

2   It can begin to organize a special responsiveness to the mother's mood that creates an imbalance in the integration of aggressive drives (cf. Sperling, 1950; Winnicott, 1948b).

3   The involvement of precocious functions with the mother's collusive response militates against developmentally arriving at a differentiated separate 'coherent ego' (Freud, 1920g) and self. This in turn leads to a dissociation through which an archaic dependency bond is exploited on the one hand and a precipitate independence is asserted on the other. A specific result is that what should have been a silent, unregistered dependency state now becomes an engineered exploitation of instinctual and ego-dependence, with a precocious narcissistic cathexis of the mother.

4   As a further consequence the disillusionment that belongs to maturational separating off from mother is side-tracked and a false identificatory oneness is manipulated (cf. Searles, 1962). This way, instead of disillusionment and mourning, an ego–attitude of concern for the mother and excessive craving for concern from the mother becomes established. This concern is quite different from the concern that belongs to sadistic instinctual attack on the mother and the ensuing feelings of guilt (cf. Klein, 1932). This concern is an ego–interest that substitutes for a true object cathexis (cf. Winnicott, 1948b).

5   Through the impingements that derive from failure of mother's role as protective shield, a precocious cathexis of external and internal reality takes place. This organization of inner and outer reality leaves out a very important function of the ego's subjective awareness and experience of itself as a coherent entity. Its synthetic function is also disrupted (cf. James, 1960).

6   The strain and impingements from the failure of mother's role as protective shield, which I am designating here as cumulative trauma, have their most specific effect on the vicissitudes of body-ego development in the infant and the child. The researches of Coleman, Kris, and Provence (1953), Greenacre (1958, 1960b), Hoffer (1950, 1952), Kris (1951), Milner (1952), Spitz (1951, 1962), and Winnicott (1949a, 1949c, 1951) have stressed the importance of the maternal caretaking procedures (protective-shield role) for the development of the body ego in the context of the earliest stages of the ego–id differentiation and the gradual integration of a sense of self. Here I want to refer, only very

116

briefly, to my inference from clinical material that the breaches in the mother's role as protective shield leave their precipitates most sentiently and effectively in the body-ego development of the child. These residues over the course of maturation and development gather into a specific type of body-ego organization and form the substratum of the psychological personality. Pertinent here are the observational data offered by Coleman, Kris and Provence (1953), Kris (1951), and Ritvo and Solnit (1958). In the adult patient it is through the clinical observation of the idiosyncrasies of the body-ego behaviour in the transference-neurosis and the total analytic setting that we can hope to reconstruct what are the particular genetic patterns of the cumulative trauma in a given case (Khan, 1963b). The concept of cumulative trauma tentatively offers, in terms of early ego-development and in the context of infant–mother relationship, a complementary hypothesis to the concept of fixation points in libido development. In this sense it tries to map out what were the significant points of stress and strain in the evolving mother–infant (child) relationship that gradually gather into a dynamic substratum in the morphology of a particular character or personality.

Once this interplay between infant and mother starts, it brings into its sphere of action all new developmental experiences and object relations. In many significant aspects this later pathogenic interplay between mother and child aims to correct the earlier distortions through impingements. This is what I think Greenacre (1959) refers to as the drive behind 'the union of the child's special need with the parent's special sensitivity'. That these attempts at recovery only complicate the pathology is an irony of human experience. This is perhaps at the root of many attempts at cure through love and passionate involvement in our adult patients. I have tried to discuss this aspect in my (1962) paper 'The Role of Polymorph-Perverse Body-Experiences and Object-Relations in Ego-Integration' (see also Alpert, 1959; Khan, 1963b; Lichtenstein, 1961).

I have so far stressed only the pathogenic effects on infant development from breaches in the mother's role as protective shield. It would, however, be a gross misrepresentation of the total complexity of the interplay between mother and infant if we fail to state that although the infant ego is weak, vulnerable, and extremely dependent on the mother's role as protective shield, the infant has also a great inherent resilience and potentiality (strength). It not

117

only can and does recover from breaches in the protective shield, but it can use such impingements and strains as 'nutriment' (Rapaport, 1958) toward further growth and structuration (cf. Kris, 1951; Rubinfine, 1962). It is important to remember that though the ego can survive and overcome such strains, exploit them to good purpose, manage to mute the cumulative trauma into abeyance, and arrive at a fairly healthy and effective normal functioning, it nevertheless can in later life break down as a result of acute stress and crisis. When it does so – and this is of great clinical importance – we cannot diagnostically evaluate the genetics and economics of the total processes involved if we do not have a concept like cumulative trauma to guide our attention and expectancy. It has often been remarked in our literature during the past three decades that the character disorders of a schizoid type, which have become the more frequent type of patient in our practice, present a clinical picture whose aetiology needs concepts that include disturbances of infant–mother relationship that were at the time neither gross nor acute (Khan, 1960a; Kris, 1951). I am suggesting that the concept of cumulative trauma can help us a great deal here. The human infant is well endowed to struggle with the vicissitudes of his internal and environmental stresses. What is important for us is to be able to identify in the clinical process what effects this struggle has left and how it has shaped the adult character (cf. Greenacre, 1954, 1960b; Khan, 1963a; Lichtenstein, 1961).

One treacherous aspect of cumulative trauma is that it operates and builds up silently throughout childhood right up to adolescence. It is only in recent years that we have learned to evaluate as pathogenic a certain precocious development in children. Such precocity had previously been celebrated as giftedness or strong ego–emergence or a happy independence in the child. We are also inclined to view with much more caution and reserve, if not suspicion, a mother's boasts of a specially close rapport and understanding between herself and her child.

Clinical experience shows that the phases of maturational development where these impingements from mother's failure in her role as protective shield tend to get organized into an active collusive relationship between mother and child are the late oral, early anal, and phallic phases – the phases where the emergent instinctual process and maturational ego-process test the mother with their full need and demand. It is also these stages where the stimulus hunger asks for maximal psychological adaptation, response, and restraint from the mother in her role as protective shield. The chief psychic process involved in such collusive relationships is identification, as Kris (1951) and Ritvo and Solnit (1958) have stressed. This identification remains essentially of an incorporative and projective type, interfering with internalization and assimilation of new object-representations, and thus confuses a proper differentiation and growth of internal psychic structures. This holds true also of the distortion of the libidinal strivings and object relations of the Oedipal phase (cf. Schmale, 1962).

The phase at which the child himself acutely becomes aware of the distorting and disruptive effects of this collusive bond with the mother is at adolescence. Then the reaction is dramatically rejective of the mother and all the past cathexes of her (Khan, 1963c). This, of course, makes the adolescent process of integration at once tortuous and impossible. At this point attempts at integration which wilfully negate past libidinal investments, ego-interests, and object ties are instituted. This leads either to collapse of personality development into inertia and futility, or a short, magical recovery into omnipotent isolation, or a passionate craving for new ideals, new objects, and new ego-interests (Beres and Obers, 1950; Erikson, 1956; Geleerd, 1958; Khan, 1963a; Spiegel, 1951).

Conclusion

The concept of cumulative trauma takes into consideration psycho-physical events that happen at the pre-verbal stage of relationship between mother and infant. It correlates their effects on what later becomes operative as a disturbed relationship between mother and child or as a *bias* in ego and psychosexual development (Khan, 1962, 1963b). Once an infant emerges out of the pre-verbal stage we can never see directly the first impingements and failures in the mother's role as the protective shield. What we see in direct observation or clinically are derivatives of these mental processes and capacities. What I am conceptualizing here as cumulative trauma has been described by Anna Freud (1958) in another context. She states 'that subtle harm is being inflicted on this child, and that the consequences of it will become manifest at some future date.'

Even though we have now available many sensitive accounts of direct observations of the feeding situations and the total relationship between infant and mother (Robertson, 1962), there is still doubt as to whether we can identify at the point of its actuality the breakdown of the mother's role as protective shield in relation to the infant's anaclitic needs. As Kris's (1962) account of the infant Anne makes abundantly clear, even though an infant was observed by a team of highly skilled professionals, it was only in retrospect that the effects of such breakdown of a good-enough provision of maternal care began to be visible. In the case of Anne we see how the impingements from the mother's handling already began to gather into the structure and function of the cumulative trauma. It is important for us to be able to chart out clearly the earliest nature and role of these failures, because only thus can we organize our clinical expectancy and arrive at true diagnosis. As Anna Freud (1962) expressed it:

> . . . if our present direction of interest is no more than a turning of our glance from the effects of dependence on to the contents and processes in the period of dependence, it is still a turning-point of decisive importance. By taking this line we change the direction of our interest from the illnesses themselves – neurotic or psychotic – to their preconditions, to the matrix from which they arise, i.e., to the era where such important matters are decided as the selection of neurosis and the selection of the types of defence.

Note

1   The classifications Winnicott gave were, in fact, 'absolute dependence' and 'relative dependence' (1960c, p. 46). [*ed.*]

10

FEAR OF BREAKDOWN

Donald W. Winnicott

My clinical experiences have brought me recently to a new under-standing, as I believe, of the meaning of a fear of breakdown.

It is my purpose here to state as simply as possible this under-standing, which is new for me and which perhaps is new for others who work in psychotherapy. Naturally, if what I say has truth in it, this will already have been dealt with by the world's poets, but the flashes of insight that come in poetry cannot absolve us from our painful task of getting step by step away from ignorance towards our goal. It is my opinion that a study of this limited area leads to a restatement of several other problems that puzzle us as we fail to do as well clinically as we would wish to do, and I shall indicate at the end what extensions of the theory I propose for discussion.

Individual variations

Fear of breakdown is a feature of significance in some of our patients, but not in others. From this observation, if it be a correct one, the conclusion can be drawn that fear of breakdown is related to the individual's past experience, and to environmental vagaries. At the same time there must be expected a common denominator of the same fear, indicating the existence of universal phenomena; these indeed make it possible for everyone to know empathetically what it feels like when one of our patients shows this fear in a big way. (The same can be said, indeed, of every detail of the insane person's insanity. We all know about it, although this particular detail may not be bothering us.)

Emergence of the symptom

Not all our patients who have this fear complain of it at the outset of a treatment. Some do; but others have their defences so well organized that it is only after a treatment has made considerable progress that the fear of breakdown comes to the fore as a dominating factor.

For instance, a patient may have various phobias and a complex organization for dealing with these phobias, so that dependence does not come quickly into the transference. At length, dependence becomes a main feature, and then the analyst's mistakes and failures become direct causes of localized phobias and so of the outbreak of fear of breakdown.

Meaning of 'breakdown'

I have purposely used the term 'breakdown' because it is rather vague and because it could mean various things. On the whole, the word can be taken in this context to mean a failure of a defence organization. But immediately we ask: a defence against what? And this leads us to the deeper meaning of the term, since we need to use the word 'breakdown' to describe the unthinkable state of affairs that underlies the defence organization.

It will be noted that whereas there is value in thinking that in the area of psychoneurosis it is castration anxiety that lies behind the defences, in the more psychotic phenomena that we are examining it is a breakdown of the establishment of the unit self that is indicated. The ego organizes defences against breakdown of the ego organization, and it is the ego organization that is threatened. But the ego cannot organize against environmental failure in so far as dependence is a living fact.

In other words, we are examining a reversal of the individual's maturational process. This makes it necessary for me briefly to reformulate the early stages of emotional growth.

Emotional growth, early stages

The individual inherits a maturational process. This carries the individual along in so far as there exists a facilitating environment, and only in so far as this exists. The facilitating environment is itself a complex phenomenon and needs special study in its own right; the

122

essential feature is that it has a kind of growth of its own, being adapted to the changing needs of the growing individual.

The individual proceeds from absolute dependence to relative independence and towards independence. In health the development takes place at a pace that does not outstrip the development of complexity in the mental mechanisms, this being linked to neurophysiological development.

The facilitating environment can be described as *holding*, developing into *handling*, to which is added *object-presenting*.

In such a facilitating environment the individual undergoes development which can be classified as *integrating*, to which is added *indwelling* (or *psychosomatic collusion*) and then *object-relating*.

This is a gross oversimplification but it must suffice in this context.

It will be observed that in such a description forward movement in development corresponds closely with the threat of retrograde movement (and defences against this threat) in schizophrenic illness.

Absolute dependence

At the time of absolute dependence, with the mother supplying an auxiliary ego-function, it has to be remembered that the infant has not yet separated out the 'not-me' from the 'me' – this cannot happen apart from the establishment of 'me'.

Primitive agonies

From this chart it is possible to make a list of primitive agonies (anxiety is not a strong enough word here).

Here are a few:

1 A return to an unintegrated state. (Defence: disintegration.)
2 Falling for ever. (Defence: self-holding.)
3 Loss of psychosomatic collusion, failure of indwelling. (Defence: depersonalization.)
4 Loss of sense of real. (Defence: exploitation of primary narcissism, etc.)
5 Loss of capacity to relate to objects. (Defence: autistic states, relating only to self-phenomena.)

And so on.

Psychotic illness as a defence

It is my intention to show here that what we see clinically is always a defence organization, even in the autism of childhood schizophrenia. The underlying agony is unthinkable.

It is wrong to think of psychotic illness as a breakdown, it is a defence organization relative to a primitive agony, and it is usually successful (except when the facilitating environment has been not deficient but tantalizing, perhaps the worst thing that can happen to a human baby).

Statement of main theme

I can now state my main contention, and it turns out to be very simple. I contend that clinical fear of breakdown is *the fear of a break-down that has already been experienced*. It is a fear of the original agony which caused the defence organization which the patient displays as an illness syndrome.

This idea may or may not prove immediately useful to the clinician. We cannot hurry up our patients. Nevertheless, we can hold up their progress because of genuinely not knowing; any little piece of our understanding may help us to keep up with a patient's needs.

There are moments, according to my experience, when a patient needs to be told that the breakdown, a fear of which destroys his or her life, *has already been*. It is a fact that is carried round hidden away in the unconscious. The unconscious here is not exactly the repressed unconscious of psychoneurosis, nor is it the unconscious of Freud's formulation of the part of the psyche that is very close to neurophysiological functioning. Nor is it the unconscious of Jung's which I would call: all those things that go on in underground caves, or (in other words) the world's mythology, in which there is collusion between the individual and the maternal inner psychic realities. In this special context the unconscious means that the ego integration is not able to encompass something. The ego is too immature to gather all the phenomena into the area of personal omnipotence.

It must be asked here: why does the patient go on being worried by this that belongs to the past? The answer must be that the original experience of primitive agony cannot get into the past tense unless the ego can first gather it into its own present time experience and into omnipotent control now (assuming the auxiliary ego-supporting function of the mother (analyst)).

124

In other words, the patient must go on looking for the past detail which is *not yet experienced*. This search takes the form of a looking for this detail in the future.

Unless the therapist can work successfully on the basis that this detail is already a fact, the patient must go on fearing to find what is being compulsively looked for in the future.

On the other hand, if the patient is ready for some kind of acceptance of this queer kind of truth, that what is not yet experienced did nevertheless happen in the past, then the way is open for the agony to be experienced in the transference, in reaction to the analyst's failures and mistakes. These latter can be dealt with by the patient in doses that are not excessive, and the patient can account for each technical failure of the analyst as countertransference. In other words, gradually the patient gathers the original failure of the facilitating environment into the area of his or her omnipotence and the experience of omnipotence which belongs to the state of dependence (transference fact).

All this is very difficult, time-consuming and painful, but at any rate it is not futile. What is futile is the alternative, and it is this that must now be examined.

Futility in analysis

I must take for granted an understanding and acceptance of the analysis of psychoneurosis. On the basis of this assumption, I say that in the cases I am discussing the analysis starts off well, the analysis goes with a swing; what is happening, however, is that the analyst and the patient are having a good time colluding in a psychoneurotic analysis, when in fact the illness is psychotic.

Over and over again the analysing couple are pleased with what they have done together. It was valid, it was clever, it was cosy because of the collusion. But each so-called advance ends in destruction. The patient breaks it up and says: So what? In fact, the advance was not an advance; it was a new example of the analyst's playing the patient's game of postponing the main issue. And who can blame either the patient or the analyst (unless of course there can be an analyst who plays the psychotic fish on a very long psychoneurotic line, and hopes thereby to avoid the final catch by some trick of fate, such as the death of one or other of the couple, or a failure of financial backing).

We must assume that both patient and analyst really do wish to end the analysis, but alas, there is no end unless the bottom of the trough has been reached, unless *the thing feared has been experienced*. And indeed one way out is for the patient to have a breakdown (physical or mental) and this can work very well. However, the solution is not good enough if it does not include analytic understanding and insight on the part of the patient, and indeed, many of the patients I am referring to are valuable people who cannot afford to break down in the sense of going to a mental hospital.

The purpose of this paper is to draw attention to the possibility that the breakdown has already happened, near the beginning of the individual's life. The patient needs to 'remember' this but it is not possible to remember something that has not yet happened, and this thing of the past has not happened yet because the patient was not there for it to happen to. The only way to 'remember' in this case is for the patient to experience this past thing for the first time in the present, that is to say, in the transference. This past and future thing then becomes a matter of the here-and-now, and becomes experienced by the patient for the first time. This is the equivalent of remembering, and this outcome is the equivalent of the lifting of repression that occurs in the analysis of the psychoneurotic patient (classical Freudian analysis).

Further applications of this theory

Fear of death

Little alteration is needed to transfer the general thesis of fear of breakdown to a specific fear of death. This is perhaps a more common fear, and one that is absorbed in the religious teachings about an afterlife, as if to deny the fact of death.

When fear of death is a significant symptom the promise of an afterlife fails to give relief, and the reason is that the patient has a compulsion to look for death. Again, it is the death that happened but was not experienced that is sought.

When Keats was 'half in love with easeful death' he was, according to the idea that I am putting forward here, longing for the ease that would come if he could 'remember' having died; but to remember he must experience death now.

Most of my ideas are inspired by patients, to whom I acknowledge my debt. It is to one of these that I *owe* the phrase 'phenomenal death'. What happened in the past was death as a phenomenon, but not as the sort of fact that we observe. Many men and *women* spend their lives wondering whether to find a solution by suicide, that is, sending the body to death which has already happened to the psyche. Suicide is no answer, however, but is a despair gesture. I now understand for the first time what my schizophrenic patient (who did kill herself) meant when she said: 'All I ask you to do is to help me to commit suicide for the right reason instead of for the wrong reason.' I did not succeed and she killed herself in despair of finding the solution. Her aim (as I now see) was to get it stated by me that she died in early infancy. On this basis I think she and I could have enabled her to put off body death till old age took its toll.

Death, looked at in this way as something that happened to the patient but which the patient was not mature enough to experience, has the meaning of annihilation. It is like this, that a pattern developed in which the continuity of being was interrupted by the patient's infantile reactions to impingement, these being environmental factors that were allowed to impinge by failures of the facilitating environment. (In the case of this patient troubles started very early, for there was a premature awareness awakened before birth because of a maternal panic, and added to this the birth was complicated by undiagnosed placenta praevia.)

Emptiness

Again my patients show me that the concept of emptiness can be looked at through these same spectacles.

In some patients emptiness needs to be experienced, and this emptiness belongs to the past, to the time before the degree of maturity had made it possible for emptiness to be experienced.

To understand this it is necessary to think not of trauma but of nothing happening when something might profitably have happened.

It is easier for a patient to remember trauma than to remember nothing happening when it might have happened. At the time, the patient did not know what might have happened, and so could not experience anything except to note that something might have been.

Example

A phase in a patient's treatment illustrates this. This young woman lay uselessly on the couch, and all she could do was to say: 'Nothing is happening in this analysis!'

At the stage that I am describing, the patient had supplied material of an indirect kind so that I could know that she was probably feeling something. I was able to say that she had been feeling feelings, and she had been experiencing these gradually fading, according to her pattern, a pattern which made her despair. The feelings were sexual and female. They did not show clinically.

Here in the transference was myself (nearly) being the cause now of her female sexuality fizzling out; when this was properly stated we had an example in the present of what had happened to her innumerable times. In her case (to simplify for the sake of description) there was a father who at first was scarcely ever present, and then when he came to her home when she was a little girl he did not want his daughter's female self, and had nothing to give by way of male stimulus.

Now, emptiness is a prerequisite for eagerness to gather in. Primary emptiness simply means: before starting to fill up. A considerable maturity is needed for this state to be meaningful.

Emptiness occurring in a treatment is a state that the patient is trying to experience, a past state that cannot be remembered except by being experienced for the first time now.

In practice, the difficulty is that the patient fears the awfulness of emptiness, and in defence will organize a controlled emptiness by not eating or not learning, or else will ruthlessly fill up by a greediness which is compulsive and which feels mad. When the patient can reach to emptiness itself and tolerate this state because of dependence on the auxiliary ego of the analyst, then, taking in can start up as a pleasurable function; here can begin eating that is not a function dissociated (or split-off) as part of the personality; also it is in this way that some of our patients who cannot learn can begin to learn pleasurably.

The basis of all learning (as well as of eating) is emptiness. But if emptiness was not experienced as such at the beginning, then it turns up as a state that is feared, yet compulsively sought after.

Non-existence

The search for personal non-existence can be examined in the same way. It will be found that non-existence here is part of a defence. Personal existence is represented by the projection elements, and the person is making an attempt to project everything that could be personal. This can be a relatively sophisticated defence, and the aim is to avoid responsibility (at the depressive position) or to avoid persecution (at what I would call the stage of self-assertion, i.e., the stage of *I am* with the inherent implication *I repudiate everything that is not me*). It is convenient here to use in illustration the childhood game of 'I'm the King of the Castle – You're the Dirty Rascal'.

In the religions, this idea can appear in the concept of oneness with God or with the Universe. It is possible to see this defence being negated in existentialist writings and teachings, in which existing is made into a cult, in an attempt to counter the personal tendency towards a non-existence that is part of an organized defence.

There can be a positive element in all this, that is, an element that is not a defence. It can be said that *only out of non-existence can existence start*. It is surprising how early (even before birth, certainly during the birth process) awareness of a premature ego can be mobilized. But the individual cannot develop from an ego root if this is divorced from psychosomatic experience and from primary narcissism. It is just here that begins the intellectualization of the ego-functions. It can be noted here that all this is a long distance in time prior to the establishment of anything that could usefully be called the self.

THE PSYCHOANALYTIC ENCOUNTER

Transference and countertransference

PART IV

11

MAKING SENSE TOGETHER

New directions in Independent clinical thinking

Steven Groarke

If we start with the assumption that the papers in this section on technique by Nina Coltart, John Klauber, Adam Limentani and Neville Symington are all influential papers, this raises an interesting question: what do we mean when we describe a psychoanalytic paper as 'influential'? A tradition is always in the process of becoming one, and the Independent tradition, initially the group of non-affiliated analysts of the British Psychoanalytical Society, is no exception to this rule. Considering the thirty years, then, since Gregorio Kohon first selected these four papers for publication, it will be instructive, I think, to look back and, in retrospect, take a measure of their seminal value.

The question of the papers' historical standing entails a more rigorous assessment of significance than we might expect from a mere checklist or audit of current usage. Based on the model of the dead father (Freud, 1912–13), influence becomes a question of the living context where the judgement of our predecessors, the summons of 'breathless mouths' (to borrow Yeats's exacting phrase), far outweighs that of our contemporaries. The effect goes both ways, however. The Freudian emphasis on foundations renders tradition as an object of renewal in the present, as well as an authoritative call from the past. As keepers of the flame, descendants are both trustful guardians and oedipal usurpers. This applies to all forms of cultural life: rather than stand-alone contributions, ideas and thoughts are influential as

133

part of the influx of a tradition, while at the same time our under-standing of the tradition is subject to the retrospective influence of new ideas. Subject as a matter of course to delay or lateness, traditions survive by calling upon us to make use of them, and in doing so we breathe new life into their origins.

Insofar as we credit the retrospective/prospective breadth of the four papers, two questions present themselves: first, how do these papers stand up to the call of their own tradition? Second, what do the papers add to our understanding of Independent thought going forward? The following remarks on Independent clinical thinking, therefore, are guided by the inextricably linked questions of legacy and renewal.

The analytic environment

While the term 'Independent' was not used in British psychoanalysis until around the middle of the twentieth century – at the original suggestion of Paula Heimann (King, 1989, p. 8) – the tradition itself is nonetheless rooted in the variously talented group formed around Ernest Jones in the early part of the century. The four papers under discussion elaborate on the practical and epistemological issues that have been passed down through this tradition, with respect to the analytic process and the analytic setting (Green, 1975). To single out one of the most prescient clinical thinkers among the founders of the British school, Ella Sharpe remains something of a touchstone, and her lectures on technique, delivered first to candidates in training at the British Psycho-Analytical Institute in the 1920s, form an essential part of the groundwork for the theory of Independent clinical thinking.

The provision of what Sharpe called a 'favourable atmosphere' (1943; quoted in King and Steiner, 1991, p. 641) need not be a matter of heightened presentation. In fact, it remains a central tenet of Independent thought that the environmental context enables the patient to make use of the analytic process by *not* drawing attention to itself. We might expect patients to take in the underlying atmos-phere in the room, but would not want them to feel pushed, against the grain of their own immediate instinctual and affective needs, into becoming preoccupied with its source. Patients are likely to feel disturbed when the defining peculiarities of the analytic situation become gratuitous, or when the restlessness of the environment itself encroaches on the patient's needs. Symington, in his paper, describes a patient who found herself in this situation on the day that her analyst received some deeply disturbing news just prior to her session, news that weighed on the quality of his listening in such a way that it was perceptible to the patient.

In advancing his main argument – namely, that 'the analyst's inner act of freedom causes a therapeutic shift in the patient' (p. 199 herein) – Symington emphasizes the extent to which 'atmosphere' affects the psychotic and borderline patient with a peculiar intensity. The technical implications of environmental influence – in particular, the problem of how to maintain the analysing situation in 'an essentially pre-verbal and "acting out" area' (Polmear, 2012, p. 361) – are no less important in the other three papers. This is evident in Klauber's focus on the amalgam of fantasy and reality that becomes attached through the transference to the analyst *in situ*; in Limentani's reference to the 'unique atmosphere' (p. 177 herein) that comes about in conjunction with the vicissitudes of affects in the transference–countertransference; and in Coltart's reflections on the therapeutic benefits of attentive waiting in the process of 'working towards a deeper nexus of feeling, fantasy, and wordless experience' (p. 150 herein).

Parsons (2007) has taken up the question of the analytic environ-ment, and the concomitant question of attention, in terms of the analyst's internal setting. A secure framework in the analyst's mind, according to Parsons, allows for sufficient flexibility in the external environment. The idea of 'flexibility' has a rich genealogy in Independent thought. Thus, sufficient ease in oneself, a distaste for compulsive analysing, and, not least of all, an underlying tact rendered the tradition of Ella Sharpe peculiarly receptive to the influence of Sándor Ferenczi. As it happens, a natural affinity between the early British and Budapest schools did not prevent the long occlusion of Ferenczi's work in the British Society. Nevertheless, reference to the 'unhampered mobility of the libido', which characterizes the 'ideal result of a completed analysis' for Ferenczi (1928, p. 99), turns up contemporaneously in Sharpe (1930, p. 369) as an 'elasticity' of psychic orientation, and in Glover (1927, p. 325) as an 'elasticity' pertaining to technical freedom over against the reification of theory. Thus, the recourse to theory as a defence against the difficulties of clinical practice was challenged early on by the English Freudians.

While Independent analysts today may trace their Freudian heritage back to Ferenczi, whose influence came most directly through Michael Balint (Parsons, 2014a, p. 188), the earlier generation of

135

British analysts nonetheless laid the ground for this particular line of descent. Looked at in the context of the 1941–45 controversies in the British Society, the memoranda on the fundamentals of technique are especially pertinent to the four papers in this section. As Riccardo Steiner (King and Steiner, 1991, pp. 680–681) points out, the characteristic qualities and originality of the British school are evident above all in their technical discriminations, including: the wish for flexibility; a disbelief in general assumptions or rigid preconceptions; and the willingness to adapt their technique to the particular circumstances and to the unique requirements of individual patients. Most importantly, some forty-odd years before Patrick Casement (1985) and others – via Rickman's (1951a) demarcation of the two-person relationship – adopted an interactional perspective, the Independent approach to 'learning from the patient' was explicitly set out in the memoranda on technique by Marjorie Brierley (1943, p. 617), Ella Freeman Sharpe (1943, p. 639), and Sylvia M. Payne (1943, p. 648).

The idea that valid technique cannot be settled beforehand remains essential in Independent thought. We can trace this therapeutic attitude towards singular psychic work (Green, 1977, p. 210) from the first generation of English Freudians to the contemporary emphasis on the patient's experience as the primary focus of technique (Parsons, 2014a, p. 189). The fallible analyst, who embodies the Independent attitude towards the irreducible singularity of analysis, relies on first-hand experience as the vital source of valid technique. And what is judged technically sound, according to Ella Sharpe (1943; quoted in King and Steiner, 1991, p. 644), cannot be taught 'in the way that facts are taught' – a more stringent conclusion, perhaps, than Sylvia Payne's acknowledgment that therapy is not an exact science.

Affect in the British school

The focus on affect in each of the four papers clarifies, in retrospect, the central position of Marjorie Brierley in the English school of psychoanalysis. We are reminded, when reading these papers, of a somewhat forgotten figure, whose death in 1984 went officially unmarked by the British Society (Hayman, 1986). A proper appreciation of Brierley's contribution would undoubtedly enhance our understanding of the papers included in this section. Affectivity is a defining preoccupation of Independent thought, and we are prompted to reconsider Brierley's incomparable contribution to this way of thinking, not least of all by Limentani's account of pre-verbal areas of disturbance and blocked affect.

Limentani's paper is based on the astounding clinical observation that '[m]any patients I have met had a past which they had never lived' (p. 189 herein). The idea of an unlived life, taken up more recently by Phillips (2012) and Ogden (2014) from a largely Independent stance, is consistent with Winnicott's reflections (p. 214 herein) on the foreclosure of experience and reality as a psychotic defence against environmental failure. In what is arguably his most important clinical paper, Winnicott outlined a new approach to the negative of 'nothing happening'. Limentani, for his part, proposes that the disruption of the classical technique is most likely to occur in the treatment of patients who lack a sense of their own historicity – patients who feel they are missing a vital part of themselves. Symptomatic of an underlying emptiness, the patient's searching does not always go into words. The problem here, as Kohon (pp. 70–72 herein) points out in his Concluding Remarks above, does not involve revealing an early trauma, or resolving an internal conflict: it is a matter of acknowledging the fact that *something failed to happen at the beginning of life*, an 'environmental deficiency' resulting in a 'basic fault'. And insofar as the papers we are discussing acknowledge the prevalence of the negative manifest as unspeakable pain, they address a defining problem in contemporary psychoanalysis – namely, how to coordinate the treatment of psychotic and borderline states, and contemporary psychosomatic practice, with an updated metapsychology of affect (Matthis, 2000; Press, 2016).

Limentani presents his paper against the background of the shift in perspectives since Freud, in which it is assumed that 'any affect or feeling state exhibited by the analysand will have the analyst as the object' (p. 190 herein). The same holds for Limentani as for the authors of the other papers: clinical thinking is modelled on the object in relationship to affect. We can read these four papers, therefore, primarily as elaborations on affective states of the object-relation in the transference–countertransference. In Limentani's formulation, it is 'the objects which are invested with affects rather than ideas being affectively charged' (p. 190 herein).

The problem of narcissistic and schizoid personality disturbances, or the modification of the classical method in the treatment of psychosomatic structures and borderline states, may be singled out in the psychoanalytic research on affects. Limentani himself makes this point. The problem of affect thus predominates in the practical experience of managing psychoanalytic treatments further to the classical rules. At the same time, the task of managing what lies beneath the surface of perception, in the whole affective gamut of patients' feelings, moods and attitudes, comes to the fore as a general problem of technique. As such, the general focus on affects provides a useful framework for all four papers in this section, where the problem of affectivity covers: (a) aspects of the setting and the analytic relationship; (b) the internal work in the analyst's countertransference to the analytic process; and (c) the combined affective and epistemological movement within the psychoanalytic process – that is, in both analyst and patient – from formlessness towards meaning, from the emotional towards the intelligible, and from unknowing towards knowing.

The general view of affect in each of the four papers is indicative of the shift in psychoanalytic perspectives since Freud. Limentani draws our attention to this shift in describing a patient who, rather than being subject to the death drive, was 'surviving without being or feeling alive' (p. 182 herein). In this case, we can see how reality is something the patient passively undergoes (so to speak) rather than lives, there is no sense of a vital internal object, existence remains cut off from drives and objects. How have our thoughts about these states of blankness (p. 145 herein) developed? The question calls for some historical background before we turn more directly to the analytic relationship.

Klein provided a coherent framework for the early thinking about affects in the British school. Although she did not necessarily address affect as a topic, the change brought about by Klein in the 1920s, with respect to the understanding of primary affects, was nonetheless more important than the occlusion of affects by unconscious phantasy (Green, 1973, p. 77). Taking the representation of drives from birth onwards as given, Klein assumed that there is no affect without representation. Jones's foundational paper on affect theory, 'Fear, Guilt and Hate' (1929), may be seen in this context. In addressing what he called states of pre-ideational primal anxiety, as well as the oedipal danger that later develops out of this situation, Jones was able to rely on Klein's account of the primary defences against the fear of annihilation. The latter was seen as the primordial danger.

Furthermore, Michael Balint's arrival in Britain in the late 1930s was significant in introducing Ferenczi's emphasis on the affective nature of the psychoanalytic process. However, before Ferenczi's ideas were taken up by later Independent analysts (cf. Sklar, 2011), Marjorie Brierley (1937, p. 48) elaborated on the traumatic nature of archaic anxiety – 'the primary "traumatic situation"' (Jones, 1929, p. 392) – in conjunction with Jones's later paper on the instincts (Jones, 1936). She made the point that the primary affect of fear need not be derived from libidinal or aggressive instincts, even though it may be aroused in connection with them. For Brierley, this perspective accords with Freud's final elaboration on the theory of the affect, in which anxiety of helplessness (*Hilflosigkeit*) – i.e., the primitive distress of the human infant – is seen as the essence of anxiety. She proposes that the 'first fear situation in life' leaves an impression on the psyche and, moreover, that it tends 'to be reactivated in later situations which involve the same primary affect' (1937, p. 48).

Brierley opens a route for Independent thinking by taking her lead from William McDougall's idea that 'every primary impulse gives rise to its own qualitatively specific affect and probably also has its own quantitative thresholds' (1937, p. 48). As well as Brierley, Jones and John Flügel (1955) were also influenced by McDougall's model of instinct, affect and emotion. Similarly, Glover (1939, p. 307) maintained that 'there are as many primitive affects as there are primitive ego nuclei'. He posits a neonatal series of reflex-bound instinctual patterns connected to primitive ego nuclei, assuming that every drive or instinct involves an ego-function – a view that subsequently enters Independent thinking through Fairbairn's model of object-relations (Rayner, 1991, p. 31). For Glover, as for Brierley, the term 'primary affect' refers to the particular quality of these rudimentary instinctual patterns of mental life, and, looked at in the context of Glover's general conception of ego nuclei, their views on affects were essentially complementary. Brierley was nonetheless the key figure in the perspectival shift on the significance of affective life. She set a precedent within the British school for the extension of affectivity not only as a concept, but more importantly as a general frame of reference for clinical thinking and the analytic relationship.

The psychotherapeutic relationship

How do the papers that we are looking at engage with this line of thinking? Affect is addressed as a topic only in Limentani's paper, but affective factors are nonetheless central in the other three papers, where the connection between affect and what Klauber calls 'the psychoanalytical relationship' comes to the fore. The same holds for Klauber as for the other three authors: affectivity provides a general framework in terms of 'the setting of communication between analyst and patient and inside each of them' (Green, 1977, p. 213). The question of how best to respond to the patient's affective communication necessitates a fully articulated link between affect theory and the concept of countertransference.

Throughout the second half of the twentieth century, the link was forged, in a radical and distinctive fashion, by a number of British analysts. Following a series of important papers by Michael and Alice Balint (1939), Winnicott (1949b), Heimann (1950), Gitelson (1952) and Little (1957), it was increasingly 'realized that the way in which analysts found their functioning disturbed could be a useful indicator' (Parsons, 2014c, p. 115). The Independent emphasis on emotional contact, understood as an integral feature of the interpretative work (Kohon, pp. 54–55), may be seen as part of a more general reappraisal of the concept of countertransference (Jacobs, 1999). Further to the idea that the analyst goes only as far as 'his own complexes and internal resistances permit' (Freud, 1910d, p. 145), the usefulness of countertransference (Racker, 1968; Searles, 1979) was recognized in conjunction with the analyst's affective response to the patient's communications (King, 1978). The response depends on the analyst's capacity to pay close and careful attention to the perturbation of his or her own thinking.

Klauber's innovative approach to the problem of transference–countertransference difficulties was formulated in this context. In their paper, 'On Transference and Countertransference' (1939), the Balints convey something essential about the personal element of the analyst that links Ferenczi's innovations in technique to Klauber's concern with the extent to which the analyst's personality affects the course of treatment. The common ground here, between the Hungarian and British schools, underwrites the Independent focus on the intersubjective nature of the psychotherapeutic relationship – admittedly 'a very peculiar relationship, but a definite one' (Klauber, p. 200). For the Balints (1939, p. 219–220), there is no such thing as an absolutely good or correct technique, only a sufficiently sound one, which may be seen as doubly individual insofar as it has to satisfy two demands – namely, the objective task of helping the patient become more familiar with unconscious aspects of himself and the subjective task of affording the analyst a means of emotional expression, or providing an 'outlet' for his emotions.

Klauber confirms the Balints' main conclusion that, while there are different ways of working as an analyst, there is nonetheless only one method of psychoanalysis aimed at the vital relationship the patient has with himself and others. The analytic function is what matters, but this cannot be seen in isolation from the person who embodies the function, the acting person of the analyst. Nevertheless, the emphasis that Klauber places on what happens after the patient has left the analyst's consulting room for the last time underlines the reach of the process itself. The different affective configurations created by the analyst's personality notwithstanding, 'the analytic process initiated in the ego of the patient extends outside his personal contact with the analyst' (Klauber, 1976, p. 138). Allowing for the fact that analysts inevitably facilitate and enliven the experience of the process in different ways, it is the experience of the process itself that counts. This line of thinking runs directly from Balint through Klauber to the contemporary Independent emphasis on the internal process of the analytic experience (Parsons, 2000, p. 58ff).

Alongside the idea of technique as a means of emotional outlet for the analyst, the concept of strain or pressure comes to the fore in Winnicott's account of the emotional burden that therapeutic treatment places on the analyst (1949b). In that paper, which broke new ground in the theory of clinical technique, Winnicott identified three aspects of countertransference phenomena: (a) repressed identifications; (b) personal elements; and (c) affective reactions. What new insight did this offer? Abnormal countertransference feelings on the one hand, and, on the other, the identifications belonging to the analyst's personal experiences, were addressed by Freud and the Balints, respectively. As for the 'objective countertransference', Winnicott counted hate among the objective reactions to a patient who may be relating to the analyst, or otherwise behaving, in a hateful manner. And affective reactions are rendered meaningful precisely in terms of the *use* that the analyst is able to make of them. The pressure consists in being moved and perturbed by the affect of hate. The task involves bringing hate into the area of use.

In terms of the contact and communication that pertains under pressure, the idea that the analyst feels the strain of the psychic work that has not been done in infancy introduces an important distinction between projective identification and emotional responsiveness. The fact that the patient's negativity triggers hatred in the analyst is seen as more important than the patient's projection into the analyst. The patient's mental function generates something that actually belongs to the analyst. Kohon draws on the examples of Balint, Symington, Coltart and Bollas in registering his own objections to 'the characterization of the countertransference as based solely on the

141

process of projective identification' (p. 64 herein). The objection is underpinned by the Independent approach in general but, more particularly, by the object-relations theory of affect. The technical implications of the latter were set out by King (1978), first with respect to the monitoring of emotional responses to the analytic process *per se* and second in terms of the link between affect and early trauma in certain types of difficult patient.

While King effectively recapitulates Winnicott's argument, Klauber consolidates and augments the definition of 'objective counter-transference' as part of a therapeutic relationship. Most importantly, he identifies the mutual participation of emotional responsiveness as the agent of therapeutic change. The idea of mutual participation goes beyond notions of strain and emotional outlet; rather, the desire and needs of the analyst are seen as constitutive elements of the analytic relationship. This obviously has direct implications for the aim of treatment. The analytic task is not seen primarily in terms of what has to be done to improve the patient's mental functioning. Rather, the work of countertransference affords the analyst access – indeed, through his own fallibility – to what may have failed for the patient in the past. Klauber (p. 162 herein) reminds us that the patient derives 'the substantial part of his cure' not only on account of the analyst's capacity for objective hate, but also with respect to the shared ground of primordial vulnerability. In terms of what may be seen as the psychoanalytic contextualization of *l'homme faillible* (Ricoeur, 1960), Klauber confirmed the extent to which Winnicott developed a new way of working *within* the negative, as distinct from the work *of* the negative (Green, 1999).

Winnicott, however, was not alone in drawing a link between affect and use in post-classical theory and practice. Paula Heimann's celebrated paper, 'On Counter-Transference' (1950), remains a central reference for the difficulties of clinical practice that we are looking at through Klauber's lens. A single contribution rarely, if ever, amounts to a turning point in the history of ideas. Nevertheless, by applying Kleinian thinking to a burgeoning preoccupation in the British school with innovative approaches to countertransference, Heimann's paper provided a clearly delineated framework for the use the analyst makes of his affective response.

Klauber's paper may be seen as part of an ongoing attempt, by Independent analysts and others, to work out the therapeutic impli-cations of Heimann's definition of the analysing situation as an intersubjective situation – that is, as 'a relationship between two persons' (1950, p. 81). Heimann based her argument on the assumption that the analyst's unconscious is capable of understanding that of his patient. She applied the idea of 'rapport' to a particular clinical encounter with difficulty – namely, where the analyst unconsciously introjects the patient prior to an understanding of the patient's projections. This involves a subtle, but much narrower, definition of 'use' than the one with which Winnicott operated. The play of apprehension and comprehension is framed in terms of introjection–projection on the Kleinian model. On the one hand, far from working within the negative, the analyst employs the 'tool' of countertransference in the analysis of anxiety and defence. On the other hand, countertransference is seen not only as 'part and parcel of the analytic relationship', but also as part of the patient's 'personality' (1950, p. 83). There is a danger here of seeing everything 'created' in the analyst as countertransference (p. 54 herein). In fact, five years later, at the 19th International Psycho-Analytical Congress in Geneva, Heimann presented another paper on the dynamics of the countertransference, which marked her break with Klein and her group. Her change of orientation had been increasingly apparent since 1949 (Tonnesmann, 1989) and, on this occasion, Heimann (1956, p. 307) comes much closer to the idea of the analyst as an acting person, making it perfectly clear that the 'analyst's personality is one part of the analytic situation and of the patient's problems on a realistic as well as a phantasy level'. The acknowledgement of a 'realistic level', operating in conjunction with the projective–introjective horizon of intelligibility, was a major factor in Heimann's move away from the Kleinian group and towards a more Independent way of thinking and working, as well as a return to her classical Freudian roots.

There is a further distinction worth making, the therapeutic implications of which can hardly be overestimated. Heimann (1950, p. 83) states explicitly that she does not 'consider it right for the analyst to communicate his feelings to his patient'. This remains a matter of debate within the Independent tradition and elsewhere. For example, whereas Little (1951, p. 47) advanced the idea of 'countertransference interpretations', King (1978, p. 331) did not believe that 'anything is usually to be gained by the analyst sharing his own affective reactions with the patient'. The debate goes back to Ferenczi's technical innovations, while at the same time setting an important parameter for the papers by Klauber, Symington and Coltart with respect to the 'expressive' uses of the countertransference (Bollas, 1987). In my experience, patients, who might otherwise find it difficult to keep

143

the analytic relationship alive, can often make use of an interpretation that allows them to know something of how the analyst feels, particularly under the pressure of the patient's more disturbed states of mind.

The dialogical nature of Independent thought

The idea that 'on rare but significant occasions the analyst may analyse his experience as the object of the patient's transference in the presence of the patient' (Bollas, 1987, p. 201) is a good example of the way in which a leading contemporary analyst in the British Society addresses the Freudian tradition of Independent thought, not only as an authoritative call from the past, but also as an object of renewal in the present. Bollas is one of a group of outstanding contemporary Independent thinkers – alongside Symington, Mitchell, Parsons, Kohon and Paul Williams – whose input into British psychoanalysis is indebted to the generation of Klauber and Coltart. Looking further afield, the theoretical and countertransference difficulties highlighted by each of the four papers in this section demonstrate the extent to which developments in French psychoanalysis have played a decisive role in the renewal of the British Independent tradition.

We could cite a number of examples in support of this claim: first and foremost, perhaps, the work of André Green (Kohon, 1999a). But we could also include, for instance, the complementary analytic perspectives of Laplanche and Winnicott (Scarfone, 2005); the dialogue between Winnicottian psychosomatic theory (Winnicott, 1949c) – including what Bollas (1987, p. 282) calls the 'somatic knowledge' of the 'unthought known' – and the work of Pierre Marty and the Paris School of Psychosomatics; and the work of René Roussillon (2011) on primary homosexuality and primary agonies, which draws explicitly on the clinical innovations in Ferenczi and Winnicott, but also recalls the tradition of Brierley on the sensory and emotional elements of the earliest relationship. Furthermore, the work of César and Sára Botella (2005) on regredience – that is, a mode of formal regression that affects the analyst working within the negative – seems to me particularly relevant in the context of Independent clinical technique. If we take their work as illustrative of the British–French dialogue in Independent thought, it is important to note that the dialogue reveals blind spots as well as common themes in the respective schools.

In an attempt to account for a situation in which something failed to happen for the infant, something that should have happened as a matter of course, César and Sára Botella identify the negative of the trauma in terms of a potential effect without content. As with Limentani's patient (p. 180 herein), notwithstanding an outpouring of death fantasies, the patient was nonetheless 'plunged into a state of total inactivity' and 'blankness'. The negative thus outweighs any sense of conflict or thoughts about what the object might do. It is what the object has *not* done that comes across in the state of blank pain. In this case, the paradigm of unconscious phantasy is not adequate to the difficulty, which consists in rendering presentable that which has never been intelligible.

Coltart continues to formulate blank pain in terms of 'unthinkable content'. Similarly, Winnicott (p. 124 herein) demonstrated a degree of ambiguity in construing the fear of breakdown as a defence against something that has already happened (the break in the mother–infant relation at the level of absolute dependence) but has not yet been experienced. The idea of traumatic content (the content of the event) is central in both cases and, as such, is indicative of the Independent approach to trauma, which has 'led to diverse ways of integrating the contribution of the environment into the approach in the consulting room' (Keene, 2012, pp. 36–37).

The Botellas (2005, p. 116), on the other hand, contend that infantile trauma issues neither from the intensity of a perception nor from the content of a representation but, rather, from an incapacity to bind or gather an experience as such. The resulting state of non-cathexis, characterized by a total absence of intelligibility, is described in terms of a 'hole' or a 'gap' in both the perceptual and the representational realm. In this case, the notion of a perceptual trace – that is, as distinct from a memory-trace – is presented in contrast, first, to the Winnicottian idea of the yet-to-be-experienced event that has already occurred and, second, to the Freudian mechanism of *Verwerfung*, or the abolition of a representation.

How should we treat words that issue as impersonal reports on experiences that are in fact unthinkable? How do we help the patient to make meaningful links between strategies of evasion and states of blankness? It seems to me the analyst is especially reliant here on what Geoffrey Hill (2008) called the 'diligence of the imagination'. As for the papers under discussion, the thread that runs from unspeakable pain to a type of non-interpretative analytic action (the analyst's inner act of freedom) focuses attention on the non-representable, pre-psychic impressions that remain inaccessible to classical technique. Accordingly, Coltart (p. 155 herein) situates her signal contribution in the area where blankness appears to be, or where a gap opens in the ground. The 'profoundly silent patients' that she discusses in her paper alert the analyst to a negative duality of self and object. Language is laid open, in the devitalized uses the patient makes of it, as an appearance in which nothing appears. The Botellas (2005, p. 28), in a distinctly Hegelian vein, describe things in terms of a specular absence in the subject's capacity for self-representation, coupled with a real absence of the object.

It would appear that the negative of the trauma is discernible only in the regression of the analytic situation, and that it requires a spontaneous and eruptive act on the part of the analyst to solicit and galvanize comparable psychic work in the patient. Coltart ends up shouting at the patient who fell violently silent in the third year of his analysis, without 'the remotest idea *at that moment*' (p. 156 herein) what she had in mind. We need to think of technique in the broadest possible terms where sensation precedes understanding, and where countertransference may be seen as the counterpart to the patient's sensation of ceasing to exit. In a comparable movement to Coltart's gesture, the Botellas (2005, pp. 31–34) describe the therapist dreaming, naming and acting the wolf in the treatment of a severely traumatized four-year-old child. In both cases, the regressive movement of the patient's psyche, the silent propulsive aspect of his unlived or devitalized life, is coupled with the analyst's openness to a process of formal regression *as a lived experience*.

Coltart models this retrogressive encounter on her analysis of prolonged silence and psychosomatic structures. In her paper, which remains at the very forefront of Independent clinical thinking, she identifies the patient's regression in 'the darkness of the psychosomatic symptom' (p. 159 herein). At the same time, consistent with the emphasis in contemporary analytic theory on the backward movement towards the lived immediacy of perception, she delimits the path of return in terms of words that are sufficiently compatible 'with the physical track chosen by the mind' (this volume). Some sort of 'message' can therefore be sent back along the same track by way of the body to the mind, which constitutes a communicative link in the psyche-soma. The potentiality of affect is invested with new meaning, where the movement within the analytic process determines the technical imperative to register impressions of emptiness on the one hand and, on the other, to reclaim the experience of 'nothing happening' by revitalizing the occasion of coexistence.

The 'puzzling leap' from soma to psyche, which formed an essential part of Freud's (1916–17, p. 258) conviction that symptoms are meaningful, is put to work beyond the Freudian paradigm of hysteria, on the grounds that intersubjective communication – making sense together – provides new clinical possibilities for the more recalcitrant difficulties in the analytic encounter.

12

'SLOUCHING TOWARDS BETHLEHEM...'

Or thinking the unthinkable in psychoanalysis

Nina E.C. Coltart

After I had agreed to write this paper, my mind went blank for quite a long time. Then I began to realize that a paper for a symposium whose overall title was 'Beyond Words' appropriately had to be generated in that very area, namely, where blankness seemed to be. After a while, the title for the paper announced itself. I was wary of it, since it seemed both eccentric and religious. But it stuck tenaciously. For those of you who do not know it, it is taken from a short poem by W.B. Yeats called 'The Second Coming'. It occurred to me when I reread it closely that it is a poem about breakdown and the possibility of healing, or could be seen as such. It is mysterious, but then so is our subject. It goes like this (my italics):

> Turning and turning in the widening gyre
> The falcon cannot hear the falconer;
> Things fall apart; the centre cannot hold;
> Mere anarchy is loosed upon the world,
> The blood-dimmed tide is loosed, and everywhere
> The ceremony of innocence is drowned;
> The best lack all conviction, while the worst
> Are full of passionate intensity.

Surely some revelation is at hand;
Surely the Second Coming is at hand.
The Second Coming! Hardly are those words out
When a vast image out of Spiritus Mundi
Troubles my sight: somewhere in the sands of the desert
A shape with lion body and the head of a man,
A gaze blank and pitiless as the sun,
Is moving its slow thighs, while all about it
Reel shadows of the indignant desert birds.
The darkness drops again; but now I know
That twenty centuries of stony sleep
Were vexed to nightmare by a rocking cradle,
And what rough beast, its hour come round at last,
Slouches towards Bethlehem to be born?

This is not a paper on religion. It does not look to Messianic dogma, nor to Christian symbol to help us out of the anarchic depths of the unconscious. What caught my attention was the idea that there is a distinct metaphor for us in the poem which speaks to the whole of what analysis is about. We can move the metaphor of the poem from the religious to the analytical. Some people have seen this as pessimistic; you will gather that I have seen it differently.

It is of the essence of our impossible profession that in a very singular way we do not know what we are doing. Do not be distracted by random associations to this idea. I am not undermining our deep, exacting training; nor discounting the ways in which – unlike many people who master a subject and then just *do* it, or teach it, we have to keep *at* ourselves, our literature and our clinical crosstalk with colleagues. All these daily operations are the efficient, skilful, and thinkable tools with which we constantly approach the heart of our work, which is a mystery.

The day that one qualifies as an analyst, the analyst that one is *going to be* is a mystery. Ten years later, we may just about be able to look back and discern the shape of the rough beast – ourselves as analysts in embryo – as it slouched along under the months and years until, its hour come round at last, there is some clearer sense of ourselves as analysts. The process of doing analysis has slowly given birth to an identity which we now more or less recognize as an analyst, or at least the identity which we have become, and are still becoming, which for us approximates to the notion of 'being an analyst'. This

149

may be very different from that which we long ago had visualized or hoped for.

It is my belief that something very similar obtains also for our work with our patients. However much we gain confidence, refine our technique, decide more creatively when and how and what to interpret, each hour with each patient is also in its way an act of faith; faith in ourselves, in the process, and faith in the secret, unknown, *unthinkable* things in our patients which, in the space which is the analysis, are slouching towards the time when their hour comes round at last. When that hour comes, by dint of all our long, thoughtful, interpretative attempts to familiarize ourselves with the patient's inner world, we begin to see shaping up things that we may have guessed at; or predicted, or theoretically constructed or relied on; or even, almost like by-products of months of careful, ready work, things that take us by surprise. We have been waiting attentively, in Freud's own words, 'for the pattern to emerge'. Those of us who were fortunate enough to be taught by the late Dr Bion value the stress which he laid on the need to develop the ability to tolerate not knowing, the capacity to sit it out with a patient, often for long periods, without any real precision as to where we are, relying on our regular tools and our faith in the process, to carry us through the obfuscating darkness of resistance, complex defences, and the sheer *unconsciousness* of the unconscious.

In parenthesis, there is a possible solution or definition here of that controversial problem, the difference between psychotherapy and psychoanalysis. Although I am currently stressing our ignorance, *there is* always something going on that we more or less *know* something about; the daily *tabula rasa* of the analytic session produces a mass of information; and for a patient who comes once or twice a week, it may well be constructive and ego-supportive to get on to a track indicated by one of these signposts. In analysis we can afford to ignore them, in the slow, attentive working towards a deeper nexus of feeling, fantasy, and wordless experience, that is slouching along in an as yet unthinkable form. Clues we note and store away, but need not, often must not, hear them as distracting sirens' songs to be fallen for and followed.

I want to say something more here about the act of faith. It is to do with Wilfred Bion. I have to confess that at the time that I wrote my short paragraph above about being taught by Bion, it was pretty well a summary of what I knew about him. Of course, I knew that he had invented a Grid and I had never talked to anyone who could make real sense of it. But since writing my original paper, I felt a strong urge to read all the works of Bion, and have done so. I was both delighted and horrified by what I found. Delighted because some of it expressed so clearly some of my own ideas; horrified because it began to look as though I had been plagiarizing. But I do not think I can have been. I have concluded that, apart from perhaps being more influenced by the few seminars that I had with him than I realized, we had simply developed individually along similar lines *in some ways*. I stress this because I do not wish time or imaginative conjecture to be wasted in thinking that I am seriously comparing myself to any extent with him. Wilfred Bion was a widely cultured man and I think probably a mystic and a genius. Certain clues in his writings suggest that, in the most modest and dispassionate way, he thought the same. And I am not. Also he did invent that Grid, and he constantly refers to it, and even now that I have read him word for word, it makes little sense to me, and I cannot use it. This may be because Bion was, amongst other things, mathematically minded, and I am innumerate.

To return to the act of faith. Bion *uses* this phrase and by it intends to signify the most highly desirable stance of the psychoanalyst. He says that the act of faith is peculiar to scientific procedure and must be distinguished from the religious meaning with which it is invested in common usage. The essence of its creation – and Bion sees it, as do I, as a positive, willed act – is refraining from memory and desire, a phrase which many people *do* loosely associate with what they know of Bion. He says in *Attention and Interpretation* (1970, p. 30): 'It may be wondered what state of mind is welcome if desires and memories are not. A term that would express approximately what I need to express is "faith" – faith that there is an ultimate reality and truth – the unknown, unknowable, "formless infinite",' which can become at least partly known through evolution into objects of which the individual personality can become aware. The channel for this evolution and the transformation of the apprehension of the ultimate reality, or a bit of it, is the analyst's direct attention and perception, and his capacity to bring together hitherto meaningless fragments of the patient's mental and verbal elements into a thinking process, and communicate this back to the patient.

Bion says that this form of attention, this act of faith, must be what he calls 'unstained by any elements of memory or desire or sensation'. He means in the analyst, of course.

151

'The more the psycho-analyst occupies himself with memory and desire the more his facility for harbouring them increases and the nearer he comes to undermining his capacity for F [the act of faith]. For consider: if his mind is preoccupied with what is or is not said, or with what he does or does not hope, it must mean that he cannot allow the experience to obtrude . . .' (1970, p. 41). No-one who learns to denude himself of memory and desire, he goes on to say, and of all those elements of sense impression ordinarily present, can have any doubt of the reality of psychoanalytical experience which remains ineffable. It will be seen that Bion has intuition very high in his hierarchy of the tools at our disposal, and is advocating a constant sternly self-disciplined practice. Indeed, at one point, he actually equates intuition with 'analytic observations'.

It must be emphasized, however, in case it is not clear enough already, that Bion is not advocating random speculative commentary unrooted in a huge reservoir of experience, thought, theoretical knowledge, and the capacity to draw upon and correlate all these in the intervals *between* the dark experiencing of the act of faith, and in the interests of making the *evolution* of the total experience comprehensively available to the patient. The philosopher Immanuel Kant said: 'Intuition without concept is blind: concept without intuition is empty.' It seems to me that Bion, and I in my way in this paper, are striving for the merging of the two.

Before I move on from this section on Bion's thought, I just want to quote from a question–answer seminar recorded when Bion was in Sao Paulo in 1973. It says with such simplicity so much that elsewhere in his writings Bion goes over repetitively at length and in a complex way; the questioner asks: 'How did you come to realize the advantages of suppressing memory and desire during an analytic session?' and Bion replies: 'I found I could experience a flash of the obvious. One is usually so busy looking for something out of the ordinary that one ignores the obvious as if it were of no importance.' Whereas, again in *Attention and Interpretation*, he says, unhelpfully if challengingly, 'There can be no *rules* about the nature of the emotional experience that will show that it is ripe for interpretation.' Here I would add that faith and self-reliance are indeed needed!

The crucial thing about our technical development is that it hinges on a paradox. There is a delicate balance between our reliance on our theories and on our knowledge of human nature in many of its dimensions – (and experience tells us that human nature continually reveals similar patterns which generates good theory) – the balance, I repeat, is between this *reliance*, and our willingness to be continually open to the emergence of the unexpected. *Plus ça change, plus c'est la même chose* may be a good truism for analysts but it is only true in a restricted sense; it is the changes that are rung that are the essentials of individual humanity. There is a grim stage when we are *learning to be* analysts when we are endangered by our own templates, our theories, and our teachers. We may detect the faint shuffle of the slouching beast, and be tempted to throw a set of grappling irons into the darkness, seize him, label him, hang him round with words, and haul him prematurely to birth. We may then often be stuck with a deformed monster that we have largely created by our own precipitate verbosity; we may then proceed laboriously onwards with a sort of analytic mistake, while the true creature who is not yet ready for the light of day retreats backwards into the darkness again.

The use of the metaphor of the poem here says what I want to say, but perhaps I should explain it a little, and less poetically. The seductive impulse to use the power of one's thinking and theorizing to take possession of the patient too soon can be great, but will, as suggested, be of little ultimate value to him. Precipitate control of the material may lead to a sense of satisfaction in the analyst, and often to quite conscious layers of the patient, whose resistance to exposing his true unknown reality to the light will have been served by it.

Heisenberg's Uncertainty Principle is a hard taskmaster in the everyday life of the consulting room; it seems to me undesirable that one should communicate certainty about a patient to a patient, or, at least, only very occasionally. The whole of our subject, psycho-analysis, can be, and often is, attacked on the grounds that it is unscientific and cannot be supported by any scientific evidence. The most that can be claimed for it is that it is *probable*, and what we use is not rigorous scientific investigation, but the act of faith, supported by rational and imaginative conjectures, themselves inevitably con-ditioned by our learning and our experience. The act of faith may feel like a spontaneous regression to complete unknowing, and may well be accompanied by dread; it can be disturbing to the analyst and seem like a serious self-induced attack on his ego, which in a way it is. To quote Bion again, with particular reference to trying to capture the rough beast too soon: 'Such depths of ignorance are difficult to dare to contemplate, though I am bound to feel a wish to believe how Godlike I am, how intelligent, as a change from being appalled by my ignorance.' But it may be at the expense of the *true* pattern emerging that we do this.

I am sure I am not saying anything heretical or unfamiliar to analysts at least, if I confess that I sometimes wish ardently, as I settle down for the opening sessions of what promises to be a long analysis, that the first year were already over. This is part of the paradoxical nature of our work. I would not for the world pass up that first year with all its subtle demands on the technique of getting the patient rooted in the analysis, feeling for the available transferences, learning history, and doing first aid, which is often so necessary when things have fallen apart and anarchy has been loosed upon the world.

But after this preliminary work, there comes a time which is exhilarating, when the pace quickens and the gears change. Paradoxically again, this is often the time when darkness begins to close in, but it is a darkness having that special quality of the unknown which is moving towards being known. Freud was speaking of a time like this, I imagine, when he said that sometimes he had to 'blind himself in order to focus on the light in one dark spot'. There is a textural richness which begins to draw deeper analysis out of one's own darkness, and stretch oneself towards the limit of ingenuity, technique, and a rapid use of identifications and intuition, combined with imaginative intensity. During phases like this in analysis it is true to say that one does not *think* at all during some sessions, at least in the ordinary cognitive use of the word. Indeed, one of the most satisfying elements about entering the stage of doing an analysis when the anxiety of the early years is left behind and senility has not yet come, is this freedom from actually thinking while one is actively engaged in working; i.e., when the act of faith is becoming easier. Of course, to say this is not to detract from the high value attaching to the power of attention and total concern with the patient. In fact there is plenty of evidence, not only in our literature, but in that of philosophy and religion, that the attention is more total when temporarily freed from concurrent cognitive processes. This switch into fifth gear cannot exactly be legislated for, although Bion's advice that we should rigorously practise for it is relevant, and it does not by any means always happen. Then we fall back again on thinking, and theorizing, and trying things out in our heads, or just waiting. But in the fifth gear phases, when the act of faith is most fully deployed, when our listening ear seems to be directly connected with our tongue and speech, interpretative dialogue is not a process which I would regard as being under everyday conscious control. Fascinating data derived from bio-feedback experiments show that the nature of the brain-waves actually changes in the states to which I am referring and predominantly alpha rhythm on the EEG takes over from normal waking mixed beta and theta waves. When I gave this paper to the English-speaking Conference, one of the analysts in the discussion took up what I have just said and asked me rather peevishly what I meant by saying that this was fascinating. I fear I was unable to answer satisfactorily. I had myself participated in bio-feedback experiments and had learned to alter my brainwaves, blood pressure and skin resistance. If the phenomenon I have just described is not self-evidently fascinating, then we are on different wavelengths and I cannot justify the use of such a personalized word.

Certain recurring problems in analytic work give valuable encouragement to our reliance on the process that I have just attempted to describe. These are problems which may be rather specially regarded as falling into the arena entitled Beyond Words. One of them is silence. Any silence of more than about 40 minutes in analysis begins to have its own peculiar interest. But there is a very particular challenge issued by profoundly silent patients, who are often, by the way, not diagnosable as such during a careful assessment interview. I make this point because it indicates that profound silence itself, as well as what it conceals, can be a rough beast which is slouching along in the depths of a communicative, articulate patient and whose time may need to come round and *be endured* in the analysis.

I have treated eleven patients in 25 years who have been deeply silent for long periods during the analysis. One for nearly a year, several for months or weeks.

One of these was a man who was in his mid-50s when he started treatment with the complaint of near-suicidal depression. He was unmarried, sexually virginal, powerful, charismatic, and a successful captain of industry. He was not, I decided in the first year, a False Self personality, nor was he, apparently, homosexual or perverse. He had a huge number of acquaintances, but no really close friends. He was a clubbable man. The very fact of starting analysis, and that he had never really talked deeply to anyone about himself, meant that in his case the first couple of years were full of interchange and improvement. But I was suspicious that something else was gathering its forces in the depths of his inner world. He slowly made an eroticized transference, and was somewhat elated for months. I could not exactly predict what the shape of the beast was going to be, but that there was something completely different that had to emerge in time if the analysis was going to work, I did not doubt. He had come to me with his centre not holding, and with things falling apart; and the initial improvement had not truly touched that. In his third year, he suddenly ground to a halt, and fell violently silent, exuding ever-stronger black waves of hatred and despair. I slowly tried out the various technical manoeuvres that I had learned over the years for approaching and entering silence. To no avail. The change in him from late midlife crisis neurosis to something which breathed psychosis was heavy in the atmosphere. He never failed to attend, but his body movements and even his shape seemed to have altered. Very close attention to these things is of the essence when faced with such a massive Beyond Words challenge. He slouched and humped himself grimly and disjointedly up and down my stairs and in and out of my room. His gaze, when he glanced at me, was shifty, evil, and terrified. He was as if possessed. When I spoke about what I saw and felt, he glowered, grunted and sank further into an ungainly heap. He had never wanted to lie on the couch, so all this was face-to-face. I carried dark and heavy projective identifications, to put it one way, which I tried in vain to decode to him, until I was almost as saturated in despair as he was.

One day, without really thinking it out clearly, I suddenly demon-strated an example of what Neville Symington in a recent paper has called the analyst's act of freedom [pp. 192–206 herein (ed.)]. I simply and suddenly became furious and bawled him out for his prolonged lethal attack on me and on the analysis. I wasn't going to stand for it a second longer, I shouted, without the remotest idea *at that moment* of what alternative I was proposing! This outburst of mine changed the course of the analysis.

It was only in the subsequent interpretative understanding of that parameter, as my outburst would be called, and of the preceding black months, that we came to see how much, to his own surprise and horror, this man had needed to live out, and have *experienced and endured by another person without retaliation*, his primary hatred of a genuinely powerful mother. He had, so to speak, lost her to his only brother who was born when he was eleven months old, and he had been required by her throughout his life to love and revere her unstintingly. He had solved this first great problem of his life by remaining unswervingly loyal to her and it had nearly cost *him* his life. You will see that the act of freedom arose from the exercise of an act of faith. I had given up trying to 'understand' this patient, given

156

up theorizing and just sat there day after day without memory or desire in a state of suspension, attending only with an empty mind to him and the unknowable truth of himself, which had shaped his life, until such a moment as I was so *at one* with it that I *knew it* for the murderous hatred it was, and had to make a jump for freedom – his as well as mine, though I did not think that out at the time – by shouting. These acts of faith can feel dangerous.

I would like to speak briefly here for a moment of another thing that is often, I have the distinct impression, felt to be dangerous in psychoanalysis, albeit in a different way from the encounter with murderous hatred via the act of faith. This is laughing. You hardly ever hear analysts talk about laughing in sessions, and you do not find papers written about it either. Again I return to Bion for a comment though he nowhere has developed it as much as I could have wished. In one of his São Paulo seminars (Bion, 1980), he is talking about how psychoanalysis has changed and developed; he wonders would Freud even understand what some of us are doing now? Then, apparently at random, he goes straight on to say:

> I wonder if it is within the rules of psychoanalysis to be able to laugh at ourselves? Is it according to the rules of psychoanalysis that we should be amused and find things funny? Is it permissible to enjoy a psychoanalytic meeting? I suggest that, having broken through in this revolutionary matter of being amused in the sacred progress of psychoanalysis, we might as well continue to see where that more joyous state of mind might take us.
>
> (pp. 94–95)

Then, rather maddeningly, but very characteristically, he says no more about this explicitly, but I think it is significant that he goes straight into a short passage which ends like this:

> . . . I sometimes think analysts are sunk in gloom; so much so that they are often taken by surprise when they discover that there is such a thing as mental pain. One feels that they have only learned that there is a *theory* that there is mental pain, but that they don't believe it exists, or that psychoanalysis is a method of treating it. So when a patient gets better they are surprised. They do not believe it has anything to do with the work they are doing; but if we are to go on growing and developing, I believe that the psychoanalytical procedure does a great deal to help that

development to take place. Psychoanalysis helps the spirit or the soul . . . to continue; we can help the soul or the psyche to be *born* even, and help it to continue to develop after it is born.

Now the immediate juxtaposition of those two passages makes me think that implicit in the second passage is the message of the first; to put it very simply, that laughter and enjoyment can be therapeutic factors in psychoanalysis. Certainly I believe that one not only can but should enjoy psychoanalytical sessions.

I once thought about writing a paper on laughing in psychoanalysis and perhaps this is the nearest I shall get. I suppose there is a fear that I may be deluding myself, and not noticing that what it really means is that my technique has got sloppy, or that I have developed a special sort of defence, or both, or many more horrendous things, but certainly with advancing age laughter in sessions seems to occur more often than it did. Of course, it is important to try to continue to analyse and monitor what is happening. I remember that when I was still training, I started to treat a patient in what had to be called five-times-a-week psychotherapy, because I was not yet an analyst. He was not one of my Clinic training cases. He was a man who could make people laugh. He was quite ill, but he was really extremely amusing. I was so serious about my training and what I thought were the sacred rules of psychoanalysis that I used to use a lot of energy trying not to laugh. Of course I analysed the aggression in his jokes, and there was plenty of it, and what was defensive, distracting and seductive about it all. And so I would now. But I also think now that I would laugh first if I felt like it. I am now of the opinion that I deprived both him and me unnecessarily by being so prim. I think I might have got nearer to some true shape or pattern in him *faster*, by responding with a natural reaction and *then* talking about it. If we are too protective of our self-presentation and of what we consider grimly to be the sacred rules of True Psychoanalysis, then we may suffocate something in the patient, in ourselves, and in the process.

Another category of patients who present one with specific Beyond Words problems are those with psychosomatic symptoms. In this I include, of course, the fairly straightforward, pure, and now relatively rare hysterical conversions. The overlap between these and some psychosomatic symptoms of different aetiology can be extending and confusing. For example, I have had the opportunity to treat five cases of asthma of late onset in adults, two in analysis, and three in focal analytic psychotherapy. They could not exactly be classified as hysterics, because I believe hysterical symptoms are rooted in a pathological disablement of the will, while willing and breathing, which is what goes wrong in asthma, do not connect up properly in a psychological sense, i.e., we do not breathe at will. A paralysed limb where the voluntary muscles cease to work hysterically is a different matter. But they were certainly conveying a message of conflict through their asthma attacks, and this *is* what hysterics do. They were also threatening life itself, and two of them very nearly did die in status asthmaticus. If I were to condense into one sentence what the hidden central dynamic was, I would say it was pre-verbal never-thinkable, never-expressible rage with the mother, rooted in a period before the attainment of the depressive position. In silence, eventually, I had to experience this rage directly myself as raged at, before being able to evolve this shape into suitable words.

The special interest of psychosomatic symptoms, to pick up the main metaphor of this paper, is that the rough beast whose hour is not yet come is holed up in the body. There is a lovely quotation from the poet John Donne which refers to the non-pathological aspect of this:

The blood spoke in her cheek,
as if her body thought.

The beast has crossed that mysterious barrier whose location eludes us, and moved over into a stronghold from which it is only on rare occasions easy to deliver him. Mostly, he seems inaccessible, and we perceive that part of the mind has lodged on a psychotic island in the body. This image arises from a paper by Herbert Rosenfeld (1985), which sheds light on the treatment of women who not infrequently select the uterus as their psychotic island. We could say that a psychosomatic symptom represents that which is determined to remain unconscious, or unknowable, but which at the same time has actually made itself conscious in a very heavy disguise; it is speakable about only in a dense and enigmatic code. In terms of the metaphor of my paper, we have to ask what is the unthinkable content slouching along in the darkness of the psychosomatic symptom? How do we build a bridge which *really holds* over the secret area of the body–mind divide? Can the unthinkable become thinkable? Can we possibly devise words which have enough compatibility with the physical track chosen by the mind, so that we can send some sort of message down back along that same track via the body to the mind? By ordinary, careful analysis laced with inspiration one may at length interpret the psychosomatic symptom so irresistibly that it yields. A rush of new affects may appear. The now more verbal material may be enriched by new–old memories. Or the symptom may just quietly fade away. Nevertheless, there is a certain mystery which we do well not to ignore. It would be unwise to conclude that because we have apparently cured a genuine psychosomatic symptom by dynamic interpretation we actually *know* how it was *done*. We may be able to derive further theory from it. We may even be able to repeat the performance with another patient with a similar problem. But we do not quite know how it was done. Where and how did our laboriously evolved words and thoughts meet and capture the resolutely unthinkable beast in the unconscious process?

There is a way of visualizing analysis as a spiral process. The seemingly same ground is ploughed over and over again. And yet there is always something new about it. I refer to this spiral effect here because it has a special relevance to our work with psychosomatic symptoms. We may have undermined such a symptom to the point of its yielding. The patient may be in completely different territory, a long way up the spiral. Suddenly the symptom returns. It requires investigation all over again. The original understanding does not influence it in the same way. The mind is so protean that it can colonize the body in a new spirit and skilfully enlist the symptom under a new banner in the ongoing war of resistance in the transference.

Perhaps I may end here by saying that patients with such symptoms, and silent patients, teach us most vividly and memorably that there is always in our work a dimension that is beyond words. Some people *suffer* more from the unthinkable than others, and for these we have to do all in our power to help towards the therapeutic transformation, to bring thoughts to the unthinkable and words to the inexpressible. Gradually the rough beast may, within the framework of the analytic relationship, slouch towards being born, and the new creature emerging from the birth is the increased happiness and peace of mind of the patient. But in all of us there are some things which will never be within our reach; there is always a mystery at the heart of every person, and therefore in our job as analysts.

13

ELEMENTS OF THE PSYCHOANALYTIC RELATIONSHIP AND THEIR THERAPEUTIC IMPLICATIONS

John Klauber

Confidence in the therapeutic success of the analytic method tempts analysts to overlook some of the strains it imposes on both patient and analyst. The development of transference is always traumatic for the patient, as is the longing for relationship with the analyst as a result of their intimacy. The development of psychoanalytic objectivity and distance, which have to be combined with ready empathy, are similarly an arduous task for the analyst. The period of depression which the analyst must endure before he acquires his skill is described, with its accompanying danger of the prolonged dependence of the psychoanalyst on his own training analyst.

The most neglected feature of the psychoanalytic relationship still seems to me to be that it is a relationship: a very peculiar relationship, but a definite one. Patient and analyst need one another. The patient comes to the analyst because of internal conflicts that prevent him from enjoying life, and he begins to use the analyst not only to resolve them, but increasingly as a receptacle for his pent-up feelings. But the analyst also needs the patient in order to crystallize and communicate his own thoughts, including some of his inmost thoughts on intimate human problems which can only grow organically in the context of this relationship. They cannot be shared and experienced in the same immediate way with a colleague, or even with a husband or wife. It is also in his relationship with his patients that the analyst refreshes his own analysis. It is from this mutual participation in analytic understanding that the patient derives the substantial part of his cure and the analyst his deepest confidence and satisfaction.

The evolution of the theory of technique might be thought of as a gradual victory, but only a partial victory, for the recognition of the relationship. This clearly had its reasons as it was liable to get out of hand in the early days when wild analysis was a danger, as it still does occasionally today. And the technique of interpreting unconscious impulses aggravated resistance, resulting in the sort of sexual battle that Freud described (1915a) in his 'Observations on Transference-Love'. In his last clinical paper (Freud, 1937c) he was struggling similarly with the problem of the negative transference, protesting that the hostility of a former pupil was nowhere to be seen at the time of his analysis. The path to an approach which is less threatened by the patient's feelings was opened gradually between 1928 and 1950 by Wilhelm Reich (1928, 1945), Anna Freud (1936), Melanie Klein (1948), with her concentration on the interplay of object-relationship and character formation and the subtleties of the transference, by Winnicott (1949b) and Paula Heimann (1950) with their utilization of the countertransference, and Hartmann (1950a) who began to map an area of functioning outside the 'seething cauldron' of the impulse life. All this supplemented the libido theory, which was too stiff on its own for an adequate description of the affective life, with a series of articulations which would make it more acceptable to the patient and ease the atmosphere of the consulting room. The way was open for an easier discussion of the actual relationship, exemplified by such contributors as Nacht (1957), with his stress on the analyst's 'presence' and Greenson (1974), who regards the analyst's capacity for loving his patient as essential equipment for his job. However, there remains little description of what actually happens between patient and analyst except in transference/countertransference terms or any details of the strains imposed on the analyst by fulfilling his obligations.

The strength of the emotions generated in the psychoanalytical relationship is in fact played down. According to a personal communication by Willi Hoffer there was a time when many analysts wore white coats, no doubt to protect themselves. The ubiquity of acting out, to which Limentani (1966) drew attention, provides evidence that tensions which are temporarily unmasterable are regularly generated in the course of analysis. In 1972 I suggested that there was an element of a tease in psychoanalytic therapy since emotions are constantly aroused which the analyst will never satisfy. The patient has to be content with an interpretation instead, and I thought that the capacity to use analysis might be connected with the capacity to cathect the analyst's interpretations, which all patients libidinize, instead of his person. There seems to be little discussion of the possible long-term vicissitudes of the patient's longings and of the question of how far our techniques of analysis of the terminal transference, so far as we can judge them, actually stand up to the hopes that we place in them. It is strange, too, that there seems to be no discussion of the effects on the analyst of forming relationship after relationship of the deepest and most intimate kind with patient after patient, and the mourning which at some level must be involved for each one of them.

Clinical theory and the physical arrangements in the consulting room are designed to protect analyst and patient from these problems. On the whole they are very successful, but I think that the conduct of analysis could often be improved if certain neglected problems were recognized. I should therefore like to consider the nature of the analytical relationship in more detail.

The psychoanalytic relationship consists partly in the replacement of an object-relationship by a mutual identification, or rather by identification supplemented by an attenuated ('aim-inhibited') object-relationship. The nature of the identification is different, however, on the two sides.

The actual operation of these processes remains somewhat mysterious, but an attempt may be made to conceptualize them as follows. The patient withdraws his unsublimated instinctual energies from the analyst as a person, but cathects him increasingly with them as a fantasy object. His instinctual desires for the analyst of fantasy are reduced, or even neutralized, by interpretations elucidating the archaic origins of his fantasies. The extent to which the ego's functioning can remain autonomous against the massive stimulation of fantasy in the transference and retain a realistic picture of the analyst, and the means by which it does so, are not well clarified. This was clearly the area with which Freud was struggling in 1915 when he decided that the patient's love for the analyst was 'genuine' and compared the dangers of the analyst's position with a seductive patient to that of the pastor who visited the dying insurance agent: the insurance agent

163

was not converted but the pastor left the house insured. On the other hand, the patient's ego clearly makes an affective relationship with the analyst as a person and forms an identification with the therapeutically orientated aspects of the analyst's ego. This identification lasts him in favourable cases for the rest of his life, while the unsublimated aspects of the transference are analysed away during the treatment. This theory implies that the distortion of the person of the analyst by fantasy has been too unrealistic to last and that the patient's passion for truth, his *amor intellectualis*, has been great enough to result in the formation of a powerful new analytic ego and ego-ideal. The fact that the formation of an ego-ideal normally depends on object loss suggests that this is also an area of theory in need of further clarification. Freud was never tired of repeating, however, that there were patients who were not amenable to this transformation; for them only the logic of soup and the argument of dumplings had any effect. One may legitimately wonder whether a great many patients do not fall into an intermediate class between these two extremes.

The analyst does not cathect the patient as a fantasy object in the same way. Occasionally he makes a transference to the patient, typically as a response to the patient's transference, but this is quickly brought under control by his own continuing state of spontaneous self–analysis (Gitelson, 1952). The analyst has to identify with his patient's mental and emotional processes in order to achieve empathy, but the identification involved in empathy is not enough. It is too transient and too uncontrolled. In order to achieve continued and deeper understanding, he must not only empathize with his patients but scrutinize their mental processes critically, continually testing the empathetic identifications which he holds inside him with his intellect and with the affects which finally determine his judgement. That is, he must hold the patient inside himself cathected with just the right degree of ambivalence, absorbing some parts of the image into himself and holding others at a distance. Any object-relationship which he forms with the patient will be on a highly sublimated level, any instinctual expression being subjected to considerable modification through the analyst's absorbing preoccupation with the patient as an inner object. The conditions under which he maintains this preoccupation are not the easiest. Into the isolated, physically immobile life of the analyst come a succession of intelligent, mostly personable younger people who bring with them the breath of many different lives. They share with him their deepest feelings, as well as feeding into him considerable instinctual stimulation by the stories they tell,

164

by their appearance, their voices and their smell. On the whole, analysts manage this situation well, but considerable instinctual inhibition is involved. It is perhaps not surprising that their repressed object-relationship occasionally overflows into massive identification, as when they embrace a patient's point of view (for instance of a marriage) or even – occasionally – introject his symptoms.

In order to attain and maintain this high achievement, however, measures have to be taken the drastic nature of which is overlooked. The usual psychoanalytic arrangement of chair and couch abrogates the characteristic cue for human responses. The infant at the breast fixes his eyes on his mother's eyes as he feeds, and the human adult makes love face to face, and not *more ferarum*, 'in the manner of the animals'. For the most intimate and prolonged exchange of secret thoughts that humans have devised the patient is prevented from seeing the analyst's face, while the analyst sees only the back of the patient's head or perhaps the rear side of his face. Sometimes he sits where he can see the patient's eyelids or sclera, thus (among his other reasons for it) allowing himself a small piece of reassurance of which the patient is deprived unless he turns round. The reciprocity of normal human response is also abrogated in other ways. The patient lies down, normally on his back, while the analyst sits. The analyst addresses the patient, or half addresses him; the patient addresses the analyst via the air. The intimacy of the relationship is being offset – perhaps as a necessary precaution – by a set-up perpetuating the authoritarianism and perhaps the magical aura of the nineteenth-century hypnotist. It receives its theoretical justification in the rather Helmholtzian notion that, by turning away from the stimulus of the analyst's appearance, the patient is freed from the pull of reality and can produce the derivatives of his unconscious mental processes in less distorted form. There are practical experiences which correspond to this. The use of the couch does facilitate regression and free association in the most neurotic patients. (I will give a more detailed explanation of the mechanism whereby it does so, later.)

It will be more convenient at this point, however, to draw attention to some possible effects of these arrangements on the analyst, in addition to the privacy of thought which they secure him. If the effect of turning away from the analyst is so momentous for the patient, what is the effect of turning away from the patient on the analyst? How does the analyst accommodate himself to being without the basic cue of human expression for ten hours, 200 days a year? Does it impose a strain on him? If so, what is its nature and what means are available for him to alleviate it? I will return to this later. But first I would like to sketch out some aspects of the analytical relationship in more detail. I hope it will not be thought that I exaggerate the difficulties. If I do, I believe that I err in the right direction because I think that they require more open consideration than they receive.

I should like to start with a description of the position of the newly qualified psychoanalyst. This description may not apply with the same force to those who have practised psychotherapy for many years in a psychoanalytically orientated institution as to those who come fresh to more or less full-time analytic work after being students. The newly qualified analyst is confronted by quite severe object loss. First, he probably loses his analyst, and this at a time when analytical support might be very useful to him. Next, he loses the object relations of his daily working life if he gives up his previous career completely, or at any rate a good many of them – the undervalued but important exchanges which do so much to give us the sense of belonging to a community. Above all, his instinctive desire to form object-relationships with his patients is frustrated, lying at the root, perhaps, of much countertransference difficulty until he can accommodate himself to the psychoanalytic way of life. All this may be obscured to some extent and for a time by the relief of qualifying and the excitement of starting his longed-for career. What will not be obscured is the sense of loss of an ego: the intellectual task of fol-lowing the evolution of unconscious themes in his patients' words and behaviour, relating them to an effective notation and considering them in such a way as to be able to produce a spontaneous and more or less effortless interpretation, is immensely difficult. When it is achieved, it restores the sense of reality to the analyst's ego. Many analysts admit, however, that it took them many years to feel themselves to be analysts and to be able to accept most patients who were recommended, without experiencing some degree of anxiety and guilt. The analyst's professional role is thus for a long time alienated from his full sense of identity. In this plight he must cathect the inner representations of his teachers, first of his analyst, then of the idealized image of the great man or woman who represents authority to him. This feeling of therapeutic inadequacy might be called the depressive position of the newly qualified analyst. The great figures will have a tendency to operate in him as introjects, he will look for opportunities to apply their formulations rather than his own, and he may ever find himself occasionally mouthing bad interpretations from the book twenty years later.

To sum up, it will be seen that I regard the beginning of psycho-analytic practice as involving, in addition to its satisfactions, a depressive experience as a result of object loss and separation between the ego and the ego-ideal, against which the analyst tries to defend himself by introjection. Of course, he also defends himself by seeking new teachers in the external world and discussing cases with his colleagues in seminars. I do not think that he can entirely escape the effects of having to relate to patients as internal objects rather than external objects in this way, however. And while he clearly needs support and further education, there may come a danger point at which the search for his own originality and authority becomes submerged by further introjections. This way also lies the danger of idealization of ambivalently cathected leaders, which may overwhelm individual judgment.

If beginning the practice of analysis holds these strains for the analyst, what strains does beginning analysis hold for the patient? To my mind, though it may be heavily concealed by improvement, beginning analysis must be described as a trauma for the patient.

The essence of a traumatic situation, according to Freud, is an experience of helplessness on the part of the ego in the face of accumulation of excitation whether of external or internal origin' (1926d), and also 'a breach in an otherwise efficacious barrier against stimuli' (1920g). The barrier that is breached in analysis is, of course, the barrier against the excitation of unconscious fantasy and unconscious memory. The psychoanalytic arrangements are designed to effect this breach for therapeutic purposes. I should say at once that the arrangements and interpretation are also designed to contain the trauma and reduce it from the start. I believe, however, that our confidence in our therapeutic efficiency and the quickening of object-relationship that characterizes the start of a new analysis induce in us a tendency to underrate the drastic nature of what we do.

The patient is asked to sacrifice the reassurance of his previous contact with the analyst, eye to eye, ego to ego. The reason why patients are often, or perhaps always, afraid to lie on the couch is that they understand one of its essential meanings. This is the loosening of the grip of their ego on reality at the very time when enormous intrapsychic demands are imposed on its synthetic function under the influence of a powerful new object-relationship. The abrogation of response by the analyst is compounded by the withholding of a great many normal comments and answers to questions. The patient is thus, so to speak, dropped by the analyst from the point of view of the role that he exercised at the consultation as a member of the externally

167

real, holding environment. The patient who has been 'dropped' in this way has to clutch at a new object–relationship, in the first instance hypercathecting the analyst's words. He is reassured by the genuine object cathexis which he feels from the analyst, but a split has occurred in his ego. The experience of being dropped from the analyst's holding environment to being held by the Word alone results in the analyst's being jet-propelled in the patient's mind into magical status. The patient's new, intensified object–relationship with the analyst becomes steadily more invested with fantasy. Transference phenomena begin to occur. The realistic ego which operates with energies further removed than the fantasies from their instinctual sources, and which makes a realistic relationship with the analyst, is rendered less potent. It is confronted by strange, involuntary thoughts which it tends to repudiate. The patient has begun to enter the world of waking dreams. These dreams take over, or partially take over, in the consulting room, and sometimes outside it, for several years. What the development of the transference has shown is the power of analysis, aided by the couch/chair arrangement, to remobilize the past traumatic introjections which the patient can now no longer contain. He has to rely on a stranger to help him with his problems and, sensing their complexity, he may rightly apprehend that the stranger, whatever his capacity to respond, will fail to understand him adequately in some important areas with which he will have to struggle on his own after the analysis is over. His confidence in his power to continue his own analysis may have been diminished by an assault on the ego, of whose dangers Ernst Kris (1956b) was well aware: the sudden release of repressed memories, to which might be added the effect of wonderful interpretations and sometimes of interpretations which speak too quickly of the patient's aggression rather than of the anxieties behind it. All this aggravates the trauma, and it seems justified to conclude from the recognized phenomenon of the honeymoon period, that the patient instinctively copes with it by employing manic defences.

Of course, the therapeutic action of psychoanalysis starts immediately. In spite of his anxieties, the patient will usually feel enormously reassured by the analyst's ability to demonstrate his capacity to accept and understand his feelings in a way which is a totally new experience for him.

The problem is: to what extent can interpretation resolve the developing wishes directed at the amalgam of the analyst as a real and fantasy object? According to the classical theory only pregenital impulses could be sublimated, though this is now generally doubted. The nature of the capacity for sublimation is clearly relevant, however, to the question of what elements of the transference can reasonably be expected to be resolved. Freud recognized that there was a problem in this area when he referred to the fact that in some respects the patient's love was 'genuine', that is, presumably that it included an element which could not simply be analysed away. The question of how far analysis in fact leaves the patient to struggle with these residual feelings, in spite of our efforts to resolve them, is clearly important for the patient's development in the lifetime that should await him undisturbed after he has left the analyst's room for the last time. If he is left with unreciprocated love and unresolved hostility then this is a difficulty of the psychoanalytic procedure which must be examined.

The residual bond (to which the analyst always responds in some way) is most clearly seen in training analysis. Freud, still rather naive about transference matters, regarded the bond that springs up between the candidate and his analyst as 'not least' of the gains of analysis. Perhaps we are now entitled to be more suspicious that a prolonged dependency of thought may also sometimes arise. Although a similar bond is less easy to observe in former patients who are not analysts, we may suspect that it remains strong in some of them – those patients, for instance, who, in spite of the gains of analysis, still lead unsatisfying lives; in some depressed patients; and patients whose lives have been dramatically changed by analysis. It has remained strong in those patients who, in spite of their ambivalence, return to the same analyst in an attempt to put things right between them, and in those patients who move over a period of twenty years from one analyst to another. Two other phenomena, or possible phenomena, may also give rise to thought. One is that it seems to be not uncommon for patients to harbour resentment against their former analysts. There must, of course, be many explanations for this, but the tease inherent in stimulating and frustrating emotions could be one of them. The second phenomenon, if it exists, is of a comparable kind on the part of the analyst. There sometimes seems to be almost a tendency among psychoanalysts, or at any rate a temptation, to sabotage their relationship with their patient after termination. If this impression has any truth in it, then it implies that the strain of countertransference feelings is also not easily dealt with. After all, how can we be expected to allow patients to impose so much instinctual restraint on us and not to resent them for it?

Whether it is true or not, it raises questions of the long-term effect of analytic work on the analyst which deserve consideration. The mourning of an analyst for his patients would not be directly comparable in kind to the residual mourning of his patients. Nonetheless, if it is true that the inhibition of object-relationship with the patient imposes a strain, then it is likely to result in some form or degree of introjection to compensate for the gratifying object that has been lost. This may operate in manifold ways, but it could, for instance, be in part by the introjection of the uncivilized parts of particular patients with whom the analyst has to deal, resulting in an excessive tolerance of aggression in certain areas, with strong reaction formations against it in others. My own opinion is that such a process probably does affect many analysts early in their career, but they work through it with maturity. If this is true, it is very important to consider how the atmosphere of psychoanalytic training and the organization of a psychoanalytical society could foster it or diminish it.

The therapeutic implications of the views of the psychoanalytical relationship which I have presented centre, as far as the patient is concerned, on the resolution of two problems: the trauma that he has undergone and the mourning that he may be left with. The two problems are related.

Whom does the patient mourn? Is it the analyst with whom his ego makes a relationship, or is it the analyst of fantasy who has attracted to himself previously unconscious impulses and longings? As in normal love and hate, it must always in some degree be both, since the analyst of reality could not mean so much to him unless he also represented the archaic figures with which we need to maintain a relationship throughout our lives. This is the crux of the matter. In the psychoanalyst the patient finds again the amalgam of fantasy and reality that he met in his first analyst of childhood – the mother who understood the thoughts he could not verbalize.

If the patient is to overcome his attachment to the analyst, more is required than simply interpretation of the transference fantasies because, put more accurately, it can only be a question of the interpretation of such transference fantasies as the patient is able, consciously or unconsciously, to make available to the analyst, and the analyst able to recognize and understand. The patient must therefore also reach a less intense relationship with the person of the analyst which has been bathed and interpenetrated by the transference fantasies by a route which allows his ego opportunity to assess the analyst's real attributes.

This underlines that the first requirements of analytic technique must therefore be to facilitate the patient's capacity to communicate his feelings and thoughts as fully as possible. In order to do this, it is of the greatest importance that the analyst should not reinforce the trauma the patient has experienced by behaving in an unnecessarily traumatic way himself. In order to reduce the split between the analyst of fantasy and the analyst apprehended in detail by the ego, a constant aim must be to facilitate the integration of the two images by the interpretation of the patient's warded-off perceptions of reality and, sometimes, in my opinion, by the acknowledgment of their accuracy by the analyst.

Much of this may be considered to be the common ground of all analysts, but I believe that in fact pinpointing the problems of trauma and mourning leads to a subtly different attitude and technique. For instance, analysts will be less inclined toward the traumatic use of silence, which drives the patient into silence or into concealing his feelings of rejection and his depression. The use of prolonged silence has already been criticized on these grounds by the Kleinian school. But although we know too little of what our colleagues really do, it seems to me that analysts are often oversensitive in their fear of disturbing the transference. If they become more aware of the traumatic factors involved, they may examine their techniques and be surprised to discover unnecessary areas of traumatization or failure to detraumatize. Do we sometimes pay too high a price for the sophistication of our techniques, for instance, if we reply only with an interpretation? To take another example: some analysts do not reply to Christmas cards. They analyse the patient's motives for sending one when he returns. Is it really sound to imagine that more is to be gained by rebuffing the patient in this way than by recipro-cating as a member of society with a common culture and still analysing the motives when they come up? Is it really sound to act as though the patient had no knowledge of one's private life and family, or even of the severe blows that fate may deal one? It seems to me important that the patient should be relieved so far as possible (it is a delicate area) of the oppressive feeling, which he does not necessarily express, that the analyst has adopted a Jehovah-like stance, able to control completely the irruption into the consulting room of human joy or sorrow. Of course there are dangers in this procedure in comparison with the classical idea of the analyst's prime function as remaining, so far as possible, simply a mirror; but these disadvantages have to be weighed against the disadvantages of the patient's suppressing responses through negative attitudes to the analyst's rejection, which may then become difficult to elicit.

The gradual acknowledgement of reality increases the sense of reciprocity with his patient for the analyst too. He feels more real: the split between his professional personality and his real personality is reduced. I am not here suggesting – and I hope I will not be misunderstood – that he should step out of his role or have any objectrelationship with his patient which is not confined, and remains confined, within the framework of analysis and termination. The sort of relationship I am describing does not interfere with the development of a hostile transference, though this would clearly be its danger if abused. But it does, I believe, help to prevent the suppression of a secret hostile relationship and transference, and of defensive idealization.

The maintenance of a relationship between patient and analyst that is a hint, and only a hint more reciprocal than is envisaged in the usual model, also protects the analyst against the dangers of introjecting a fantasied ideal of psychoanalysis, which may impose on him an illusory standard of normality. This may affect his treatment of patients deleteriously and even disturb his emotional balance for many years. Man does not live by reality alone, even less by psychic reality. It is good for analyst and patient to have to admit some of the analyst's weaknesses as they are revealed in the interchange in the consulting room. The admission of deficiencies may help patient and analyst to let go of one another more easily when they have had enough. In other words, the somewhat freer admission of realities – but not too free – facilitates the process of mourning which enables an analysis to end satisfactorily. The end of analysis is in this way prepared from the beginning.

AFFECTS AND THE
PSYCHOANALYTIC SITUATION
Adam Limentani

In announcing the main topic for the 30th International Psycho-Analytical Congress in Jerusalem in 1977, the Programme Committee noted that the problem concerning affects seemed appropriate as a focus for the discussions, since no two theories agree on it. The truth of this statement is affirmed by the most casual reappraisal of the literature as stated in a number of outstanding contributions such as those of Brierley (1951), Rapaport (1953), Rangell (1967) and Green (1973). Green's *Le Discours vivant* (1973), a very comprehensive work on the subject, has not attracted sufficient attention because it has appeared only in French and in Spanish (1975). Papers written in more recent years have continued to highlight the discrepancy of approach to the problem in various parts of the world, due not entirely to parochialism on the part of some writers, but rather because of the disparities between theory, technique and clinical practice. The major areas of theoretical research are: (1) the drive discharge theory, (2) the debate on the existence of unconscious affects, (3) the relationship to their mental representations and fantasies, (4) the issue concerning the possibility of affects dissociated from the object, (5) the ego as the only seat of anxiety, (6) the problem of narcissistic and schizoid personality disturbances, and (7) the widespread calls for adjustments and modifications of the classical method in the treatment of borderline and narcissistic states, which has generated further complications in the matching of theory with practice. Although the task of reviewing the literature has been undertaken by André Green (1977) the subject of the affects in the analytic situation remains vast. In this paper I shall not concentrate on any one aspect of the theory of the affects or of a specific clinical phenomenon, nor will I attempt to supply any answers. I shall, however, underline certain diagnostic features which are fundamental to an understanding of the state of *malaise* existing in the relationship between theory and our clinical daily work.

In the course of a recent address to the British Society, Bion (1976) remarked that 'feelings are the few things which analysts have the luxury of being able to regard as facts.' He added that when analysts embark on theory, they lose their sense of direction 'as they have an inexhaustible fund of ignorance they can draw upon.' As few would dispute so simple yet profound a statement, it is, however, difficult to see how we have reached a situation which was so well summed up by Rangell (1967) when he wrote: 'affects, the original centre, in giving way to subsequent developments have become, wrongly, "the forgotten man". In spite of their ubiquity clinically, [the affects] have in a sense been bypassed, or at least minimized out of proportion, and receive a good deal less of systematic attention than they deserve in our total theoretical metapsychological system.' Rangell was clearly referring to Freud's (1933a) shift of emphasis from representations to the instinctual impulses and to the description of the id as the reservoir of the life and death instincts, later responsible for the developments expressed in the work of Ferenczi and Melanie Klein. The immediate result of this thinking was to link affects with the unconscious fantasies or to regard them as the expression of instincts. The work and experiences described in Balint's and Winnicott's writings have also made us all the more aware of the patient's predicament occasioned by the closeness of bodily feelings to the psychic apparatus. It is prolonged contact with borderline patients that has opened our eyes to the continuous attempts to impinge on the analyst as the object. The understanding of object relations and their implications from the point of view of the countertransference has gained momentum during the last quarter of a century. I am referring to these develop-ments here because it is possible that Rangell's statement may not be easily understood unless it is stressed that his remarks apply to the lack of systematic attention in trying to incorporate the affects in a total metapsychological system.

In our actual clinical work we could hardly overlook the affects as they are often the immediate reason why patients seek treatment, and

174

during analysis the patients continue to note the qualitative and quantitative changes in their affects when assessing their own progress or lack of it.

The success and failure of an analysis could in fact be said to rest on the degree of affective change which takes place during its course. An analysis is most often remembered through the recall of a particular affect which had probably been dominant. Statements such as 'an altogether overwhelming emotional experience'; 'it was very distressing'; 'I could not go through it again'; 'I was depressed all the time'; are not infrequently heard from analysands. Analysts will speak of an analysis as having been a 'stimulating' or 'interesting' one, or, when nothing seemed to be happening for months at a time: 'boring'. Neither analysts nor patients are prepared to admit that a treatment was entirely 'intellectual' whereas it may clearly appear to be so to the observer. Some analyses, on the other hand, are stormy from start to finish, and it is surprising how two people are able to keep their interest going in the face of the strain and stress generated over the years; a factor which must have been aggravated by the very considerable length of most contemporary treatments. Considering the large number of patients seen by a psychoanalyst in the course of a day, it is to be expected that he will have to do something in order somewhat to insulate himself. Some therapists are more successful than others in handling the impact on themselves of their patients' emotional response to the psychoanalytic process, and are therefore able to avoid losing touch with the analysands even when their direct emotional involvement in the relationship is at a low point. The less successful will not infrequently himself become the victim of psychosomatic disorders, and it should be noted here that the defence of intellectualization affords no protection to the analyst against such an eventuality (Sandler, 1972).

I make no apology for focusing on the emotional position of the analyst in the psychoanalytic situation, so vividly described in Gitelson's courageous paper published in 1952. The literature on affects has in fact shown a curious neglect of this aspect of the therapeutic relationship and one has to turn to papers mainly devoted to the countertransference to see it adequately discussed. It was Paula Heimann (1950) who introduced the then revolutionary notion that the countertransference did not simply mean the transference of the analyst towards his patient but that, rather, it was an instrument of research into the patient's unconscious. She also regarded it as being not only 'part and parcel' of the analytic relationship but also a *creation* of the patient and therefore part of the latter's personality. She did warn, however, against its usage as a screen for the analyst's shortcomings and also deprecated the practice of the analyst's disclosing his feelings to the patient, views which the present writer wishes to endorse very strongly. An example of the consequence of such behaviour in the analytic relationship was observed by me in the course of supervisory work. A student–analyst had explained a recent lapse of his attentiveness to his patient as being due to a feeling state which had affected him. The patient's reaction was to become overanxious and deeply concerned about her therapist's mental health. The opportunity was missed for understanding the impact of the analyst's 'unusual' state on the patient in terms of early life experience of a mother who made heavy demands on her child. Further, the patient was not ready to deal with reality. Such unburdening is much more in keeping with Gitelson's view of the therapist's transference which, he believes, should be brought right out into the open. If this is the case, we can assume that the analyst expects something in return for his admission (confession) and such expectation will be coloured by unresolved infantile wishes and needs on his part.

In theory, by turning to the countertransference, the analyst has the tools (his psychoanalytical concepts and his feelings) to control the affective state of the analytic situation at any given moment. The first few years of my life as a psychoanalyst were profoundly affected by a remark from my supervisor, Dr Sylvia Payne, when she was advising me on the timing of a genetic interpretation. Having made a good case for early intervention, she added as an afterthought, 'In the last resort it really depends on how quickly you wish to decrease the level of anxiety in the patient and how much of it you can take.'

It is fashionable nowadays for analysts to believe they can do just that by giving what they consider is a transference interpretation, which allegedly also includes an examination of the countertransference, by imparting it in terms such as 'You want to make me angry.' This 'you and me' interpretation must fail to elicit an appropriate affective response in so far as it leaves out any clarification of the patient's role at the time. It does not say whether he is in the role of a baby or a child who is experimenting or, say, an adolescent who is deliberately provoking an adult; and it is of course quite meaningless in terms of object relations theory, as it gives no indication who the analyst is at that precise moment. Some analysts, no doubt, would argue that so challenging a remark could lead up to an explanation of the use of the analyst as a particular object. But there is little reason for withholding such knowledge if the analyst has it at his disposal. The vicissitudes of affects in the analytic situation can be, and in my contention are, controlled by the analyst; a point which I shall take up again. His personal attitudes, training and theoretical position will all influence him in his interventions, creating a unique atmosphere. The dissociation of his faculties of thinking and feeling will have far-reaching effects on the course of an analysis. A patient will often respond with increasing persecutory anxiety to an excessively *feeling* approach because it can be experienced as seduction, teasing and, finally, frustrating. A collusive approach at the intellectual level can hide the failure to respond to the patient's attempt to escape from his emotions. This situation could be gleaned from the statement of a drug addict: 'My analyst and I agreed to stop after two years because there was no transference.' In my view that was indicative of a two-way transference block and needed careful elucidation *in* analysis rather than termination of the encounter.

In our work we are constantly exposed to both external and internal experiences. Some, but very limited, protection is afforded by placing oneself out of sight. Our narcissism, however, whether healthy or unhealthy, will always be threatened. The situation is further complicated by the ambiguity in the analytic situation which plays a part not always fully appreciated. For instance, at the outset, we invite the patient to enter into a relationship which offers a mixture of satisfaction and frustrations, and with a demand for utter trust which he can hardly experience towards a total stranger. We stipulate that words shall be the method of communication, knowing full well that most affects cannot be adequately described in words. We assure the analysand that both of us will be able to work better if we are not to stare at each other, yet we know how difficult it is for an infant in the first months of life to take his eyes off his mother. We, further, impose restriction on his movements, thus removing one important element from the triad of cognition, affect and motion, which are intensely and intricately interrelated throughout the individual's development. The time limit imposed on the sessions and their periodicity are 'natural expressions of love, and symbolical of good food and care', as Winnicott noted as far back as 1945 (Winnicott, 1945b). It should cause little surprise if certain patients may wish from time to time to use every means at their disposal to express their feelings and to create unforeseen situations which can exercise the analyst's emotional responses as well as his technical skills. This is most likely to occur in borderline states and narcissistic character and personality disorders, when the impact on the analyst from the patient's affects, projections and projective identifications will be at its greatest. Problems of management overlap with the difficulty of understanding the patient.

Allowing the fulfilment of wishes for a physical contact with the therapist and the introduction of non-verbal ways of dealing with outbursts of violence are explained as a genuine and honest desire to maintain contact with the analysand. Yet it is difficult to see how it could be claimed that the psychoanalytic process is not thereby affected or prejudiced.

Psychoanalysts tend to rationalize, hence to justify, taking steps which are outside ordinary practice, but they seldom acknowledge that such steps may be gratifying or defensive. There are also those who, as a result of rigidity in their personality, cannot tolerate the behaviour of a patient when it is clearly disruptive and often incompatible with the classical technique. This is often associated with a blunting of the analyst's capacity for effective response, leading to stagnation or the discontinuation of treatment. The use of reassurance, humouring and an avoidance of transference interpretation is less difficult to understand in this context but, in my opinion, is more likely to produce further complications and an interference, possibly total, with the psychoanalytic process.

Before proceeding to the next section, I should explain that my understanding of the term 'affect' is in accordance with that suggested by Laplanche and Pontalis (1967): 'any affective state, whether painful or pleasant, whether vague or well defined and whether it is manifested in the form of a massive discharge or in the form of a general mood, therefore linking it with states of tension.' Affects are linked with ideas or mental representations. A feeling, as an affective presentation, is an internal rather than an overt activity, yet it is seldom out of touch with the external situation. Muscular, glandular and physiological activities can be associated with feelings.

The concept of 'feeling state' as suggested by Joffe and Sandler (1968) is also valuable in differentiating conditions where somatic changes are not in immediate direct evidence.

The disruption of the classical method is most likely to occur in the treatment of persons, men or women, who are inarticulate and unable to remember many details of their childhood. They may be highly intelligent and often possess outstanding intellect and exceptional talent. The obvious difficulty in verbalization is almost invariably linked with an incapacity to express valid and genuine feelings and emotions. Love and hate are unavailable to them, love even more than hate. They may complain of depression without displaying it, but we do not believe them to be capable of it. On the other hand, should there be anxiety, this will be of a pervasive, inhibiting, paralysing and primitive quality.

The case material which I wish to present is fairly typical of a situation met in contemporary psychoanalytic work when a patient's affective disturbance has a profound effect on the psychoanalytic process. Negative therapeutic reactions expose the analyst to massive countertransference responses. In this clinical outline, I shall deal only with those aspects relevant to our topic. There were two particular features: a major one being that for months on end the patient would be unable to use the couch; and a minor, but no less irritating, one in her attempt to control omnipotently everything in the external and internal world to such a degree that the analyst was unable to elicit any emotional response from her without feeling tempted to abandon the analytic and therapeutic role.

Clinical material

Mrs A. began her analysis at the age of 27, on account of severe, intractable anxiety associated with poorly described feelings of depression and suicidal thoughts. She also complained, from true incapacity, about being inarticulate. She had given up a lucrative occupation which she had pursued without appropriate training, and which had caused her to feel a fraud. She had been married for some years, but there seemed to be little left in the marriage besides devotion on the husband's part and admiration on hers, coupled with a fear that he might leave her. There was little physical contact, neither partner being greatly concerned about it.

Mrs A. had been brought up under unusual circumstances. Her family at first lived in a small village in southern England, in total isolation. An older sister and brother excluded her in every way, forcing her to become totally immersed in an ambivalent relationship with her parents. Her father, from all accounts a very disturbed man, had taken over her toilet training from the start and insisted, with her connivance, on 'cleaning her' until she was nearly eleven years old.

The mother, a teacher, preoccupied with supplementing the family income and looking after her own mother, seemed to be almost unaware, or at least unconcerned, about the father's intrusions into the daughter's life. Mother's father had died the day after Mrs A.'s birth. After three months of breast feeding, mother had to go away for some weeks, leaving the child in the care of the maternal grand-mother. This shattering episode in Mrs A.'s life was brought into the analysis at the time of the first separation three months after work had begun, when she plunged into a state of total inactivity, blankness, and a whole stream of death fantasies. This incident also marked the disappearance of the early, explosive, erotized transference. On my return I found a patient who had only thoughts and no feelings, and she was soon to discover that she had no more control over her thoughts than her feelings.

After the next separation Mrs A. returned, having lost not only her feelings but her thoughts as well. Her blankness, however, had an excruciating as well as exquisitely painful quality to it which, having communicated itself to me, I could then tell her about. When she complained that she was now suffering again, I recalled reading in a story by Chekhov of a doctor telling his patient: 'You must feel the pain, otherwise you are dead.' However, what was causing such intense psychic pain to my patient was still out of our reach; but it was also clear, to both of us, that the anxiety was there to fend off the experience of other affects of a dangerously intense nature. When I tried to put her in touch with her aggression, or rage, easily available in the transference and in her relationships to a number of clearly bad external objects, she would gesture with her hands as if hoping to touch something, saying: 'Where is it, I cannot feel it.' It was at this time that I would become conscious of the rift created by deep splitting and my patient's capacity for dissociation. The occurrence of negative therapeutic reactions would also make heavy demands on my patience and resilience. One serious relapse occurred after an Easter vacation, when she reported having been present at a Jewish Passover celebration. (She, a Protestant, had always been attracted to the Jewish religion as a further escape from her untenable identity.) She had been impressed by a part of the service and had written down her recollection of it on a piece of paper which she handed to me. It read: 'Mouths but they speak not; eyes but they see not; noses but they smell not; hands but they touch not; feet but they walk not; throats but they make no sounds.' This time she had no thoughts, no mind and no body. However, she reported a dream she had had during the vacation in which *she was standing in a street, waiting for a taxi; there were hundreds of them but they were all full. A doctor standing behind her was urging her to get away.* She appreciated the irony in that she had identified me both in the taxis full of people and also in the doctor behind her. She had remembered I existed, but that was no good if there were so many people able to hire me. As she got in touch with the idea of having longed for me during the holidays, she became panicky and no more was possible for that session. The next day she reported having read a book for the first time in years (Mrs A. did not read either books or newspapers). To my surprise it was a book which popularized the understanding of somatic illnesses. She was shocked at reading that repressed anger could cause arthritis and that a baby feels so much when left. This had reminded her of the taxi dream. Mrs A.'s stare during this exchange had become unbearable to me. I was at a loss what to say, having tried in the past every possible approach to get her to use the couch again; I reminded her that in the dream the doctor had been standing behind her, which was how it should be. She then pointed out that the reason why the dream had been so painful was that she could not see me. She was now distinctly irritated and mentioned my persistence in suggesting the use of the couch. She went on to remind me of a 'knocking game' she used to play with her mother when a small infant, in which she would knock with her hand on the side of the cot and her mother would reply with gentle knocks, standing behind her, out of her sight (this was a new detail). She had known about this game all her life but she now had a conviction of remembering the feeling of it. With feeling hitherto unknown to either of us, she asked if I understood that she did not want me to act in the same way as her mother, at least not when I was available to her.

As analysts we often forget that patients do not always attempt to repeat past affective experiences in their analyses; they also try to avoid them. However, persistence in interpreting an obvious resistance had paid well, as it had brought back an early infantile memory of a feeling, linking it with the transference and promoting insight. The feeling had led us to the idea of the disappearance and unavailability of the mother–analyst. This of course does not mean that Mrs A. at other times had not used the eye to eye opportunity she herself had provided, for indulging in her cannibalistic impulses; or as a substitute for instinctual wishes involving the skin; or for hiding defences and for preventing memories from getting through. Writing down and handing over to me on paper her thoughts and fantasies was a symptomatic action used by Mrs A. when under stress. I regarded this as a 'transitional space' valuable in preventing acting out (Khan, 1972b). On the other hand, it is possible that I was not sufficiently discouraging because I welcomed such an action from a patient who had been so inarticulate.

This brief account would be incomplete without the mention of Mrs A.'s love affair with death, which had started when she was four years old. She then played a 'game' in which she would throw herself on the ground and would lie there thinking she was dead until she was disturbed or resuscitated by magical internal means. Her assurances that she would not kill herself had little effect on me until the recovery of this early memory. Afterwards and in the light of all available material, I came to the conclusion that Mrs A., rather than being under the influence of the death instinct, was quite simply anti-life, as she seemed to seek a way of surviving without being or feeling alive. She longed for death, but real death filled her with horror. There must be many meanings attached to the patient's dealings with death and her feeling of deadness which was frequently traced to her mother's similar feeling dating back to the loss of her own father. On the other hand, acting the part of being dead was the ultimate defence against the eruption, into the Conscious system, of un-conscious affects linked to destructive instinctual drives and impulses (Laplanche, 1975). A clue to such a possibility was the references to be gathered from an affective response dream which I had during a difficult phase in the treatment. In the dream *the shadowy figure of a woman shows me a life-size rag-doll which I pick up and throw across several rooms, until it lands out of sight in a corner. With the female figure I follow the flight of the doll. As we reach it, it suddenly comes to life. I feel anxious, darkness descends. In the next scene I am in my car with a figure again next to me. An electrical wire is on fire and the engine is about to be set alight. A woman appears and offers to repair the car for a fee which seems excessive.* I wake up with a feeling of curiosity and refreshed. I immediately associated the woman who had offered to repair the car to Mrs A., whose conflicts about the lack of reparative drive had dominated the analysis recently. The doll was similar to a puppet which I had had as a child, and which was safely out of the way in the attic. The reason for having such a dream did not emerge fully until the Monday session when Mrs A. reported having had a dream about loving. As she was reflecting that on Friday she had been upset as she thought I was pushing her too hard, I suddenly recalled that I had been preoccupied with external matters and that I had been somewhat irritable and less than attentive to the patient's relapse into a state of severe anxiety. In the silence that followed, I recalled a third part of the dream in which *balloons containing a bugging device* (day residue) *were floating about my analytic room. As I tried to shoot them down I was aware I should not destroy them.* It may be self-evident that over the weekend I had become conscious of my lapsing from free-floating attention, but what is more relevant is that the dream made me aware that an excess of therapeutic zeal was getting through to the patient, increasing her anxiety and fear of recovery, quite apart from causing me to feel irritable and impatient. I do not propose to go into the personal aspects of the dream material, but I note that having got in touch with my aggressiveness and frustration, a direct response to the negative therapeutic reaction displayed by Mrs A. at the time, I was able to recover my analytic curiosity, hence the feeling of well-being on waking.

Comment

My understanding of this woman's predicament was that a fragmentation of the ego (or a regression to unintegrated state; Winnicott, 1945b) had taken place in the first few months of her life, causing the kind of disintegration which deals with anxiety that cannot be contained by other means such as projection, denial, negation, projective and introjective identification (Segal, 1964). The slightest attempt at integration is followed by a fresh outburst of massive anxiety which screens off every emerging feeling state. Unconscious affects in such cases may never see the light of day. My further attempts to understand her illness have led me to a re-examination of Khan's concept of cumulative trauma which I believe is applicable to this case. Khan [pp. 104–120 herein (ed.)] has underlined the effects of a type of maternal stress in which the mother's protective shield is lost and in the analysis such task falls on the therapist, who should not attempt to be a 'mother'. Also, Khan's idea, formulated in his writings included in *The Privacy of the Self* (1974) concerning affects and threat of annihilation staying hidden and dissociated rather than repressed, appears valid as does his suggestion that when someone has taken himself as an internal object, the fear of annihilation is indeed paralysing. Outstanding in Mrs A.'s was the fact that anxiety linked with psychic pain was equal to anxiety about emptiness and blankness. Concepts such as that of signal anxiety or 'feeling safe' (Sandler, 1972) or splitting processes being responsible for the lack of availability of emotions (Klein, 1946) are not only essential to the comprehension of the material but indispensable.

I shall now discuss, briefly, some problems linked with 'anxiety' and the role of words and reconstructions in relation to the affects.

'Anxiety' in the psychoanalytic situation

Clinically, we recognize the existence of signal, primary, castration, separation, paranoid, depressive, neurotic and psychotic anxiety. Each type carries a specific meaning, function and origin. The list is a formidable one and not encouraging to our hope of finding a single basic theory of the affects. Green (1973, p. 104) has commented on the absence of such a theory in the writings of Melanie Klein, who has influenced many authors who have dealt with this subject. My understanding of this apparent omission is that the stress placed on the analysis of paranoid and depressive anxieties must be taken in conjunction with the concepts of primitive fantasies, early development and object relations. A theory of affects, as such, may be irrelevant to the Kleinian psychology, which could hardly be said to neglect them. However, some among our Kleinian colleagues create the impression that all one has to do in order to clarify the most obscure clinical situation is to locate the paranoid or depressive anxiety. It is not always easy to relate this attitude to clinical experience. There are, for instance, individuals (of whom Mrs A. is a clinical example) in whom anxiety dominates their lives to the point of freezing or pushing everything else out of the picture. When they come into analysis, we soon· realize that we are not dealing with straightforward signal anxiety. It is more the case of anxiety being used as a screen to conceal other affects, rather than a particular idea or mental representation (see also Jones, 1929; Lewin, 1965). This is a massive effort on the part of the ego to block the affective path to the exploration and study of the thought processes which have gone into the formation of symptoms. To launch into an investigation of a precise genetic and developmental source of the anxiety could be misleading and confusing to the patient.

An interesting hypothesis recently advanced by Calef (1976; working in conjunction with Weinshel), if proved valid, might have interesting repercussions on our clinical work. From the starting point that some instinctual conflicts may terminate in unrepressed satisfactory resolutions (as part of character formation), this author argues that the signal affects determined by such conflicts would be conceived as reliable and trustworthy. In so far as neurotic conflict clouds perceptual consciousness and those functions which demand the development of affect signals, affective signals will be distorted. This in turn will lead to distortions of the more complex secondary affects. (In this context see also Kohut, 1973.) Should this hypothesis be correct, it follows that certain internal structures or functions, as they are functions of functions, may not be direct products of conflict and need not be relegated to the unconscious. According to Calef, we are dealing here with a form of internalization, not necessarily introjection. Some signal affects may therefore be considered as only indirect and not direct products of conflict.

Words, affects and the psychoanalytic situation

Those who have experience in treating cases of sexual perversions and delinquency are quite familiar with the observation of the direct discharge of an impulse in a seemingly total absence of anxiety or guilt. Pre-verbal areas of disturbance, common in these conditions, are linked with feelings being resisted in an entirely autonomous way; the impulsive behaviour being designed to short-circuit affect development. Brierley (1951) has pointed out that affective language is older than words. She regards affects as part of a primitive system of the ego. Uncovering them, tracing their origin and interpreting their relation to the associated impulses and thoughts permits the integration of the primitive ego into the principal ego. The difficulty here is that words will constantly fail us, particularly when they are most needed. The good analytic hour and the rapport with the psychotic or borderline patient will be disrupted by failure to find the correct words for describing a feeling state. Patient and analyst share the frustration. In general we tend to ascribe such difficulties to the material being derivative of some pre-verbal experience. Less attention has been paid to the possibility of the analyst's having unconsciously recognized the patient's feeling in so far as it reminds him of a similar, personal and early pre-verbal experience. Help is impeded as even a long personal analysis may not succeed in supplying us with the exact and precise word which is needed at a given moment. In my supervisions I have noted that some very gifted but disturbed students have a capacity for dealing with such situations, perhaps because they have had very similar experiences in their own analysis. On the other hand, the less gifted but intellectually bound student may be inclined to use cliché or jargon expressions which may be quite difficult to eradicate. Bion (1976) has commented on our having to use words which are debased by common usage, and also on the fact that the analyst needs a discipline beyond that which can be provided by any training. He believes that forging words, which the analyst must keep in working order, will give him a language which he can use and value. It is perhaps in this use of technical language that the most serious collusion occurs between analyst and patient, as if each needed to create a barrier between feelings, impulses and thoughts.

Words are also at the centre of the controversy to which I have already made brief reference, concerning explosive affective situations, actual or threatened violence and a variety of acting in, which occur in the course of treating the more disturbed patients, especially those with borderline conditions. I believe that the absolutely correct interpretation which could quell the storm exists only in theory. In practice, a theoretically correct interpretation may be quite inadequate for the situation and should not be repeated in exactly the same form. Those who believe that a failure of an intervention to produce a change in a tense situation is always due to incorrect understanding, must either believe in magic or subscribe to a theoretical position which they dare not challenge. Because words are or are assumed to be ineffective, the analyst feels inclined to abandon the analytical stance and he may do so at the slightest sign of approaching trouble.

A parallel situation to that obtaining in psychoanalytic work occurs in the physical treatment of similar states. The neuroleptic drug fluo-ethixol decanoate, notable for its anti-psychotic action and anxiolytic effect in certain overactive and excitable patients, can have a biphasic effect on mood, low doses tending to be activating and high doses sedating. The following example shows the predicament we face when searching for the correct dosage in our interpretative work.

A girl in her early 20s, Miss B., had a history of sudden outbursts of violent behaviour requiring periods of isolation in her room or in hospital. She warned me about this in the first interview when she told me that her therapist had her ejected from his office by the police. She now wanted 'to get this man out of her system'. Within days she developed a state of mind towards the analyst which was a mixture of animosity and sexualization of the relationship. An interpretation of her increasing ambivalent dependence on the analyst–mother, aimed at decreasing the erotization of the transference, was followed by a session in which she screamed incessantly, keeping up

186

a barrage of insult against him. Her behaviour was then linked with the interpretation given on the previous day, but I only succeeded in increasing what now seemed to be an expression of intolerable tension and narcissistic rage. Preparing for the next intervention, it occurred to me that people outside the room might be afraid. This led to my becoming aware that I was frightened, and I then began to consider the possibility of this feeling being due to projective identification. The situation became clear when she shouted that I had made her feel ugly and unattractive. I rejected the *idea* that this referred to physical ugliness and told her that my interpretation had aggravated her feelings of greed and dependence, and as she anticipated frustration she felt angry and aggressive and in consequence ugly and unattractive inside herself. I felt considerable anxiety in making this type of intervention because I was not sure that the patient could tolerate my abrupt entry into her inner world, and I was also aware that I was dealing with a nearly, but not quite, conscious affect.

In dealing with Miss B. and patients with such narcissistic problems, more than repression is involved in the analysis of their affects, which strike us forcibly as being related to tension phenomena. The most thorough exploration of the ambivalence, basic as it is, is not sufficient in relieving tension unless it is accompanied by the analysis of the inner world fantasies and of those 'primitive agonies (anxiety being not a strong enough word)' which Winnicott [p. 124 herein (ed.)] has described as lying behind 'the fear of a breakdown that has already been experienced'. In the case in point, a deeper interpretation had the required sedating effect, preferable to reassurance or calling the police. The patient left in a calm state with the feeling of having been understood. As the session was followed by sustained improvement, it is right to speculate on the possible change in the mental representation from that of a persecuting analyst–mother to one able to contain the aggression and greed.

A very different situation from the one just described arises when wordless communications, in the form of acting out and symptomatic actions, occur suddenly in an attempt by the patient to show that all is not lost in the course of analyses which appear satisfactory, both partners doing their duties. The only other clue that the affects are not brought into the analysis as a part of knowing and experiencing (Khan, 1969) is that the countertransference is seldom in question.

Space does not allow me to enter into a discussion of the connection between the lack of expression of the primary affects and psychosomatic states, and the clinically observed phenomenon of the closeness between explosive acting out and implosion leading to somatic manifestations, a Hobson's choice for so many unhappy individuals (Limentani, 1966; McDougall, 1974).

Some important questions remain. How do the words we use relate to an infant's or child's original experience? The language we use reflects the sophistication of the adult mind, and we know how we value the capacity in the analysand to abstract. What have we achieved when a patient responds to a correct interpretation of his repetitive compulsion, which is aimed at undoing an unpleasant weaning experience, saying, 'You are telling me that I am banging my head against a brick wall.' Is that what a baby feels at the time? Does it feel more than an adult? Are we not expecting an internal change to take place irrespective of verbal inadequacies? Are words the music of thoughts, as a woman said in acknowledgement of the analytic work done? On the other hand, are words, often such shallow and poor mediators of the affective states, all that important to the psychoanalytic process?

Years ago, I had a patient who seldom spoke during the second phase of a very long analysis. He broke his silence once, after some months, to say in answer to a further attempt at interpretation on my part, that I suffered from the delusion that words were necessary in psychoanalysis. We parted when he decided he was well enough to continue his analysis on his own. I never discovered whether he agreed or disagreed with my construction that in making me silent he was undoing the experience of having had a psychotic mother who had talked incessantly and irrelevantly all her life before being removed to a mental hospital. During the long silences I learned to understand his tensions, moods, depressions and a host of non-verbal communications. I have never been able to pass on that emotional experience to my students or my colleagues.

The role of affects in reconstruction

In a timely reappraisal of reconstruction in psychoanalysis, Greenacre (1975) clearly defines the obligatory contributions of the analysand and those of the analyst, which she finds more difficult to define. This is so because the analyst's thinking and cognitive processes are constantly under 'the ebb and flow of his personal and mental and emotional reactions. He may sometimes be clearly aware of this, at other times they are almost or completely subliminal. This part of the analytic work cannot be faked, computerized or even taped . . .' and,

I would add, seldom, if ever, accurately reported. But more relevant to our topic is Greenacre's remark that it is 'the language of the specific reconstruction of actual emotional experiences that furnishes a reliving with a new perspective'. Having further noted that verbal communications must be the most important channel to be used towards the achievement of real knowing, she reminds us of the large number of non-verbal and pre-verbal communications available to the partners in the analytical relationship and asks 'not whether and how these physical eruptions may be analysed but rather how they operate in the basic transference relationship'. I have quoted extensively from this important paper because it touches on the core of the problem we face in the analysis of adults. Although it seems impossible to improve on Greenacre's final statement that the reconstruction brings the child and adult together, in the present writer's view this will not occur in every analysis. In a large number of cases it seems to happen more readily in the course of a second analysis, which almost invariably includes a reconstruction of the previous one. Many patients I have met had a past which they had never lived. A first analysis can restore the past to them, but the affects are swamped by an avalanche of recollections and intellectual constructions (often mainly contributed by the analyst) and reconstructions. The real working through of old and discarded feeling-states can in these patients take place only in the course of a second analysis.

Adherence to theoretical beliefs plays a part in the work of reconstruction of traumatic experiences, which have occurred in early life, in association with appropriate affective states. An example of this arose in the course of a discussion in the British Society, when it was agreed that fear of strangers was central to the understanding of the psychopathology of an adult patient. However, one speaker dated the traumatic experience to the eighth month of life while another felt that such fear *had* to be related to the paranoid position and therefore it would have to be put back a few months. It seems inevitable that this time difference in the theoretical arguments would itself reflect on the analytic situation and any feeling state which might then be recaptured. Five months is a large slice of an infant's life.

Afterthoughts

When we speak of the psychoanalytic situation, it is obvious that we are referring to the relationship of a special type which is born out of the specific, and in some way peculiar, nature of the encounter; the affects generated in it will, to some extent, reproduce those which occur or have occurred outside it. The mere fact that reciprocal actual sexual gratification is missing underlines the difference. The opportunity of thinking about the topic discussed in this paper has confirmed the view, which I have held throughout my psychoanalytic career, that any affect or feeling state exhibited by the analysand will have the analyst as the object, in fantasy or in person. It can therefore be best understood in terms of object relations theory. I am less convinced of the possibility of an affect being unrelated to an object, although in theory such an event could be observed outside the analytic relationship. I believe this could happen in the case of a *feeling dream* for example, in the absence of any particular imagery, but again it could well be that such a dream is derived from a pre-objectal state. With Brierley (1951) I would also say that it is the objects which are invested with affects rather than ideas being affectively charged.

Looking at the problem from the point of view of the therapist, it is my belief that although he will follow every lead offered by the patient, he will remain in control of the climate and temperature of the psychoanalytic situation. This requires the development of a special sensibility, a kind of internal pacemaker, which improves in its function with experience. This sensibility is of course part of the countertransference, but it has the special quality of operating mostly at a subliminal level and is therefore not in the immediate field of awareness of the therapist, as is the case with many other counter-transference elements. A sudden and excessive demand, stimulated by the patient, will increase the affective load. The analyst's training will prevent immediate discharge and if all is well this internal information will maintain an appropriate level of fruitful emotional exchange. The average level of anxiety will be similarly regulated. Calef (1976) has gone even further in suggesting that a therapist uses 'the individual influencing machine' and that 'theoretical bias fre-quently functions more for the purpose of rationalizing the influen-cing machine than for the therapeutic work itself'. Although the term used by Calef is rather sinister, it deserves serious examination because of the indirect effect on the analysis of the affects generated at certain times in the psychoanalytic situation by the work of reconstruction. Although we are well aware that the affects are only one of many phenomena observed and developed in psychoanalysis, the different ways of handling them by those who practise contribute to the particular quality of the patient's total experience. A number of psychoanalysts (Ferenczi was the first among them) will provide a totally emotive analysis by utilizing all the available intellectual abilities in themselves and their patients. At the other end of the psychoanalytic spectrum are those who will rely on a clearly formulated theoretical and technical approach, reaching the basic emotions through the use of their brains. Both extreme groups have their detractors and poor imitators, whose psychoanalytic identity was perhaps never adequately established. Where a satisfactory identification is lacking, imitation may provide a substitute (Gaddini, 1969).

Psychoanalysis is an art but, unlike art itself, it cannot be isolated from meaning. Psychoanalysts, in common with artists, are dissatisfied with their capacity to interpret and externalize the total innermost experiences in themselves and their analysands. Unlike artists, however, they must constantly struggle with the imperative of distinguishing imagination from reality. It is almost a cliché to observe that even in the most talented, artistic expression confers no guarantee of freedom from emotional turbulence, neurosis or psychosis. Writers may long to give musical effect to the words they employ. Musicians, who claim the privilege of an ability to express feelings without being too troubled by precise meaning, will, if pressed, confess to the superiority of language as the true mediator in object relations. Have not painters expressed their frustration by writing on their canvases? It is possible that in the case of the artist we are dealing with an exclusive, albeit highly satisfactory, process of reparation in relation to the internal object, leading to affective tension only being discharged. Psychoanalysis, contrary to commonly held fears, can be helpful to the artist in providing a further outlet in the psychoanalytic situation for the appropriate release of the affects. Greater integration derived from intellectual *and* emotional working through reduces acting out and symptomatic actions quite apart from mobilizing new areas in the personality. As many analysts know, this would enhance rather than impede artistic expression.

It cannot be of little value to remind ourselves that we are not alone in seeking appropriate affective discharges. As psychoanalysts, we are only too aware that our profession is not only impossible (Greenson, 1966), but also extremely difficult.

15

THE ANALYST'S ACT OF
FREEDOM AS AGENT OF
THERAPEUTIC CHANGE

Neville Symington

In this chapter I intend to explore a phenomenon with which all analysts are familiar. I will first describe it and then examine what its implications are for theory. I shall refer to it as the 'x-phenomenon'. I shall start with some clinical examples.

I was charging Miss M. a little more than half what my other patients were paying. She had been a clinic patient and I used to sigh to myself and say inwardly, 'Poor Miss M., £X is the most that I can charge her.'

I did not in fact articulate it so clearly as that. In my mind it was like an acknowledged fact that everyone knows, like the unreliability of the English weather. It was part of the furniture of my mind and I had resigned myself to it in the same way as I reluctantly resign myself to the English weather. So the analysis went on and on with that assumption as its unquestioned concomitant until one day a startling thought occurred to me: 'Why can't Miss M. pay the same as all my other patients?'

Then I remembered the resentment she frequently expressed towards her boss who always called her *'Little Mary'*. A certainty began to grow in me that I was the prisoner of an illusion about the patient's capacities. I had been lassoed into the patient's self-perception and I was just beginning to extricate myself from it. I then brought up the question of her fee and in the course of a discussion she said, 'If I *had* to pay more then I know I would.'

She had now clearly told me that she had the capacity in her to pay more and that this could be mobilized if I changed my inner attitude towards her. A few sessions later I said to her, 'I have been thinking over our discussion about the fee. I charge most of my other patients £X and in our discussion I have not heard anything that makes me think that I should not charge you the same.'

For two sessions she cried rather pitifully but then became resolved that she would meet the challenge. Soon she found a job that paid her one third more than her previous salary. In moving job she extricated herself from the patronizing tutelage of the boss who called her 'Little Mary'. She had been able to do this because she had first been freed from the patronizing attitude of her analyst. Shortly after this she finally gave the push to a parasitic boyfriend. Again, I think she had been able to do this because she had been able to give the push to a parasitic analyst. These two events were soon followed by other favourable developments. I think the source of these beneficial changes was in that moment of inner freedom when I had the unexpected thought: 'Why can't Miss M. pay the same as my other patients?' I am calling this act of inner freedom the 'x-phenomenon'.

Now I want to take another example. This patient was an obsessional man who used to hesitate sometimes in the middle of telling me something, usually as he was about to tell me some thought he had had since the previous session. As he had often expressed his apprehension that I would think him pathetic I would say to him something like, 'I think you are afraid that if you tell me about the incident in your mind I shall think you are pathetic.'

Of course I was thereby clearly inferring that I would not think him pathetic. With this assurance he would then obligingly tell me the thought in his mind. Then one day I was reading the following passage from *Four Discussions with W.R. Bion*:

Q. . . . She wouldn't be put off by what you suggest; she would get irritated with your reply and insist that you call her by her first name.

B. Why not the second one? Why not whore? Or prostitute? If she isn't one, then what's the trouble? Is she wanting to be called a prostitute or a whore? If not, what is the point of the story? What convinced her that her father was right?

Q. She wants sex with other men besides her husband, therefore in her view, she must be a whore. She's afraid that if she got a divorce from her husband she would run around and have sex with all sorts of men – behave like a free whore.

B. In view of what you are saying I think I would try to draw her attention to the way in which she wishes to limit my freedom about what I call her. It is just as much a limitation if the patient wants you to give the correct interpretation. Why shouldn't I be free to form my own opinion that she's a whore or that she is something quite different? Why be angry with me because in fact I am free to come to my own conclusions?

Q. Her fear is that your own conclusion will be that she is a whore.

B. But why shouldn't I be allowed to come to that conclusion?

Q. So you conclude she is a whore – now where are you?

B. But I haven't said that I do. The point I want to show is that there is a wish to limit my freedom of thought . . .

(Bion, 1978, pp. 15–16)

As I read this I had a moment of illumination about my obsessional patient. I had been a prisoner of this patient's controlling impulses and at the moment of reading this passage from Bion I had a new understanding in which I felt freed inwardly (though this had outward concomitants). The next time he expressed his apprehension that I would think him pathetic I said to him quietly, 'But I am quite free to think that.'

He was much taken aback. It was possible then to see how much he operated by controlling my thoughts and the thoughts of others. A great fear was that if he allowed me to think my own thoughts then I might have the thought: 'How nice it would be to get away from Mr X.'

Then on to his feeling that no one ever *wanted* to be with him. This was linked to childhood experiences where his parents never wanted to be with him but farmed him out with child minders while they pursued their business interests in various parts of the world. We were able to look at his need to wind himself around me like a boa-constrictor and try to substitute my thinking and feeling for his, to make me into his ego, as it were. It was then possible to link his failure to be able to think and feel with the absence of a mother or analyst

194

who wanted to be with him. The foundation of the thinking capacity seems to lie in the internalization of this maternal desire. Again the source of all this interpretative work and insight started from the moment of my own inner act of freedom. So this was another case of the 'x-phenomenon'. The remaining examples I want to take are from a patient about whom I shall need to give more background.

This patient was referred after an episode of hallucinatory psychosis. I took her on largely because of her strong motivation to get better. She regularly hallucinated in the sessions and communicated with what I shall call 'telegraphic bits'. It may have been a regression to holophrastic speech. After a long silence she would just say 'crocodile' and then some minutes later she would look at some point in the room and say 'blue circle'. I found myself reading *Alice in Wonderland* to help me into the right gear. I abandoned myself to crazy fantasy through which I linked these discrete elements. This phase of treatment progressed satisfactorily and eventually the hallucinations disappeared and she was able to address me if not as a person, at least as a distinct entity. I learned later that until that point she had not been able to distinguish between me and her boyfriend and in fact thought that I was him. From the moment that she saw me as distinct the honeymoon period of treatment was over for me.

In the initial interview she had told me the content of the hallucinations which had led her to seek treatment. In these hallucinations she was merged with her mother and savagely attacking her boyfriend. It became clear, only slowly, that one of the principal reasons why she wanted treatment was to overcome her sadistic fantasies and actions towards any object of her love. The honeymoon period was over when I became the target of her sadism. Her sadistic attacks were subtle, unrelenting and certainly threw me off balance. She honed in on those areas of my own vulnerability with a devastating precision and she was unrelenting. For instance for a long period she said she felt I was not the right person for her and she began to investigate other possible therapists. She twice sought the advice of a female colleague. In all this she reiterated frequently that in my attitudes, tones of voice, gestures and in my manner of dressing I conveyed male chauvinist attitudes and that I was unsympathetic to the needs and predicaments of women. This was not articulated neatly like that. It was hinted at on occasions, raged about at others and only slowly was it possible to decipher what she was saying. At other times she would scream exasperatedly at me, and so intensively that I was unable to think. She would reproach me with fury for not attending to the matters which she had insistently brought to my attention. I was usually quite in the dark and realized that she probably thought she had asked me something or told me about some thought or event but had not in fact done so or had told me so elliptically that either the phenomenon itself or its import had escaped me.

Now, in her persistent accusation that I was dominating towards her because she was a woman and I was a man, I was aware of two things. In the first place I knew that she was sadistically attacking me and secondly, that, operating at a psychotic level of perception, she was more sensitive to my own unconscious attitudes than a patient in a classical transference neurosis. My problem therefore was on the one hand not to allow myself masochistically to become a victim of her sadism and yet not to dismiss out of hand the content of what she was saying. Yet, of course, in that hesitant and divided state of mind, I was the perfect victim. The treatment went through a particularly bad patch that lasted for about a year. I thought to myself that perhaps I was not the right person for her, perhaps she did need a woman, perhaps my male chauvinist attitudes were getting in the way of clear interpretation and so on. And the more I wavered inwardly the more furious and attacking she became. During this time she also complained regularly about rigidity, that I needed to be more flexible, I needed to consider other approaches or needed more analysis myself. For a long time I wavered inwardly, as if I were standing on marshy ground.

Then about three years into treatment she adopted a new manner of behaving in the sessions. Instead of sitting in her normal chair (she did not use the couch) she walked past me and sat in a chair behind me. I resolutely remained in my chair. Sometimes she pulled her chair right up behind mine and on one occasion she poked my arm with her finger. Then, instead of sitting behind me, she took to standing behind me and I continued to keep to my chair determinedly interpreting and continued to do this for some eight sessions. Then one day I became uncomfortable with this procedure. I did not feel at ease and I was not able to respond spontaneously. Although I was interpreting, it was not out of an inner freedom but defensive in character. I decided that next time she walked past me and stationed herself behind my chair I would move across to the other side of the room. I could not say quite why I decided to do this but I knew that I could not interpret freely when I felt this discomfort. So the next time she took up her standing routine I got up calmly and moved to a settee on the other side of the room. As she saw me do this she turned and said in tormented fury, 'Why did you move?' (it had a tone which denoted that I had no right to move as I had just done) and at the same time she moved back to her own chair and I moved back to mine. 'What thoughts do you have about why I moved?' I asked. 'Just sheer male dominance', she said in defiant rage. Now, at this point I had an inner conviction that it was no such thing. I felt an inner certainty which I had not possessed before. I felt quietly confident that I had not acted out of any such motive and that I was not reacting to her sadistically.

'Can you think of no other possible interpretation of my action?' I asked her. 'No,' she said, 'it's just sheer male dominance'. Where-upon I said that it seemed that we had reached a deadlock and then there was a tense silence and there was an atmosphere that was pregnant with fury. Then at the end of about twenty minutes the atmosphere began to ease and I felt that we both had come through a crisis like two swimmers who had just managed to cross a turbulent river and reached terra firma. Some ten minutes after that she said, 'I don't know about you but I am feeling better', smiling slightly. That composite moment when I acted and then when in response to her I experienced an inner certainty that I had not had before is another instance of the 'x-phenomenon'. She was more able to listen from then on and in certain ways communication became easier and there was greater clarity, although a great deal remained obscure and communication was still badly impaired.

With the same patient there was another instance that is less easy to describe but I shall attempt to do so. I had a very clear notion that my role as analyst was to interpret to the patient my understanding of the unconscious import of what lay behind her manifest com-munications but a stage was reached with her when she could not bear any interpretations. She screamed that she could not sort anything out unless I accepted the surface meaning of what she said and also unless I accepted responsibility for what belonged to me in the process. She could not sort out what was her, could get no insight into herself, until she was clear who she was and who I was. In other words she needed to separate out the two elements that made up herself and me from the agglutinous mass that they were for her at the time. At this stage the only way in which it was possible for her to do this was, at various junctures, for me to express what my feelings were. It was important to her to know that they were really mine; several times she asked me if these were my feelings or those of all analysts; I told her that they were mine. Sometimes she would ask whether these were feelings shared by all analysts and I told her truthfully that I did not know.

After a period of this type of communication it became possible for her to express some separateness and then it was possible to interpret in the normal way again. (I say 'in the normal way' because I think the communications about my feelings were interpretations. They were interpretations about the way she was merged with me through the superego structure of her personality. I will come back to this later in the paper.) There was a transitional stage when I would couch interpretations in this sort of way, 'I want to express to you the thought that is in my mind . . .' and then I would go on with the substance of the interpretation.

Finally I was able to interpret what I thought was in her mind. I understood this as being a transition from being a fused object in the transference to a separate one and that the interpretations had to be in a mode that was acceptable to the different psychological states that accompanied those phases. Again when I acted from personal freedom rather than follow some specific technical regulation that is supposed to be followed in an analysis then therapeutic shifts occurred and, I might add, a great deal of insights and learning in the analyst. (I hope it will not be inferred that I am scorning analytic technique; this would be the very opposite of what I am intending to say. After all the soul of analytic technique is to free analyst and patient from the normal social constraints and so favour development of the inner world. The problem is when 'classical technique' becomes the agent of a new social constraint.) I hope that these illustrations of the 'x-phenomenon' are sufficient to convey my meaning.

My contention is that the inner act of freedom in the analyst causes a therapeutic shift in the patient and new insight, learning and development in the analyst. The interpretation is essential in that it gives *expression* to the shift that has already occurred and makes it available to consciousness. The point though is that the essential agent of change is the *inner* act of the analyst and that this inner act is perceived by the patient and causes change. Even the most inner mental act has some manifest correlate that is perceptible, though this perceptibility may be unconscious and probably is. The psychotic is particularly sensitized to these minute changes. I will give two examples of this from the last patient that I took my clinical material from. In the first example it was an instance of an inner emotional state and in the second a specific inner mental act. Shortly before seeing my patient one day I received news that another patient of mine had committed suicide and I was upset, to put it mildly. There was a silence for the first twenty minutes of the session, then she looked at my desk and I made an interpretation that I cannot now remember but I shall not forget her response, 'I am not taking stick for your bad experience.' She was in tune with my emotional state in relation to which my interpretation bore little importance and she sensed this. She perceived it in the atmosphere. I am quite sure that she had no external knowledge of what had occurred.

The other occasion was when I was trying to decide on which day to finish prior to Christmas and I was thinking about this during a silence. The moment I said to myself inwardly that I would make Tuesday the last session she said at that precise moment, 'You have interrupted my thoughts, you have just stolen something from me.' I had of course. Instead of being in reverie with her I had stolen a chunk of shared thinking in favour of an administrative decision. As far as she was concerned I might just as well have spoken my thoughts out loud because she felt my inner act so that even an inner judgement has some perceptible external correlate. I do not think that the mental, emotional and sensational spheres ever exist in isolation. The most inward mental act reverberates through the sensational and perceptual spheres. The psychotic patient is tuned in to these inner spheres in a way that is not so of neurotics or normal people. The psychotic is not cut off from reality but rather one minute aspect of reality is enlarged so that the rest of the mental or emotional field is crowded out. It is like the zoom lens on a television camera that swoops down on one object of interest and that one object then takes up the whole television screen. I am insisting therefore that the inner act of the analyst affects the patient, especially is this so in the psychotic and borderline patient. The focus of this paper though is that the analyst's inner act of freedom causes a therapeutic shift in the patient. To account for this further contention, it seems that some theoretical ramparts are needed to support it.

I think at one level the analyst and patient together make a single system. Together they form an entity which we might call a corporate personality. From the moment that patient and analyst engage in what we call an analysis the two are together part of an illusory system. Both are caught into it. Recent literature stresses that the analyst is not just a mirror but this is a gross understatement. The analyst is lassoed into the patient's illusory world. He is more involved in it, more victim to it than the average social contact. As the analytical work proceeds the analyst slowly disengages himself from it. In this way transference and countertransference are two parts of a single system; together they form a unity. They are the shared illusions which the work of analysis slowly undoes. Psychoanalysis is a process which catalyses the ego to ego contact: that area of the personality that is non-corporate, personal and individual. In this way psychoanalysis is working in the opposite way to religion, whose central social function is to bind people together into corporate entities. We need to look at this corporateness as belonging to a part of the personality where fusing takes place and how we can assimilate this to psychoanalytic theory.

In all the instances of x-phenomenon that I have given, the analyst's personal feelings have been shrouded by illusory feelings, emanating from the patient's unconscious superego. This could be formulated by saying that the feelings belonging to the superego have cloaked the feelings belonging to the ego. However the term superego needs to be amplified in the way that the sociologist Talcott Parsons (1952) has done:

> the place of the superego as part of the structure of the personality must be understood in terms of the relation between personality and the total common culture, by virtue of which a stable system of social interaction on the human levels becomes possible. Freud's insight was profoundly correct when he focused on the element of moral standards. This is, indeed, central and crucial, but it does seem that Freud's view was too narrow. The inescapable conclusion is that not only moral standards, but *all the components of the common culture* are internalized as part of the personality structure. Moral standards, indeed, cannot in this respect be dissociated from the *content* of the orientation patterns which they regulate.
>
> (p. 23)

These illusory feelings in the patient are partly the internalized values of the family of origin, of his class and national allegiances together with the impulses, especially the destructive ones, from within. The impulses from within are strengthened and supported by the cultural values. At the beginning of the analysis (and often for a long time), the patient and analyst are held in thrall by the power of this personal–cultural illusion. This is possible because the patient and analyst become part of a system through which communication takes place. In his passive role where he does not assert his own view of the world, the analyst allows himself to be swept into the personal–

cultural contents of the patient's superego and interprets within that framework. Analyst and patient are part of a system and are joined through the superego parts of their personalities. It is through the superegos that corporate personality is effected. When the patient first comes to the analyst's consulting room it is probable that a fusing takes place of the analyst and patient via the superegos of each. Transference and countertransference are emotional expressions of this fusion.

If this model is accepted, then it follows that within the corporate personality there is a process of resistance and transference occurring in the whole entity, in other words in the patient and analyst. There is, however, also a process of analysis occurring in both persons, in the total entity. The process of analysis is the guarantee that there can be movement out of a locked situation. A female patient once asked me, 'What guarantee have I that something in your unconscious will not block my progress? You may unconsciously envy my desire to have a baby and my capacity to have one and therefore block me subtly.' I observed that it seemed she assumed that all the analytic power lay within me. She immediately retorted that it did not lie within her. I pointed out that she seemed to feel that if it was not in her and not in me then it did not exist at all. This was linked to her view that I had possession of the process. When she began to realize that this was not so she felt grief and realized that neither she nor I had control over the speed of development. She often said that she could not move until I moved first.

For a very long time I did not understand this. Only after about three years of treatment I suddenly realized that she meant that she could only move when an inner act of freedom had occurred within me. I had not realized at this stage that she was able to 'know' when these occurred. She was reliant on x-phenomenon but for a long time she had the fantasy that it was within my power to summon it at will. She became sad as it began to dawn on her that I had to wait, just as she did. So in the corporate entity there is a shared illusion or delusion (transference/ countertransference) and shared resistance and there is also a process which we call psychoanalysis which fights a slow but persistent battle in both against the shared resistance and illusion. The analytic process catalyses the individual to individual existent reality. The x-phenomenon is a product of the analytic process. The latter works at a deep level, at a pre-verbal, primary process level. It finds its verbal expression in interpretation. Interpretation expresses this deep change and effects the final consummation of it at the conscious and manifest level. The sudden access of personal feeling in the analyst that breaks another bond of the illusory stranglehold in which both patient and analyst are held in thrall is immediately experienced by the patient and exists prior to insight. It implies a form of communication between analyst and patient that supersedes man's methods of perceiving the nonhuman world. The analytic procedure capitalizes on this special form of human communication.

It could be argued that what I am describing is a particular instance of projective identification but I do not think this does justice to those psychological events which, for want of a better term, I have called the x-phenomenon. Projective identification means that feelings which belong to the patient are projected into the analyst and lodge there like a foreign body. What I am describing is a joint process in which the real feelings of analyst and patient are aroused by the resistant process. The analyst's feelings are *his* feelings even though they may have been stirred up by the patient. Patient and analyst are responsible for the feelings that are generated in the situation. Often the patient is 'blamed' for feelings experienced by the analyst and this is called projective identification. This type of description implies that there are only two blameable objects in the room: patient and analyst. There is a third term: the process in which both are involved.

What I have said so far may seem to contradict Freud's view that our only knowledge of the external world is through perception, mediated consciously by the ego. In nearly all Freud's writings he followed the scientific view of his day which was that man's knowledge of his fellow man is via his senses and does not differ essentially from his knowledge of the nonhuman world. Before Freud formulated the structural model he ascribed this type of knowledge to consciousness and thought that the unconscious did not have *direct* access to the external world. When he came to formulate the structural model he thought that the agency whose role is to mediate the external world to the organism is the ego and that the superego and id do not have direct contact with it. Now he does not specifically say whether he considers that this mediating role of the ego is just the conscious part of the ego but there are two passages which contradict all his other assertions on this matter:

I have had good reason for asserting that everyone possesses in his own unconscious an instrument with which he can interpret the utterances of the unconscious in other people.

(1913i, p. 320)

It is a very remarkable thing that the *Ucs.* of one human being can react upon that of another, without passing through the *Cs.* This deserves closer investigation, especially with a view to finding out whether preconscious activity can be excluded as playing a part in it; but, descriptively speaking, the fact is incontestable.

(1915e, p. 194)

He is here talking about a special type of knowledge that exists between human beings that does not pass through the normal sense organs or through that conscious part of the personality inhabited by word-presentations. This particular type of knowledge therefore antedates any interpretation that the analyst may give.

That there is a special type of knowledge by which human beings know each other that is quite different in kind from the way in which men know the physical universe was, I think, first articulated by Giambattista Vico. Until Vico all knowledge had been divided into three different kinds: metaphysical or theological, deductive and perceptual. Under this last category were included empirical observation and experiment. To these three types of knowledge Vico added another: knowledge that we have of ourselves and other human beings. In the case of human beings we are not just passive observers, he said, because we have a special knowledge 'from the inside' and we have a right to ask why it is that human beings act in the way they do. This type of knowledge is active and not passive because we can only know something from the inside if human beings have created it. God is therefore, according to Vico, the one who has perfect knowledge as he is the creator of all, but in the case of the special knowledge that human beings can have of each other it is a similar type of knowledge: it is knowledge *per causas*. But Vico has not had a great following among thinkers within the human sciences. What he has asserted has been taken for granted by all great writers of prose or poetry but has not been studied seriously within the social sciences. Probably Max Weber, the sociologist, is the best-known follower of Vico's viewpoint. He distinguished between the ordinary knowledge by which we know the physical universe which he called *Wissen* and that special type of knowledge proper only to the knowledge of human beings by human beings and this he called *Verstehen*. Although this special type of knowledge has been central to clinical work in psychoanalytic practice there does not seem to be a metapsychology to account for it. The idea that a scientist might

203

take this type of knowledge seriously is also scorned by almost all schools of thinking within academic psychology.

Vico said that it was possible to enter into the world of past cultures 'from the inside' by studying the poetry and myths that belonged to them. To gain this special type of knowledge man needs to be equipped with *fantasia*. Vico considered that this type of knowledge was superior to the knowledge that we have of the non-human world; this is because human culture has been created and can therefore be known from the inside. Now this idea that culture is a human creation and can therefore be known from the inside can, I think, be applied to the sort of knowledge that we have of a patient in the psychoanalytic situation. Once we accept clearly that there is the 'constitutional factor', or the biological given with its associated drives, then the rest of what we are concerned with is the product of human creation. What we analyse is a product of the inner fantasy life in interaction with first the mother, then the mother and father, siblings and finally the whole social environment. Theoretically it would be possible for all these elements to be analysed and understood. This understanding is of a special kind and arises through an act of insight which has been generated and made possible by the analytical process. We need to get some clue as to how this act of insight occurs.

Let us say I take hold of Kant's *Critique of Pure Reason* and read this statement: 'If we have a proposition which contains the idea of necessity in its very conception, it is a judgement *a priori* (1781, p. 26), I may understand it straight away but, on the other hand, I may not. If I do not it is because I have a false idea and this blinds the intellect. I will be able to understand when I can banish the false idea and allow the idea that Kant is proposing to be grasped by my intellect. I may be quite resistant to doing so because it may mean I have to give up many fond ideas which are comfortable to my way of life or habit of mind. To understand Kant I need to adopt a passive attitude so that I can become receptive to his ideas but I must actively be prepared to banish mine. At the moment of understanding I become Kant, as it were, through an action of the ego, whereby I dispel my superego contents and because of this I remain separated and become slightly more of an individual. At the moment of understanding activity and passivity come together and form a single psychological event.

Now, in the psychoanalytical situation, something very similar occurs. The patient's communications and the analyst's feelings and thoughts become the raw material out of which understanding arises.

The analyst does not only have his own false ideas to clear away but needs to be passive to the analytical process and combating the resistance that he and the patient are locked into. The attempt to understand is being continually sabotaged by a parallel process that stimulates and fosters false ideas. Received theoretical positions may be used by the resistant process, as they also may be used by the benign psychoanalytical process. The patient and analyst as a corporate entity are involved in these two processes. Belief in the psychoanalytical process seems to be the essential ingredient for both parties. However, it seems that it may be the special role of the analyst to carry this belief for the patient as well as for himself, especially early on in treatment.

The act of understanding is rooted in what is most personal, in the ego, but the false ideas are located in the superego. At the moment of insight, expressed in interpretation, the illusions or false ideas are banished both in analyst and in patient. A personal, ego to ego, contact is established and replaced by an illusion or false belief that held the two together until that time. This belief that held both together is that social glue in microcosm that binds together the numerous communities and groupings of society. This type of togetherness is quite different from the ego to ego contact that occurs at particular moments in analysis. This type of contact is a revolution because new reality, new growth begins. In fact, it is the only true revolution that does occur within human affairs. Because, subsequent to this personal act of understanding new concepts have to be imported into the superego in order that the latter agency can now reflect the new changes that have taken place in the ego.

In order to separate, the patient needs to get access to the analyst's core feelings. His interpretations need to flow from here to as great an extent as possible if the patient is to be able to separate. This is most especially true for the psychotic patient whose fusion at the superego level is greatest and whose need for ego to ego contact is also greatest. It greatly concerned one patient whether what I said to him was what *I* thought or felt or was just a received dictum of the psychoanalytical tradition and therefore just a superego content. Each time a resistance was overcome it was then possible to reach further into what I truly thought or felt and then he was able to separate himself a bit more from that mother glue. He became more able to separate himself from the analyst and from his maternal object intrapsychically. My greatest problem in his analysis was to reach those feelings which were most truly mine. In the case of that patient the problem was particularly acute but on reflection I think this may be a central problem in every analysis.

The psychoanalytical setting is concerned to foster a particular type of communication which is demonstrated most clearly in those moments which I have called the 'x-phenomenon'. This level of communication occurs from the very first moment when the patient enters the consulting room and with it a certain patterning of unconscious knowledge. The goal of the interpretative work is to make this conscious. At the same time there is another process at work, in both the analyst and the patient, whose goal is to sabotage the analysis. This process is located in the superego and makes use of illusions and cultural myths as its instrument. We call this process resistance but I have wanted to emphasize that this is a system in which both analyst and patient are involved, not something that is just located in the patient. The 'x-phenomenon' implies that there is a knowledge that is pre-verbal and that it is anterior to speech and therefore to interpretation. At this level of knowledge the patient knows unconsciously the analyst's internal attitudes. If, for example, the analyst is unconsciously envious of the patient in some particular way then the patient perceives it and only a change in the analyst's inner attitude will enable the patient to move forward psychically. The moment the analyst becomes aware of his or her attitude and is freed from it then the patient perceives it. That is to say he or she perceives a change within the self and may make declarations to that effect without knowing the cause. The interpretations that follow the x-phenomenon become conscious articulations of a change that has already occurred unconsciously at the ego to ego level. The interpretations help them to re-establish the superego so that its myths and values change and become tuned in to the changes that have occurred within the ego.

With the exception of Winnicott I think that most analysts operate on the assumption that people are separate entities. I think that the x-phenomenon and the particular form of knowledge that it must imply means that people are individuals and yet part of a corporate entity. Because we are parts of a corporate entity then as soon as analyst and patient come together in the same room there is an immediate adaptation and fusing. The corporate entity instantly establishes itself. Socially this occurs when two people meet, but, in this case, ego-to-ego contact is kept to a minimum, so also the joint illusion is kept to a minimum. In psychoanalysis the latter is enhanced but only, so to speak, so as to hypercathect it and work through it and give place to the personal.

PART V

REGRESSION AND THE PSYCHOANALYTIC SITUATION

16

REGRESSION

Allowing the future to be re-imagined

Hannah Browne

He came home. Said nothing.
It was clear, though, that something had gone wrong.
He lay down fully dressed.
Pulled the blanket over his head.
Tucked up his knees.
He's nearly forty, but not at the moment.
He exists just as he did inside his mother's womb,
clad in seven walls of skin, in sheltered darkness.
Tomorrow he'll give a lecture
on homeostasis in megagalactic cosmonautics,
For now, though, he has curled up and gone to sleep.

Wisława Szymborska, Going Home (2015)

When I was invited to write this chapter, I had the unsettling realization that I had never thought much about regression. Unsettling, because regression is a concept at the heart of the psychoanalytic endeavour, which the psychoanalytic situation facilitates. The transference by its very nature is regressive, containing the patient's earliest relation with himself and his objects. Without regression there would be no psychoanalysis.[1] So why did I, a British psychoanalyst trained in the twenty-first century, feel that I knew so little about it? Had I resisted thinking about it or, simply, taken it for granted?

In a recent clinical discussion, I was struck by a senior analyst's suggestion that what the patient needed was a therapeutic regression. I realized that, in fourteen years of attending clinical discussions at the Institute of Psychoanalysis, I could not recall anyone making this suggestion before. By contrast, I could think of a number of occasions where there had been discussions about whether patients should be made to sit up, come at a lower frequency, or perhaps be given an ending date for their analysis. These were all for a variety of apparently good reasons but it made me think that, perhaps, there was a more widespread resistance to regression.

This seems to be confirmed by the difference in emphasis between two panel discussions on the topic taking place in 1958 and 1999 in the United States (Spurling, 2008, p. 524). The first was on 'Technical aspects of regression during psychoanalysis', and the second 'Regression: essential clinical condition or iatrogenic phenomenon?' Spurling suggests this reflects a general unease with the whole idea of regression. And yet perhaps this is not a new phenomenon. In 1954, Winnicott addressed the British Society with these words:

> The study of the place of regression in analytic work is one of the tasks Freud left us to carry out, and I think it is a subject for which this Society is ready. I am trying to put something into words, something which belongs to psycho-analysis to-day, and I base this idea on the fact that material relevant to the subject occurs frequently in papers read before the Society. Usually attention is not specifically drawn to this aspect of our work.
>
> (1954a/1955, p. 16)

In writing this chapter, I have had to (re)mind myself of regression. Once I began to explore it, there was so much to say – far more than can be said here. This is not a comprehensive overview but the beginning of a conversation that I feel has been largely missing from my development as an analyst.[2]

The present book serves as a reminder that there was a time in the British Independent tradition when regression and its implications for technique was a defining feature. The three papers bring this vividly alive: voices that remain as vital today as thirty years ago.

Regress comes from the Latin 'go back, return', meaning to return to a former or less developed state (*Oxford English Dictionary*). Dimensions of time and space are implicit: to move to an earlier time or more primitive form, thus putting it at the heart of the 'here-and-now' of the analytic situation, which contains the 'there-and-then' of early psychic life.

As a phenomenon, it was well recognized in hypnosis, so it is there from the very beginning of psychoanalysis. It is not particular to the analytic situation: regression accompanies all of us, throughout our lives. The concept is predominantly a descriptive one, and, yet, its recognition is at the heart of some of Freud's most important meta-psychological concepts, integral to the repetition–compulsion, return of the repressed and the death instinct itself.

Michael Balint describes the curious way in which regression appears and disappears in Freud's thinking (1968, p. 122). The term is first used by Freud in 1900 to explain why dream thoughts arise primarily in the form of sensory images (1900a). In 1914, he adds a footnote distinguishing three types (Laplanche and Pontalis, 1967, p. 386).

Topographical describes how, when excitation cannot travel 'forward' from perception to motor discharge, it returns to its perceptual origins as in dreams, hallucinations or mnemic traces. *Temporal* is the reversion to past phases of development such as libidinal stages, object-relationships, or early dependence: 'the bringing back into play of what has been inscribed' (p. 388). *Formal* denotes a transition to more primitive modes of expression and representation.

Freud initially regarded regression as defensive, as a pathogenic factor in the neuroses, psychoses and perversions. Afterwards, he began to recognize regression's importance in the transference, eventually regarding it as the most potent form of resistance. It can also be an ally in analytic therapy, although Freud rarely mentions this (Balint, 1968, p. 119). In 1914, Freud says,

> The patient's associations moved back from the scene which we were trying to elucidate to earlier experiences . . . This regressive direction became an important characteristic of analysis. It appeared that psycho-analysis could explain nothing belonging to the present without referring back to something past. . . . The temptation to confine one's attention to the known present exciting cause was so strong, however, that even in later analyses I gave way to it. . . what a degree of scientific regression is represented by the neglect of regression in analytic technique.
>
> (1914d, p. 10)

Here Freud recognizes his own tendency to ignore what he knows.[3]

One year later he writes:

Unconscious processes only become cognizable by us under the conditions of dreaming and of neurosis – that is to say, when processes of the higher, Pcs., system are set back to an earlier stage by being lowered (by regression).

(Freud, 1915e, p. 186)

For Freud regression was essential if we are to have access to the Unconscious. In spite of this, Balint points out his inconsistency:

Regression during treatment was recognized as an important factor of therapy in the early cathartic cases. . . . Equally, we have printed evidence that the theoretical idea of regression was one of the oldest; and still it had to wait until 1900 to appear in print, and more than another ten years till its full significance as a factor in pathogenesis was fully recognized. From then on it had a spectacular career, but only in its pejorative aspects, as a redoubtable form of resistance, then as a symptom of the repetition compulsion and, lastly, as the most important clinical example of the death instinct. On the other hand, its role as a therapeutic ally was mentioned only very cursorily, and then apparently forgotten or overshadowed by its threatening aspects.

(Balint, 1968, p. 122)

And yet, is it really that surprising? All of us are equivocal about our infantile past that is never really past. It begins when we are barely out of infancy ourselves – consider the contempt a toddler shows the new baby which disguises both a horror of his own helplessness and the longing to be in blissful union with the mother once more:

Hans is very jealous of the new arrival, and whenever any one praises her, says she is a lovely baby, and so on, he at once declares scornfully: 'But she's not got any teeth yet.'

(Freud, 1909b, p. 11)

The Sandlers developed the concept of an anti-regressive function:

We believe this . . . to be operative throughout our development, and for most of our daily lives. It requires mental work and effort to be maintained, and is the source of so-called 'civilised' behaviour. Society has found it necessary to create situations in which licensed regression can take place. . . We are referring here to parties, having a drink in the evening, reading novels, watching films, crowd behaviour, making love, and a myriad other ways in which . . . we relax the anti-regressive function. Those who cannot relax this function from time to time are psychologically at risk.

(Sandler and Sandler, 1994, p. 433)

Indeed. Yet, the issue of regression in the consulting room remains contentious. Breuer fled when he encountered it with Anna O., her regression turning into an intense and extreme erotic transference, which Breuer could not contend with. Freud did not run away from his patient's transferences, and so psychoanalysis was born; nevertheless, he remained cautious concerning regression and its influence in the situation of transference. He consistently warned his colleagues that 'The treatment must be carried out in abstinence' (1915a, p. 165).

Ferenczi was the first to explore the therapeutic importance of regression to primitive object relations during the course of an analysis. This was rooted in his recognition of early trauma and the impact this has on the developing mind. In such patients, Ferenczi felt that first the analyst and patient needed to allow the experience to unfold, and that interpretation and understanding would follow later.

It was Ferenczi's experiments with a more elastic technique when dealing with regressed patients that led to his disagreements with Freud (Balint, 1968, p. 125). Freud was concerned by reports of Ferenczi allowing physical contact with his patients. Michael Balint, who was analysed and trained by Ferenczi, argued that a distinction between benign and malignant regression may have helped bridge their differences, as it allows a technique that does not gratify the demands of the patient but recognizes them as a way of communicating unspeakable early psychic trauma. Balint suggests that Ferenczi would have concluded that his methods were not effective. However, Ferenczi's premature death in 1933 prevented any rapprochement with Freud. The impact on the analytic world was so traumatic that further exploration of therapeutic regression was repressed.

Perelberg (2008, p. 106) has pointed out how the concept of regression and the issue of temporality were at the heart of disagreements during the Controversial Discussions, centring on whether unconscious phantasy was a product of an earlier event (Kleinian

213

view), or a later one that acquired earlier aspects through regression (as emphasized by both the Freudian and the Independent group). Missing from the discussions was any consideration of après-coup.[4] Perelberg comments that:

> My sense is that the concept of *après-coup* solves the dichotomy of whether earlier or later events are more important as it indicates the way in which . . . later events resignify earlier ones, which then emerge with a new meaning.
>
> (Perelberg, 2008, p. 119)

However, this is not a concept that prevails in the discourse of British psychoanalysis – for many, it remains a missing concept (Sodré, 2005). Nevertheless, it has been present in the writings of Dana Birksted-Breen, Christopher Bollas, Gregorio Kohon, Juliet Mitchell, Rosine Jozef Perelberg, and others.

After Ferenczi's death, his ideas on regression were elaborated by Balint, who moved to the United Kingdom in 1939 and became a central figure in the Independents. Balint's theories on therapeutic regression and psychoanalytic technique culminated in his book *The Basic Fault* (1968). The increasing complexity of cases being analysed challenged classical technique, as did the increasing recognition of the importance of early object relations in the shaping of the psyche.

Winnicott theorized that early environmental failure could lead to the development of a false self as a way of protecting the true self. He recognized that regression to dependence within the analytic relationship was a way for these patients to re-live the not-yet-experienced trauma, which in turn enabled them to discover their true self (Abram, 2007, p. 275). Regression to dependence meant that the ego was temporarily impaired and someone had to take over care.

Winnicott attracted much criticism because he took on a large part of the care-taking role himself, with prolonged or extra sessions and physical holding (Rayner, 1991, p. 195). In his defence, Rayner points out that he was trying to help patients who had not been helped by classical analysis and his experiments took place in an age when physical-holding techniques were fashionable. It should be emphasized that Winnicott was talking about some patients at some point in their analyses (Caldwell and Joyce, 2011, p. 23). Indeed, Winnicott said that:

The idea is sometimes put forward: . . . Winnicott likes or invites his patients to regress. . . . There are no reasons why an analyst should *want* a patient to regress, except grossly pathological reasons.

(1954a/1955, p. 24)

There is a danger of a rather reductive approach to regression: something to be either promoted or guarded against. The concept of *après-coup*, as elucidated by Perelberg, transforms regression into a dimension that is in dynamic relation with multiple other dimensions:

Après-coup acquires meaning in the context of a structure that contains many other concepts and includes multiple temporalities – progressive and regressive movements take place together and reciprocally influence each other. These include development, regression, repression, fixation, repetition compulsion, the return of the repressed and the timelessness of the unconscious. This creates a complex structure that gives Freud's concepts of time a multi-dimensional perspective. *My image is that of a heptagon in motion.*

(2008, p. 108, italics in original)

Regression is not something to be considered in isolation. Topographical, temporal and formal regressions all operate in a complex matrix, interacting with each other and with other dimensions in the day-to-day life of the individual and in the moment-by-moment life of the analytic session in perpetual motion. Changes in setting and technique have been at the heart of the controversy surrounding regression, so it is worth considering the psychoanalytic situation itself.

Bleger distinguishes the *process* – what goes on in the relationship between analyst and patient – from the *setting* (or *frame*, depending on the alternative translations offered), which is understood as a *non-process*, providing the framework in which the process occurs (2013, p. 228).[5] The most psychotic and regressed parts of the patient are contained by the constancy of the setting, so they can go unrecognized; in it resides the symbiotic relationship with the mother/analyst. Ultimately, this too must be analysed.

The setting both invites and frustrates regression. Donnet calls it an ambiguous rather than a 'neutral' setting, and suggests that, in exploring his active techniques, Ferenczi was simply accentuating what already existed (2010, p. 164).

215

For Parsons, the setting embodies unconscious processes encompassing, on the one hand, Lewin's idea that the setting represents the mind in a dream-state (1955), and, on the other, Green's idea that the setting represents the Oedipus complex uniting the dream (narcissism), maternal caring and paternal prohibition (1984) (Parsons, 2000, pp. 176–178).

Parsons also explores the analyst's internal setting, saying that:

> This . . . defines and protects an area of the analyst's mind where whatever happens, including what happens to the external setting, can be considered from a psychoanalytic viewpoint.
>
> (2014, p. 154)

Parsons argues that this concept makes possible a considerable flexibility of the external setting, without any sacrifice of its analytic quality. He suggests that the concept of an internal framework might have helped Ferenczi and Winnicott contain their very disturbed patients without altering the external setting to such a degree (p. 157).

For Perelberg, the paternal prohibition of violence and incest is present in the abstinence of both analyst and patient. This 'establishes a link with the past, not only of our patients but also of our theories that are part of the analyst's repertoire and of his *internal setting*' (2015b, p. 79, italics in original).

Contained within the setting is the evolving relationship between the patient and analyst. How the analyst meets and responds to regression plays a key part in how it unfolds in the analysis. In his Introduction, Kohon quotes Freud, who argued that '. . . no psychoanalyst goes further than his own complexes and internal resistances permit' (1910d, p. 145). Kohon goes on to say 'the resistances that we traditionally place on the side of the patient belong to the analyst as well. It might happen that they belong more to the analyst than to the patient' (p. 61 herein).

Perelberg cautions that this should not lull one into a belief in a democratic process where mutuality and harmony are emphasized; she argues that there is a 'profound dissymmetry, trauma and violence inherent in the analytic situation. It is inherent because this is the stuff of unconscious phantasies' (2015b, p. 69).[6] It is precisely this asymmetry and the trauma inherent in it that makes it so important that we take seriously the need, not just for the analyst to survive, but for the analyst to behave (Winnicott, 1954a/1955, p. 21).[7]

Abuses within the analytic situation have been part of the founding trauma of psychoanalysis (Gabbard, 1995).[8] While the risk is inherent in any professional situation where one person is in a position of authority, prestige or power over another, in psychoanalysis our need to be open to primitive mental states in ourselves and our patients makes it particularly hard to know at times when a boundary crossing becomes a boundary violation (Sandler and Godley, 2004, p. 29). Minor boundary variations always precede more major violations (Gabbard, 2003). Perhaps we cannot be permanently aware of the danger at all times, but we must certainly always stay alert to the possibility. Maintaining an inflexible neutral stance is no solution, as Gabbard and Lester point out, '. . . a central paradox of the analytic situation is that professional boundaries must be maintained so that both participants have the freedom to cross them psychologically (Gabbard and Lester, 1995, p. 42).

There is an added paradox: the seductive dimension at the heart of the psychoanalytic situation. Laplanche sees the analyst's offer of an analysis as re-actualizing the primal seduction of the child by the parents (1987, p. 156). Furthermore, Chetrit-Vatine explores the 'ethical seduction' of the patient by the analyst, linking the analyst's passion with his responsibility for the patient (2011, p. 253). Hence, the issue of parameters[9] is important, and it is highlighted and discussed in both Stewart's and Casement's papers.

Stewart did not take the decision to physically restrain his female patient lightly. He had an intuition that, if he threatened to end the analysis, she would have challenged this; she would have wanted to see if he was serious, thus ending a treatment which time proved she needed and could be helped by. He wondered if she would have chosen this form of acting out if he was physically smaller, for example, and decided she would, as it appeared to be compulsive.

It is possible that patients have an intuitive sense of what their analyst can tolerate. In this particular analysis, there was a gentle testing of the analyst before the fully fledged acting out. A female analyst could presumably analyse such a patient, but any parameters would unfold differently. This is a creative process and unique to each analytic couple, who have to work out together how primitive experiences can be brought safely into the analytic setting in a way that allows meaning to be constructed. To quote Kohon (p. 52 herein): 'The Object Relations view is that the psychoanalytic situation is always created and developed from the specific and unique interaction between the patient and the analyst.'

Stewart reflects on the possible meanings and dangers of this parameter, working with the patient to understand what it represents. In this sense, his internal setting remains intact, which is what allows this parameter with this patient to remain analytic.

The work of *après-coup* is vivid in Stewart's description of the analysis: the regressive and progressive movements; the different temporalities; the return of the repressed; the patient's development as seen in her ability to work out that the ghost was a hallucination; and even why she may have needed to have this hallucination. A startling developmental leap, and a generational leap at that, since her grandmother had also seen ghosts. This kind of achievement was possible because she had an analyst who respected her need to explore different ways of communicating, from physical action to letters to drawings, and who gave her time and space to work something through. This, in turn, allowed her to bring her madness more fully into the consulting room, while beginning to be able to get on with her life outside. Eventually, her terror of her imagined violent genitals could find representation for the first time, allowing her to contemplate marriage and children of her own.

It can sound a little too easy put like this. I was left wondering about the emotional impact of each session and the toll it must have taken on the analyst. I can imagine the turmoil: desire, doubt, terror, loneliness, all intermingled; having to bear it with no guaranteed outcome, no certainty of where it was leading.

If the reader could only imagine the impact on Stewart, Casement graphically conveys the sense of pressure he was under. Here, again, is a struggle with a parameter – again the question of physical contact. If Stewart had to physically wrestle with his patient, Casement had to wrestle with the fearsome consequences of first allowing, and then refusing the possibility of physical contact. Casement uses Bion's concept of nameless dread to understand how, by refusing the holding and being able to tolerate his patient's projections, she was eventually able to receive them back again in tolerable form. I would add that his initial agreement to the possibility of hand-holding was equally important. If he had refused outright, he might have been refusing the initial projection, thus not having the opportunity of doing the psychic work that took place afterwards, with the withdrawal of the offer – both movements seem to have been necessary for the elaboration of this particular trauma.

At the time of this paper being written, Casement and his patient did not know that there had been an earlier trauma, which had been re-enacted in the analysis (Casement, 2002, p. 93). Perhaps it is not quite right to say that the patient did not know – rather, that this knowledge existed as an *unthought known* (Bollas, 1987). When Mrs B. was burnt at the age of 10 months, the doctor feared that admission to the only hospital available would lead to her death, and that her only chance was to be barrier-nursed at home by her mother. This meant that the mother could only touch her baby with sterile gloves, and then only for the bare essentials, feeding and cleaning, in order to avoid deadly infection – this was in the days before antibiotics. In other words, no matter how much her baby might scream and cry, she was not to be picked up and held. As Casement says, 'what a parallel!' (p. 94). Here, again, we see how *après-coup* links the here-and-now of the transference with the there-and-then of early trauma, thus initiating a triadic structure that allows symbolic functioning to develop (Perelberg, 2015a, p. 1472).

There is an analytic genealogy that links these three papers: Stewart acknowledges Balint as his analytic grandfather (1996, p. ix). Stewart was Casement's training analyst (2006, p. xi). Balint's emphasis on the need to go beyond words if early trauma is to find representation, to journey alongside the patient, sharing in the uncertainty and confusion, to allow the patient to make something of himself without 'attention-seeking interpretations', finds elaboration in the work of Stewart and Casement. These aspects of technique are what I regard as characteristic of the Independent tradition; it was what I was searching for, many years ago, when I came across *On Learning from the Patient* in a psychoanalytic bookshop (Casement, 1985).

The analytic thinking I was familiar with at the time had helped me to make sense of my experiences as a psychiatric trainee. However, the clinical technique left me feeling troubled. There was often an impression of an all-knowing analyst proclaiming from on high. Casement's book led me to explore writers in the Independent analytic tradition, where I found analysts prepared to allow space for the patient's thoughts, ever mindful to 'avoid putting alien feelings into the analysand's heart, and foreign words into the analysand's mouth' (Kohon, p. 69 herein).

This brings me to Balint's area of creation, a concept that remains underestimated, even today. I believe that we analysts find it so hard not to pre-empt the patient. Winnicott puts it rather provocatively: 'It appals me to think how much deep change I have prevented or delayed in patients . . . by my personal need to interpret (1969, p. 219).

219

Sklar suggests that one way for the patient to deal with profound early trauma is to shut down:

> The very regressed patient needs to deal with life by having very little of it . . . Analysis then is a provision of a space and an environment for the possibility of a return to life. . . . Prior to such a return to hope, the analysand has first to find a creative part of himself as a form of becoming alive.
>
> (Sklar, 2011, p. 16)

Sklar quotes Enid Balint:

> This state is overcome only when the patient painfully allows himself to feel alone, in the analyst's presence but with no other person being there. He may then begin to perceive for himself and to enter the Area of Creativity.
>
> (1993, p. 104)

The importance of this solitude in psychic life is explored by Kohon (2016, p. 25), who makes a crucial distinction between *psychic refuges*, which are human beings' normal, healthy need for privacy and solitude, and Steiner's well-known concept of *psychic retreats* (1993). Kohon suggests that it is only when the withdrawal takes on an excessively rigid form that it should be labelled 'pathological'. We all have a realm of experience which is incapable of being put into words, much of this must remain hidden (Cohen, 2013). It is the traumatic past that needs to find representation, for, if it does not, then 'it will continue to beckon us from the future, changing the course of the story. . . . This is what is at the core of the compulsion to repeat' (Kohon, 2016, p. 17).

As psychoanalysts, what we try to do is to unfasten the circular temporality of the compulsion to repeat, so as to inaugurate a more open one – a temporality that would allow for the possibility of different futures. Regression plays a key role in enabling this. A way for the patient to (re)experience the past in the analysis, which allows restructuring of psychic experience.[10]

This clearly echoes with Winnicott's idea of the fear of breakdown – a breakdown that has already happened but has not yet been experienced (pp. 121–129 herein). As the Botellas put it 'the absence of representable content does not mean the absence of an event' (2005, p. 164). This is the territory of psychic figurability, where, by allowing his own regression, something is revealed in the analyst's mind which was already in existence in the patient as a non-representable state. In making this possible, the analyst is working as a double for the patient (Botella and Botella, 2005, p. 67).[11]

Earlier writers focused on the more dramatic aspects of regression, including the need to introduce parameters, and this has dominated the debate so that the more 'ordinary' aspects of regression have been overlooked (Bollas, 1987, p. 258). Bollas' example of such an episode, contained within the everyday psychoanalytic setting, reminds us that it is part and parcel of analytic work. Kohon gives a moving account of regression that did not entail challenging acting out but, none-theless, required the analyst to bear being there, doing 'nothing', which was a very important 'something' (1999b, p. 159).

Regression interweaves the analytic work during each session and over the months and years. We invite it every time we allow our patient to come in, lie down and say whatever comes to mind. It is not a case of encouraging or discouraging – it is inherent in the psychoanalytic encounter. Emphasizing the essential day-to-dayness of regression is not to minimize the formidable demands it can place on us. If we do not hold regression in mind, then we will overlook it, mistake it for resistance, respond by organizing our thoughts and our patients' thoughts too quickly, intrude on their creative space, depriving them of a chance to understand something for themselves, to reach a place and finally know it for the first time.

Baranger *et al.* convincingly argued that:

> Progress in analytic theory and technique must be situated at the frontiers of psychoanalysis, in the difficulties that may seem impossible to overcome in order to go farther in the psychoanalytic process. . . . The frontier is not precisely defined, being a large 'No Man's Land', open both to eventual progress in analysis as well as to spectacular failures. It is a risk zone where the *Unheimlich* reigns, where the dangers have no name, where the analyst cannot go forward without anxiety about his own action. We could say: the zone of the unborn trauma (unborn for both the analyst and his analysand).
>
> (Baranger *et al.*, 1988, p. 127)

In his Concluding Remarks in the Introduction, Kohon speaks of the courage needed to believe in psychoanalysis. An openness to regression requires boldness too – not just because of censure from society or our colleagues, but because regression is a risky business. It is unpredictable. We do not know when or how it will emerge, or where it will take us: we can find ourselves in a wilderness that is unnamed, untraveled; we may feel lost, bewildered, estranged from ourselves. However, by allowing it to come into play, it can enrich and enlighten our work in the here-and-now and, in so doing, the there-and-then can be transformed, allowing the future to be re-imagined.

Notes

1 In truth, this view is not widespread in British psychoanalysis. By contrast, French psychoanalysts regard regression as what characterizes psychoanalysis (Birksted-Breen and Flanders, 2010, p. 41).
2 Of course, I can only speak for my own experience. When I did the course on the Independent tradition in 2003, there was no seminar devoted to regression; in 2016, there is. Perhaps, this is reflective of the way regression comes in and out of focus.
3 See Chapter 8, 'Knowledge and Its Vicissitudes', in Kohon (1999b, pp. 149–173).
4 *Après-coup* is the French translation of Freud's concept of *Nachträglichkeit*, which was translated into English as 'deferred action'. However, deferred action is not felt to be a good translation, given that it implies a linear forward movement, not the complexity of temporalities developed by French psychoanalysis (see Birksted-Breen and Flanders, 2010, p. 20; Laplanche and Pontalis, 1967, p. 111; Perelberg, 2008). It is not lived experience in general that is revised, but whatever it has been impossible to represent at the time. This is the link with trauma (see Kohon, 2016, p. 16).
5 Churcher and Bleger translate the Spanish '*encuadre*' as '*setting*', in English (Bleger, 1967b, p. xli). In the original, the word originates from '*encuadrar*', which means 'to set a painting in a frame' (Kohon, personal communication). The French use the same word, '*le cadre*' (Birksted-Breen and Flanders, 2010, p. 42). See also Kohon, in Green and Kohon (2005, p. 93).
6 See also Kohon, in Green and Kohon (2005, p. 81).
7 In February 2001, seven months before I began my psychoanalytic training, *The London Review of Books* published an article by Wynne Godley detailing his analysis with Masud Khan (Godley, 2001). Godley's description of Khan's boundary violations and abusive behaviour is deeply disturbing; according to his account, Khan was in analysis with Winnicott at the time. New evidence, based on Winnicott's appointment diaries, suggest Winnicott was not in fact Khan's analyst at this

time (Abram, 2013, p. 455; Caldwell and Joyce, 2011, p. 25). Further details about this are being prepared for publication (Jan Abram, personal communication). Nonetheless, Godley's disclosures about such prominent proponents of therapeutic regression may well have negatively affected further theoretical and clinical discussions about the subject. Regrettably, the silence in institutions after such events of abuse is well-documented (Gabbard and Peltz, 2001).

8 Dimen has coined the term 'primal crime' (2011, p. 73). See also Levin (2016, p. 381).

9 A term introduced by Eissler (1953) and defined by Rycroft (1968) as 'aspects of psychoanalytical technique which can (arguably) be modified to meet the needs of particular classes of patients' (Stewart, 1992, p. 82).

10 Brazelton (1992) has developed the concept of touchpoints. Before a developmental leap the child can become disorganized and appear to take a step backwards: crying, not feeding, and no longer sleeping through the night. If accommodated, rather than being resisted, the child soon reorganizes and takes a further step forward. Brazelton suggests that this happens throughout an individual's life.

11 See Perelberg (2015a) for an evocative account of this work of figurability.

17

THE UNOBTRUSIVE ANALYST

Michael Balint

The more the analyst's technique and behaviour are suggestive of omniscience and omnipotence, the greater is the danger of a malignant form of regression. On the other hand, the more the analyst can reduce the inequality between his patient and himself, and the more unobtrusive and ordinary he can remain in his patient's eyes, the better are the chances of a benign form of regression.

Thus we have arrived at one of the most important problems of modern analytic technique, which is how much of the two therapeutic agents – interpretation and object-relationship – should be used in any one case; when, in what proportion, and in what succession should they be used? This problem is important in every case, but is especially acute in the treatment of a regressed patient when the work has reached the area of the basic fault. Since, as we have found, words have only a limited and uncertain usefulness in these areas, it seems to follow that object-relationship is the more important and more reliable therapeutic factor during these periods, while in the states after the patient has emerged from his regression, interpretations will regain their importance.

The question now arises as to what sort of technique the analyst can use to create the object-relationship which, in his opinion, is the most suitable for that particular patient; or, in other words, will probably have the best therapeutic effect. The first analyst who experimented with these effects fairly systematically was Ferenczi. Viewed from this angle his 'active technique' and his 'principle of relaxation' were deliberate attempts at creating object-relationships which, in his opinion, were better suited to the needs of some patients than the atmosphere of an analytic setting created according to Freud's classical recommendations. Ferenczi recognized fairly soon that, whatever he tried to do, the result was that his patients became more dependent on him, that is, he became more and more important for them; on the other hand he could not recognize the reasons why this had to happen. Today we may add that his technique, instead of reducing, increased the inequality between the patients and himself, whom they felt to be really omniscient and all-important.

It was fairly early in my career that I realized that keeping to the parameters of classical technique meant accepting strict selection of patients. In my beginner's enthusiasm this was unacceptable, and under Ferenczi's influence I experimented with non-verbal communications; starting with 1932 I reported on my experiments and results in several papers; most of them reprinted in *Primary Love and Psycho-Analytic Technique* (M. Balint, 1965). Of course, my techniques and my ways of thinking have undergone considerable change during the years, and though I am fully aware that my present ideas are anything but final, they have again reached a stage at which I can 'organize' them, that is, express them in sufficiently concrete form so that they can be discussed and, above all, criticized.

In my endeavour to overcome the difficulties just mentioned, for some years now I have experimented with a technique that allows the patient to experience a two-person relationship which cannot, need not, and perhaps even must not, be expressed in words, but at times merely by what is customarily called 'acting out' in the analytic situation. I hasten to add that in all these non-verbal communications, the acting out will of course be worked through after the patient has emerged from this level and reached the Oedipal level again – but not till then.

May I recapitulate here the several trains of thought that led me to these experiments. On many occasions I have found to my annoyance and despair that words cease to be reliable means of communication when the analytic work reaches the areas beyond the Oedipal level. The analyst may try, as hard as he can, to make his interpretations clear and unequivocal; the patient, somehow, always manages to experience them as something utterly different from that which the analyst intended them to be. At this level explanations, arguments, improved or amended versions, if tried, prove of no avail; the analyst cannot but accept the bitter fact that his words in these areas, instead of clarifying the situation, are often misunderstood, misinterpreted, and tend to increase the confusion of tongues between his patient and himself. Words become, in fact, unreliable and unpredictable.

This clinical observation is so important to my train of thought that I will show it from yet another angle. Words – at these periods – cease to be vehicles for free association; they have become lifeless, repetitious, and stereotyped; they strike one as an old worn-out gramophone record, with the needle running endlessly in the same groove. By the way, this is often equally true about the analyst's interpretations; during these periods they, too, seem to be running endlessly in the same groove. The analyst then discovers to his despair and dismay that, in these periods, there is no point whatever in going on interpreting the patient's verbal communications. At the Oedipal – and even at some of the so-called 'pre-Oedipal' – levels a proper interpretation, which makes a repressed conflict conscious and thereby resolves a resistance or undoes a split, gets the patient's free associations going again; at the level of the basic fault this does not necessarily happen. The interpretation is either experienced as interference, cruelty, unwarranted demand or unfair impingement, as a hostile act, or a sign of affection, or is felt so lifeless, in fact dead, that it has no effect at all.

Another train of thought started with the discovery of the ocno-philic bias of our technique (M. Balint, 1959, 1968). Nowadays analysts are enjoined to interpret everything that happens in the ana-lytic situation also, or even foremost, in terms of transference, i.e., of object-relationship. This otherwise sensible and efficient technique means that we offer ourselves to our patients incessantly as objects to cling to, and interpret anything contrary to clinging as resistance, aggressiveness, narcissism, touchiness, paranoid anxiety, castration fear, and so on. A highly ambivalent and strained atmosphere is created in this way, the patient struggling, prompted by his desire for inde-pendence, but finding his way barred at every point by ocnophilic 'transference' interpretations.

The third train of thought originated from my study of 'the silent patient'. Silence, as is more and more recognized, may have many meanings, each of them requiring different technical handling. Silence may be an arid and frightening emptiness, inimical to life and growth, in which case the patient ought to be got out of it as soon as possible; it may be a friendly exciting expanse, inviting the patient to undertake adventurous journeys into the uncharted lands of his fantasy life, in which case any ocnophilic transference interpretation may be utterly out of place, in fact disturbing; silence may also mean an attempt at re-establishing the harmonious mix-up of primary love that existed between the individual and his environment before the emergence of objects, in which case any interference either by interpretation or in any other way is strictly contraindicated as it may destroy the harmony by making demands on the patient.

The last train of thought is connected with my ideas about the area of creation, an area of the mind in which there is no external organized object, and any intrusion of such an object by attention-seeking interpretations inevitably destroys for the patient the possibility of creating something out of himself.

Objects in this area are as yet unorganized, and the process of creation leading to their organization needs, above all, time. This time may be short or very long; but whatever its length, it cannot be influenced from outside. Almost certainly the same will be true about our patients' creations out of their unconscious. This may be one of the reasons why the analyst's usual interpretations are felt by patients regressed to this area as inadmissible; interpretations are indeed whole, 'organized', thoughts or objects whose interactions with the hazy, dream-like, as yet 'unorganized' contents of the area of creation might cause either havoc or an unnatural, premature, organization.

The outward appearance of all these, widely different, states is a silent patient, seemingly withdrawn from normal analytic work, 'acting out' instead of associating, or possibly even repeating something instead of recollecting it; and, last but not least, he may also be described as regressing towards some primitive behaviour instead of progressing towards complying with our fundamental rule. All these descriptions – withdrawal, acting out, repetition instead of remembering, regression – are correct but incomplete and thus may lead to mistaken technical measures.

Thus the technique that I found usually profitable with patients who regressed to the level of the basic fault or of creation, was to bear with their regression for the time being, without any forceful attempt at intervening with an interpretation. This time may amount only to some minutes, but equally to a more or less long stretch of sessions. As I have mentioned several times, words at these periods have anyhow ceased to be reliable means of communication; the patient's words are no longer vehicles for free associations, they have become lifeless, repetitive, and stereotyped, they do not mean what they seem to say. The standard technical advice is correct in this case too; the analyst's task is to understand what lies behind the patient's words; the problem is only how to communicate this understanding to a regressed patient. My answer is in accepting unreservedly the fact that words have become unreliable and by sincerely giving up, for the time being, any attempt at forcing the patient back to the verbal level. This means abandoning any attempt at 'organizing' the material produced by the patient it is not the 'right' material anyway – and tolerating it so that it may remain incoherent, nonsensical, unorganized, till the patient – after returning to the Oedipal level of conventional language – will be able to give the analyst the key to understand it.

In other words, the analyst must accept the regression. This means that he must create an environment, a climate, in which he and his patient can tolerate the regression in a mutual experience. This is essential because in these states any outside pressure reinforces the anyhow strong tendency in the patient to develop relationships of inequality between himself and his objects, perpetuating thereby his proneness to regression.

I wish to illustrate what I have just said by referring to an episode from an analysis which, at that time, had been going on for about two years. The patient remained silent right from the start of the session for more than 30 minutes; the analyst accepted this and, realizing what possibly was happening, waited without any attempt whatever at interference; in fact, he did not even feel uncomfortable or under pressure to do something. I should add that in this treatment silences had occurred previously on several occasions, and patient and analyst had thus had some training in tolerating them. The silence was eventually broken by the patient starting to sob, relieved, and soon after he was able to speak. He told his analyst that at long last he was able to reach himself; ever since childhood he had never been left alone, there had always been someone telling him what to do. Some sessions later he reported that during the silence he had all sorts of associations, but rejected each of them as irrelevant, as nothing but an annoying superficial nuisance.

Of course, the silence could easily have been interpreted as resistance, withdrawal, a sign of persecutory fear, inability to cope with depressive anxieties, a symptom of a repetition compulsion, etc.; moreover since the analyst knew his patient fairly well, he could even have interpreted or guessed one or the other topic emerging in the associations and also some of the reasons why the patient felt that particular idea irrelevant and was rejecting it. All these might have been correct interpretations in every respect – except in one: they would have destroyed the silence and the patient would not have been able to 'reach himself', at any rate, not on that occasion. There is one more unintended side-effect of any, however correct, interpretation: it would inevitably reinforce the patient's strong repetition-compulsion, there would again be someone there, telling him what to feel, to think, in fact what to do.

Furthermore, all this happened in an exclusively two-person relationship; the dynamic problem to be dealt with did not have the structure of a conflict for which a 'solution' had to be found. The situation demanded somewhat more skill from the analyst than, say, the understanding of verbal association; by finding a correct answer to the silence, the· analyst was running the risk of raising expectations in his patient that this would possibly happen time and again and trigger in this way the development of addiction-like states; another risk was to impress the patient that he has got an analyst so wise and so powerful that he can read his patient's unspoken thoughts and respond to them correctly, the risk of becoming 'omnipotent'; and lastly, words would have been unreliable in this situation, more likely than not they would have forced the patient prematurely into the Oedipal area and created further obstacles to the therapeutic work instead of removing some. Of course, all these are characteristic signs that the analytic work has reached the area of the basic fault.

The right technique, as long as the patient is regressed to this level, is to accept 'acting out' in the analytic situation as valid means of communication without any attempt at speedily 'organizing' it by interpretations. Emphatically, this does not mean that in these periods the analyst's role becomes negligible or is restricted to sympathetic passivity; on the contrary, his presence is most important, not only in that he must be felt to be present but must be all the time at the right distance – neither so far that the patient might feel lost or abandoned, nor so close that the patient might feel encumbered and unfree – in fact, at a distance that corresponds to the patient's actual need; in general the analyst must know what are his patient's needs, why they are as they are, and why they fluctuate and change.

From another angle, the technical problem is how to offer 'something' to the patient which might function as a primary object, or at any rate as a suitable substitute for it, or in still other words, on to which he can project his primary love.

Should this 'something' be (a) the analyst himself (the analyst who undertakes to treat a regression), or (b) the therapeutic situation? The question is which of these two is the more likely to achieve sufficient harmony with the patient so that there may be only minimal clash of interest between the patient and one available object in the present. On the whole, it is safer if the patient can use the therapeutic situation as a substitute, if for no other reason than because it diminishes the risk of the analyst becoming a most important, omniscient, and omnipotent object.

This offering to the patient a 'primary object', of course, is not tantamount to giving primary love; in any case mothers do not *give* it either. What they do is to behave truly as primary objects, that is, to offer themselves as primary objects to be cathected by primary love. This difference between 'giving primary love' and 'offering oneself to be cathected by primary love' may be of fundamental importance for our technique not only with regressed patients, but also with a number of difficult treatment situations.

To describe the same role from a different angle, i.e., using different 'words': the analyst must function during these periods as a provider of time and of milieu. This does not mean that he is under obligation to compensate for the patient's early privations and give more care, love, affection than the patient's parents have given originally (and even if he tried, he would almost certainly fail). What the analyst must provide – and, if at all possible, during the regular sessions only – is sufficient time free from extrinsic temptations, stimuli, and demands, including those originating from himself (the analyst). The aim is that the patient should be able to find himself, to accept himself, and to get on with himself, knowing all the time that there is a scar in himself, his basic fault, which cannot be 'analysed' out of existence; moreover, he must be allowed to discover *his* way to the world of objects – and not be shown the 'right' way by some profound or correct interpretation. If this can be done, the patient will not feel that the objects impinge on, and oppress, him. It is only to this extent that the analyst should provide a better, more 'understanding' environment, but in no other way, in particular not in the form of more care, love, attention, gratification, or protection. Perhaps it ought to be stressed that considerations of this kind may serve as criteria for deciding whether a certain 'craving' or 'need' should be satisfied, or recognized but left unsatisfied.

The guiding principle during these periods is to avoid any interference not absolutely necessary; interpretations particularly should be scrutinized most meticulously, since they are felt more often than not as unwarranted demand, attack, criticism, seduction, or stimulation; they should be given only if the analyst is certain that the patient *needs* them, for at such times *not giving* them would be felt as unwarranted demand or stimulation. From this angle, what I have called the dangers of ocnophilic interpretations may be understood better; though the patient is in need of an environment, of a world of objects, such objects – foremost among them the analyst – must not be felt as in any way demanding, interfering, intruding, as this would reinforce the old oppressive inequality between subject and object.

I hope this clinical description will help the reader to understand why so many analysts have quite so many different terms to describe it. All of them had the following features in common: there was the suggestion that no oppressive or demanding object should be present; that the environment should be quiet, peaceful, safe, and unobtrusive; that it should be there and that it should be favourable to the subject, but that the subject should be in no way obliged to take notice, to acknowledge, or to be concerned about it. Once again, these common features are the exact characteristics of what I called primary objects or primary substance.

To provide this sort of object or environment is certainly an important part of the therapeutic task. Clearly, it is only a part, not the whole of the task. Apart from being a 'need-recognizing' and perhaps even a 'need-satisfying' object, the analyst must be also a 'need-understanding' object who, in addition, must be able to communicate his understanding to his patient.

18

SOME PRESSURES ON THE ANALYST FOR PHYSICAL CONTACT DURING THE RELIVING OF AN EARLY TRAUMA

Patrick J. Casement

Is physical contact with the patient, even of a token kind, always to be precluded without question under the classical rule of abstinence? Or are there some occasions when this might be appropriate, even necessary, as Margaret Little has suggested in relation to episodes of delusional transference (1957, 1958), or as Balint and Winnicott have illustrated in relation to periods of deep regression? (M. Balint, 1952, 1968; Winnicott, 1954b, 1963c).

I shall present a clinical sequence during which the possibility of physical contact was approached as an open issue. There seemed to be a case for allowing a patient the possibility of holding my hand. The decision to reconsider this was arrived at from listening to the patient and from following closely the available cues from the countertransference. The clinical material clearly illustrates some of the issues involved in this decision.

The patient, whom I shall call Mrs B., is in her 30s. She had been in analysis about two and a half years. A son had been born during the second year of the analysis.

When she was eleven months old Mrs B. had been severely scalded, having pulled boiling water onto herself while her mother was out of the room. She could have died from the burns. When she was seventeen months old she had to be operated on to release growing skin from the dead scar tissue. The operation was done under a local anaesthetic. During this the mother had fainted. (It is relevant to the childhood history that the father was largely absent during the first five years.)

Soon after the summer holiday Mrs B. presented the following dream. She had been trying to feed a despairing child. The child was standing and was about ten months old. It wasn't clear whether the child was a boy or a girl. Mrs B. wondered about the age of the child. Her son was soon to be ten months old. He was now able to stand. She too would have been standing at ten months. (That would have been before the accident.) 'Why is the child in my dream so despairing?' she asked. Her son was a lively child and she assumed that she too had been a normal happy child until the accident. This prompted me to recall how Mrs B. had clung to an idealized view of her pre-accident childhood. I thought she was now daring to question this. I therefore commented that maybe she was beginning to wonder about the time before the accident. Perhaps not everything had been quite so happy as she had always needed to assume. She immediately held up her hand to signal me to stop.

During the following silence I wondered why there was this present anxiety. Was it the patient's need still not to look at anything from before the accident unless it was seen as perfect? Was the accident itself being used as a screen memory? I thought this probable. After a while I said she seemed to be afraid of finding any element of bad experience during the time before the accident, as if she still felt that the good that had been there before must be kept entirely separate from the bad that had followed. She listened in silence, making no perceptible response during the rest of the session.

The next day Mrs B. came to her session with a look of terror on her face. For this session, and the five sessions following, she could not lie on the couch. She explained that when I had gone on talking, after she had signalled me to stop, the couch had 'become' the operating table with me as the surgeon, who had gone on operating regardless, after her mother had fainted. She now couldn't lie down 'because the experience will go on'. Nothing could stop it then, she felt sure.

In one of these sitting-up sessions Mrs B. showed me a photograph of her holiday house, built into the side of a mountain with high retaining walls. She stressed how essential these walls are to hold the house from falling. She was afraid of falling for ever.[1] She felt this had happened to her after her mother had fainted.

(Here I should mention that Mrs B. had previously recalled thinking that her mother had died, when she had fallen out of her sight during the operation, and how she had felt that she was left alone with no one to protect her from the surgeon who seemed to be about to kill her with his knife.) Now, in this session, Mrs B. told me a detail of that experience which she had never mentioned before. At the start of the operation her mother had been holding her hands in hers, and Mrs B. remembered her terror upon finding her mother's hands slipping out of hers as she fainted and disappeared. She now thought she had been trying to re-find her mother's hands ever since, and she began to stress the importance of physical contact for her. She said she couldn't lie down on the couch again unless she knew she could, if necessary, hold my hand in order to get through the reliving of the operation experience. Would I allow this or would I refuse? If I refused she wasn't sure that she could continue with her analysis.

My initial response was to acknowledge to her that she needed me to be 'in touch' with the intensity of her anxiety. However, she insisted she had to know whether or not I would actually allow her to hold my hand. I felt under increased pressure due to this being near the end of a Friday session, and I was beginning to fear that the patient might indeed leave the analysis. My next comment was defensively equivocal. I said some analysts would not contemplate allowing this, but I realized that she might need to have the possibility of holding my hand if it seemed to be the only way for her to get through this experience. She showed some relief upon my saying this.[2]

Over the weekend I reviewed the implications of this possibility of the patient holding my hand. While reflecting upon my counter-transference around this issue I came to recognize the following key points:

1   I was in effect offering to be the 'better mother' who would remain holding her hand, in contrast to the actual mother who had not been able to bear what was happening.
2   My offer had been partly motivated by my fear of losing this patient, which was especially threatening to me just then as I was about to present a paper on this patient to our Society.

3   If I were to hold this patient's hand it would almost certainly
     not, as she assumed, help her to get through a re-experiencing of
     the original trauma. (A central factor of this had been the *absence*
     of her mother's hands.) It would instead amount to a bypassing
     of this aspect of the trauma, and could reinforce the patient's
     perception of this as something too terrible ever fully to be re-
     membered or to be experienced.

I therefore decided that I must review with the patient the
implications of this offer as soon as I had an opportunity to do so.

On the Sunday I received a hand-delivered letter in which the
patient said she had had another dream of the despairing child, but
this time there were signs of hope. *The child was crawling towards a
motionless figure with the excited expectation of reaching this figure.*

On the Monday, although she was somewhat reassured by her
dream, Mrs B. remained sitting on the couch. She saw the central
figure as me representing her missing mother. She also stressed that
she hadn't wanted me to have to wait to know about the dream. I
interpreted her fear that I might not have been able to wait to be
reassured, and she agreed. She had been afraid I might have collapsed
over the weekend, under the weight of the Friday session, if I had
been left until Monday without knowing that she was beginning to
feel more hopeful.

As this session continued, what emerged was a clear impression
that Mrs B. was seeing the possibility of holding my hand as a 'short-
cut' to feeling safer. She wanted me to be the motionless figure,
controlled by her and not allowed to move, towards whom she could
crawl with the excited expectation that she would eventually be
allowed to touch me. Mrs B. then reported an image, which was a
continuation in the session of the written dream. She saw the dream-
child reaching the central figure, but as she touched this it had
crumbled and collapsed. With this cue as my lead I told her I had
thought very carefully about this, and I had come to the conclusion
that this tentative offer of my hand might have appeared to provide
a way of getting through the experience she was so terrified of, but
I now realized it would instead become a side-stepping of that experience as it had been rather than a living through it. I knew that if
I seemed to be inviting an avoidance of this central aspect of the
original experience I would be failing her as her analyst. I therefore
did not think that I should leave the possibility of holding my hand
still open to her. Mrs B looked stunned. She asked me if I realized

what I had just done. I had taken my hand away from her just as her mother had, and she immediately assumed that this must be because I too couldn't bear to remain in touch with what she was going through. Nothing I said could alter her assumption that I was afraid to let her touch me.

The following day the patient's response to what I had said was devastating. Still sitting on the couch she told me her left arm (the one nearest to me) was 'steaming'. I had burned her. She couldn't accept any interpretation from me. Only a real physical response from me could do anything about it. She wanted to stop her analysis to get away from what was happening to her in her sessions. She could never trust me again. I tried to interpret that her trust in her mother, which had in a fragile way been restored after the accident, seemed to have been finally broken after her mother had fainted. It was this ultimate breach of that trust which had got in the way of her subsequent relationship to her. I felt it was this that she was now in the process of re-enacting with me in order to find that this unresolved breach of trust could be repaired. She listened to this, and was nodding understanding, but she repeated that it was impossible to repair.

The following day Mrs B. raged at me still for what she saw as my withdrawing from her. The possibility of holding my hand had been the same to her as actual holding. She felt sure she would not have abused the offer. It had been vitally important to her that I had been prepared to allow this, but my change of mind had become to her a real dropping away of the hand she needed to hold on to. To her I was now her mother who had become afraid. Her arm seemed to be on fire. To her I was afraid of being burned too.

Mrs B. told me that the previous day, immediately after her session with me, she had become 'fully suicidal'. She had only got out of this by asking a friend if she could go round to see her, at any time, if she felt that she couldn't carry on. She had ultimately needed to see her friend. It had been her friend's availability which had prevented her from killing herself. She then rebuked me with the fact that her friend could get it right. Why couldn't I? I told her she did not need from me what she could get from others. She needed something different from me. She needed me not to buy off her anger by offering to be the 'better mother'. It was important I should not be afraid of her anger, or of her despair, in order that I stay with her throughout the relived experience of no longer having her mother's hands to hold on to. She needed me to remain analyst rather than

236

have me as a 'pretend' mother. It was also crucial I do nothing that could suggest I needed to protect myself from what she was experiencing or was feeling towards me. She listened and became calmer. Then, momentarily before leaving the session, she lay down on the couch. She thus resumed the lying position.

I shall now summarize the next two weeks. Mrs B. dreamt of *being lost and unsafe amongst a strange people with whom she could not find a common language.* I interpreted her anxiety as to whether I could find a common language with her. In one session she had a visual image of a child crying stone tears which I interpreted as the tears of a petrified child (herself). She dreamt of *a baby being dropped and left to die.* She dreamt of *being very small and being denied the only food she wanted. It was there but a tall person would not let her have it.* In another dream *she was in terror anticipating some kind of explosion.* Throughout this she persisted in her conviction that she could never trust me again, and she experienced me as afraid of her. Alongside this she told me her husband had become very supporting of her continuing her analysis, even though he was getting a lot of 'kick-back' from it. This was quite new. I interpreted that at some level she was becoming more aware of me as able to take the kick-back from her, in her analysis.

Shortly after this Mrs B. reported the following two dreams in the same session. In the first *she was taking a child every day to meet her mother to get some order into the chaos,* which I interpreted as her bringing her child-self to me in order to work through the chaos of her feelings towards me as the mother she still couldn't trust. She agreed with this but added she didn't bring the child to me by the hand. She had to drag her child-self by the hair. In the second dream *she was falling through the air, convinced that she was going to die despite the fact that she was held by a parachute with a helicopter watching over her.* She could see the contradictions (sure of dying whilst actually being safe) but this did not stop her feeling terrified in the dream, and still terrified of me in the session. She stressed that she didn't know if I realized she was still feeling sure she was dying inside.

On the following Monday Mrs B. told me she had dreamt that she had come for her last session as she couldn't go on. She had begun falling for ever, the couch and the room falling with her. There was no bottom and no end to it.

The next day the patient felt she was going insane. She had dreamt there was a sheet of glass between herself and me so that she couldn't touch me or see me clearly. It was like a car windscreen with no wipers in a storm. I interpreted her inability to feel that I could get in touch with what she was feeling, because of the barrier between her and me created by the storm of her feelings inside her. This prevented her seeing me clearly, just as it had with her mother. She agreed and collapsed into uncontrolled crying, twisting on the couch, tortured with pain. At the end of this session she became panicked that I wouldn't be able to tolerate having experienced this degree of her distress.

On the Friday she spoke of a new worker in her office. She had asked him how long he had been trained. She then realized she was asking him for his credentials. I interpreted her anxiety about my credentials and whether I had the necessary experience to be able to see her through. I added that maybe she used the word 'credentials' because of the allusion to 'believe'. She replied 'Of course, credo.' She said that she wanted to believe that I could see her through, and to trust me, but she still couldn't.

The next week Mrs B. continued to say she didn't think she could go on. She had had many terrible dreams over the weekend. The following day she again sat up for the session. For much of this session she seemed to be quite deluded. Awareness of reality was fleeting and tenuous. For the greater part of the session she was a child. She began by saying she didn't just talk to her baby, she picks him up and holds him. Then, looking straight at me she said, 'I am a baby and you are the person I need to be my mother. I need you to realize this, because unless you are prepared to hold me I cannot go on. You have got to understand this.' She was putting me under immense pressure. Finally she stared accusingly at me and said 'You *are* my mother and you are *not* holding me.'

Throughout this I was aware of the delusional quality of her perception of me.[3] In this session there was little 'as if' sense left in her experience of me, and at times there seemed to be none. It was meaningless to her when I attempted to interpret this as transference, as a reliving of her childhood experience. Not only was I the mother who was not holding her, in her terror of me I had also become the surgeon with a knife in his hand who seemed to be about to kill her. At this point there seemed to be no remaining contact with me as analyst.

I reflected upon my dilemma. If I did *not* give in to her demands I might lose the patient, or she might really go psychotic and need to be hospitalized. If I *did* give in to her I would be colluding with her delusional perception of me, and the avoided elements of the

238

trauma could become encapsulated as too terrible ever to confront. I felt placed in an impossible position. However, once I came to recognize the projective identification process operating here I began to surface from this feeling of complete helplessness. This enabled me eventually to interpret from my countertransference feelings. Very slowly, and with pauses to check that the patient was following me, I said to her, 'You are making me experience in myself the sense of despair, and the impossibility of going on, that you are feeling. I am aware of being in what feels to me like a total paradox. In one sense I am feeling it is impossible to reach you just now, and yet in another sense I feel that my telling you this may be the only way I can reach you.' She followed what I was saying very carefully, and slightly nodded her head. I continued, 'Similarly I feel as if it could be impossible to go on, and yet I feel that the only way I can help you through this is by my being prepared to tolerate what you are making me feel, and going on.' After a long silence Mrs B. began to speak to me again as analyst. She said, 'For the first time I can believe you, that you *are* in touch with what I have been feeling, and what is so amazing is that you can bear it.' I was then able to interpret to her that her desperate wish for me to let her touch me had been her way of letting me know she needed me to be really in touch with what she was going through. This time she could agree. She remained in silence for the last ten minutes of this session, and I sensed that it was important that I should do nothing to interrupt this in any way.

The next day Mrs B. told me what had been happening during that silence. She had been able to smell her mother's presence, and she had felt her mother's hands again holding hers. She felt that it was her mother from before the fainting that she had got in touch with, as she had never felt held like that since then. I commented that she had been able to find the internal mother that she had lost touch with, as distinct from the 'pretend' mother she had been wanting me to become. We could now see that if I had agreed to hold her physically it would have been a way of shutting off what she was experiencing, not only for her but also for me, as if I really couldn't bear to remain with her through this. She immediately recognized the implications of what I was saying and replied. 'Yes. You would have become a collapsed analyst. I could not realize it at the time but I can now see you would then have become the same as my mother who fainted. I am so glad you didn't let that happen.'

To conclude I will summarize part of the last session in this week. Mrs B. had woken feeling happy and had later found herself singing extracts from the opera *Der Freischütz*, the plot of which (she explained) includes the triumph of light over darkness. She had also dreamt *she was in a car which had got out of control having taken on a life of its own. The car crashed into a barrier which had prevented her from running into the oncoming traffic. The barrier had saved her because it had remained firm. If it had collapsed she would have been killed.* She showed great relief that I had withstood her angry demands. My remaining firm had been able to stop the process which had taken on a life of its own, during which she had felt completely out of control. The same dream ended with *the patient reaching out to safety through the car windscreen which had opened to her like two glass doors.*

Discussion

This case illustrates the interplay between the various dynamics operating. My initial offer of possible physical contact was, paradoxically, tantamount to the countertransference withdrawal which the patient later attributed to me in my decision not to leave this offer of that easier option open to her. In terms of Bion's (1962b) concept of 'a projective-identification-rejecting-object' the countertransference here became *the container's fear of the contained.* A further complicating pressure came from the fact that I was shortly to present a paper on this patient to our Society, and I was genuinely afraid of being exposed there as having failed had my patient left the analysis, or had she needed to be hospitalized, just prior to my presenting that paper concerning her. By offering the possibility of the patient holding my hand I was in effect seeking to lessen these risks to myself, and this is an example of Racker's (1968) concept of *indirect countertransference*, in that my response to the patient here was being influenced by some degree of persecutory superego being projected by me on to my professional colleagues.

The resulting sequence can be understood in the interactional terms of Sandler's (1976) concept of *role-responsiveness* or in terms of Winnicott's description of the patient's need to be able to experience in the present, in relation to a real situation between patient and analyst, the extremes of feeling which belonged to an early traumatic experience but which had been 'frozen' because of being too intense for the primitive ego to encompass *at that time* (Winnicott, 1954a, 1963b. See also Winnicott [pp. 121–129 herein (ed.)]. There had come to be a real issue between this patient and me, in the withdrawal of my earlier offer of the possibility of holding my hand. In using this to represent the central element of the original trauma the patient entered into an intensely real experience of the past as she had perceived it. In so doing she was able, as it were, to 'join up with' her own feelings, now unfrozen and available to her. The repressed past became, in the present, a conscious psychic reality from which (this time) she did not have defensively to be psychically absent. During this I had to continue to be the surviving analyst, and not become a collapsed analyst, in order that she could defuse the earlier fantasy that it had been the intensity of her need for her mother that had caused her mother to faint.

The eventual interpretative resolution within this session grew out of my awareness of the *projective identification process* then operating. I am understanding this here as the product of interactional pressures upon the analyst from the patient, which are unconsciously aiming to evoke in him the unbearable feeling state which the patient could not on her own yet contain within herself (cf. Ogden, 1979). It is a matter for speculation whether I would have been so fully subjected to the necessary impact of this patient's experience had I not first approached the question of possible physical contact as an open issue. Had I gone by the book, following the classical rule of no physical contact under any circumstance, I would certainly have been taking the safer course for me but I would probably then have been accurately perceived by the patient as actually afraid even to consider such contact. I am not sure that the reliving of this early trauma would have been as real as it was to the patient, or in the end so therapeutically effective, if I had been preserving myself through-out at that safer distance of classical 'correctness'. Instead I acted upon my intuition of the moment, and it is uncanny how precisely and unwittingly this led me to re-enact with the patient this detail of the original trauma, which she needed to be able to experience within the analytic relationship and to be genuinely angry about. It is this unconscious responsiveness to unconscious cues from the patient to which Sandler refers in his (1976) paper 'Countertransference and Role-Responsiveness'. Winnicott also speaks of this when he says: 'In the end the patient uses the analyst's failures, often quite small ones, perhaps manoeuvred by the patient . . . and we have to put up with being in a limited context misunderstood. The operative factor is that the patient now hates the analyst for the failure that originally came as an environmental factor, outside the infant's area of omni-potent control, but that is *now* staged in the transference. So in the end we succeed by failing – failing the patient's way. This is a long

241

distance from the simple theory of cure by corrective experience.' (1963b, p. 258).

With regard to the recovered analytic holding I wish to add one further point. Because this was arrived at experientially with the patient, rather than by rule of thumb, it did more than prove a rightness of the classical position concerning no physical contact. 'En route' this had instead acquired a specificity for this patient which, in my opinion, allowed a fuller reliving of this early trauma than might otherwise have been possible.

I shall conclude with a quotation from Bion's (1962b) paper 'A Theory of Thinking'. He says:

> If the infant *feels* [my italics] it is dying it can arouse fears that it is dying in the mother. A well-balanced mother can accept these and respond therapeutically: that is to say in a manner that makes the infant feel it is receiving its frightened personality back again but in a form that it can tolerate – the fears are manageable by the infant personality. If the mother cannot tolerate these projections the infant is reduced to continued projective identification carried out with increasing force and frequence.
>
> (pp. 114f)

Bion continues:

> Normal development follows if the relationship between infant and breast permits the infant to project a feeling, say, that it is dying into the mother and to reintroject it after its sojourn in the breast has made it tolerable to the infant psyche. If the projection is not accepted by the mother the infant feels that its feeling that it is dying is stripped of such meaning as it has. It therefore reintrojects, not a fear of dying made tolerable, but a nameless dread.
>
> (p. 116)

I know that Bion is here describing an infant's relationship to the breast. Nevertheless, I believe that a similar process, at a later developmental stage, is illustrated in the clinical sequence I have described. I consider that it was my readiness to preserve the restored psychoanalytical holding, in the face of considerable pressures upon me to relinquish it, which eventually enabled my patient to receive her own frightened personality back again in a form that she could tolerate. Had I resorted to the physical holding that she demanded, the central

242

trauma would have remained frozen, and could have been regarded as perhaps for ever unmanageable. The patient would then have reintrojected, not a fear of dying made tolerable, but instead a nameless dread.

Notes

1   'Falling for ever' is referred to by Winnicott as one of the 'unthinkable anxieties' along with 'going to pieces', 'having no relationship to the body' and 'having no orientation' (1962, p. 58).
2   At the time I was thinking that this offer of the possibility of holding my hand might, in Eissler's (1953) terms, be a permissible 'parameter'.
3   I now understand this in terms of the psychic immediacy of the transference experience.

19

PROBLEMS OF MANAGEMENT
IN THE ANALYSIS OF A
HALLUCINATING HYSTERIC

Harold Stewart

It is not often that one has the opportunity of analysing a patient who fights with a 'ghost' during the course of treatment, and so I thought the case merited clinical discussion. I shall have little to say about the theoretical aspects of hallucinatory phenomena, but there are grounds for a discussion about various parameters that I used during the analysis which I think were necessary to sustain the analysis and bring it to a fairly successful conclusion.

Elizabeth Zetzel in her paper 'The So-called Good Hysteric' (1968), which mainly concerns women patients, made a useful classification of hysterical patients into four grades according to their psychopathology and prospects of analysability. My patient would, I think, fall somewhere between her third and fourth grades and I shall briefly delineate what these grades represent. To quote:

> Third, there are women with an underlying depressive character structure who frequently manifest hysterical symptomatology to a degree which disguises their deeper pathology. Fourth, there are women whose manifest hysterical symptomatology proves to be pseudo-Oedipal and pseudo-genital. Such patients seldom meet the most important criteria for analysability.

She describes the fourth group as follows:

However, while their symptoms may present a facade which looks genital, they prove in treatment to be incapable of recognizing a genuine triangular situation. For them, as for Oedipus himself, the parent of the same sex has not remained a real object in any meaningful way. Such patients all too readily express intense sexualized transference phantasies. They tend, however, to regard such phantasies as potential areas of realistic gratification. They are genuinely incapable of the meaningful distinction between external and internal reality which is a prerequisite for the establishment of a therapeutic alliance and the emergence of an analysable transference neurosis.

My patient was not quite as ill as this and was, perhaps, also not a typical hysteric since severe depressions were one of her presenting symptoms. A panel discussion on hysteria in Paris (Laplanche, 1974) showed the difficulties in defining the hysterical character, when compared say to the obsessional, and I do not wish to enter into that discussion here. I will, therefore, arbitrarily label her as a hysterical depressive character and proceed to describe her and the relevant aspects of the analysis which has lasted now for seven years.

She was referred to me by a colleague working in a hospital to whom a physician, on realizing that my patient might have some emotional disturbances to account for the recurrent fevers which had been present over a four-year period, had referred her. She was 29 years old, looked rather wild and scruffy, wore torn jeans, and although she complained of depressions which had started with her first sexual experience ten years previously, did not have the typical depressive *facies*. During these depressions, she said she felt split in two, one part of herself wanting to be bad, in fact, turned out to be almost a compulsion. She felt unloved and unwanted by everyone including her family, and was unable to involve herself in any real way with anyone. She had obtained a good degree in sociology but was now working in a situation far below her capabilities. She was having an affair with a married man, was sexually subservient to him, was frigid and felt vaguely guilty about sex. There was little sense of identity or self-esteem. At the second session, she told me she wanted to be a man, that she felt that she was like a man and was a compulsive clitoral masturbator. This masturbation was experienced as if she was masturbating a penis that felt real, even though she knew that she did not possess one in reality, and she felt herself to be a man attacking a young child.

Her attitude towards her father, a successful professional man, was of scorn and contempt for his feebleness in the family circle, and she was frightened to some extent of her mother, who apparently held the family together, but who, in the patient's childhood, had shown uncontrollable tempers towards her children, doing them physical violence and then complaining to the children that they had hurt her by making her be violent towards them. She had a sister two years older than herself and two brothers, two and eight years younger, none of whom she really got on with. She had a delusional idea that her father was not her actual father but that she had someone called her 'real father', whom she had seen only once when she was five years old. This was by a canal near her home when she was out walking and he was described as a tall, dark man wearing an overcoat which, however, was buttoned-up in the female fashion. Her actual father had been in the Forces since her birth in 1939 and had only occasionally been home until his demobilization in 1946. At about this time she also thought she remembered her father's batman, her father being an officer, exposing himself or doing something to her when he was staying in her parents' home.

The only pleasurable experiences that she remembered from childhood were of her maternal grandmother who stayed with them during the war. She had been a kind, gentle, motherly woman, the only sane adult of the family and her departure at the end of the war, when her father returned, was a great loss to the patient. However, just to complicate matters, this grandmother used to see ghosts that no-one else saw, but as these ghosts were benevolent by nature they were not seen as frightening experiences.

The early stages of analysis were characterized by a careful and suspicious attitude towards me while she talked and expanded on her themes, but interspersed were runs of sessions when she would become mocking, provocative, denigrating towards me and the analysis and anything I might say was twisted in these ways against me. These attacks of her being bad ended by her saying she was sorry about them and hoped she had not hurt me. The attacks were based on her father's attitudes and behaviour towards her since childhood, as he had constantly mocked, undermined or ignored anything constructive that she had tried to do. Her saying she was sorry was more placatory than genuine. Her mother's attacks were rather different and I shall now come to these.

After this initial gentle testing of me, the situation changed and I was faced with a difficult technical problem. For much of the time she wanted to be like a baby, to be with me or inside me, and hated the ends of sessions and weekend breaks. The problem arose from the fact that on occasions she would impulsively rush off the couch during a session and try to overpower me in a physical struggle, principally in order to find out, by feeling with her hand, whether I had an erection or not. At first I could stop her with verbal interpretations but these soon became useless and I had to decide what to do. This uselessness at times of verbal interpretations is a phenomenon well recognized by all psychoanalysts who deal with very disturbed patients. I could have used threats by telling her that if she continued with this behaviour, I would have no alternative but to stop treatment, and possibly this threat might have worked. But I suspected that because of the very unrealistic nature of her desires, her behaviour was more compulsive than impulsive. Furthermore, I knew that she was the sort of person who, if prohibited from doing something, would immediately have to do it in order to see if the prohibitor meant what he said, and this would have meant the end of the analysis. I therefore adopted a different course, which was my first parameter, but which depended on a specific factor. This was that, physically, I was bigger and stronger than she, and hence I could physically prevent her from finding out what she wanted to know. This meant physical struggles with the patient and I was concerned that this might then become a form of instinctual gratification for her with the danger of an addiction to an actual physical surrender to me becoming part of the analysis for her. I also had to examine my own countertransference concerning close physical contact with a female patient, but I decided that this was not the motivation of my decision. I wondered whether, if I were smaller, her acting out would not have occurred, but I doubt it because of the compulsive nature of her actions.

The result of doing this was very satisfactory for the course of the analysis. Over a period of months, instead of her becoming addicted to this behaviour, it slowly decreased in frequency as she discovered that I and not she had control of the situation, that I was being the sane, responsible person in the situation – perhaps like her grandmother – and she was gradually able to introject me as a sane control who did not punish or denigrate her or make her feel terribly guilty about her activities. In the analysis of her acting out activities that is essential if parameters are used, it became clear that I was regarded

247

as a phallic mother or a combined-parent figure and she was attempting to try to differentiate the sexes by the presence or absence of the penis. She herself was also the phallic mother, violent and uncontrollable, and I, the helpless child-victim of her childhood experiences. I was also the narcissistic extension of herself, the phallic mother to do with as she pleased, with my penis being her penis. She was also envying and wishing to damage my penis, particularly its symbolic use as a penetrating analytic organ, since her father always thought of himself as intellectually superior to her. Last, but not least, she also wished to see if, as a woman, she was arousing and conquering me sexually.

Gradually she became intensely dependent but ambivalent towards me, confused, empty and depressed and was now unable to work at her job. She dragged herself to her sessions and for the rest of the day did little but stay in her room. Her parents, who lived in a provincial town, were paying for her analytic fees and she existed on sickness and social security benefits.

She now started writing letters to me to keep in contact over weekends and holidays and these were indicative of her state of mind. I quote from one letter:

Dear Darling Dr Harold, I love you, I adore you, I worship you, and I cannot bear to be away from you. I hate you for arousing such feelings in me and not giving them any real outlet . . . Take me back to your womb. I want to experience the world from inside you. I cannot exist separated from you . . . Take off all your clothes. Show me that you have a penis. Show me that you can erect. I cannot bear it if you don't want me . . . Go back to the devil you sprang from. Stop torturing me. Take your claws out of my body. Take your pick and shovel from my mind. You are plunging me into chaos. I want my hatred to worry you, to provoke in you the same degree of anxiety that I have to cope with. I hate your placid, self-sufficient manner. I think you are the most undesirable, unattractive, unsexy, uneverything object I have ever seen. I want to rip your clothes off. I want to whip you till the thickness of the lash is doubled by the particles of your flesh and blood tumbles from it like a waterfall.

Other letters were quite incoherent and unreadable. She was afraid of madness and of driving others mad. She was keeping contact with me for the whole week by means of letters as well as sessions and was fearful that this constant contact and dependence would drive us mad. But at least the contact was now verbal and no longer physical and I believe she was now experiencing me not only as the phallic mother but also as her phantasy 'real father'; you will recall the feminine aspect of him in the way the overcoat was buttoned-up.

It was about a month before the Easter break of the third year of analysis that I became very concerned about her. After a Friday session, I developed the strong feeling that she might conceivably attempt to kill herself to escape from her torment and the coming weekend and Easter break, and I decided to act on my countertransference feeling. I telephoned her to suggest that if she felt she could not cope with the weekend she could telephone me if she so wanted to. She thanked me, did not telephone and for the next week was more cheerful, presumably as a result of my display of concern about her. However, the outcome was the introduction into the analysis of a new form of communication that needed to be dealt with.

She came to the session with a packet containing some drawings. She placed the packet on my desk, left it unopened, and showed every sign of severe anxiety. She sat on the couch and told me she had done the drawings over the weekend and that she wanted me to see them. Yet at the same time she was quite terrified of their possible effect on me and did not want me to look at them then. Towards the end of the session she was fairly silent, rather hostile and anxious about me, saying she felt a looming black shape in the room. She was terrified about being in the room with the drawings which I had left still in their packet on my desk. She could not bear the anxiety and, most unusually for her, left fifteen minutes early; usually she did not want to leave. At the next session, however, she felt more confident and was now prepared to look at them and discuss them with me.

The drawings were of three distinct types. The first was of separate discrete drawings done in charcoal, several to a sheet, the drawings varying from simple representations of objects to a more complex design of objects. The second type was a sheet covered completely with a highly organized complex design, particularly of faces, done in black and white with a felt pen. The outlines within the design were quite sharp. The third type was also a complex design covering the sheet but the outlines were less clear, there were no recognizable objects and, most significantly, the outlines were in colour. It was these last drawings that were so very frightening to her, particularly one in black and red which she described as showing her obscenity and violence. It is perhaps to be expected that colour and indeterminate shapes would be the vehicle for the expression of a person's primitive aggressive sexual phantasies, rather than clearcut black and white drawings.

Her initial terror of my response concerned what I might think of her having such phantasies and at the same time she must have felt that she had projected the blackness of the aggression in the form of the looming black shape into my room and so made it unsafe, but the reality of my normal response to her had allowed her to distinguish the reality of me and my room from her projections.

These sort of pictures continued to be brought along to sessions and my problem was of knowing how to deal with them. Because of the similarity of the styles, I had realized from the first that the patient had probably read Marion Milner's (1969) book *The Hands of the Living God* and this she confirmed. This was probably another reason why the coloured pictures were so frightening to her, since they had not been copied from Milner's patient's style. But I also realized that I could never understand or interpret her drawings as Marion Milner did, as I do not possess her sort of artistic creativity, intuition and insight for such use in the analytic situation. So I had to treat them like dreams, asking for her associations to the drawings and attempting to link them with her past and with the transference in the usual manner. But I also did not show an overinterest in them since I thought that if I did, my patient would most probably flood me with drawings. In the event she drew until the Easter break and after that almost dried up pictorially. It is of some interest that she later went to art classes for the first time in her life and has proved to have a good deal of talent, a good example of a removal of an inhibition.

The drawings were concerned with problems of separation together with her sexual and sadistic phantasies on almost every libidinal level or type of object–relationship. Perhaps the most important aspects were her fear of the nature of her vagina, which was shown as having teeth or a beak, and fears of vaginal orgasm, as opposed to clitoral orgasm. The vaginal orgasm was seen as destructive not only to the erect penis of her partner, but also to the penis which she felt was hidden away inside her and only came out when she felt sexually excited and frustrated in her near-delusional phantasy. She had experienced puberty as castrating, as it meant that a real adult male penis had not developed at that time and hence if she now properly experienced her vagina, this would be the final blow to her desires to possess a penis of her own. The main threat to this blow was the

250

analysis and the emergence of her femininity. She now had intercourse with a man, had no orgasm, but for the first time realized the terror of her vagina being the way it was in her drawings.

Her last picture was a complete coloured mess on the paper and it was done just before a holiday break. This came after one of her mocking, denigrating sessions and she described the picture as a smearing of shit all over my walls. This followed reading an account of the treatment of a woman called Mary Barnes. It could be shown to her that her behaviour had represented this shit-smearing over my insides to destroy everything inside me, including the potential babies I might return with after the break, and also to damage me for abandoning her and leaving her to hold her mad baby inside which she saw as empty and worthless. A dream also connected this with feelings of her abandonment by her mother when she, the patient, had been hospitalized for a fortnight when she was three years old, and for being abandoned when she had started going to school.

We have now arrived at the time when her hallucinations began, in the third year of analysis, during the summer break. I received a letter from her during the holiday when she was motoring in Europe – although she was unable to work, she could still drive. I shall quote the relevant passages from it:

This holiday is proving disastrous. I have been attacked by a ghost, abandoned by the bloke I went with, and raped by a madman. I was staying in a youth hostel when I was assaulted in the night by an ancient Spanish roué, dressed in clothes from the Regency period, perhaps. I struggled with him for what seemed ages, finally fighting him off. Then I put my hand straight through him and realized he was a ghost. Up till then I had been convinced he was real. Then I was aware of his decaying body rotting away beside me on the bed, and I sat at the end of the bed frozen with horror for about an hour. After a very long time, it dawned on me that perhaps it wasn't a real ghost but a hallucination. I didn't know what alternative was the worst, but I began semi-automatically to analyse my reasons for producing such a vicious ghost. Anger seemed to be predominant in me. I was angry with the fellow I went with because he's a lazy, insensitive, self-satisfied bastard and there was no real contact between us. But I think I pushed onto him my angry transference feelings, also my sexual feelings, to a lesser extent.

It seems to me that her analysis of the situation is essentially correct in relating the hallucination to her experience of me although I do not think I am quite as bad as all that, but I think' her feelings were of murder and fear of murder, rather than anger, as shown by her horror of the decaying, rotting body. This is one of the points made by Bion (1958) in his paper 'On Hallucination', where he quotes Freud to the effect that the patient's state of mind and feeling is under the sway of the pleasure principle, and in that phase of development the patient's actions are not directed towards a change in the environment but are intended to unburden the psychic apparatus of accretions of stimuli. My patient seemed to be doing this as well as trying to change the environment in that she did fight with her hallucination.

I expect I could be phantasized as an ancient Spanish roué, and the fight she was having could also reflect her actual experiences of her physical struggles with me, but her mention of the Regency period clothes is very significant. She comes from one of the English towns that are graced by the Regency style and atmosphere and there seems little doubt that this ancient roué also contains the reference to her father and her childhood. This well fits in with Freud's view, mentioned in 'Constructions in Analysis' (1937d), that this is method in madness, and it is the fragments of historical truth which give the compulsive belief in delusions and hallucinations its strength, since it derives from infantile sources. I also think that this mixture of present and past experience that is contained within the hallucination is a good example of a compromise symptom.

Two further incidents occurred on this holiday which confirmed the feelings of anxiety concerning suicide that I had had, by her flirting with death in a near-suicidal way. She went swimming in the sea but so far out in a heavy current that she had to be saved by local fishermen while clinging to some rocks. After this she drove back about a thousand miles across Europe with the rubber on her tyres so worn that the canvas was exposed. These actions represent an extreme challenge to death and also help to confirm my method of dealing with her challenging acting out in the early stages of the analysis.

On her return she had intense desires for intercourse with me and, when thwarted, masturbated continuously. She then saw another ghost in her bedroom, and this was a little man three feet tall with fair hair and blue eyes who carried a rope and a bucket. She had a great fear on seeing it but then said to herself that it was a ghost and it disappeared. Apparently it resembled her younger brother, who was born when she was eight years old. She then had more mocking, denigrating sessions and behaved badly to her parents while at their home. I was able to show her that the attacks on me followed the separations of the holiday and my refusal to have intercourse with her, and also displayed the envy of her mother for having the younger brother. The three-foot-high ghost probably represented the third year of her analysis and was her baby in the form of a hallucination. The attacks on her parents were to destroy their intercourse and happiness and also to destroy her own treatment, since they were paying for it, out of guilt for her attacks and also to show what a useless analyst I was. At the next session she told me she realized the correctness of this and then disclosed her phantasy of having two babies inside her, one a mocking, green, envious baby and the other a pale, almost lifeless baby that she had to keep starved. This one was the sensitive, feminine baby that could easily be hurt. The compulsive, angry, envious penis phantasies came from the first baby and her problem was that the more loving she felt, the more she hated the separations from me and so this second baby had to be kept starved of love although she desperately desired it. This corresponds with Bion's views on hallucinations.

At the session after this she told me that she had seen her 'real father' again for the first time since childhood and he had said some-thing to her but she didn't know what. She realized she had been hallucinating, but following this experience she felt that her mind had altered and somehow come together for the better, and she now started to make herself a dress. This was the first breakthrough of her feminine self. This 'real father' was probably me representing some good split-off infantile aspect of her actual father for whom she had always longed.

At the next session she told me of having had a hallucination of a large penis on herself, then she became her mocking, biting, attacking self, but at the end of the session wanted to kiss me better. She then saw the film *The Devils*, which is about the nuns of Loudon, and later that evening had a persistent vision of her genitals rotting away. On putting her hand there, she felt a large hole where they had rotted away and was terrified. She then realized that this was another hallucination, a negative hallucination this time, and was then able to feel her genitals. She wanted to know if she was going mad and I said that for that moment she had been mad. She broke down and cried, but then linked her hallucination with the hysterical mad nun

253

in the film who had licked the blood of her beloved priest's wounds after his torture, putting her tongue into them. I linked up her torturing treatment of me in the previous sessions with the priest's torture and of her intense desire to remove the source of her sexual desires by hallucinating away her genitals or to give herself the penis instead. She accepted this and told me that I tormented her with desire but did not gratify her, and so she tortured me in return but was then afraid of driving me away. She was also tortured by humiliation at her failure to seduce me, but she then became afraid that she would hallucinate me away completely and that she would not be able to see or hear me and then she would be quite mad. This so bothered her that she gave my telephone number to her sister in case this might occur. She also broke down in tears at her art class. These events were important since, for the first time, she was really acknowledging to herself and to others that she was ill.

She now had a significant dream of my wife being pregnant and her feeling left out. Her associations were to a period of her childhood when her father had recently returned from the Forces; her parents had then quarrelled a lot and temporarily separated into different bedrooms, her father's being next to hers. She had then been shattered when her younger brother had been born when she was eight years old. This dream was soon followed by a pregnancy phantasy where she felt very heavy and wanted to urinate excessively. Apart from the transference aspects, she came out with the idea that her father had wanted to kill her when she was two years old. This was the time when her first brother was born and the conclusion must be that she had wanted to kill her father when the brother had been born. Thus her murderous feelings of jealousy and abandonment by her father at the birth of both brothers, together with desires for their disappearance, came out more fully into the open. By now she was wearing the new dresses that she had made, used cosmetics and perfume and in every way was more feminine. After eighteen months off work, she was now able to return and, of equal importance, she was able to allow herself to regress much further during her sessions since she was developing the confidence that at the end of the session she would reintegrate and not stay in a regressed chaotic state. She was developing a real sense of self.

By this time she had had several types of hallucinating experience and we began to recognize that there were various levels of this experience. The first was in recognizing that she could see things around her, but knew all the time that the experiences were not real and came from her imagination. The second was a state where she was not sure if the experiences were real or not, which made her feel afraid and so she switched her mind off in case they did become real.

The third state was where things came on her very suddenly out of the blue with the conviction of reality and it took some time before she was able to recognize that these experiences were not real. This state was usually preceded by feelings of anxiety, and she could not say why she should feel anxious. In my view the third state contains truly dynamic unconscious experience-phantasies coming from the id and the anxiety preceding their emergence is probably a subliminal awareness of them by the deeper layers of the ego. In a previous paper (Stewart, 1966) I have discussed hallucinations in terms of ego-splitting. Since they represent instinctual and affective state, the anxiety on the ego's part is hardly surprising when the danger of their becoming conscious arises. The first state, when she is aware of their unreality from the start, must represent preconscious ego phantasies, and the second state a borderline area between the first and third states.

So far, the third state had always occurred outside the sessions and I pointed out that she was keeping these experiences in their immediacy away from me. The effect of this statement was to make her feel I was persecuting her by trying to drive her mad in the sessions by asking her to hallucinate. She felt I was not interested in her as a person but only as an object from which I could learn about mental functioning – a statement with some truth in it. She also felt that she could now triumph over me by keeping me frustrated in not producing these phenomena. Yet, at the same time she knew and acknowledged that I was right and that the chances were that she would not be driven mad by them. But I also knew that in showing this interest in her hallucinating states, it was quite on the cards that she would produce them for me in abundance in typical hysterical fashion. In the event, I do not think she did, but before getting on to them, another phenomenon turned up which was in fact rather similar to a proper hallucination.

While talking on the couch, she would suddenly shout out a word or phrase that could have had meaning in the context of the rest of what she was saying, yet by its nature seemed to come from another layer of the mind as an intrusion of a rather explosive nature. It often contained a parapraxis that altered the sense of what she was meaning to say. For example, during the session when she felt I was trying to drive her mad by suggesting she bring her hallucinations into the consulting room, she felt confused with the knowledge that I was also the person who was trying to help her and had enabled her to return to work. She felt she loved me, wanted to put her arms around me, wanted me to put my penis inside her, and then shouted, 'Perhaps the penis is too exciting for you.' She then said that she had been going to say quietly, 'The penis is too exciting for me.' The problem here was to know (a) whether she was talking to herself and admonishing herself as though she were two people, like Lewis Carroll's Alice in Wonderland, or (b) whether she was telling me that I, the analyst, could not cope with the excitement that I might have in my penis and so was perhaps driving her mad by overstimulating her and so creating confusion, or (c) whether both were correct. Since she started the next session by telling me I was analysing myself, having just seen my new copy of Kohut's *Analysis of the Self* (1971) and also telling me that I was writing notes to myself, on seeing a scrap of paper with writing on it on my desk, it seemed that the notion that I could not cope with the excitement in my penis was correct. But when she next said that last night she thought that I was inside her and that she was me, it seemed that the possibility of the penis being too exciting for her might also be correct and that she dealt with the exciting penis by incorporating and identifying with it. So in analysing her, I was also analysing myself. Furthermore, 'you' and 'me' could represent projected and introjected objects from the past. This may illustrate some of the problems involved in interpretation and under-standing and the potential overdetermination of these statements.

I was seeing her in the early evenings and it being winter, it was dark outside and she now wanted to have only one light on in the consulting room so that it was rather dim and peaceful. She would go into a reverie-like state, like a child in a nursery with the dim light, and I had to remain very still in my chair, since any undue movement on my part would disturb her reverie and also make her feel, in a near-delusional way, that I was undoing my trousers or masturbating and this frightened her. She had the phantasy of being a small child sitting on my knee and of being bounced up and down on it by me, exciting her until she wet my trousers. She wanted to suck my penis, my breast or her thumb, and had an intense desire to masturbate. She then suddenly jerked round, felt that I was hitting her and shouted that she mustn't do that. This seemed to refer either to her wetting with excitement or to her desires to masturbate. At the next session she felt she was being driven mad by her desires to urinate and to masturbate and wanted to cut off my hands. She also had the compulsive phantasy that I had undone trousers and was playing with my penis. She then jerked round, shouting, 'You shouldn't do things like that.' She then thought that she had meant to say, 'say things like that', instead of 'do things like that', which again contains the problem of who the 'you' is, but she went on quickly. She covered herself with her coat, which had been on the couch, and held her genitals, saying, I must masturbate. She then felt horrified at this action of hers. I moved slightly in my chair and she screamed, 'I don't know what I'm so frightened of.' I did not know whether she was afraid she might have excited me sexually and that I might assault her sexually in some way, since there had been so many references during the analysis to a real or phantasied traumatic sexual assault on her as a child; or whether she was having the phantasy that she was me, or I her, and that she was secretly masturbating in phantasy and controlling me and that my punishment was towards this aspect of her masturbation rather than a straightforward Oedipal punishment. It was even more complicated since I did not know whether the penis was father's or mother's, although I strongly suspect the latter since mother was felt to possess everything.

The next session was devoted to her playing a very complex game with various objects in my room, having them stand for various part-objects or aspects of mother, father, analyst or herself. It was like watching a child playing with its toys. A most important object was my ashtray, which is a container on a tall column, kept by the side of the couch for the use of patients, and this stood for the phantasy penis. It emerged that her possession of this was essential to prevent the confusion in her mind of all the other parts moving around and splitting. She made a slip about her being the 'baby analyst', which I think referred to her feeling of not being the adult analyst, who has the penis with its penetrating and understanding qualities to bring things together, but only a baby amateur analyst; but I also think it referred to her feeling of having had to try to understand the confusing aspects of her family from an early age and to be the father, who was absent and later devalued.

This was followed at the next session by her telling me that the batman, her father's army valet, always used to wash his hands. She then placed her hand on her genitals and told me she could notice a strong smell of soap in the room. I could not smell anything myself, but she then bit her hand which, she screamed, was 'his soapy hand'. Here was the first hallucination, an olfactory one, during the session and it was associated with a fairly obvious identification with this person, concerning the hand and the genitals and linked with a

257

masturbatory action. I must confess that I could not clearly see the transference aspect unless this was an attempt to wash away the guilt she experienced from having tried to possess my analytic penis for herself only and using me as her batman. A great deal of the analysis concerned her desire to be a man, and for her to possess the penis represented a defence against internal chaos, depression and emptiness. On one occasion when I collected her from the waiting room, she hallucinated that my trousers were undone and my penis was showing, but her associations were to the fact that she had seen my trousers in a different colour from the one they were and that this colour corresponded to her mother's trousers. This led her on to realizing that she also experienced me as a mother who was false and phoney, untrustworthy and interested only in money and sex. I had always felt quite sure that one aspect of her emphasis on the penis and its possession was a defence against her vaginal desires and phantasies with the jealous rivalries and envies of her mother's vagina and womb at both Oedipal and pre-Oedipal levels, and as I previously mentioned, in the transference I was usually either a phallic mother or the phantasy 'real father' with his feminine overcoat, making it a bisexual transference figure. Yet at the same time, the hallucinations and verbal interruptions continued to suggest early traumatic assault by a man, not by her violent mother, and of her having witnessed parental intercourse. I had the classical difficulty of not knowing if I was dealing with actual traumatic experience or with unconscious phantasy. In one session she shouted, 'No, don't,' and then had the phantasy of a large man bending over her and her feeling little. She suddenly realized that she had used the same words to the little ghost who had resembled her younger brother but there was now a reversal of sizes, and this realization caused more mind-clearing.

There were other hallucinations but, most interestingly, she revealed a strange practice that she used in her bedroom. She would construct an artificial penis for herself with a stuffed rubber glove tied around her, and also make a female doll-like figure. She would then draw the curtains so that the room was very dim and would then have intercourse with the doll, she being a man and the doll a little girl. At times she would reverse the constructions and make a man and she would be the little girl and the man-doll would have intercourse with her. This was an acting out of her masturbation phantasy. Perhaps the most important aspect of this is the negative one that the two figures were never equal, i.e., man and woman, and this corresponded with her view that, in spite of everything she said, her mother was basically seen as having a worse deal out of life than her father and was always in the inferior position.

She was by now feeling greatly improved, was working hard at her job, cleaning and painting her flat, painting well at art classes and also doing some writing, which she had always wanted to do. She had also found herself a proper boyfriend and he was an interesting choice. He was a large man who suffered from impotence and she treated him on behavioural therapy lines sexually and gave him the sexual potency he had lacked. It was as though she was creating a potent adult penis for herself and at the same time repairing the damage the penis had suffered for which she had felt guilty throughout her analysis. It was just before having intercourse with him on one occasion that she had what she described as a 'devastating hallucin-ation'. It was not of a penis this time, but of a 'violent cunt', twisted and distorted like a Francis Bacon painting, and she now realized how terrified she was and had been of her mother and of her mother's violence which she had experienced as a child, together with the violence that she felt existing in herself and her genitals. The penis phantasy had long been a defence against this 'violent cunt' phantasy and she now in experience realized that I had been right in this assessment from the start. She is now capable of vaginal orgasm, is married to this man and wanting children, knowing she will have her violence towards them under control; and I continue to see her once a week.

I realize that this has been a rather patchy picture of an analysis, but I hope it has illustrated the problems I faced in what many people would describe as an almost unanalysable patient. I believe that without the introduction of the various parameters mentioned, this analysis would not have survived. A word should be said about the sort of parents found in these severe hysterical patients. Brenman, in the Panel on 'Hysteria Today' (see Laplanche, 1974), considered that one of the ingredients specific to the hysterogenic mother is a mother overwhelmed by anxiety and unconsciously conveying to the infant that the infant's anxieties are really catastrophic. My experience has also been that this process has not been unconscious but that the mothers have been both physically violent and unpredictable in reaction to their infants, so that the situation really was catastrophic for the infant. Furthermore, the fathers have usually been absent or disillusioningly disappointing to their infants, leaving both mother and infant to deal with each other without adequate support.

To finish, I would like to quote the nursery rhyme from the beginning of Zetzel's paper. The second and third lines even contain the mechanism of displacement upwards:

> There was a little girl,
> And she had a little curl,
> Right in the middle of her forehead,
> And when she was good,
> She was very, very, good,
> But when she was bad,
> She was horrid.

PART VI

FEMALE SEXUALITY

20

THE CENTRALITY OF SEXUAL
DIFFERENCE IN FREUD

The work of Gregorio Kohon
and Juliet Mitchell

Megan Virtue

At times it is argued that hysteria has vanished from the clinical stage in the twenty-first century. Interest in hysteria is thereby confined to historians of psychoanalysis, or to feminist theorists who look back to the use of the hysteria diagnosis to socially control women in the nineteenth century. Contemporary psychotherapists have other diagnoses to employ, such as borderline and narcissistic disorders.

In the paper included in this collection, originally published in the *International Journal of Psychoanalysis*, Kohon asks, 'Is hysteria really a thing of the past?' His answer is clear:

> The liberation of sexual morality, the loss of a certain 'innocence' in women, the change in the 'feminine ideal', the social acceptance of sexuality, would all have been contributory factors in the disappearance of hysteria as such. There is a certain theoretical simplicity behind all of this which considers the presence of a neurotic conflict as a conflict about present sexual impulses.
>
> (Kohon, p. 280 herein)

Kohon then proceeds to enumerate a series of important contemporary changes that have taken place in the theory of psychoanalysis.

These include the exclusion of sexuality from theoretical and clinical considerations in the aetiology of the neuroses (Fairbairn, 1941); the abandoning of the concept of the Oedipus complex as 'the model of sexuality and meaning for the subject'; the consideration of the differentiation of sexes as something 'natural' and 'given'; the theoretical dismissal of the concept of penis envy; the naturalism present in the theoretical stress on the processes of identification with either member of the parental couple; and the emphasis on the threat of the loss of the mother, at the expense of ignoring the presence (or absence) of the father. He concludes that, given these theoretical and ideological changes, the theory may be looking for something else in the patients seen by psychoanalysts, and, as a consequence, clinicians also find something else.

In 2000, Mitchell was still rightly asking, 'where are the hysterics?' She adds yet another important item to Kohon's list: the diagnosis of hysteria might have disappeared with the inauguration of *psychosomatics*, a new diagnostic category. In fact, complaints of the body, the causes of which appeared to be mysterious or unknown, broadly fell under the umbrella of psychosomatic illnesses, currently designated by the acronym MUS: 'Medically Unexplained Symptoms'.

The following two papers on female sexuality, both first published in 1984, take hysteria as their subject. The background to these papers is a panel debate that had taken place eleven years earlier, in Paris, at the 28th IPA Congress on *Transference and Hysteria Today* (Laplanche, 1974). The members of the panel discussing the place of hysteria in psychoanalysis were David Beres, Alfredo Namnum, Eric Brenman and André Green; leading the discussion were Serge Lebovici and Walter Joffe. At the conference, there was a generalized consensus whereby psychoanalysts recognized the necessity of including aggression, as well as the libidinal drive, in the genesis of hysteria. More recently, Mitchell (2000) also remarked upon the need to integrate the destructive drive in understanding hysteria. However, the main theme explored at the congress was whether hysteria continued to exist as a clinical structural entity, or if it was only one of many modes of defence against psychosis, a response to anxieties that are early, psychotic and non-sexual. In his summing up, Laplanche noted that the latter formulation constituted a major shift from Freud's idea of the sexual as fundamental in the aetiology of neurosis; it considered hysteria as secondary and defensive, via a sexualization of conflicts related to survival anxiety. While some participants at the conference confirmed the disappearance of conversion hysteria from their consulting-rooms, Laplanche noted that, in the nineteenth century, hysterics were found in the Salpêtrière hospital; he suggested that in the twentieth century, hysterics might still be found, if not in mental hospitals, then in the wards of neurological hospitals.

Recent publications by neurologists support Laplanche's suggestion made over four decades ago. In 2015, *The Lancet* published an article by Suzanne O'Sullivan, a consultant neurologist and neurophysiologist, highlighting the plight of numbers of patients seen in neurology clinics with 'dissociative' or hysterical seizures (O'Sullivan, 2015). O'Sullivan states the frequency with which such patients present to neurologists and notes that health professionals underestimate the seriousness of the problem. One consequence of the failure to diagnose and treat hysterical seizures is that patients can be unnecessarily exposed to multiple toxic drugs over many years. Although the cause is understood to be psychological, she states that neurologists can only speculate about the mechanisms underlying these conditions. She conveys her astonishment that there has been little improvement in treatment for hysterical patients, underlining this by including as an illustration in her article one of the best-known paintings in the history of medicine, *Une Leçon clinique a la Salpêtrière* – André Brouillet's painting of Charcot and his students examining a hysteric. O'Sullivan appeals for compassion for those afflicted, whose condition, though psychologically generated, is not under their control; undoubtedly, paralysis caused by hysteria is as debilitating as that due to infection or degenerative disease.[1]

The above report indicates that, far from having vanished, hysteria is often present in neurological settings. Terminology may have changed, but hysteria remains to be understood and explained. Against this background, it is fitting and rewarding to explore the influence and on-going relevance of these two papers by Kohon and Mitchell, thirty years after they were included in the first edition of the present book. They are particularly relevant to the handful of psychoanalysts who are working in acute hospital settings, for whom knowledge of hysteria may be helpful to understand and treat certain patients; they are equally important for psychoanalysts in private practice, where hysteria may manifest more in terms of character formation than focal symptoms (Laplanche, 1974).

Kohon and Mitchell's papers read Freud through Lacan's 'return to Freud' – an important re-evaluation and re-interpretation of Freud's original texts, which had great influence, in the first instance, on French psychoanalysis and, more recently, on the rest of the psychoanalytic world. Through their writings, Kohon and Mitchell elaborate Lacan's reading of Freud's theory of female sexuality and sexual difference for an Anglo-Saxon readership. Both papers begin with hysteria as the pathology that enabled Freud to create the theory of psychoanalysis, but which also points to its limits, in what he called the 'bedrock': the repudiation of femininity.

Kohon returns to the classical case history of Dora, showing the move Freud makes from hysteria, understood as a biological condition, to its being seen as a psychic illness, one from which both men and women can suffer, although arguably there is a specific association between hysteria and women. Kohon uses the concept of divalence developed by Enrique Pichon-Rivière (1970, 1971; see also Bleger, 1967b) to posit a hysterical phase – what he calls a *divalent stage* in the development of all women. Stuck in what he describes as her divalence, not being able to choose between her father and her mother, the hysteric becomes unable to decide whether she is a man or a woman (Leclaire, 1971).

Invoking the Freudian tenet that theorizing is intertwined with the vicissitudes of the drive, Mitchell explores hysteria and theories of female sexuality in relation to the construction of psychoanalytic theory itself. Kohon writes that: 'Hysteria is not just a psychiatric diagnosis which would include conversion hysteria, anxiety hysteria etc., but is a human problematic, specifically female, *present in all of us*' (p. 275, italics added).

Both authors stress that hysteria is much more than a psycho-pathology. In fact the papers emphasize the centrality of the Freudian psychoanalytic understanding of sexual difference and the mode of its internalization, highlighting the role of the castration complex in psychic structuring.

Basing their arguments on Lacan's contributions, the authors understand the pivotal role of the castration complex fundamentally as a symbolic passage, during which both boys and girls initially desire the mother. During the phallic phase (Freud, 1923e), the child believes that he or she has the phallus, thus becoming, in phantasy, the object of mother's desire. The castration complex instantiates the prohibition against being the sole object of mother's desire, bringing about the differences between the sexes and the generations. In this way, the boy's Oedipus complex is brought to an end, while the girl's Oedipus complex is inaugurated: she identifies with her mother and transfers her desired object from mother to father. This trajectory shows the complex psychic task for the girl in the change of object from mother to father and demonstrates the asymmetry of the Oedipus complex in boys and girls.

Following Freud's description of the universal castration complex (1923e), there was much resistance to this concept: it was at the centre of the 'Jones–Freud controversy' of the 1920s and 1930s. Mitchell (1982) notes that the change of emphasis away from sexual difference to female sexuality during those debates reflected some of Freud's colleagues' rejection of the castration complex. She attributes this to the rise of object relations theories, with their emphasis on the primary relationship with the mother. In his paper, as already mentioned, Kohon also notes the absence of the father from the Oedipal scene in a psychoanalytic milieu that privileges object relationships. It is perhaps ironic that these two papers on the subject of female sexuality both encourage reconsideration of the castration complex as a valuable heuristic for psychoanalytic understanding.

Despite Freud's later speculations about the more daemonic aspects of human functioning, exemplified in the repetition compulsion as a way of understanding unconscious guilt and masochism (Freud, 1920g), he never turned away from sexuality, considering it crucial for psychic structuring (Freud, 1923b). Mitchell shows how, from the studies on hysteria onwards (Freud, 1895d) until the late unfinished paper on the splitting of the ego (Freud, 1940e), Freud consistently tried to understand the impact of sexual difference on the psyche. This links to an important theme in both papers: the desexualization of psychoanalytic theory. Laplanche already remarked upon this in his report following the 1973 IPA panel on hysteria (Laplanche, 1974), and it has been discussed in subsequent literature (Davies, 2012; Green, 1995, 2000b; Kohon, 1999b; Mitchell, 1996). As stated above, the hysteria panel noted a change in formulations of hysteria from seeing it as an expression of psychosexual conflict to viewing the pathology as a secondary defence covering over psychotic anxieties (Brenman, 1985; Riesenberg-Malcolm, 1996). Through her studies of the male hysterics of the First World War, Mitchell (1996) also critically described this move away from Oedipal explanation towards regression to the early mother–infant relationship. Other authors have also commented on how this move away from 'the sexual breast' to 'the nursing breast' exemplifies the desexualization of psycho-analysis and the tendency to overlook hysteria (Bollas, 2000). This spotlight on the pre-oedipal has had a bearing on psychoanalytic technique, with a greater emphasis being placed on the interpretation of separation anxiety than on castration anxiety (Davies, 2012). Green argues that versions of object relations theory are based on an artificially created bipolarity between drive and object (Green, 2000b), which denies the mother's sexuality and the complexities of the maternal erotics in the primary relationship (Green, 2000a). This also suggests that what is primitive and archaic is prior to sexuality, rather than an early form of sexuality, which brings into focus the difference between pleasure and anxiety (*as dissociated, rather than as forces in conflict*). Kohon and Mitchell's papers are scholarly calls to reconsider sexuality as constitutive of the human psyche and its role in the understanding of psychopathology.

Both papers refer to Freud's eschewing of biological and sociological explanations of sexual difference and his theory of psychosexuality. At the end of 'A Child Is Being Beaten', Freud (1919e) rejected Fliess's biological explanation of sexual difference and Adler's sociological explanation of the masculine protest. Mitchell addresses this in her examination of Kleinian theory, in which, she argues, both biological and sociological influences are privileged by Melanie Klein.

More recently, Mitchell has continued the broad terms of this debate with Judith Butler (Butler, 2015; Mitchell, 2015). Butler holds that gender is socially constructed through performativity. In viewing masculinity and femininity as socially constructed, Butler (1990) does away with the seeming intractability of sexual difference. Mitchell, like Kohon, affirms that whatever changes occur in social processes, psychoanalysis is about unconscious structures: these structures are human features recurring in all societies, which, in turn, construct their own norms regarding masculinity and femininity. Similarly, Kohon argues that, in the light of sexual liberation, knowledge of sex does not necessarily reduce the role of incestuous phantasies in life; it is the *unconscious* repression of these sexual wishes that makes human sexuality human.

Mitchell (2003) has also rethought the distinction between the psychoanalytic concept of *sexual difference* and that of gender. She argues for retaining the concept of sexual difference alongside the concept of gender, which she further elaborates to include sexuality. According to Mitchell, sexual difference implicates subject/object interaction and heterosexuality; in contrast, the concept of gender includes sexual difference but is not *constituted* by it.

In her paper, following Lacan, Mitchell refers to the importance of the notion of *absence* in Freud's theory. It is around absence that sexual difference is symbolized: the absence of the mother, the absence of the penis. The void is where meaning vanishes, like the unknowable navel of the dream (Freud, 1900a), leaving only the chaos of the unconscious. The universal repudiation of femininity, of the space marking the absent penis, and of passivity, Freud saw as the psychic bedrock in men and women, pointing to the limits of psychoanalysis. The absence of the mother and the loss of the penis link separation anxiety to castration anxiety; the earlier anxieties being re-transcribed *après-coup* (Davies, 2012). For Freud it is what will come to occupy the space created by absence that will create psychic structure. Mitchell contrasts the role of absence in Freud's theory with Klein's understanding of infantile phantasies, which are ubiquitous. For Klein, it is the presence of the good/bad breast and, therefore, what the infant has *got* that is transformed by phantasies; the envy of the Kleinian mother is of a mother who is the source of all plenitude and *has* everything.

Both papers exemplify themes that Freud will go on to elaborate after his work on hysteria, including mourning, repetition and splitting. Kohon illustrates the impasse of the hysteric who is suspended between her parents, unable to make a choice. She does not renounce her original objects but, instead, she moves between mother and father, wishing to hold on to both, not allowing for substitutes. Kohon describes how, unable to mourn her objects, the hysteric becomes incapable of investing in a real sexual relationship. Here, Kohon implicitly links the hysteric's failure to mourn with Freud's theory of melancholia (Freud, 1917e), which has also been described in the case of Anna O (Perelberg, 1999). Kohon's elaboration of the hysteric's predicament, repeatedly moving between shifting identifications, illustrates the sterility of the repetition compulsion (Freud, 1920g). Mitchell refers to the subject's solution to the loss of the object (penis) in the form of an expeditious move towards the creation of a fetish. This attempt to cover over the gaping hole draws on Freud's later thinking on splitting (Freud, 1940e). The creation of the fetish, on the model of the delusion and hallucination, connects sexuality and psychosis, the confluence of which Kohon explored in his paper 'Love in a time of Madness' (Kohon, 2005a).

The life and academic history of these particular authors account for their rich theoretical contributions in these papers. Mitchell, with her background in the academy, her scholarly reclaiming of Freudian/ Lacanian psychoanalysis for feminism in *Psychoanalysis and Feminism* (1974), and her 'Introduction' to Lacan (in Mitchell and Rose, 1982), makes Lacan available to British psychoanalysts. Kohon, originally from Argentina, learnt about Lacan's work through Oscar Masotta's teaching and writings and the early translations of Lacan's works in Spanish; he also brings to his published work a familiarity with continental philosophy and theory that is uncommon in Anglo-Saxon settings. He draws from Pichon-Rivière, the Swiss-Argentine psychoanalyst who exercised great influence in South-America. Kohon modifies the use of Pichon-Rivière's concept of 'divalence', offering a description of a 'divalent stage', which marks the di-phasic predicament of the hysteric. These authors' papers are important contributions to on-going discussions of sexuality in the British Society.

Discussion and elaboration of hysteria and sexuality in the British Psychoanalytical Society

Following the 1920s and 1930s, psychoanalysts focused on the earliest phases of life; their theorizing increasingly addressed borderline and narcissistic pathologies, and the category of psychosomatics rose to prominence; in the wake of this, hysteria went backstage. The two papers on female sexuality included in this section formed part of a groundswell of reawakened interest in hysteria by British psychoanalysts from across the traditions. Published works on hysteria include those by Brenman (1985), Stewart (pp. 244–260 herein), Riesenberg-Malcolm (1996), Mitchell (1996, 2000), Perelberg (1997, 1999), Britton (1999, 2003, 2005), Kohon (1999b) and Bollas (2000).

As mentioned above, in the 1920s and 1930s there was the 'Jones–Freud controversy' about female sexuality, in which Sigmund Freud, Melanie Klein, Ernest Jones and others participated. Jones questioned and criticized Freud's version of the genesis and structure of the superego and the nature of the feminine castration complex. Influenced by Melanie Klein, Karen Horney and other colleagues from Berlin, Jones argued for the existence of a 'primary femininity' as an alternative to the idea of penis envy – an envy that would arise, according to these authors, as a defensive formation. The framing of this debate, according to Mitchell (1982), was an attempt early on to move away from the concept of castration anxiety.

It is worth quoting Freud at length:

I object to all of you (Horney, Jones, Rado, etc.) to the extent that you do not distinguish more clearly and cleanly between what is psychic and what is biological, that you try to establish a neat parallelism between the two and that you, motivated by such intent, unthinkingly construe psychic facts which are unprovable and that you, in the process of doing so, must declare as reactive or regressive much that without doubt is primary. Of course, these reproaches must remain obscure. In addition, I would only like to emphasize that we must keep psychoanalysis separate from biology just as we have kept it separate from anatomy and physiology . . .

(Freud, letter to Carl Müller-Braunschweig, 1935)

The 'Jones–Freud controversy' remained unresolved. The Controversial Discussions of the 1940s, which were, in part, a consequence of the earlier debate in the 1920s and 1930s, were focused nevertheless on the question of phantasy, rather than on sexuality. The debate on female sexuality was not revived in Britain for a while, even in the wake of the sexual revolution of the 1960s, unlike in America, where it was discussed again. Influenced by the earlier debate, attention in Britain had largely become directed towards separation anxiety in the context of early psychic life (Birksted-Breen, 2005), without reference to the relevance of sexuality in the earliest relationship of mother and infant.

The shift in focus towards earliest mental life led to the idea that British psychoanalysts are not very interested in sexuality (Budd, 2001). This observation appears accurate, especially when compared with French psychoanalysts, but it is not representative of all British analysts. Renewed attention to hysteria encouraged a plurality of theorization, some of which emphasized underlying psychotic, *non-sexual* anxieties (Brenman, 1985; Riesenberg-Malcolm, 1996). Other authors, in contrast, referred to phantasies of parental sexuality (Britton, 1999). In his paper on female sexuality (1931b), Freud considered the early phase of intense attachment of the girl to her mother as being 'especially intimately related to the aetiology of hysteria' (Freud, 1931b, p. 227). He commented that this was not surprising, as the phase and the neurosis are characteristically feminine. In 1997, a book was published edited by two British analysts from the Independent and Contemporary Freudian traditions, entitled *Female Experience: Three Generations of British Women Psychoanalysts on Work with Women* (Raphael-Leff and Perelberg, 1997); it was republished in 2008 to include the fourth generation. Perelberg (1997) described bodily symptoms experienced by women in analysis with women, hysterical 'solutions' to conflicts of separation from their mothers. At the same time, the author also referred to the structuring

271

effects of castration, clearly drawing on Freud's ideas on sexuality (Raphael-Leff and Perelberg, 1997).

Psychoanalysts from within the Contemporary Freudian tradition have continued to address the role of infantile sexuality in psychic structuring (Perelberg, 2009). Working within a developmental model, analysts, including Eglé and Moses Laufer, Mervin Glasser, Clifford York, Donald Campbell, Peter Fonagy, Mary Target, Rosine Perelberg, Rosemary Davies, and Joan Schachter, have written on sexuality, perversion and the role of the father. Some of this work has been generated in clinical institutions, including the Portman Clinic (M. Glasser, D. Campbell), the Brent Adolescent Centre (E. and M. Laufer), and the Anna Freud Centre (Rose Edgecumbe, Marion Burgner, C. York, P. Fonagy, M. Target). As part of the Anna Freud Young Adults Research Group, analysts treated patients for whom difficulties related to sexuality and, in the case of those analysts who were working at the Portman Clinic, sexual perversions, were prominent. These and other authors produced a considerable volume of psychoanalytic literature, generating theoretical ideas, as well developing techniques for treating clinical problems. Some of the theory that was developed was naturally influenced by the British Society milieu. For example, Glasser's (1979, 1985) concept of the core complex, which he developed while working with perverse patients, addresses the fusional matrix of the mother-and-infant relationship and the vicissitudes of early separation; the role of castration anxiety was thereby somewhat overshadowed by an emphasis on the pre-genital. In her paper on *après-coup*, Perelberg (2006) discusses the reworking of earlier memories following later psychic developments. *Après-coup* removes the dichotomization of separation anxiety/castration anxiety as the earliest anxieties are refracted in the light of later ones. In restating the relevance of castration anxiety, Kohon and Mitchell's papers on female sexuality were a timely and valuable contribution to discussions of sexuality in Britain; they have contributed to an understanding of Lacan's view of desire, which keeps the focus on the psychic construction of subjectivity, rather than on biological determinants.

Sexuality has continued to be discussed through interest in French psychoanalysis and via international meetings with French colleagues. For two decades, a group of analysts from France and Great Britain has met annually for clinical discussions, while other courses of the psychoanalytic training include bibliographical references to French authors.

Mitchell's paper was originally published in *Women: The Longest Revolution. Essays in Feminism Literature and Psychoanalysis* (1984), a collection of political and literary essays, rather than in a clinical psychoanalytic journal. This may account for it being less well known to psychoanalytic audiences than her seminal book, *Psychoanalysis and Feminism* (1974), and her 'Introduction' to Lacan in her volume *Feminine Sexuality: Jacques Lacan and the école freudienne* (Mitchell and Rose, 1982). Kohon draws on this introduction, which also forms a backdrop to Mitchell's paper here. Kohon's paper, with its reference to hysteria and to the Dora case history, has frequently been prescribed for the teaching of candidates of the British Society and is used in associated educational settings; Dora's case clearly demonstrates the presence of sexuality in the clinical situation, something that, given the emphasis on early object relations, can easily be ignored.

These papers demonstrate the importance of hysteria for the theorization of psychoanalysis; their republication provides another opportunity to think afresh about sexuality and its role in psychic structure. In an age of increasing interest in psychosomatic illnesses, these papers also help us to think about the mind/body relationship and its foundational relevance for psychoanalysis.

Note

1   Recent large-scale epidemiological studies have suggested that functional (psychogenic) neurological disorders account for over 16 per cent of all new neurology outpatient referrals. Many of these patients remain high users of health and social services (Edwards and Bhatia, 2012). It is important to acknowledge here that current psychoanalytic theorizing of functional conditions is aetiologically complex. While some functional disorders can be understood as hysterical in form and therefore predicated on symbolized conflicts, the Paris School of Psychosomatics theorize certain functional conditions as somatic solutions to deficits in psychic representation (Smadja, 2010).

21

REFLECTIONS ON DORA

The case of hysteria

Gregorio Kohon

Freud in 1886, in his 'Report from Paris' – the first paper in the English Standard Edition of his complete works – separates hysteria as a psychic illness from biological sex (1956a [1886]). This is what he has learned from Charcot in Paris, he tells us, and to which he adds the notion of hysteria as caused by a psychic trauma which occurred at some point in the past history of the subject. In the same way that they were formerly treated as witches, nowadays – says Freud – female hysterical patients can easily be identified as 'liars', women who 'deceive us'. In the discussion that followed the presentation of this report to the College of Professors of the Faculty of Medicine in Vienna (Andersson, 1962), it was suggested that Freud should present the case of a male hysteric, which in fact he does a few months later (Freud, 1886d). This last lecture becomes his first published paper on hysteria.

By including men among hysterical patients, Freud joins in the attempt to give scientific status to the proposition of hysteria as a psychiatric diagnosis.[1] Nevertheless, despite this separation between hysteria and biological sex, the cases of hysteria in women form the entire contribution to the *Studies on Hysteria* (Freud, 1895d). Psychoanalysis truly began with women. As will be suggested in the third part of this paper, the connection between women and hysteria makes sense to me, and Freud never seems to have abandoned this idea, which in fact has been present in psychoanalysis ever since (see for example Zetzel, 1968).[2] Freud first mentioned it in 'Heredity and the Aetiology of the Neuroses' (1896a); reaffirmed it in the *Three Essays* (1905d); and finally stated it in 'Inhibitions, Symptoms and Anxiety' thus: 'there is no doubt that hysteria has a strong affinity with femininity, just as obsessional neurosis has with masculinity' (1926d, p. 143).

I think that in the development of the Oedipal drama of the women there is a hysterical stage, in which the subject – caught up in her need to change object from mother to father – can get 'fixed', unable to make the necessary choice. If it were true then – as Freud suspected – that a woman will choose a husband according to the image of her father, and establish with him in fantasy the same relationship that she had with her mother (Freud, 1931b), I would like to suggest that a woman always at heart remains a hysteric. What I am referring to is not unknown to psychoanalysts in their practice: a female patient will say that she is in love with her male analyst but nevertheless make a maternal transference to him, 'and one that is often fiercely denied and frequently has delusional undertones' (Green, 1972).

It is with Dora that psychoanalysis becomes what we know it to be: the problem of transference is introduced for the first time in her case, and in doing so, Freud opens a different window to a hitherto very obscure world. In the historical continuity of thinking about hysteria there is, at this point, a rupture, a necessary conversion from the study of hysteria as carried out up to the time of Charcot, to that done by Freud (Pontalis, 1977). It is an irrevocable change of direction which will eventually make possible, in its ultimate consequences, the invention of the analytic situation. It is to hysterical patients that we must be grateful, and it is to Freud's genius that we owe the discovery that what happens in dreams also happens in hysteria: in both cases, by disguising itself, desire can then find its satisfaction. Hysteria, after Freud, can no longer be considered as a syndrome from which both men and women could suffer, but rather as a reflection of an internal conflict: it exists independently of the symptoms presented by hysterical patients. Freud's attempt took him even further than he intended at the beginning: hysteria is not just a psychiatric diagnosis which would include conversion hysteria, anxiety hysteria, etc., but is a human problematic, specifically female, present in all of us. In 'Dora', for example, Freud's position is already clear: what is important is that she reacts to a sexual encounter reflecting a certain conflict in a particular way; what is relevant in her sexual life resides in her unconscious fantasy (Namnum, quoted in Laplanche, 1974).

The number of papers written on the case of Dora is astonishing, and there seems to be no end to our wish to know more about her. Those concerned with sociology, history and political science, literary critics and novelists, all seem interested – for one reason or another – in her case. In 1979, a film was made about her (McCall *et al.*, 1979); and, three years before, the Company of Renaud-Barrault put on a play in the Theatre d'Orsay dedicated to her (Cixous, 1976). Why such a fuss? And what is the connection – if any – between our wish to know, our curiosity, and hysteria?

Of the five so-called 'clinical cases' of Freud[3] the 'Fragment of an Analysis . . .' (1905e) is the only one that refers to a woman. The history of Dora is extraordinary. It is a 'literary masterpiece', which according to Marcus initiates a new genre, and thanks to which he associates – with a certain irony – Freud with Nabokov, Proust, Mann, Joyce, Ibsen and Borges (Marcus, 1974).[4] What is admired is its literary value and the Ibsenian way in which Freud holds his readers in suspense (Ellenberger, 1970; Meltzer, 1978). The story unfolds before our eyes, suggesting more and more complexities in the relationships created between the various characters. Dora might well arrive at Freud's door with 'her script written in advance' (Mannoni, 1969), but Freud takes possession of the script and transforms it. What could have been a 'classic Victorian domestic drama' is now a family novel of mysterious complexity: time passes in it, but the repressed comes back once and again in the form of stories within other stories, in the various betrayals of the characters who were themselves betrayed (Marcus, 1974).

Freud seems exalted – and perhaps also excited? – by the way in which he discovers the connection between Dora's sucking of her finger and her knowledge of fellatio; how he interprets the sensation of pressure on her thorax and associates it with Herr K.'s erect penis; how he comes to the association between her playing with the reticule and masturbation. His exaltation is no longer that of a young doctor on an ambitious quest for a name and fame; there is now a persistent search for the truth – although we do not know whether it is Dora's truth or Freud's. The intolerant therapist of the *Studies* has now been transformed into a psychoanalyst (Meltzer, 1978).

Freud knows that he has a powerful instrument which will permit him – by following a method which he considers precise, namely the analysis of dreams – to uncover the secret of the symptoms of his patients. The conversion in this is total: he not only is convinced that he can do it, but, according to him, anybody can. Apparently Dora satisfies Freud's desires and his special interest in sexual matters by offering him her 'pathogenic material' without major obstacles, but she arouses his curiosity when, for example, 'she plays at having secrets', quickly hiding that unimportant letter in the waiting room. Dora speaks about the little jewel box in her first dream, and there is a box to be opened in the second, while Freud, in a letter to Fliess, talks about his collection of picklocks with which he is gently unlocking the case of an eighteen-year-old girl (Freud, 1954). And in analysing that first dream, Freud (1905e) states: 'A regularly formed dream stands, as it were, upon two legs.' The development of a mutual seduction in the relationship between Dora and Freud seems fairly evident.[5] Many of his interpretations, and the way they were made, could not be understood by Dora except as an attempt at a parental, incestuous seduction (Bion, 1972).

According to Dora's account, Herr K. had found a way of being alone with her in his shop, from which they could see a religious procession in the main square. After closing the outer door and the shutters, Herr K. 'suddenly clasped the girl to him and pressed a kiss upon her lips. This was surely just the situation to call up a distinct feeling of sexual excitement in a girl of fourteen who had never before been approached. But Dora had at that moment a violent feeling of disgust . . .' (Freud, 1905e, p. 28). This is where Freud makes the connection between one of her symptoms and the possibility that Dora had felt the pressure of the erect penis of her father's friend. But Freud goes further, defining Dora's conduct in the same scene and her reaction as 'already entirely and completely hysterical'. Freud shows here his prejudice, his intolerance and frustration: there is a parallel, a repetition of the same scene in the analysis, in which a new friend of her father's, this time Freud, not only tries to impose his will and what could be seen as his penetrating interpretations, but also his 'not too impractical' solution: the possibility of marrying Herr K.

Freud is going to feel as rejected as Herr K. Dora, instead of responding in a supposedly 'healthy' way on both occasions, disappoints not only Herr K. but also Freud. Freud's frustration is evident in various ways. When he insists upon the necessity of speaking plainly on sexual matters and of being frank and open with our patients, Freud says: 'It is possible for a man to talk to girls and women upon sexual matters of every kind without . . . bringing suspicion upon himself . . . The best way of speaking about such things is to be dry and direct . . . I call bodily organs and processes by their technical names, and I tell these to the patient if they – the names, I mean – happen to be unknown to her' (p. 48). It is at this precise moment that Freud resorts to French: '*J'appelle un chat un chat*'; and a few lines later: 'The right attitude is: "*pour faire une omelette il faut casser des oeufs*".' We could think, with Marcus (1974), that Freud would have been the first to smile at the observation that in this splendid declaration about direct and frank language, its author disappears, not once but twice, into quotations in French.

The criticisms of Freud, leaving aside here those that come from feminist authors, have been multiple and varied. Freud's mistake was in failing to interpret the transference enough (Muslin and Gill, 1978); in not maintaining a neutral attitude in the treatment (Langs, 1976); in having ignored the pathology of the milieu (Rieff, 1971); in not having recognized that what Dora wanted was the total, exclusive and absolute love of her mother (Lewin, 1973); in not having understood Dora's problems in terms of her genetic, adolescent development (Erikson, 1961); in failing to recognize the defence mechanisms typical of the adolescent period, or his own counter-transference reactions to them (Glenn, 1980); in not having paid enough attention to the real disappointment with her father and other men during Dora's years of development (Scharfman, 1980).

Some of these criticisms – and here I can only consider them globally without necessarily doing them justice – are undoubtedly valid. Whether they are based on what would have been Freud's 'technical' errors, or on 'theoretical' deficiencies, they are all concerned to find a more exact alternative 'model'. Almost a century later, it is relatively easy to see what Freud might have done 'wrong'. It happens in our daily work: with hindsight we can always make the 'right' interpretation. However, for me there is still a different question: since we have the opportunity to know a bit more about Freud's intervention, what can we learn about Dora?

More than twenty years after her treatment with Freud, Dora was referred by her own doctor for a consultation with Felix Deutsch (F. Deutsch, 1957). Her symptoms are hysterical ones: *tinnitus*, loss of hearing in one ear, dizziness. Very rapidly Dora starts making a list of her complaints: the indifference of her husband, how her son has abandoned her, her unhappy life, her frigidity, her disgust and dislike of sexual relations, her rejection of a second pregnancy because of her fear of labour pains, her sleeplessness (she waits insomniac every night until her son comes home and she attributes his lateness to his interest in girls), her conviction that her husband is unfaithful to her

278

with other women, and how she considers that all men are mean and selfish. What a change is produced in Dora, the unbeloved, when she realizes that Deutsch, being an analyst, also knows Freud's work: how could she miss such an opportunity? Dora is transformed: she becomes flirtatious, seductive and with great pride reveals her identity to Deutsch.

Her symptoms disappear at the time of her second visit in which she now describes her chronic premenstrual pain, her vaginal discharges, her unhappy childhood, her mother's compulsions and obsessions, her lack of love, her constipation (her mother's only real preoccupation and from which she now also suffers). Miraculous and rapid cure! A few days later, Dora's brother calls Deutsch to thank him.[6] He tells Deutsch how difficult it is to get along well with Dora, how suspicious she is of everybody, that she always and chronically tries to put people against each other. Dora was jealous and possessive of her son who, contrary to his mother's hopes, developed a successful career as a musician. She clung to him in the same way that she had clung to her husband who died of a heart attack, tortured by his own inhibitions and by the paranoid and suffocating behaviour of Dora. Dora's palpitations, her anxiety attacks, her chronic fear of death, kept everybody in a constant state of alarm all through her life and, finally, her death from cancer of the colon was an acknowledged blessing for all those who surrounded her. From all points of view, Dora seems to have been 'one of the most repulsive hysterics' (F. Deutsch, 1957).

From reading his 'Fragment', it is clear that Freud did not like Dora. It is also clear that Freud did perhaps feel attracted and seduced by Dora; perhaps there are reasons for thinking that they had both embarked on a game of mutual seduction, but this need not necessarily imply that he liked her. To think, as some authors suggest, that if only Freud had taken her on again as a patient when she returned to him fifteen months later, Dora would have developed differently, is the result of groundless optimism. Dora's insincerity is quite evident: when she asks for more, what she wants is more revenge, and this is, in effect, the content of the communication that she makes to Freud. Freud appears to our eyes as seduced and abandoned; he obviously felt hurt and offended by Dora's behaviour but, nevertheless, this could not come as a surprise since, in the first dream she told him, Freud had understood that Dora had decided to abandon the treatment. His struggle was irremediably lost from the start.

We know that Freud found his reasons to explain his failure: Dora forced new questions, principally related to the problem of the transference and the question of homosexuality. The problems that were presented forced new theoretical positions and we find ourselves, through the years, with his need to revise his previous conceptions. We have then a Freud of the footnotes, different from that of the original text, still stuck to a notion of genital heterosexuality, Oedipal and simple (Mitchell, 1982). We see him, confronted with the homosexuality of his patient, struggling with himself and with that simplistic, initial Oedipal theory. Lacan points out the true prejudice which leads Freud astray in his intervention: from his belief in an ideal, natural Oedipus complex arises 'his need to insist upon Dora's love for Herr K. as a displacement of her love for her father' (Lacan, 1951). The vacillations and the confusion about the history of the publication of his work do not now seem so mysterious: Freud had placed himself 'rather excessively in the place of Herr K.' (Lacan, 1951).

Dora had managed to provide Freud with the illusion of power only to take it away. She convinced him that he could 'be the analyst', an infernal game in which all Freud seemed to have done was to follow the designs of Dora's neurosis. The comparison of a hysteric with a bullfight is very appropriate here: at all times the bullfighter, like the hysteric, does nothing which is not designed *to make the bull do something* (Racamier, 1952). *Dora continues waving her cape in front of us, as she did in front of Freud. And Freud's text, in its turn, continues provoking in us this wish to know more, and we never seem to be satisfied. In this sense, Freud's text – and perhaps any text on hysteria – is 'hysterical' too: it tantalizes us, waving a cape that hides nothing behind it. But it is that illusion of power, that very blindness which, ironically, will allow Freud to move forward. At the end, Freud confesses: 'I do not know what kind of help she wanted from me.' It is in this confession that psychoanalysis has found its object.*

★ ★ ★

Today we face the question of the existence or non-existence of hysteria. The word has disappeared from certain psychiatric manuals, and at one of the last International Congresses of Psychoanalysis there was a panel dedicated to this subject (Laplanche, 1974). Is hysteria really a thing of the past? The liberation of sexual morality, the loss of a certain 'innocence' in women, the change in the 'feminine ideal', the social acceptance of sexuality, would all have been contributory factors in the disappearance of hysteria as such. There is a certain theoretical simplicity behind all of this which considers the presence of a neurotic conflict as a conflict about present sexual impulses. The liberation of sexual morality has, of course, had innumerable consequences for the individual and society, but only with difficulty could it affect the Oedipal unconscious fantasy, the unconscious psychic scenario, the incestuous fantasies. A certain contemporary sexualism has slowly pervaded psychoanalysis, turning sexuality (as understood by Freud) into genitality. This has been the misunderstanding of the sexologists who believe that what is repressed is the 'knowledge' about sex. For them the sexual process would be a more or less physiological 'need', equivalent to other physiological needs: all that is required is 'information' about it. The liberation of desire – which is different from the liberation of sexual morality – would originate in the informed knowledge about the 'sexual facts', which nowadays includes knowledge about the Oedipus complex. Therefore, the resolution of conflicts would result from a 'healthy sexual practice'. The Oedipal drama has been transformed into a totally banal sequence of 'events' and 'anecdotes': everybody can talk – and even joke about it. But the joke is on us: *what makes sexuality in human beings specifically human is repression*, that is to say, sexuality owes its existence to our unconscious incestuous fantasies. Desire, in human sexuality, is always transgression; and being something that is never completely fulfilled, its object cannot ever offer full satisfaction.

Theoretical simplistic 'naturalism' has gone hand in hand with the desexualization of the theory, a question that has been a fundamental, controversial issue in the history of psychoanalysis?[7] What I am referring to, for example, is present in the discussion reported by Laplanche, in which psychoanalysts of different persuasions discuss *hysteria*. Many of our colleagues would hold – as was suggested in that Panel – that hysteria is only a defensive technique to maintain at a distance and under control anxieties which are defined as primitive, psychotic and not sexual (Laplanche, 1974). This way of defining hysteria as a defence is best illustrated in the work of authors like Fairbairn. It is the result of the elimination from the theory of the role of sexuality in the aetiology of the neuroses, which is the central pillar of Freudian thought. In Fairbairn's theories, drives are not pleasure-seeking but object-seeking; hysteria always reveals the presence of oral conflicts, which in his view are the ones that really count; he believes that the Oedipal conflict has been 'overestimated' – 'it involves a certain misconception', he claims – being for him a sociological phenomenon more than a psychological one; guilt is not connected to incestuous wishes in a triangular situation but to fantasies of theft of love that was not freely given; the father as an object is a rather 'poor second' (Fairbairn, 1941).

Hysteria is then torn away from the Oedipal constellation, and the Oedipus complex is relegated to a secondary place: it is no longer that through which the relationship between baby and mother is transcended; it no longer serves as the principal agent of the psychic structuring of the child. Not only is the Oedipus complex made to appear earlier in life but it is transformed into something radically different: it ceases to be the model of sexuality and meaning for the subject.

In changing the concept of the Oedipus complex, the idea of the existence of a prohibition of incest and the castration complex is, consequently, also changed. By eliminating the castration complex as the mark that distinguishes the difference between the sexes; and by attempting, at the same time, a supposed revaluation of the concept of femininity and of women, we meet up again with a belief in a process of biological identification based on a differentiation of the sexes which is supposedly 'natural' and 'given'; we return to the notion that women and men are 'created in nature' (Mitchell, 1974).

However, it is not possible for us as psychoanalysts to appeal to biology to explain the difference between the sexes. We must not confuse the universal uncertainty of the unconscious with the apparent biological reality. What there is in the unconscious is *a danger and a threat* for the man, and *a desire and an envy* for the woman, and not – as is assumed – an overvalued penis and an undervalued vagina. A penis, just as much as a vagina, does not secure or guarantee anything for the subject about becoming a sexual human being (Masotta, 1976). What the idea of bisexuality denotes is precisely the uncertainty of that process and the struggle through which all human beings *become* either a woman or a man.[8]

There are also those authors who stress the processes of identification with either parent as the cause and explanation for the differentiation of the sexes. In this case, the 'naturalism' resides in believing that the sexual difference is imposed on the already 'created' man or woman, by the culturally determined roles. This position also accounts for many of the separations and divisions in the psychoanalytic movement. Freud opposed both the biological as much as the sociological determinism in the theories that tried to explain the differentiation of the sexes from those points of view. As Mitchell points out: all these explanations look similar to Freud's, 'but the place accorded to the castration complex pushes them poles apart'

(Mitchell, 1982, p. 22). Lacan had insisted on this very same point in his comments on Jones' theories, asking himself how Jones managed to be so much in agreement with Freud when his ideas were so radically different (Lacan, 1955–6).

In the development of psychoanalytic theory it has been justly recognized that – independently of the sex of the child – what counts is the threat of the loss of the mother. This has produced a remarkable progress in both our theoretical and clinical practices but what has been left still unresolved is the mystery of the presence of the father (Le Guen, 1974). The father has disappeared from the theory. For Freud, the mere existence of the father brought about the castration complex and the Oedipus complex. In trying to vindicate the mother, the theory has transformed the father into a kind of appendage of the mother.[9]

The relevance of these important changes in psychoanalytic theory for the consideration of hysteria can be seen more clearly at this point. We can understand why, for example, psychoanalysts claim not to find hysterics any more in their consulting rooms:[10] patients may be hysterics but since the theory looks for something else, it also finds something else. One could take this even further: we can turn around, look at the cases of hysteria treated by Freud, and maintain that they were in fact more disturbed, borderline patients. As a result of the change in the theory, we would be in the position of concluding that hysteria does not exist now, nor did it exist then.

* * *

Psychoanalysis is like a nomadic tribe, never settling in any one place (Pontalis, 1977). There is no map or boundary other than those that psychoanalysis has created for itself. Hysteria has not only motivated the emergence of psychoanalysis but it also perpetuates its existence. In this context, it makes sense to talk about the double vision that the analyst needs to have: analysis has to invent the patient, not only investigate him (Malcolm, 1980). Psychoanalysis created, in the first instance, the possibility of its existence by inventing a new illness: the transference neurosis. Identified as a nomadic people, sometimes we may not see the frontiers, the innumerable paths which lead us to narcissism, to the different psychoses, to the obsessional phenomena. But hysteria is always there, defining the Freudian psychoanalytic field, and 'not as a witness to dogmatic orthodoxy, but as a central element of a psychopathology which offers its meaning to our thinking' (Green, 1964). This is where hysteria and obsessional neurosis come together as transference neurosis, giving a central place to the castration complex within the Oedipal drama: the inevitable presence of the proto-fantasies of the primal scene; paternal or maternal seduction; the disguises by displacement and condensation; the possibility of a coexistence between regression and the reality principle; and the ever-present prohibition of the taboos (Green, 1964).

If we bring hysteria back to the constellation of the Oedipus complex, we could then see that together with the parallelism of the development of men and women, we have to stress the differences and the asymmetry that exist. In so far as the Oedipal developments are asymmetrical there is, for example, an important difference between female and male homosexuality, and in the general structure of perversions in women and men.

In the case of women, the question is not the change from clitoral pleasure to vaginal pleasure but the need to change the object from mother (and the acceptance of her castration) to father (and the possibility of having his babies). In connection with the acceptance of the castration of the mother, it should be stressed that the notion of penis envy only makes sense in reference to, and in connection with, the notion of a phallic mother: it originates in the universal belief of children that the mother has a phallus, *not in the existence of a real penis in the father*. The misunderstanding about penis envy (the assumption that this concept undervalues women) has created a concept of compensation: envy of the womb. Of course men are envious of women but the issue here is a different one: instead of trying to explain the difference of the sexes, this concept would do away with the differences!

The change of object from mother to father is what is problematic for the woman – as relevant and problematic as not having to change objects is for the man. In this sense, bisexuality might be more relevant for women than for men, and it is in this connection that hysteria – with what I propose as the divalence of the hysterical stage – 'has more affinity with femininity' than with masculinity. While the question that the obsessional neurotic asks is: *Am I dead or alive?*, the question that the hysteric poses is: *Am I a man or a woman?* (Leclaire, 1971). Many hysterics would try to resolve this dilemma by forcing themselves to be a woman by making a child (see the case described by Lemoine-Luccioni, 1976). In other cases, they would remain dissatisfied heterosexuals, only being able to reach orgasm

284

through fantasizing either that they are making love to another woman, or that they are active participants in their partner's sexual encounters with other women. A frequent case nowadays is that of a more or less active bisexual woman, struggling to decide – in her supposed 'process of sexual liberation' – whether to be homosexual or heterosexual.

It is said that the hysteric is made for psychoanalysis and, in effect, hysteria is what encouraged its development, forced its birth. Nonetheless, I would like to suggest that *that which defines psychoanalysis also limits it.* Hysteria is considered the neurosis closest to normality, the prototype of the neurotic individual. It is all apparently there, nothing could be clearer: the question of the third one, the Oedipal conflict, the enigma of sexuality through somatizations. It is, however, present only in appearance for when we look at it, there is nothing really there. Dora characterizes the issue of female desire only in that hysteria is a caricature of 'normality'. The hysteric disguises herself: she will pretend to be a woman, she will put on the fancy dress of what she thinks will constitute her 'feminine self'. What must remain hidden under the disguise is her castration, which she rejects and which paradoxically is what defines her as a woman. The 'feminine' will appear only in her symptoms. The hysteric takes her own masked body and dresses up with it, uses it as if it were a brand-new dress, just bought, resplendent, full of sequins, but not very satisfying. Joan Riviere, in fact, extended this to all women: 'Womanliness . . . could be assumed and worn as a mask . . . much as a thief will turn out his pockets and ask to be searched to prove that he has not the stolen goods' (Riviere, 1929). Could this be a rebellion against the law of the father in this patriarchal society? Perhaps, but then the hysteric is the result of the failure of that rebellion. Men support her in this failure, nourish her and respond to her seductions,[11] which they enjoy. They are united with her in the reassuring and comforting fantasy which seems to tell us that femininity lies after all in the guise of what the hysteric wants us to believe is a 'real woman'. Being a true caricature of the feminine, it is also a caricature of everything else: heterosexuality, homosexuality, perversions, the couple, desire – and psychoanalysis – *attempting to change the truth of what the analyst is, and is doing, and of what the patient is, and is doing* (Brenman, quoted in Laplanche, 1974).

Whilst at the root of the Oedipal conflict lies ambivalence, that 'simultaneous existence of contradictory tendencies, attitudes or feelings in relation to a single object, especially the coexistence of love and hate' (Laplanche and Pontalis, 1967), I would like to suggest that what characterizes hysteria is divalence. This concept was created by Pichon-Rivière, but he used it in a different way and in a different context. For him, divalence was what characterized – in his version of Melanie Klein – the paranoid-schizoid position, and it refers to the double aspect of good and bad within each partial object. Divalence would be for him 'primary', since ambivalence can only take place after the constitution of a total object (Bleger, 1967a; Pichon-Rivière, 1970, 1971). However, I would like to use the notion of divalence to suggest that it develops together with the constitution of whole objects, father and mother, and it defines a specific moment in the development of the individual, in which the subject is confronted with the choice between these two objects. It is a *hysterical stage*, present in every woman, probably throughout her life. It characterizes, within the context of the Oedipal drama, something specifically female.

Nagera has delineated two sub-stages of the Oedipus complex in the girl. In the first one, which he calls the phallic-oedipal, the mother is still the primary libidinal object; the girl is in an active position in relation to the mother. In the second, which would be the Oedipal phase proper, the father has become the primary object of the girl's libidinal interest, and her position is receptive in relation to him (Nagera, 1975). The hysterical stage I am describing would come in between these two phases, it would take place at that precise moment in which the subject, after the full recognition of sexual differences, has to make the change from mother to father. However, I am referring to it as a *stage*, not in a developmental sense, but more as a place where something happens, on which a performance takes place, a drama is developed, and at the same time, as a distance between two stopping places.

This change of objects – a movement between two places, between two positions – is a very problematic one: we know about it through the failures in achieving it. To my mind, the patient described so richly by Stewart [pp. 244–260 herein (ed.)] is an example of what could happen with some hysterics who fail – for whatever reasons – to overcome this stage. Through the patient's confusion, and through her divalence, the analyst becomes a 'bisexual transference figure'.

While the obsessional subject must decide if he loves or hates his object, how the scales of his ambivalence will tip, and is paralysed by this conflict between love and hate which seems impossible to resolve, the hysteric wanders between one object and the other, paralysed between the two, unable to choose between them, frozen in a gesture of apparent resolution. Thus the conflict of ambivalence is superimposed, and is 'secondary' to that of divalence in hysteria, so that the subject can feel ambivalent towards either one of her objects at a given moment, without being able to choose one or the other. Although playing the role of a seductress, trying to win her idealized father on to her side, she is also in strong phallic competition with him for the mother. Freud speaks of Dora's love for her father as a 'reactive symptom', as a defence against her love for Herr K. It makes more sense though to think that what 'still exercised power in the unconscious' in Dora, what was suppressed, was her phallic attachment to her mother. There is plenty of evidence to suggest an unconscious identification of Dora with her father, and Krohn and Krohn (1972) suggested that this identification could be seen as 'a defence against her hostility and rivalry with him or as an expression of an unconscious wish to love woman as a man' (see also Lacan, 1951; and Mitchell, 1982).

In fact, 'stuck' in her divalent stage, the hysteric seems to map one triangular situation on top of the other in her unconscious: in one triangular set, she occupies the place of her mother – whom she displaces through her rivalry with her, and tries to seduce father. In another set, she is in an aggressive rivalry with father for the conquest of mother. The two situations combine but never quite mix, nor are they resolved: at the end, the hysteric will always feel betrayed by both mother and father, and will never find satisfaction. The 'extreme ambivalence' that we find described in the literature, and that would mark the relationship of the hysteric with men, stems from her divalent position. The hysteric cannot define herself as a man or as a woman because she cannot finally choose between her father or her mother. The hysteric will always remain in the middle, moving constantly between one and the other, without getting close to either one: petrified half-way, she postulates the impossible. She is half participating, half excluded: 'Thanks to the support of a possible double identification, she will remain in an unsatisfied desire, with a more or less intense verbosity and relative happiness, sheltered from a frigidity which is her safeguard and the guarantee of her ambiguous disinterest' (Perrier, 1974).

The beautiful butcher's wife will continue to desire caviar, of precisely which she will deprive herself (Lacan, 1958); or like that other one who, liking good meat, when invited to a restaurant where excellent meat is served, ends up ordering fish (Israel, 1972). Thus we can understand why an author like Masud Khan (1975a) casts doubt on the treatability of hysterics, recommending his students not to interpret to hysterical patients the erotic transference (Khan, 1975b). Extraordinary teaching, ironic comment, which would turn psychoanalysis upside-down and which, nevertheless, makes sense: *to speak of sexual desire to an hysteric is to try to impose a notion which is inaccessible to the subject.* In spite of the apparent transparency of her discourse, the hysteric 'cannot determine the object of her desire' (Masotta, 1976). Because of her divalence, she will be condemned to be a 'go-between' (Slipp, 1977). She will reject whoever loves her, and will die in desperate passion for an inaccessible other, always believing that all she dreams of is 'a desire that would be born of love' (Safouan, 1974), when in fact her problem is how to bear love when sex is present (Green, 1982). For Dora it is Herr K. but it is not Herr K., in the same way that it is Frau K. but it is not Frau K. either. What Dora does is to get interested in the relationship between two people, never as two separate people. The identification with one of them only makes sense to her if seen from the perspective of the other one. That creates the game of multiple identifications, which ultimately leaves the hysteric empty and desperate: the labyrinths of her desire lead nowhere, except to the preservation of that very desire.

In that blind alley the hysteric cannot answer the fundamental problem that is posed to her: since there is a difference between the sexes, *who is she, a woman or a man?* Anna O., in 1922, transformed now into a social reformer and a campaigner for universal love, shows her confusion when she says: 'If there were any justice in the world, women would make laws and men would have babies' (quoted in Ellenberger, 1970).

Notes

1 For a historical view of the development of the concept of hysteria and the various attempts to distinguish between the biological sex and the illness, see Ilza Veith's (1975) book.
2 It has also been present, in a different way, in everyday language, retaining in this case the derogatory meanings attached to the word.
3 For some – no doubt, interesting – reason, the case of female homosexuality is never included in this group (Freud, 1920a).
4 Today we find works of fiction attempting to imitate Freud's style and presentation. See, for example, the first part of *The White Hotel* (Thomas, 1981).

5 With reference to the erotic link between Dora and Freud, see the interpretation that Anzieu (1959) makes of Freud's dream of the round table. Cf. also the comments that Decker (1982) makes about Freud's libidinal involvement in the choice of Dora's name.

6 We know that Dora was in reality Ida Bauer, Otto Bauer's sister. He was one of the main socialist leaders in Austria (Rogow, 1979).

7 This issue was, of course, at the centre of the disagreements between Freud and some of his followers and formed the basis for many of the splits in the psychoanalytic movement. More recently, Lacan and the French authors whom he influenced so strongly have developed a criticism of what is seen as the desexualization of the theory, and its 'naturalistic' assumptions. It would not fall within the scope of this paper to expand on this point. I would like to refer the reader to Mitchell's and Rose's 'Introductions' to the writings of Lacan on feminine sexuality (Mitchell, 1982; Rose, 1982).

8 This is not to argue that there might be anatomical, physiological and endocrinological evidence that points to the existence of a potential bisexuality in both sexes. There seems to be some evidence too that this bisexuality develops in different forms for men and women (Nagera, 1975). At every stage in the process of development in the human embryo the female precedes the male; males are developmentally retarded in comparison with females, except for their sexual differentiation: this is the only aspect in which the male precedes the female. The male differentiation is completed at sixteen weeks, while the female is at twenty weeks (Hutt, 1972). This could suggest that bisexuality is more relevant for women, which also seems to be indicated by the presence of two fully developed leading sexual organs, the clitoris and the vagina. It was this presence that made Freud think of women as having two phases in their sexual life, and the controversial notion of the change from clitoral pleasure to vaginal pleasure (Freud, 1925j, 1931b).

9 The natural figure of the father will be confused again and again with the normative figure throughout Freud's work, thus causing an ambiguous reading of many of his ideas. This confusion is central in the text of 'Dora', and we can understand why it has aroused so much interest among feminists: the question of the father relates to the status of the transference; the problem of the transference takes us to consider the place of the father in the aetiology of the neuroses (see Cixous and Clement, 1975; Gearhart, 1979; Moi, 1981; Rose, 1978).

10 French analysts seem to have less difficulty in finding hysterical patients than their English colleagues. This is the result of their different theoretical outlooks.

11 See Temperley's (1975) paper on the complicity of the husbands of hysterics with their wives.

22

THE QUESTION OF FEMININITY AND THE THEORY OF PSYCHOANALYSIS

Juliet Mitchell

This paper is not about psychoanalytic concepts of femininity; it is about the connection between the question of femininity and the construction of psychoanalytic theory. I suggest that for Freud, 'femininity' sets the limits – the starting- and the endpoint – of his theory, just as its repudiation marked the limits of the possibility of psychotherapeutic cure:

> We often have the impression that with the wish for a penis and the masculine protest we have penetrated through all the psychological strata and have reached bedrock, and that thus our activities are at an end. This is probably true . . . The repudiation of femininity can be nothing else than a biological fact . . .
>
> (1937c, p. 252)

This intimate relationship between the problem of femininity and the creation of theory has not characterized other psycho-analytic work. This is largely to do with the shifting orientation: from neuroses to their underlying psychoses; from Oedipal to pre–Oedipal. In part it is to do with a difference to the nature of the theoretical constructions. After Freud, the theoretical concepts belonging to psychoanalysis were there to be added to, repudiated, and confirmed.

By and large, alterations and alternatives emanate directly from the clinical work. But Freud had a different task: it was to make *other* concepts psychoanalytical.

For Freud the notion of the unconscious is there, an idea waiting in the circumambient literature; it is transformed into a theory by his application of it to the material he observed. Freud's patients correct, repudiate or confirm his concepts which remain always larger, wider in application than their particularity in the clinical setting. But if we take Melanie Klein as an example we can see a different intellectual process. When she starts her work the theory and practice of psychoanalysis is already established. Immersed in her practice she comes to question specific aspects of the existent psychoanalytic theory. Her patients do not lead her back into an overarching theory but forward to a new description which relates only to what is observed and experienced. There is no preoccupation with the nature of theory as such, or with the nature of science, or with making psychoanalysis scientific. This is assumed. Not so for Freud.

What did Freud consider to be the nature of theory? I am going to give two quotations which will mark the framework. First, from the *New Introductory Lectures*:

We cannot do justice to the characteristics of the mind by linear outlines like those in a drawing or in a primitive painting, but rather by areas of colour melting into one another as they are represented by modern artists. After making the separation we must allow what we have separated to merge together once more.

(1933a, p. 79)

And in 'Why War?', his address to Einstein:

It may perhaps seem to you as though our theories are a kind of mythology and, in the present case, not even an agreeable one. But does not every science come in the end to be a kind of mythology like this? Cannot the same be said today of your own Physics?

(1933b, p. 211)

Lines drawn to communicate what we know is only a blurred merging. Myths – symbolical stories set up to explain other stories.

When he first used hypnosis with patients, Freud (like others) was aware that the treatment echoed an important hypnoid state within

291

the hysterical attack itself. At least within Freud's psychoanalytic theory, there remains, I believe, always this homologous structure: a characteristic element of the illness is taken up and repeated in the treatment and then, in its turn, finds a place at the centre of the theoretical construction. The famous reflection at the end of the Schreber case is an indication:

> Since I neither fear the criticism of others nor shrink from criticizing myself, I have no motive for avoiding the mention of a similarity which may possibly damage our libido theory in the estimation of many of my readers. Schreber's 'rays of God' which are made up of a condensation of the sun's rays, of nerve fibres, and of spermatozoa, are in reality nothing else than a concrete representation and projection outwards of libidinal cathexes, and they thus lend his delusions a striking conformity with our theory . . . It remains for the future to decide whether there is more delusion in my theory than I should like to admit, or whether there is more truth in Schreber's delusion than other people are as yet prepared to believe.
>
> (1911c, pp. 78–79)

And later:

> I have not been able to resist the seduction of an analogy. The delusions of patients appear to me to be the equivalent of the constructions which we built up in the course of analytic treatment – attempts at explanations and cure . . .
>
> (1937d, p. 268)

If for Freud a scientific theory was a myth (there is nothing pejorative in this), then we should remember both how his case histories read like *romans-à-clef* and how, if uneasily, he was well aware of this:

> I have not always been a psychotherapist. Like other neuropathologists, I was trained to employ local diagnosis and electro-prognosis, and it still strikes me myself as strange that the case histories I write should read like short stories and that, as one might say, they lack the serious stamp of science.
>
> (1893c, p. 160)

If the theory is a myth, the case history a short story, then of course the essence of the illness is in some way a story too. As one commentator has put it: 'Charcot sees, Freud will hear. Perhaps the whole of psychoanalysis is in that shift' (Heath, 1982, p. 38). I don't believe that this particular transition is the whole of psychoanalysis; but I do feel that it is important. Rather than stress language, the talking cure, I would emphasize here the listening treatment. Hysterics are creative artists, they suffer from reminiscences, they have heard something that has made them ill:

> The point that escaped me in the solution of hysteria lies in the discovery of a new source from which a new element of unconscious production arises. What I have in mind are hysterical phantasies, which regularly, as it seems to me, *go back to things heard* by children at an early age and only understood later. The age at which they take in information of this kind is very remarkable – from the age of six to seven months onwards.
>
> (1950a, Letter 59)

In these early papers – before *The Interpretation of Dreams* and an interest once more in the visual and in perception – the stress is on the aural and its connection with the formation of unconscious phantasies. Charcot saw and classified and dismissed what he heard:

> You see how hysterics shout. Much ado about nothing . . . [She is said to talk] of someone with a beard, man or woman . . . Whether man or woman is not without importance, but let us slide over that mystery.
>
> (quoted in Heath, 1982, p. 38)

But Freud decided that these tales of sound and fury did signify something. The move from seeing to hearing, from Charcot to Freud, is the move away from observation and the attendant blindness of the seeing eye.

Stories had two dimensions: what they are about and who tells them. Freud first believed that the stories were true and then that they were true as stories. Hysterics tell tales and fabricate stories – particularly for doctors who will listen. At first Freud was over-credulous. He thought they were about what they said they were about on a realistic plane, he then realized his patients were telling stories. The stories were about psychic reality: the object of psychoanalysis. What they are about, then, is first seduction and then phantasy; who tells them – this is the beginning of psychoanalysis as a theory and therapy of subjectivity.

Social historians of western Europe and America consider that hysteria reached epidemic proportions during the nineteenth century. It was primarily a disease of women. Alice James, sister of the novelist Henry and philosopher William James, will do to illustrate my theme here. Like Dora, Alice's conversion symptoms seem mainly to have been constructed from an identification with her father: a hysterical paralysis of the leg for his amputation. No one doubted that Alice was as able as her brothers; but she made her illness into her career, writing her diaries to parallel the communications of her body. She described her own feelings:

As I used to sit immovable reading in the library with waves of violent inclination suddenly invading my muscles taking some one of their myriad forms such as throwing myself out of the window, or knocking off the head of the benignant pater as he sat with silver locks, writing at his table, it used to seem to me that the only difference between me and the insane was that I had all the horrors and suffering of insanity but the duties of doctors, nurse and strait-jacket imposed upon me, too. Conceive of never being without the sense that if you let yourself go for a moment you must abandon all, let the dykes break and the flood sweep in, acknowledging yourself abjectly impotent before immutable laws.

(quoted in Strouse, 1980, p. 118)

She also commented:

When I am gone pray don't think of me simply as a creature who might have been something else, had neurotic science been born.

(p. ix)

Many nineteenth-century doctors got furious with their hysterical patients, finding themselves locked in a power struggle in which their opponent's best weapon was the refusal to be cured. Freud and subsequent analysts are familiar with the problem. Freud's understanding of this – in characteristic fashion – moved from the notion of a social gain in illness (removal of middle-class women from intolerable situations) to a psychological one where it bifurcated. It became on the one hand, the theories of resistance, the negative therapeutic reaction, and, particularly, after the case of Dora, of transference and countertransference. On the other hand, after a difficult trajectory which I am going to try to trace here, it led to the concept of a

294

fundamental human repudiation of femininity – a repudiation which, for Freud, was the bedrock of psychoanalysis both as theory and therapy.

I think – and I want to be tentative here – that psychoanalysis had to start from an understanding of hysteria. It could not have developed – or certainly not in the same way – from one of the other neuroses or psychoses. Hysteria led Freud to what is universal in psychic construction and it led him there in a particular way – by the route of a prolonged and central preoccupation with the difference between the sexes. The sexual aetiology of hysteria spoke to Freud from the symptoms, stories and associations of his patients and the otherwise unattended to, accidental comments of his colleagues. But the question of sexual difference – femininity and masculinity – was built into the very structure of the illness.

There are two aspects to Freud's interest in Charcot's work that I think should be stressed. They are separate, but I suggest Freud brought them together. Charcot emphasized the existence of male hysteria. He also organized the disease. When Freud returned from Paris to Vienna the first paper he presented was on male hysteria. In his report, he commented of Charcot's work:

Hysteria was lifted out of the chaos of the neuroses, was differentiated from other conditions with a similar appearance, and was provided with a symptomatology which, though sufficiently multifarious, nevertheless makes it impossible any longer to doubt the rule of law and order.

(1956a [1886], p. 12)

At the same time, when Freud's friendship with Fliess was at its height, he wrote to him congratulating him on his work on menstruation with these words: '[Fliess had] stemmed the power of the female sex so that it bears its share of obedience to the law' (quoted in Heath, 1982, p. 46). The search for laws, lines to sort out and the blurred picture; laws that in the end are anyway only myths.

The laws about the human psyche will be one and the same thing as the laws about sexual difference. Hysteria was the woman's disease: a man could have it. In Freud's hands hysteria ceases to be a category pertaining to any given sector of the population, it becomes a general human possibility. And a possibility not only in the sense that anyone can have it, but in that it provides the clues to the human psyche itself.

We can see Freud stumbling from the specificity of hysteria to the construction of subjectivity in the general human condition in these early writings from the 1880s and 1890s. Always it is via the dilemma of sexual difference.

Conditions related *functionally* to sexual life play a great part in the aetiology of hysteria . . . and they do so on account of the high psychical significance of this function especially in the female sex.
(1888b, p. 51)

Hysteria necessarily presupposes a primary experience of unplea- sure – that is, of a passive nature. The natural sexual passivity of women explains their being more inclined to hysteria. Where I have found hysteria in men, I have been able to prove the presence of abundant sexual passivity in their anamnesis.
(1950a, Draft K.)

Her hysteria can therefore be described as an acquired one, and it presupposed nothing more than the possession of what is probably a very widespread proclivity – the proclivity to acquire hysteria.
(Freud, 1895d, p. 122)

Freud tried all sorts of explanations as to why an illness so clearly found predominantly in women, should also occur in men. But it was a cry of Eureka! when he wrote enthusiastically to Fliess: 'Bisexuality! I'm sure you are right!' Bisexuality was a postulate of something universal in the human psyche. But while bisexuality explained why men and women could be hysterics, it did not account for why it was their femininity that was called into play.

At the level of the story, the tale Freud heard was of paternal seduction. After holding on to this information with conviction he writes to Fliess that something is hindering his work. The obstacle has something to do with Freud's relationship to Fliess – the rela- tionship of a man to a man which, by 1937, was to be the other expression of the bedrock of psychoanalytic theory and therapy, once more, a repudiation – this time, on the man's side – of femininity, of passivity in relation to a man.

Many commentators, including Freud himself, have observed that it was Freud's femininity that predominated in this relationship with Fliess; it is possible that it was his femininity that rendered that friend- ship eventually untenable. Freud referred on several occasions to his own neurosis as 'my mild hysteria'. He did so frequently at the time when he was blocked in his work on hysteria. He has a breakthrough: 'I no longer believe in my neurotica.' Hysterics are not suffering the trauma of paternal seduction, they are expressing the phantasy of infantile desire. Is this true of hysterics or of everyone? Freud's clinical listening and his self-analysis come together:

> One single thought of general value has been revealed to me. I have found, in my own case too, falling in love with the mother and jealousy of the father, and I regard it as a universal event of early childhood, even if not so early as in children who have been made hysterical . . . If that is so, we can understand the riveting power of *Oedipus Rex* . . .
>
> (1950a, Letter 71)

Hysteria, the Oedipal illness; source of the concept of the Oedipus complex, discovered through the hysteria of Freud, a male analyst. Universal bisexuality; universal Oedipus complex; hysteria the most Oedipal neurosis, the one that most utilizes bisexuality. Women more Oedipal, more bisexual, more hysterical. These connections were to remain for many years in search of a theory that explained them. What was universal, what specific to hysteria, what to femininity?

Something else that came to be connected was going on with Freud's investigations. These early texts are preoccupied with two aspects of hysteria: the absences or gaps in consciousness and the splitting of consciousness. Anna O.'s illness reveals the absences, Miss Lucy R.'s the splitting.

> [The] idea is not annihilated by a repudiation of this kind, but merely repressed into the unconscious. When this process occurs for the first time there comes into being a nucleus group divorced from the ego – a group around which everything which would imply an acceptance of the incompatible idea subsequently collects. The splitting of consciousness in these cases of acquired hysteria is accordingly a deliberate and intentional one. At least it is often *introduced* by an act of volition; for the actual outcome is something different from what the subject intended. What he wanted was to do away with an idea, as though it had never appeared, but all he succeeds in doing is to isolate it psychically.
>
> (Freud, 1895d, p. 123)

297

The splitting of consciousness, the disappearance of meaning, the unconscious – these cease to be confined as characteristics of hysteria and again become universalized. Freud finally distinguishes his theory of hysteria from Pierre Janet's on the grounds that Janet argues that hysteria's defining feature was splitting and Freud that it was conversion. For Freud, splitting was a general condition. Freud came back to the question at the end of his life. In the fragmentary paper on 'Splitting of the Ego in the Process of Defence' (1940e) he is uncertain whether, in 1938, he is on to something new or merely saying again what he has said before. It is a return to the preoccupation with splitting that had marked his work on hysteria 50 to 60 years before. I shall argue that what he says at the end is both old and new. What is new is that by the end of the 1930s he has brought it into line with the problem of sexual difference. In the early days, it went only side by side with that question – he had not yet established the point of their connection.

Not yet connected with splitting, then, in the early work on hysteria there remained the problem of the division into masculinity and femininity. In the 1890s Freud came very close to sexualizing repression. Fliess offered one version of this argument, the other was to be Adler's mistake. In a draft entitled 'The Architecture of Hysteria', Freud wrote: 'It is to be expected that the essentially repressed element is always what is feminine. What men: essentially repress is the paederastic element' (1950a, Draft M.). How close to and yet how different is this from the repudiation of femininity as the bedrock of psychoanalysis in 'Analysis Terminable and Interminable' in 1937. But sexualizing repression was not an idea that Freud held on to for long. Six months later, in the letter to Fliess in which he tells of the hold-up in his self-analysis, he comments: 'I have also given up the idea of explaining libido as the masculine factor and repression as the feminine one . . .' (1950 [1892–1899], Letter 75). And yet – with all the difference in the world – in Freud's theory, libido remains 'masculine' and it is not that repression is feminine, but that femininity is repudiated.

The concept that brought together Freud's observation of splitting and the dilemma of sexual difference as it was posed in hysteria, was the castration complex. I don't want to go into details of the concept here – merely to note whence it arose, what it explained and how forcefully it was (and maybe still is), rejected by other analysts. It came from Freud's pursuit of the internal logic of what he needed to describe. He used both Fliess's biological and Adler's sociological accounts as buffers from which his theory needed to bump away. In a fascinating two pages at the end of the paper on 'A Child Is being Beaten' (1919e), he explains why these accounts fail. The concept of castration arose, too, from a listening ear tuned to the problem in the case histories, in particular, in that of Little Hans. What it explained was briefly this: how the formation of the human psyche was inextricably linked with the construction of a psychological notion of sexual difference.

For Freud, the child's first question is hypothesized as 'Where do babies come from?' The second (or maybe chronologically the other way round for girls) is: 'What is the difference between the sexes?' The theoretician in Freud reformulated his own hypothesis – the child's imagined questions as the myth (or theory) of the castration complex: lines around blurred fields of colour.

The splitting that set up the unconscious is repeated in a split that sets up the division between the sexes. For this reason, the 1938 paper on the splitting of the ego uses as its exemplary instance the conscious acceptance of the castration complex and the simultaneous unconscious repudiation of the possibility of its implications (femininity) as expressed in the setting up of a fetish object.

For Freud the final formation of the human psyche is coincident with the psychological acquisition of the meaning of sexual difference. In Freud's theory this is not there from the beginning, it has to be acquired:

> If we could divest ourselves of our corporal existence, and could view the things of this earth with a fresh eye as purely thinking beings, from another planet for instance, nothing perhaps would strike our attention more forcibly than the fact of the existence of two sexes among human beings, who, though so much alike in other respects, yet mark the difference between them with such obvious external signs. But it does not seem that children choose this fundamental fact in the same way as the starting point of their researches into sexual problems . . . A child's desire for knowledge on this point does not in fact awaken spontaneously, prompted perhaps by some inborn need for established causes.
>
> (1908c, pp. 211–12)

The story told is about the acquisition and repudiation of this knowledge.

Sexual difference – but why should it be femininity that is repudiated? Before Freud, many doctors and commentators thought that hysterics were women trying to escape or protest their female role; Freud toyed with the possibility that all that was feminine was repressed, the repressed feminine would thus have been the content of the unconscious itself. We are all familiar with how often women are thought to be more in touch with the unconscious, more intuitive, nearer the roots of nature.

Freud's answer was: no, 'we must keep psychoanalysis separate from biology'; repression must not be sexualized. But femininity *does* come to represent this point where meaning and consciousness vanish. Because this point is chaos, that which has been made to stand in for it – made to indicate the gap – is unbearable and will be repudiated. In the loss of balance, something to fill the gap will be hallucinated, a breast; produced as fetish, envied – a penis. The clinical experience of splitting and of castration is horror – penis envy, hallucination, fetishism are quick relief.

It is commonly held that castration rests on deprivation – what is taken away from one, as, for instance, in weaning. I would suggest, however, that what it rests on and organizes into its sexual meanings is, on the contrary, splitting. It only then 'subsequently' uses deprivation. One cannot experience absence, a gap – mankind, like nature, abhors a vacuum – one can only experience this unexperienceable as something taken away. One *uses* deprivation to describe the indescribable – the indescribable are splitting and the castration complex.

Freud talks of splitting where Klein perceives 'split-off parts' which can be communicated to the analyst by projection. The similarity of vocabulary conceals essential differences. I am not sure that the splitting of which Freud talks could be experienced in the transference. It can be witnessed in fetishism, but on the other side of the fetish object there is nothing there: no object, therefore, no subject. In my limited experience all the analyst can do is bear witness; all the patient can do is experience the most intense horror, a horror that is about absence but which can become filled with phantasmagoria. The emptiness of chaos made carnate, a plethora of unorganized feelings and objects.

In splitting, the subjectivity of the subject disappears. The horror is about the loss of oneself into one's own unconscious into the gap. But, because human subjectivity cannot ultimately exist outside a division into one of two sexes, then it is castration that finally comes to symbolize this split. The feminine comes to stand over the point of disappearance, the loss. In popular imagery, castration is usually thought of as something cut off, missing, absent, a wound, a scar. Analytically, I believe it is experienced not only in these pallid indicators of absence but as something appallingly out of place: something there which should not be there. The trauma captured in splitting is that one isn't there; the same trauma that castration comes to symbolize is that one is incomplete; the trauma that can be lived over and over again in the endless byways of life's failures and imperfections. The loss can only be filled up:

> If one of the ordinary symbols for a penis occurs in a dream doubled or multiplied, it is to be regarded as a warding off of castration.
>
> (1900a, p. 357)

Because human subjectivity cannot ultimately exist outside a division between the sexes – one cannot be no sex – then castration organizes the loss of subjecthood into its sexual meanings. Something with which the subject has identified, felt to be his or herself (something that satisfies the mother, the phallic phase – *being* the phallus for the mother – completing her), disappears, is missing. Castration is 'discovered' in the mother who is no longer perceived as whole, complete – something is missing, the baby has left her. The baby goes absent – vanishes from the mirror. Bisexuality is a movement across a line, it is *not* androgyny. For Freud there is no sexual distinction symbolized before the castration complex has done its organizing of the desires expressed within the Oedipal situation. There are male and female, active and passive, multifarious *behavioural* distinctions between boy and girl infants, but no notion in the psyche that one is not complete; that something can be missing.

The castration complex is not about women, nor men, but a danger, a horror to both – a gap that has to be filled in differently by each. In the fictional ideal type this will be for the boy by the illusion that a future regaining of phallic potency will replace his totality; for a girl this will be achieved by something psychically the same: a baby. Phallic potency and maternity for men and women – come to stand for wholeness.

Hysteria was, and is – whatever the age or generational status of the man or woman who expresses it – the daughter's disease: a child's

301

phantasy about her parents: the 'daughter' in the man or woman has not found a solution in homosexuality, maternity, or a career. To 'her' femininity really seems to equal the gap indicated by castration or, in Joan Riviere's words, it is enacted as 'a masquerade' to cover it. She is good at this but it cannot satisfy.

In the 1920s some important developments took place culminating on the one hand in ego-psychology and on the other in object relations theory, both Kleinian and non-Kleinian. There was a series of important and unresolved disagreements about the nature of female sexuality, but my point here is that despite an insistence on the problem, the question of femininity ceases to be what motivates the theoretical constructions. I propose to single out a few trends within Melanie Klein's work to indicate the implications of this.

In deciphering phantasy, Freud heard the child in his adult patients. Klein worked with children and found the infant in their phantasies. But there is a difference: the child and infant merge in Klein's way of thinking – their phantasies cope with the inner and outer realities in the present. For Freud, too, through his notion of the repetition compulsion, the child is alive in the adult's present. But for Freud the present always contains a construction of the past: the subject from birth to death is first and foremost, indeed, entirely, a historical subject, nothing other than what he makes of him or herself. This sense of history is not there in Klein's theory nor in her practice. Right until the end of his life, Freud's theory emphasized the analytic task of reconstruction of a history; Klein's highlighted interpretation and the analysis of the transference experience in which the task is to understand (largely through projection and introjection) what is being communicated between two people within the analytical session. Experience of psychic mechanism elicits the story which is no longer a tale told, but something revealed, discovered in process.

Where phantasy to Freud was the story – conscious or unconscious – that the subject tells about himself, for Klein it is the mental representation of the instinct and, simultaneously, a capacity to deal with inner and outer worlds. It joins instinct to object: primitively the oral drive phantasizes an object; a breast or some substitute that can be sucked, for instance, a penis. And in turn, the object alters the inner ego; what is taken in from outside transforms the inside:

> The analysis of early projective and introjective object relationships revealed phantasies of objects introjected into the ego from earliest infancy, starting with the ideal of the persecutory breast. To begin

with part-objects were introduced, like the breast and, later, the penis; then whole objects like the mother, the father, the parental couples.

(Segal, 1964, p. 8)

The boy and the girl have both the same and different drives: where their biology is different, their urges must differ. For Klein, the instinct is biological; for Freud it is 'our main mythology'. The boy and girl have the same objects. In Klein's theory, the object they first take in is predominantly part of the mother, then the whole mother; this gives them both in Klein's theory a 'primary femininity'. There is a shift of emphasis which, I believe, is crucial. For Klein, what you have got you transform by your phantasies and then take it in and it becomes you. For Freud, it is the attachment to what you have had to abandon that you take in. Freud's subject is constituted by filling the interstices where something is missing: one hallucinates, has delusions, tells stories. Klein's person becomes him- or herself by taking in what is present. Psychically, the mother in Freud's scheme is important when she goes away (the *fort/da* game), the penis when it is not there (penis envy). Klein's concept of envy (interestingly enough also the bedrock of her theory and therapy) is for a mother who has everything.

For Klein the theory sets up a situation in which the ego phantasizes directly out of its instincts and body feelings onto an object. Whereas Freud's 'body-ego' is always a homunculus standing on its head, for Klein, the objects (despite the accreted confusing phantasies) are, in essence, taken for what they are biologically and socially. The mother is a woman, feminine. The penis, even when inside the mother, is a masculine attribute. So, for instance, when the object of the oral phase moves from breast to penis, for the girl this becomes the heterosexual moment. The projecting penis is masculine where the breast is not. The gendered object gives meaning.

For the little girl, this first oral turning to the penis is a heterosexual move paving the way to the genital situation and the wish to incorporate the penis in her vagina. But at the same time it contributes to her homosexual trends in that . . . the oral desire is linked with incorporation and identification, and the wish to be fed by the penis is accompanied by a wish to possess a penis of her own.

(Segal, 1964, p. 97)

Freud listens to a story, constructs a myth. The unconscious shows they are only stories, myths. It is the gap, the point where the story vanishes, the subject disappears. (Ego-psychologists believe the story is the whole truth and nothing but the truth the story is all.) But, what we are witnessing in Klein's description is not the unconscious as another scene, that gap which has its own laws, but an unconscious that is filled, replete with a chaos of phantasmagoria, an unconscious as full as the external world seems to be. Her theory is about such an unconscious.

Perhaps I can give another analogy, tentative; a thought-inflight. Freud's theory is a myth, a story of a story – the subject's narrative structuring of him – or herself. It stops, it fails, it needs re-telling another way. Though a novelist writes of characters of different sexes, he or she never writes of anyone of no sex or in the middle of the dividing line – Virginia Woolf's *Orlando*, whose hero/heroine must change sides, highlights this. In Freudian theory, masculinity and femininity are only their difference from each other. Difference is articulated by something imagined to be missing. From the position of something missing, each sex can be imagined as having what the other has not. In essence this is what a novelist's story is all about.

But there is another literary analogy that could act as a possibility for theory. Not a myth, but a symbolist poem. This is what Klein's theory suggests. The wish to bite indicates the oral drive; the oral drive, aggression; aggression is Klein's (not Freud's) death drive. Physical impulse becomes a conception, the conception a theory. In a symbolist poem, the symbol shapes the product. The task is not to produce hypothetical lines around blurred fields of colour but to let the image produce its own shape. The poem, however, does not speak to sexual differentiation.

As far as femininity is concerned, we have moved from the hysteric whose femininity, being about nothing, had nothing she wanted, to the feminine boy and girl who, in imaginatively taking in their mother, have everything. But I believe there is a confusion in the conceptualization here. This mother who has everything is not 'feminine'; she is complete. The poem is not, as many people – including Klein in her theory of primary femininity – argue, feminine, even if it partakes of the mother. Of course, the mother is where femininity in its positive filling in of a gap has landed and the association must retrospectively be made. But this poem and this mother are about notions of plenitude, fullness, completeness. Nothing is missing. The verb is in the infinitive. There is no 'I' nor 'other'. In the story sexual difference

304

is symbolized around absence – the abandoned object cathexis, the envy of what is missing that once, imaginatively, was there. Here in the poem, the envy is for what is there and it is everything – milk, breast, faeces, babies, penises. What Klein is describing here is the raw material, the plenitude of objects and feelings which the story relies on when it comes to construct itself, to fill in its gaps. It is perhaps poetic justice that the hysteric who must repudiate her femininity which is about nothing comes to rest on a mother who has all. But we must allow the story to tell us something about the poem as well. In describing what he calls the deployment of sexuality in the nineteenth century Michel Foucault (1976) argues that there took place:

> A hysterization of women's bodies: a threefold process whereby the feminine body was analysed – qualified and disqualified – as being thoroughly saturated with sexuality; whereby it was integrated into the sphere of medical practices, by reason of a pathology intrinsic to it; whereby, finally, it was placed in organic communication with the social body (whose regulated fecundity it was supposed to ensure), the family space (of which it had to be a substantial and functional element), and the life of children (which it produced and had to guarantee, by virtue of a biologico-moral responsibility lasting through the entire period of the children's education): *the Mother, with her negative image of 'nervous woman', constituted the most visible form of this hysterization.* (my italics)

Motherhood purports to fill in the absence which femininity covers over and which hysteria tries not to acknowledge. From their positions along a continuum, motherhood and hysteria, to have or to have not, to be or not to be, constantly question each other.

305

References

Abram, J. (2007). *The Language of Winnicott: A Dictionary of Winnicott's Use of Words*, 2nd edn. London: Karnac.

Abram, J. (ed.) (2013). *Donald Winnicott Today*. Hove: Routledge.

Alpert, A. (1959). Reversibility of pathological fixations associated with maternal deprivation in infancy. *Psychoanalytic Study of the Child*, 14: 169–185.

Andersson, O. (1962). *Studies in the Prehistory of Psychoanalysis*. Stockholm: Scandinavian University Books.

Anzieu, D. (1959). *El autoanálisis de Freud y el descubrimiento del psicoanálisis*, Vol. 2. Mexico: Siglo XXI, 1979.

Balint, A., and Balint, M. (1939). On transference and counter-transference. In M. Balint, *Primary Love and Psycho-Analytic Technique*. London: Tavistock Publications, 1965.

Balint, E. (1963). On being empty of oneself. In *Before I Was I: Psychoanalysis and the Imagination*. J. Mitchell and M. Parsons (eds). London: Free Association Books, 1993.

Balint, E. (1968). The mirror and the receiver. (Originally published as 'Remarks on Freud's metaphors about the "mirror" and the "receiver"'). In *Before I Was I: Psychoanalysis and the Imagination*. J. Mitchell and M. Parsons (eds). London: Free Association Books, 1993.

Balint, E. (1973). Technical problems in the analysis of women by a woman analyst: A contribution to the question 'What does a woman want?'. In *Before I Was I: Psychoanalysis and the Imagination*. J. Mitchell and M. Parsons (eds). London: Free Association Books, 1993.

Balint, E. (1993). *Before I Was I: Psychoanalysis and the Imagination*. J. Mitchell and M. Parsons (eds). London: Free Association Books.

Balint, M. (1933). On transference of emotions. In *Primary Love and Psycho-Analytic Technique*. London: Tavistock Publications, 1965.

Balint, M. (1949). Changing therapeutic aims and techniques in psycho-analysis. In *Primary Love and Psycho-Analytic Technique*. London: Tavistock Publications, 1965.

Balint, M. (1952). New beginning and the paranoid and depressive syndromes. In *Primary Love and Psycho-Analytic Technique*. London: Tavistock Publications, 1965.

Balint, M. (1959). *Thrills and Regressions*. London: Hogarth Press.

Balint, M. (1965). *Primary Love and Psycho-Analytic Technique*. London: Tavistock Publications.

Balint, M. (1968). *The Basic Fault*. London: Tavistock Publications.

Baranger, M., Baranger, W., and Mom, J.M. (1987). The infantile psychic trauma from us to Freud: Pure trauma, retroactivity and reconstruction. *International Journal of Psychoanalysis*, 69: 112–128, 1988.

Barossa, J., Bronstein, C., and Pajaczkowska, C. (eds). (2015). *The New Klein–Lacan Dialogues*. London: Karnac.

Benedek, T. (1952). The psychosomatic implications of the primary unit: Mother–child. In *Psychosomatic Functions in Women*. New York: Ronald Press.

Benvenuto, B., and Kennedy, R. (1986). *The Works of Jacques Lacan: An Introduction*. London: Free Association Books.

Beres, D. (1956). Ego deviation and the concept of schizophrenia. *Psychoanalytic Study of the Child*, 11: 164–235.

Beres, D., and Obers, S.J. (1950). The effects of extreme deprivation in infancy on psychic structure in adolescence. *Psychoanalytic Study of the Child*, 5: 212–235.

Bianchedi, E.T. de, Antar, R., Cortiñas, L.P. de, Boschan, L.T.S. de, Podetti, M.R.F.B. de, Piccolo E.G. de, Miravent, I., and Waserman, M. (1984). Beyond Freudian metapsychology. The metapsychological points of view of the Kleinian School. *International Journal of Psychoanalysis*, 65: 389–398.

Bion, W.R. (1958). On hallucination. *International Journal of Psychoanalysis*, 39: 341–349.

Bion, W.R. (1962a). *Learning from Experience*. London: Heinemann; New York: Basic Books.

Bion, W.R. (1962b). A theory of thinking. In *Second Thoughts*. New York: Jason Aronson, 1977.

Bion, W.R. (1970). *Attention and Interpretation*. London: Tavistock Publications.

Bion, W.R. (1973). *Brazilian Lectures 1*. Rio de Janeiro: Imago Editora, 1974.

Bion, W.R. (1976). Evidence. *Scientific Bulletin of the British Psycho-Analytical Society, No. 10* (1981). Reprinted in *Clinical Seminars and Other Works* (ed. by F. Bion). London: Karnac, 2000.

Bion, W.R. (1978). *Four Discussions with W.R. Bion*. Perthshire: Clunie Press.

Bion, W.R. (1980). *Bion in New York and São Paulo*. Perthshire: Clunie Press.

Birksted-Breen, D. (2003). Time and the *après-coup*. *International Journal of Psychoanalysis*, 84: 1501–1515.

Birksted-Breen, D. (2005). The feminine. In S. Budd and R. Rusbridger (eds), *Introducing Psychoanalysis: Essential Themes and Topics*. Hove: Routledge (pp. 142–152).

Birksted-Breen, D., and Flanders, S. (2010). General introduction. In D. Birksted-Breen, S. Flanders, and A. Gibeault (eds), *Reading French Psychoanalysis*. Hove: Routledge.

Bleger, J. (1967a). Enrique Pichon Rivière. Su aporte a la psiquiatria, y al psicoanálisis. *Acta Psiquiátrica. Psicológica América Latina*, 13: 346–350.

Bleger, J. (1967b). *Symbiosis and Ambiguity: A Psychoanalytic Study*. Hove: Routledge, 2013.

Bollas, C. (1976). Le langage secret de la mere at de l'enfant. *Nouvelle Revue de Psychanalyse*, 14: 241–246.

Bollas, C. (1978). The aesthetic moment and the search for transformation. *Annual of Psychoanalysis*, 6: 385–394.

Bollas, C. (1982). On the relation to the self as an object. *International Journal of Psychoanalysis*, 63: 347–359.

Bollas, C. (1983). Expressive uses of the countertransference: Notes to the patient from oneself. In *The Shadow of the Object: Psychoanalysis of the Unthought Known*. London: Free Association Books, 1987.

Bollas, C. (1987). *The Shadow of the Object: Psychoanalysis of the Unthought Known*. London: Free Association Books.

Bollas, C. (1989). *Forces of Destiny: Psychoanalysis and Human Idiom*. London: Free Association Books.

Bollas, C. (2000). *Hysteria*. London: Routledge.

Borgoyne, B., and Sullivan, M. (eds) (1999). *The Klein–Lacan Dialogues*. New York: Other Press (first edn).

Botella, C., and Botella, S. (2005). *The Work of Psychic Figurability: Mental States Without Representation* (trans. A. Weller). Hove: Brunner-Routledge.

Bowlby, J. (1960). Separation anxiety. *International Journal of Psychoanalysis*, 41: 89–113.

Bowlby, J. (1969). *Attachment: Attachment and Loss*, Vol. 1. London: Pimlico Books, 1997.

Brazelton, T.B. (1992). *Touchpoints: Emotional and Behavioral Development*. Reading, MA: Addison-Wesley.

Brenman, E. (1978). The narcissism of the analyst: Its effect in clinical practice. In *Recovery of the Lost Good Object*. Hove: Routledge, 2006.

Brenman, E. (1985). Hysteria. In *Recovery of the Lost Good Object*. Hove: Routledge, 2006.

Brenman Pick, I. (1985). Working through in the countertransference. *International Journal of Psychoanalysis*, 66: 157–166.

Brierley, M. (1937). Affects in theory and practice. In *Trends in Psycho-Analysis*. London: Hogarth Press, 1951 (pp. 43–56).

Brierley, M. (1943). Memorandum on her technique. In P. King and R. Steiner (eds), *The Freud–Klein Controversies 1941–45*. London: Routledge, 1991 (pp. 617–628).

Britton, R. (1999). Getting in on the act: The hysterical solution. *International Journal of Psychoanalysis*, 80: 1–14.

Britton, R. (2003). *Sex, Death, and the Superego: Experiences in Psychoanalysis*. London: Karnac.

Britton, R. (2005). Anna O: The first case, revisited and revised. In R.J. Perelberg (ed.), *Freud: A Modern Reader*. London: Whurr (pp. 31–44).

Brome, V. (1982). *Ernest Jones: Freud's Alter Ego*. London: Caliban Books.

Brown, D.G. (1977). Drowsiness in the counter-transference. *International Review of Psycho-Analysis*. 4: 481–492.

Budd, S. (2001). No sex, please – we're British: Sexuality in English and French psychoanalysis. In C. Harding (ed.), *Sexuality: Psychoanalytic Perspectives*. Hove: Routledge (pp. 52–68).

Burlingham, D. (1961). Some notes on the development of the blind. *Psychoanalytic Study of the Child*, 16: 121–145.

Butler, J. (1990). *Gender Trouble: Feminism and the Subversion of Identity*. London: Routledge.

Butler, J. (2015). Ideologies of the super-ego: Psychoanalysis and feminism, revisited. In R. Duschinsky and S. Walker (eds), *Juliet Mitchell and the Lateral Axis*. New York: Palgrave Macmillan (pp. 57–75).

Caldwell, L., and Joyce, A. (eds) (2011). *Reading Winnicott*. Hove: Routledge.

Calef, V. (1976). *The Psychoanalytic Process*. Panel discussion, Association for Child Psychoanalysis, Kansas City. Unpublished paper.

Casement, P. (1985). *On Learning from the Patient*. London: Routledge.

Casement, P. (2002). *Learning from Our Mistakes*. Hove: Brunner-Routledge.

Casement, P. (2006). *Learning from Life*. Hove: Routledge.

Chasseguet-Smirgel, J. (1975). *The Ego Ideal: Psychoanalytic Essay on the Malady of the Ideal*. London: Free Association Books, 1985.

Chetrit-Vatine, V. (2011). The frame, the analyst's passion and the ethical seduction of the analytic situation. *EPF-Bulletin*, 64: 247–260.

Cixous, H. (1976). *Portrait of Dora*. London: John Calder, 1979.

Cixous, H., and Clement, C. (1975). *La jeune née*. Paris: Union Générale d'Editions.

Clément, C. (1981). *The Lives and Legends of Jacques Lacan* (trans. A. Goldhammer). New York: Columbia University Press, 1983.

Cohen, J. (2013). *The Private Life: Why We Remain in the Dark*. London: Granta Books.

Coleman, R.W., Kris, E., and Provence, S. (1953). The study of variations of early parental attitudes. *Psychoanalytic Study of the Child*, 8: 20–47.

Cordier, S. (1977). D.W. Winnicott. *Revue L'Arc No. 69*. Aix-en-Provence.

Davies, R. (2012). Anxiety: The importunate companion. Psychoanalytic theory of castration and separation anxieties and implications for clinical technique. *International Journal of Psychoanalysis*, 93: 1101–1114.

Decker, J.S. (1982). The choice of a name: Dora and Freud's relationship with Breuer. *Journal of the American Psychoanalytic Association*, 30: 113–135.

Deutsch, F. (1957). A footnote to Freud's 'Fragment of an analysis of a case of hysteria.' In F. Deutsch (ed.), *On the Mysterious Leap from the Mind to the Body*. New York: International Universities Press, 1959.

Dimen, M. (2011). Lapsus linguae, or a slip of the tongue? A sexual violation in an analytic treatment and its personal and theoretical aftermath. *Contemporary Psychoanalysis*, 47: 35–79.

Donnet, J.-L. (2010). From the fundamental rule to the analysing situation. In D. Birksted-Breen, S. Flanders, and A. Gibeault (eds), *Reading French Psychoanalysis*. Hove: Routledge.

Duschinsky, R., and Walker, S. (eds) (2015). *Juliet Mitchell and the Lateral Axis*. New York: Palgrave Macmillan.

Edkins, A. (1979). Why I like Ess. *Bananas* [London], 21.

Edwards, M.J., and Bhatia, K.P. (2012). Functional (psychogenic) movement disorders: Merging mind and brain. *Lancet Neurology*, 11: 250–260.

Eigen, M. (1999). *Toxic Nourishment*. London: Karnac.

Eissler, K.R. (1953). The effect of the structure of the ego on psychoanalytic technique. *Journal of the American Psychoanalytic Association*, 1: 104–143.

Eissler, K.R. (1965). *Medical Orthodoxy and the Future of Psycho-Analysis*. New York: International Universities Press.

Eliot, T.S. (1921). Tradition and the individual talent. In *The Sacred Wood*. New York: Alfred A. Knopf, 1921; Bartleby.com, 1996.

Ellenberger, R.H.F. (1970). *The Discovery of the Unconscious*. London: Allen Lane.

Erikson, E.H. (1946). Ego development and historical change. *Psychoanalytic Study of the Child*, 2: 359–396.

Erikson, E.H. (1950). Growth and crises of the healthy personality. In *Identity and the Life Cycle*. New York: International Universities Press, 1959.

Erikson, E.H. (1956). The problem of ego identity. *Journal of the American Psychoanalytic Association*, 4: 16–21.

Erikson, E.H. (1961). Reality and actuality. *Journal of the American Psychoanalytic Association*, 10 (1962): 451–474.

Escalona, S. (1953). Emotional development in the first year of life. In M.J.E. Senn (ed.), *Problems of Infancy and Childhood*. New York: Josiah Macy Jr. Foundation.

Faimberg, H. (2005). *The Telescoping of Generations: Listening to the Narcissistic Links Between Generations*. Hove: Routledge.

Faimberg, H. (2012). *Nachträglichkeit* and Winnicott's 'Fear of Breakdown'. In J. Abram (ed.), *Donald Winnicott Today*. Hove: Routledge.

Fairbairn, W.R.D. (1941). A revised psychopathology of the psychoses and psychoneuroses. In *Psychoanalytic Studies of the Personality*. London: Tavistock Publications, 1952; Hove: Routledge, 1994 (pp. 28–58).

Fenichel, O. (1937). The concept of trauma in contemporary psychoanalytic theory. In *Collected Papers of Otto Fenichel*, 2nd series. New York: Norton, 1954.

Ferenczi, S. (1928). The elasticity of psychoanalytic technique. In *Final Contributions to the Problems and Methods of Psycho-Analysis*. London: Hogarth, 1955 (pp. 87–101).

Fliess, R. (1953). Countertransference and counteridentification. *Journal of the American Psychoanalytic Association*, 1: 268–284.

Flügel, J. (1955). *Studies in Feeling and Desire*. London: Duckworth.

Fonagy, P., and Target, M. (2003). *Psychoanalytic Theories: Perspectives from Developmental Psychopathology*. London: Whurr.

Fordham, M. (1960). Countertransference. *British Journal of Medical Psychology*, 33: 1–8.

Foucault, M. (1976). *The History of Sexuality*, Vol. 1. Harmondsworth: Penguin, 1981.

Frankl, L. (1961). Some observations on the development and disturbances of integration in childhood. *Psychoanalytic Study of the Child*, 16: 146–163.

Freud, A. (1929). *Introduction to the Technique of Child Analysis*. New York and Washington, DC: Nervous and Mental Disease Publ. Co.

Freud, A. (1936). *The Ego and the Mechanisms of Defence*, Revised edn 1966. London: Hogarth Press; New York: International Universities Press.

Freud, A. (1951). Observations on child development. In *Indications for Child Analysis and Other Papers*. New York: International Universities Press, 1968; London: Hogarth Press, 1969.

Freud, A. (1952). The role of bodily illness in the mental life of children. In *Indications for Child Analysis and Other Papers*. New York: International Universities Press, 1968; London: Hogarth Press, 1969.

Freud, A. (1958). Child observation and prediction of development. In *Research at the Hampstead Child-Therapy Clinic and Other Papers*. New York: International Universities Press, 1969; London: Hogarth Press, 1970.

Freud, A. (1962). The theory of the parent–infant relationship. In *Research at the Hampstead Child-Therapy Clinic and Other Papers*. New York: International Universities Press, 1969; London: Hogarth Press, 1970.

Freud, A. (1968). *Indications for Child Analysis and Other Papers*. New York: International Universities Press; London: Hogarth Press, 1969.

Freud, A. (1979). Personal memories of Ernest Jones. *International Journal of Psychoanalysis*, 60: 285–287.

Freud, A., and Burlingham, D. (1942). *War and Children*. New York: International Universities Press, 1943.

Freud, A., and Burlingham, D. (1944). *Infants without Families*, Revised edn 1973. New York: International Universities Press; London: Hogarth Press.

Freud, E., Freud, L., and Grubrich-Simitis, I. (eds) (1978). *Sigmund Freud: His Life in Pictures and Words*. New York: Harcourt Brace Jovanovich.

Freud, S. (1886d). Observation of a severe case of hemi-anaesthesia in a hysterical male. *S.E.* 1.

Freud, S. (1888b). Hysteria. *S.E.* 1.

Freud, S. (1893a) (with Breuer, J.). On the psychical mechanism of hysterical phenomena: Preliminary communication. *S.E.* 2.

Freud, S. (1893c). Some points for a comparative study of organic and hysterical motor paralyses. *S.E.* 1.

Freud, S. (1895b). On the grounds for detaching a particular syndrome from neurasthenia under the description 'Anxiety Neurosis'. *S.E.* 3.

Freud, S. (1895d) (with Breuer, J.). *Studies on Hysteria. S.E.* 2.

Freud, S. (1896a). Heredity and the aetiology of the neuroses. *S.E.* 3.

Freud, S. (1897b). Abstracts of the Scientific Writings of Dr. Sigm. Freud (1877–1897). *S.E.* 3.

Freud, S. (1900a). *The Interpretation of Dreams. S.E.* 5.

Freud, S. (1905d). *Three Essays on the Theory of Sexuality. S.E.* 7.

Freud, S. (1905e). Fragment of an analysis of a case of hysteria. *S.E.* 7.

Freud, S. (1908c). On the sexual theories of children. *S.E.* 9.

Freud, S. (1909b). Analysis of a phobia in a five-year-old boy. *S.E.* 10.

Freud, S. (1909d). Notes upon a case of obsessional neurosis. *S.E.* 10.

Freud, S. (1910d). The future prospects of psychoanalytic therapy. *S.E.* 11: 141–151.

Freud, S. (1911b). Formulations on the two principles of mental functioning. *S.E.* 12.

Freud, S. (1911c). Psycho-analytic notes on an autobiographical account of a case of paranoia (Dementia paranoides). *S.E.* 12.

Freud, S. (1912b). The dynamics of transference. *S.E.* 12.

Freud, S. (1912e). Recommendations to physicians practising psycho-analysis. *S.E.* 12.

Freud, S. (1912–13). *Totem and Taboo. S.E.* 13: 1–162.

Freud, S. (1913i). The disposition to obsessional neurosis. *S.E.* 12.

Freud, S. (1914c). On narcissism: An introduction. *S.E.* 14.

Freud, S. (1914d). On the history of the psycho-analytic movement. *S.E.* 14.

Freud, S. (1915a). Observations on transference-love (Further recommendations on the technique of psycho-analysis, Ill). *S.E.* 12.

Freud, S. (1915c). Instincts and their vicissitudes. *S.E.* 14.

Freud, S. (1915d). Repression. *S.E.* 14.

Freud, S. (1915e). The unconscious. *S.E.* 14.

Freud, S. (1916–17). *New Introductory Lectures on Psycho-Analysis. S.E.* 15, 16.

Freud, S. (1917e). Mourning and melancholia. *S.E.* 14.

Freud, S. (1918b). From the history of an infantile neurosis. *S.E.* 17: 3–122.

Freud, S. (1919e). A child is being beaten. *S.E.* 17.

Freud, S. (1920a). The psychogenesis of a case of homosexuality in a woman. *S.E.* 18.

Freud, S. (1920g). *Beyond the Pleasure Principle. S.E.* 18.

Freud, S. (1923b). *The Ego and the Id. S.E.* 19.

Freud, S. (1923e). The infantile genital organization (An interpolation into the theory of sexuality). *S.E.* 19.

Freud, S. (1925j). Some psychical consequences of the anatomical distinction between the sexes. *S.E.* 19.

Freud, S. (1926d). *Inhibitions, Symptoms and Anxiety. S.E.* 20.

Freud, S. (1926e). *The Question of Lay Analysis. S.E.* 19.

Freud, S. (1927a). Postscript to *The Question of Lay Analysis. S.E.* 20.

Freud, S. (1931b). Female sexuality. *S.E.* 21.

Freud, S. (1933a). *New Introductory Lectures on Psycho-Analysis. S.E.* 22.

Freud, S. (1933b). Why war? *S.E.* 22.

Freud, S. (1935). Letter to Carl Muller-Braunschweig, published as Freud and female sexuality: A previously unpublished letter. *Psychiatry*, 1971 (pp. 328–329).

Freud, S. (1937c). Analysis terminable and interminable. *S.E.* 23.

Freud, S. (1937d). Constructions in analysis. *S.E.* 23.

Freud, S. (1940e). Splitting of the ego in the process of defence. *S.E.* 23.

Freud, S. (1950 [1892–1899]). Extracts from the Fliess papers. *S.E.* 1.

Freud, S. (1950 [1895]). Project for a scientific psychology. *S.E.* 1: 283–387.

Freud, S. (1954). *The Origins of Psycho-Analysis: Letters to Wilhelm Fliess.* New York: Basic Books.

Freud, S. (1956a [1886]). Report on Freud's studies in Paris and Berlin. *S.E.* 1.

Fries, M.E. (1946). The child's ego development and the training of adults in his environment. *Psychoanalytic Study of the Child*, 2: 85–112.

Gabbard, G.O. (1995). The early history of boundary violations in psychoanalysis. *Journal of the American Psychoanalytic Association*, 43: 1115–1136.

Gabbard, G.O. (2003). Miscarriages of psychoanalytic treatment with suicidal patients. *International Journal of Psychoanalysis*, 84: 249–261.

Gabbard, G.O., and Lester, E. (1995). *Boundaries and Boundary Violations in Psychoanalysis.* New York: Basic Books.

Gabbard, G.O., and Peltz, M.L. (2001). Speaking the unspeakable: Institutional reactions to boundary violations by training analysts. *Journal of the American Psychoanalytic Association*, 49: 659–673.

Gaddini, E. (1969). On imitation. *International Journal of Psychoanalysis*, 50: 475–484.

García, G.L. (1980). *Psicoanálisis. Una Política del Síntoma.* Zaragoza: Alcrudo Editor.

Gearhart, S. (1979). The scene of psycho-analysis. the unanswered questions of Dora. *Diacritics*, March: 114–126.

References

Geleerd, E.R. (1956). Clinical contribution to the problem of the early mother–child relationship. *Psychoanalytic Study of the Child*, 11: 336–351.

Geleerd, E.R. (1958). Borderline states in childhood and adolescence. *Psychoanalytic Study of the Child*, 13: 279–295.

Gillespie, W.H. (1963). *Jubilee Oration. The British Psycho-Analytical Society: Retrospect and Prospect, Fiftieth Anniversary*. London: The British Psycho-Analytical Society.

Gillespie, W.H. (1979). Ernest Jones: The bonny fighter. *International Journal of Psychoanalysis*, 60: 273–279.

Gitelson, M. (1952). The emotional position of the analyst in the psychoanalytic situation. *International Journal of Psychoanalysis*, 33: 1–10.

Glasser, M. (1979). Some aspects of the role of aggression in the perversions. In I. Rosen (ed.), *Sexual Deviation*. Oxford: Oxford University Press (pp. 278–305).

Glasser, M. (1985). 'The weak spot' – Some observations on male sexuality. *International Journal of Psychoanalysis*, 66: 405–414.

Glenn, J. (1980). Freud's adolescent patients: Katharina, Dora and the 'homosexual woman'. In M. Kanzer and J. Glenn (eds), *Freud and His Patients*. New York: Jason Aronson.

Glover, E. (1927). Lectures on technique in psycho-analysis. *International Journal of Psychoanalysis*, 8: 311–338.

Glover, E. (1939). The psychoanalysis of affects. In *Selected Papers on Psycho-Analysis, Vol. 1, On the Early Development of Mind*. London: Imago, 1956.

Glover, E. (1949). The position of psycho-analysis in Britain. In *Selected Papers on Psycho-Analysis, Vol. 1, On the Early Development of Mind*. London: Imago, 1956.

Glover, E. (1966). Psycho-analysis in England. In F. Alexander, S. Eisenstein, and M. Grotjahn (eds), *Psychoanalytic Pioneers*. New York: Basic Books, 1966.

Godley, W. (2001). Saving Masud Khan. *The London Review of Books*, 22 February, pp. 3–7.

Goldstein, K. (1959). Abnormal mental conditions in infancy. *Journal of Nervous and Mental Disease*, 128: 538–557.

Green, A. (1964). Neurosis obsesiva e histeria. Sus relaciones en Freud y desde entonces. In J. Sauri (ed.), *Las Histerias*. Buenos Aires: Ediciones Nueva Visón, 1975.

Green, A. (1972). Aggression, femininity, paranoia and reality. *International Journal of Psychoanalysis*, 53: 205–211.

Green, A. (1973). *The Fabric of Affect in the Psychoanalytic Discourse* (trans. A. Sheridan). London and New York: Routledge, 1999.

Green, A. (1975). The analyst, symbolization and absence in the analytic setting. In *On Private Madness*. London: Hogarth Press & The Institute of Psychoanalysis, 1986.

Green, A. (1977). Conceptions of affect. In *On Private Madness*. London: Hogarth Press & The Institute of Psychoanalysis, 1986.

315

Green, A. (1982). *Freud and Winnicott*. Public lecture, The Squiggle Foundation, London.

Green, A. (1984). Le Langage dans la psychanalyse. In A. Green (ed.), *Langages*. Paris: Belles Lettres.

Green, A. (1986). The dead mother. In *On Private Madness*. London: Hogarth Press & The Institute of Psychoanalysis.

Green, A. (1995). Has sexuality anything to do with psychoanalysis? *International Journal of Psychoanalysis*, 76: 871–883.

Green, A. (1999). *The Work of the Negative* (trans. A. Weller). London: Free Association Books.

Green, A. (2000a). *Chains of Eros: The Sexual in Psychoanalysis*. London: Rebus.

Green, A. (2000b). The intrapsychic and the intersubjective in psychoanalysis. *Psychoanalytic Quarterly*, 69: 1–39.

Green, A., and Kohon, G. (2005). *Love and Its Vicissitudes*. Hove: Routledge.

Greenacre, P. (1954). Problems of infantile neurosis. *Psychoanalytic Study of the Child*, 9: 18–24, 37–40.

Greenacre, P. (1958). Towards the understanding of the physical nucleus of some defence reactions. *International Journal of Psychoanalysis*, 39: 69–76.

Greenacre, P. (1959). On focal symbiosis. In L. Jessner and E. Pavenstedt (eds), *Dynamic Psychopathology in Childhood*. New York: Grune & Stratton.

Greenacre, P. (1960a). Considerations regarding the parent–infant relationship. *International Journal of Psychoanalysis*, 41: 571–584.

Greenacre, P. (1960b). Further notes on fetishism. *Psychoanalytic Study of the Child*, 15: 191–207.

Greenacre, P. (1960c). Regression and fixation. *Journal of the American Psychoanalytic Association*, 8: 703–723.

Greenacre, P. (1975). On reconstruction. *Journal of the American Psychoanalytic Association*, 23: 693–712.

Greenberg, J.R., and Mitchell, S.A. (1983). *Object Relations in Psycho-Analytic Theory*. Cambridge, MA: Harvard University Press.

Greenson, R. (1966). That 'impossible' profession. *Journal of the American Psychoanalytic Association*, 14: 9–27.

Greenson, R. (1974). Loving, hating and indifference towards the patient. *International Review of Psycho-Analysis*, 1: 259–266.

Hart, B. (1911). Freud's conception of hysteria. *Brain*, 33 (131): 338–366.

Hartmann, H. (1939). *Ego Psychology and the Problem of Adaptation*. London: Hogarth Press; New York: International Universities Press, 1958.

Hartmann, H. (1950a). Comments on the psychoanalytic theory of the ego. In *Essays on Ego Psychology*. London: Hogarth Press; New York: International Universities Press, 1964.

Hartmann, H. (1950b). Psychoanalysis and developmental psychology. In *Essays on Ego Psychology*. London: Hogarth Press; New York: International Universities Press, 1964.

Hartmann, H. (1952). The mutual influences in the development of the ego and the id. In *Essays on Ego Psychology*. London: Hogarth Press; New York: International Universities Press, 1964.

Hayman, A. (1986). On Marjorie Brierley. *International Review of Psycho-Analysis*, 13: 383–392.

Heath, S. (1982). *The Sexual Fix*. London: Macmillan.

Heimann, P. (1950). On counter-transference. In M. Tonnesmann (ed.), *About Children and Children-No-Longer: Collected Papers 1942–80*. London: Routledge, 1989.

Heimann, P. (1956). Dynamics of transference interpretations. In M. Tonnesmann (ed.). *About Children and Children-No-Longer: Collected Papers 1942–80*. London: Routledge, 1989.

Heimann, P. (1960). Counter-transference. In M. Tonnesmann (ed.) *About Children and Children-No-Longer: Collected Papers 1942–80*. London: Routledge, 1989.

Hellmann, I. (1962). Hampstead Nursery follow-up studies: 1. Sudden separation and its effect over twenty years. *Psychoanalytic Study of the Child*, 17: 159–176.

Hill, G. (2008). Of diligence and jeopardy. In K. Haynes (ed.), *Collected Critical Writings*. Oxford: Oxford University Press (pp. 280–296).

Hoffer, W. (1949). Mouth, hand and ego integration. *Psychoanalytic Study of the Child*, 3–4: 49–56.

Hoffer, W. (1950). Development of the body ego. *Psychoanalytic Study of the Child*, 5: 18–23.

Hoffer, W. (1952). The mutual influences in the development of ego and id: Earliest stages. *Psychoanalytic Study of the Child*, 7: 31–41.

Hoffer, W. (1956). Symposium: Transference and transference neurosis. *International Journal of Psychoanalysis*, 37: 377–379.

Hutt, C. (1972). *Males and Females*. Harmondsworth: Penguin.

Israel, L. (1972). *El Goce de la histérica*. Barcelona: Editorial Argonauta, 1979.

Jacobs, T.J. (1999). Countertransference past and present: A review of the concept. *International Journal of Psychoanalysis*, 80: 575–594.

Jacobson, E. (1965). *The Self and the Object World*. London: Hogarth Press.

James, M. (1960). Premature ego development: Some observations on disturbances in the first three months of life. *International Journal of Psychoanalysis*, 41: 288–294.

James, M. (1962). Infantile narcissistic trauma. *International Journal of Psychoanalysis*, 43: 69–79.

James, M. (1980). Are there concepts essential to the Independent group? *The Scientific Bulletin of the British Psycho-Analytical Society*, No. 6

Joffe, W.G., and Sandler, J. (1968). Comments on the psycho-analytic psychology of adaptation, with special reference to the role of affects and the representational world. *International Journal of Psychoanalysis*, 49: 445–454.

Jones, E. (1908). Rationalization in everyday life. In *Papers on Psycho-Analysis*. London: Bailliere, Tindall and Cox, 1948.

Jones, E. (1927a). Discussion on lay analysis. *International Journal of Psychoanalysis*, 8: 174–198.

Jones, E. (1927b). The early development of female sexuality. In *Papers on Psycho-Analysis*. London: Bailliere, Tindall and Cox, 1948.

Jones, E. (1929). Fear, guilt and hate. In *Papers on Psycho-Analysis*. London: Bailliere, Tindall and Cox, 1948.

Jones, E. (1936). Psychoanalysis and the instincts. In *Papers on Psycho-Analysis*. London: Bailliere, Tindall and Cox, 1948.

Jones, E. (1953). *The Life and Work of Sigmund Freud, Vol. 1*. London: Hogarth Press; New York: Basic Books.

Jones, E. (1957). *The Life and Work of Sigmund Freud, Vol. 3*. London: Hogarth Press, 1974.

Jones, E. (1959). *Free Associations: Memories of a Psycho-Analyst*. London: Hogarth Press.

Jones, E., Strachey, J., and Rickman, J. (1927). Abbreviated report of the Sub-Committee on Lay Analysis. *International Journal of Psychoanalysis*, 8: 559–560.

Joseph, E.J., and Widlöcher, E. (eds) (1983). *The Identity of the Psycho-Analyst*. New York: International Universities Press.

Kant, I. (1781). *The Critique of Pure Reason*. London: Dent Everyman Library, 1934.

Keene, J. (2012). Reflections on the evolution of Independent psychoanalytic thought. In P. Williams, J. Keene, and S. Dermen (eds), *Independent Psychoanalysis Today*. London: Karnac, 2012 (pp. 3–62).

Kennedy, R. (2012). A severe form of breakdown of communication in the psychoanalysis of an ill adolescent. In P. Williams, J. Keene, and S. Dermen (eds), *Independent Psychoanalysis Today*. London: Karnac.

Kernberg, O. (1965). Notes on countertransference. *Journal of the American Psychoanalytic Association*, 13: 38–56.

Khan, M.M.R. (1960a). Clinical aspects of the schizoid personality: affects and technique. In *The Privacy of the Self*. London: Hogarth Press, 1974.

Khan, M.M.R. (1960b). Regression and integration in the analytic setting: A clinical essay on the transference and counter-transference aspects of these phenomena. In *The Privacy of the Self*. London: Hogarth Press, 1974.

Khan, M.M.R. (1962). The role of polymorph-perverse body experiences and object-relations in ego-integration. In *Alienation in Perversions*. London: Hogarth Press, 1979.

Khan, M.M.R. (1963a). Ego-ideal, excitement and the threat of annihilation. In *The Privacy of the Self*. London: Hogarth Press, 1974.

Khan, M.M.R. (1963b). The role of infantile sexuality and early object relations in female homosexuality. In I. Rosen (ed.), *The Pathology and Treatment of Sexual Deviation*, Oxford: Oxford University Press.

Khan, M.M.R. (1963c). Silence as communication. In *The Privacy of the Self*. London: Hogarth Press, 1974.

Khan, M.M.R. (1964). Ego distortion, cumulative trauma and the role of reconstruction. In *The Privacy of the Self*. London: Hogarth Press, 1974.

Khan, M.M.R. (1965). Foreskin fetishism and its relation to ego pathology in a male homosexual. *International Journal of Psychoanalysis*, 46: 64–80.

Khan, M.M.R. (1969). Vicissitudes of being, knowing and experiencing in the therapeutic situation. In *The Privacy of the Self*. London: Hogarth Press, 1974.

Khan, M.M.R. (1972a). Dread of surrender to resourceless dependence in the analytic situation. In *The Privacy of the Self*. London: Hogarth Press, 1974.

Khan, M.M.R. (1972b). The use and abuse of dream in psychic experience. In *The Privacy of the Self*. London: Hogarth Press, 1974.

Khan, M.M.R. (1974). *The Privacy of the Self*. London: Hogarth Press.

Khan, M.M.R. (1975a). Grudge and the hysteric. In *Hidden Selves. Between Theory and Practice in Psychoanalysis*. London: Hogarth Press, 1983.

Khan, M.M.R. (1975b). *Seminars on The Psychoanalytic Models of the Mind*. The Institute of Psycho-Analysis, London, Autumn term.

Khan, M.M.R. (1988). *When Spring Comes: Awakenings in Clinical Psychoanalysis*. London: Chatto and Windus.

King, P. (1962). Symposium discussion: The curative factors in psycho-analysis. *International Journal of Psychoanalysis*, 43: 225–227.

King, P. (1978). Affective response of the analyst to the patient's communications. *International Journal of Psychoanalysis*, 59: 329–334.

King, P. (1979). The contributions of Ernest Jones to the British Psycho-Analytical Society. *International Journal of Psychoanalysis*, 60: 280–284.

King, P. (1983). The life and work of Melanie Klein in the British Psycho-Analytical Society. *International Journal of Psychoanalysis*, 64: 251–260.

King, P. (1989). Paula Heimann's question for her own identity as a psychoanalyst: An introductory memoir. In M. Tonnesmann (ed.), *About Children and Children-No-Longer: Collected Papers 1942–80*. London: Routledge (pp. 1–9).

King, P., and Steiner, R. (eds) (1991). *The Freud–Klein Controversies 1941–45*. London: Routledge.

Klauber, J. (1972). On the relationship of transference and interpretation in psycho-analytic psychotherapy. In *Difficulties in the Analytic Encounter*. New York: Jason Aronson, 1981.

Klauber, J. (1976). The identity of the psychoanalyst. In *Difficulties in the Analytic Encounter*. London: Free Association Books, 1986 (pp. 161–180).

Klein, M. (1921). The development of a child. In *Love, Guilt and Reparation, and Other Works: 1921–1945*. London: Hogarth Press, 1981.

Klein, M. (1923). Early analysis. In *Love, Guilt and Reparation, and Other Works: 1921–1945*. London: Hogarth Press, 1981.

Klein, M. (1932). *The Psycho-Analysis of Children*, Revised edn 1975. London: Hogarth Press.

Klein, M. (1935). A contribution to the psychogenesis of manic-depressive states. In *Love, Guilt and Reparation, and Other Works: 1921–1945*. London: Hogarth Press, 1981.

Klein, M. (1946). Notes on some schizoid mechanisms. In *Envy and Gratitude, and Other Works: 1946–1963*. London: Hogarth Press, 1975.

Klein, M. (1948). *Contributions to Psycho-Analysis, 1921–1945*. London: Hogarth Press.

Klein, M. (1981). *Love, Guilt and Reparation, and Other Works: 1921–1945*. London: Hogarth Press.

Klein, M., Riviere, J., Searl, N., Sharpe, E., Glover, E., and Jones, E., (1927). Symposium on child analysis. *International Journal of Psychoanalysis*, 8: 339–391.

Kohon, G. (ed.) (1999a). *The Dead Mother: The Work of André Green*. London: Routledge.

Kohon, G. (1999b). *No Lost Certainties to Be Recovered*. London: Karnac.

Kohon, G. (2005a). Love in a time of madness. In A. Green and G. Kohon (eds), *Love and Its Vicissitudes*. London: Routledge (pp. 41–100).

Kohon, G. (2005b). The Oedipus complex. In S. Budd and R. Rusbridger (eds), *Introducing Psychoanalysis: Essential Themes and Topics*. London: Routledge.

Kohon, G. (2016). *Reflections on Aesthetic Experience: Psychoanalysis and the Uncanny*. Hove: Routledge.

Kohon, G. (2017). Some thoughts on the negative in the work of Eduardo Chillida. In R.J. Perelberg and G. Kohon (eds), *The Greening of Psychoanalysis: André Green's New Paradigm in Contemporary Theory and Practice*. London: Karnac.

Kohon, G. (2018). Bye-bye, sexuality. In R. Perelberg, *Psychic Bisexuality: A British–French Dialogue*. Hove: Routledge.

Kohon, S.J. (2014). Making contact with the primitive mind: The contact-barrier, beta-elements and the drives. *International Journal of Psychoanalysis*, 95 (2): 245–270.

Kohut, H. (1971). *The Analysis of the Self. A Systematic Approach to the Psycho-analytic Treatment of Narcissistic Personality Disorders*. Chicago, IL: University of Chicago Press, 2007.

Kohut, H. (1973). Thoughts on narcissism and narcissistic rage. *Psychoanalytic Study of the Child*, 27: 360–400.

Kris, E. (1951). Some comments and observations on early auto-erotic activities. *Psychoanalytic Study of the Child*, 6: 95–116.

Kris, E. (1956a). The personal myth. *Journal of the American Psychoanalytic Association*, 4: 653–681.

Kris, E. (1956b). The recovery of childhood memories in psychoanalysis. *Psychoanalytic Study of the Child*, 11: 54–88.

Kris, E. (1962). Decline and recovery in the life of a three-year-old. *Psychoanalytic Study of the Child*, 17: 175–215.

Krohn, A., and Krohn, J. (1972). The nature of the Oedipus complex in the Dora case. *Journal of the American Psychoanalytic Association*, 30: 555–578.

Lacan, J. (1951). Intervención sobre la transferencia. In *Lectura Estructuralista de Freud*. México: Siglo XXI, 1971.

Lacan, J. (1953). Some reflections on the ego. *International Journal of Psychoanalysis*, 34: 11–17.

Lacan, J. (1955–6). On a question preliminary to any possible treatment of psychosis. In *Écrits: A Selection*. London: Tavistock Publications, 1977.

Lacan, J. (1958). The direction of the treatment and the principles of its power. In *Écrits: A Selection*. London: Tavistock Publications, 1977.

Lacan, J. (1977). *Écrits: A Selection*. London: Tavistock Publications.

Lagache, D. (1966). La psychanalyse et la structure de la personalité. In *La Psychanalyse, Vol. 6*. Paris: Presses Universitaires de France.

Langs, R. (1976). Misalliance and framework in the case of Dora. In *Technique in Transition*. New York: Jason Aronson, 1978.

Lantos, B. (1966). Kate Friedlander. In F. Alexander, S. Eisenstein, and M. Grotjahn (eds), *Psychoanalytic Pioneers*. New York: Basic Books, 1966.

Laplanche, J. (Reporter) (1974). Panel on hysteria today. *International Journal of Psychoanalysis*, 55: 459–469.

Laplanche, J. (1975). *Life and Death in Psychoanalysis*, Baltimore, MD: Johns Hopkins University Press.

Laplanche, J. (1987). *New Foundations for Psychoanalysis*. Oxford: Basil Blackwell, 1989.

Laplanche, J. (1999). Notes on afterwardsness. In *Essays on Otherness* (trans. and ed. J. Fletcher). London: Routledge.

Laplanche, J., and Pontalis, J.B. (1967). *The Language of Psychoanalysis*. London: Hogarth Press, 1973.

Lebovici, S., and Widlöcher, D. (1980). *Psychoanalysis in France*. New York: International Universities Press.

Leclaire, S. (1971). Jerome, or death in the life of the obsessional. In S. Schneiderman (ed.), *Returning to Freud: Clinical Psychoanalysis in the School of Lacan*. New Haven, CT: Yale University Press, 1980 (pp. 94–113).

Leclaire, S. (1975). *Matan a un niño*. Barcelona: Amorrortu Editores, 1977.

Le Guen, C. (1974). *El Edipo Originario*. Buenos Aires: Amorrortu Editores, 1976.

Lemaire, A. (1970). *Jacques Lacan* (trans. D. Macey). London: Routledge & Kegan Paul, 1977.

Lemoine-Luccioni, E. (1976). The fable of the blood. In S. Schneiderman (ed.), *Returning to Freud: Clinical Psychoanalysis in the School of Lacan*. New Haven, CT: Yale University Press, 1980.

Levin, C. (2016). Fear of breakdown in the psychoanalytic group: Commentary on Dimen. *Journal of the American Psychoanalytic Association*, 64: 381–388.

Lewin, B. (1955). Dream psychology and the analytic situation. *Psychoanalytic Quarterly*, 24: 169–199.

Lewin, B. (1965). Reflections on affect. In M. Schur (ed.), *Drives, Affects, Behaviour, Vol. 2.* New York: International Universities Press.

Lewin, K.K. (1973). Dora revisited. *Psychoanalytic Review*, 60: 519–532.

Lichtenstein, H. (1961). Identity and sexuality. *Journal of the American Psychoanalytic Association*, 9: 179–260.

Lidz, T., and Fleck, S. (1959). Schizophrenia, human integration and the role of the family. In D. Jackson (ed.), *Etiology of Schizophrenia*. New York: Basic Books.

Limentani, A. (1966). A re-evaluation of acting out in relation to working through. *International Journal of Psychoanalysis*, 47: 274–282.

Little, M. (1951). Countertransference and the patient's response to it. In *Transference Neurosis and Transference Psychosis*. New York: Jason Aronson, 1981; London: Free Association Books, 1986 (pp. 33–50).

Little, M. (1957). 'R' – the analyst's total response to his patient's needs. In *Transference Neurosis and Transference Psychosis*. New York: Jason Aronson, 1981; London: Free Association Books, 1986 (pp. 51–80).

Little, M. (1958). On delusional transference. In *Transference Neurosis and Transference Psychosis*. New York: Jason Aronson, 1981; London: Free Association Books, 1986.

Little, M. (1960). On Basic Unity. *Transference Neurosis and Transference Psychosis*. New York: Aronson, 1981; London: Free Association Books, 1986.

Low, B. (1935). The psychological compensations of the analyst. *International Journal of Psychoanalysis*, 16: 1–8.

Mahler, M.S. (1952). On child psychosis and schizophrenia. *Psychoanalytic Study of the Child*, 7: 286–305.

Mahler, M.S. (1961). On sadness and grief in infancy and childhood. *Psychoanalytic Study of the Child*, 16: 332–351.

Mahler, M.S., Pine, F., and Bergman, A. (1975). *The Psychological Birth of the Human Infant: Symbiosis and Individuation*. New York: Basic Books, 2000.

Malcolm, J. (1980). *Psychoanalysis: The Impossible Profession*. London: Picador, 1982.

Mannoni, M. (1967). *The Child, His 'Illness', and the Others*. London: Tavistock Publications, 1970.

Mannoni, O. (1969). El sueño y la transferencia. In *La Otra escena. Claves de lo imaginario*. Buenos Aires: Amorrortu Editores, 1973.

Mannoni, O. (1980). *Un Comienzo que no termina. Transferencia, interpretación, teoría*. Barcelona and Buenos Aires: Ediciones Paidos, 1982.

Marcus, S. (1974). Freud and Dora: Story, history, case history. In *Representations: Essays on Literature and Society*. New York: Random House, 1976.

Masotta, O. (1976). *Lecciones de intoducción al psicoanálisis, Vol. 1*. Barcelona: Gedisa, 1977.

Matthis, I. (2000). Sketch for a metapsychology of affect. *International Journal of Psychoanalysis*, 81: 215–227.

Mayes, L., Fonagy, P., and Target, M. (eds) (2007). *Developmental Science and Psychoanalysis: Integration and Innovation*. London: Karnac.

McCall, A., Pajaczkowska, C., Tyndall, A., and Weinstock, J. (1979). *Sigmund Freud's Dora: A Case of Mistaken Identity* [Film]. BFI Distribution.

McDougall, J. (1974). The psycho-soma and the psychoanalytic process. *International Review of Psycho-Analysis*, 1: 437–459.

McGuire, W. (ed.) (1974). *The Freud/Jung Letters*. London: Hogarth Press and Routledge and Kegan Paul.

Meltzer, D. (1978). *The Kleinian Development. Part 1, Freud's Clinical Development*. Perthshire: Clunie Press.

Melville, H. (1851). *Moby-Dick*. New York: Norton, 1967.

Miller, J.A. (1979). *Cinco conferencias Caraqueiias sabre Lacan*. Caracas: Editorial de Caracas.

Milner, M. (1952). Aspects of symbolism in comprehension of the not-self. *International Journal of Psychoanalysis*, 33: 181–195.

Milner, M. (1969). *The Hands of the Living God*. London: Hogarth Press.

Mitchell, J. (1974). *Psychoanalysis and Feminism*. London: Allen Lane; Harmondsworth: Penguin, 1990.

Mitchell, J. (1982). Introduction. In J. Mitchell and J. Rose (eds), *Feminine Sexuality: Jacques Lacan and the école freudienne*. London: Macmillan (pp. 1–26).

Mitchell, J. (1984). *Women: The Longest Revolution: Essays on Feminism, Literature and Psychoanalysis*. London: Virago.

Mitchell, J. (1986). Introduction. In *The Selected Melanie Klein*. New York: The Free Press.

Mitchell, J. (1996). Sexuality and psychoanalysis: Hysteria. *British Journal of Psychotherapy*, 12: 473–479.

Mitchell, J. (2000). *Mad Men and Medusas*. London: Allen Lane.

Mitchell, J. (2003). *Siblings: Sex and Violence*. Cambridge: Polity Press.

Mitchell, J. (2015). Debating sexual difference, politics, and the unconscious: With discussant section by Jacqueline Rose. In R. Duschinsky and S. Walker (eds), *Juliet Mitchell and the Lateral Axis*. New York: Palgrave Macmillan (pp. 77–99).

Mitchell, J., and Rose, J. (eds) (1982). *Feminine Sexuality: Jacques Lacan and the école freudienne*. London: Macmillan.

Moi, T. (1981). Representations of patriarchy: Sexuality and epistemology in Freud's Dora. *Feminist Review*, Autumn, pp. 60–74.

323

Muller, J., and Richardson, W. (1982). *Lacan and Language: A Reader's Guide to Écrits*. New York: International Universities Press.

Muslin, H., and Gill, M. (1978). Transference in the Dora case. *Journal of the American Psychoanalytic Association*, 26: 311–328.

Nacht, S. (1957). Technical remarks on the handling of the transference neurosis. *International Journal of Psychoanalysis*, 38: 196–203.

Nagera, H. (1975). *Female Sexuality and the Oedipus Complex*. New York: Jason Aronson.

Ogden, T. (1979). On projective identification. *International Journal of Psychoanalysis*, 60: 357–373.

Ogden, T. (1992). *The Primitive Edge of Experience*. London: Karnac.

Ogden, T. (2005). *This Art of Psychoanalysis: Dreaming Undreamt Dreams and Uninterrupted Cries*. Hove: Routledge.

Ogden, T. (2014). Fear of breakdown and the unlived life. *International Journal of Psychoanalysis*, 95: 205–223.

O'Sullivan, S. (2015). The art of medicine: First, do no harm. *The Lancet*, 385 (9984): 2246–2247.

Parsons, M. (2000). *The Dove that Returns, the Dove that Vanishes*. London: Routledge.

Parsons, M. (2007). Raiding the inarticulate: The internal analytic setting and listening beyond countertransference. *International Journal of Psychoanalysis*, 88: 1441–1456.

Parsons, M. (2012). An Independent theory of clinical technique. In P. Williams, J. Keene, and S. Dermen (eds), *Independent Psychoanalysis Today*. London: Karnac, 2012 (pp. 63–86).

Parsons, M. (2014a). An Independent theory of clinical technique. In *Living Psychoanalysis: From Theory to Experience*. Hove: Routledge, 2014 (pp. 184–204).

Parsons, M. (2014b). Listening out, listening in, looking out, looking in. In *Living Psychoanalysis: From Theory to Experience*. Hove: Routledge, 2014.

Parsons, M. (2014c). *Living Psychoanalysis*. Hove: Routledge.

Parsons, T. (1952). Superego and theory of social systems. In *Social Structure and Personality*. New York: Free Press of Glencoe.

Payne, S.M. (1943). Memorandum on her technique. In P. King and R. Steiner (eds), *The Freud–Klein Controversies 1941–45*. London: Routledge, 1991 (pp. 648–652).

Perelberg, R.J. (1997). 'To be – or not to be – here': A woman's denial of time and memory. In J. Raphael-Leff and R.J. Perelberg (eds), *Female Experience: Three Generations of British Women Psychoanalysts on Work with Women*. London: Routledge (pp. 60–76).

Perelberg, R.J. (1999). The interplay of identifications: Violence, hysteria and the repudiation of femininity. In G. Kohon (ed.), *The Dead Mother: The Work of André Green*. London: Routledge (pp. 173–192).

Perelberg, R.J. (2006). The Controversial Discussions and *après-coup*. *International Journal of Psychoanalysis*, 87: 1199–1220.

Perelberg, R.J. (2008). *Time, Space and Phantasy*. London: Routledge.

Perelberg, R.J. (2009). On becoming a psychoanalyst. *Psychoanalytic Inquiry*, 29: 247–263.

Perelberg, R.J. (2013). *Revue Française de Psychanalyse 2011, Vols 1–5: On some of the current themes in French psychoanalysis*. D. Ribas, F. Coblence, C. Lechartier-Atlan (eds). Paris: PUF, 2011. [Review]. *International Journal of Psychoanalysis*, 94: 589–617.

Perelberg, R.J. (2015a). On excess, trauma and helplessness: Repetitions and transformations. *International Journal of Psychoanalysis*, 96: 1453–1476.

Perelberg, R.J. (2015b). *Murdered Father, Dead Father*. Abingdon: Routledge.

Perelberg, R.J. (2016). Negative hallucinations, dreams and hallucinations: The framing structure and its representation in the analytic process. *International Journal of Psychoanalysis*, 97: 1575–1590.

Perelberg, R.J. (2018). *Psychic Bisexuality: A British-French Dialogue*. Hove: Routledge.

Perelberg, R.J., and Kohon, G. (eds) (2017). *The Greening of Psychoanalysis: André Green's New Paradigm in Contemporary Theory and Practice*. London: Karnac.

Perrier, F. (1974). Estructura histérica y diálogo analítico. In J.D. Nasio (ed.), *Acto psicoanalítico, teoría y clínica*. Buenos Aires: Ediciones Nueva Visión.

Phillips, A. (2012). *Missing Out: In Praise of the Unlived Life*. London: Hamish Hamilton.

Pichon-Rivière, E. (1970). *Del Psicoanálisis a la psicologia social, Vol. 1*. Buenos Aires: Editorial Galerna.

Pichon-Rivière, E. (1971). *Del Psicoanálisis a la Psicologia Social, Vol. 2*. Buenos Aires: Editorial Galerna.

Polmear, C. (2012). The basic fault and the borderline psychotic transference. In P. Williams, J. Keene, and S. Dermen (eds), *Independent Psychoanalysis Today*. London: Karnac (pp. 361–386).

Pontalis, J.-B. (1977). *Entre le rêve et la douleur*. Paris: Gallimard.

Press, J. (2016). Metapsychological and clinical issues in psychosomatic research. *International Journal of Psychoanalysis*, 97: 89–113.

Provence, S., and Lipton, R.C. (1962). *Infants in Institutions*. New York: International Universities Press.

Racamier, P.C. (1952). Histeria y teatro. In J. Sauri (ed.), *Las Histerias*. Buenos Aires: Ediciones Nueva Visión, 1975.

Racker, H. (1968). *Transference and Countertransference*. London: Hogarth Press.

Ramzy, I., and Wallerstein, R.S. (1958). Pain, fear and anxiety. *Psychoanalytic Study of the Child*, 13: 147–189.

Rangell, L. (1967). Psychoanalysis, affects, and the human core. *Psychoanalytic Quarterly*, 36: 172–202.

Rapaport, D. (1953). On the psychoanalytic theory of the affects. *International Journal of Psychoanalysis*, 34: 177–198.

Rapaport, D. (1958). The theory of ego autonomy. *Bulletin of the Menninger Clinic*, 22: 13–35.

Raphael-Leff, J., and Perelberg, R.J. (eds) (1997). *Female Experience: Three Generations of British Women Psychoanalysts on Work with Women*. London: Routledge.

Raphael-Leff, J., and Perelberg, R.J. (eds) (2008). *Female Experience: Four Generations of British Women Psychoanalysts on Work with Women*. London: The Anna Freud Centre.

Rayner, E. (1991). *The Independent Mind in British Psychoanalysis*. London: Free Association Books.

Rayner, E., Joyce, A., Rose, J., Twyman, M., and Clulow, C. (2005). *Human Development: An Introduction to the Psychodynamics of Growth, Maturity and Ageing, 4th edn*. Hove: Routledge.

Reich, A. (1951). On countertransference. *International Journal of Psycho-analysis*, 32: 25–31.

Reich, W. (1928). On character analysis. In R. Fliess (ed.), *The Psychoanalytic Reader*. London: Hogarth Press, 1950.

Reich, W. (1945). *Character Analysis, 2nd edn*. New York: Orgone Institute Press.

Rickman, J. (1951a). Number and the human sciences. In *Selected Contributions to Psychoanalysis*. London: Karnac, 2003 (pp. 218–223).

Rickman, J. (1951b). Reflections on the function and organization of a psychoanalytic society. *International Journal of Psychoanalysis*, 32: 218–237.

Ricoeur, P. (1960). *L'Homme faillible*. Paris: Aubier, Éditions Montaigne.

Rieff, P. (1971). Introduction. In *S. Freud, Dora: An Analysis of a Case of Hysteria*. New York: Collier Books.

Riesenberg-Malcolm, R. (1985). Interpretation: The past in the present. *Scientific Bulletin of the British Psycho-Analytical Society*, No. 5.

Riesenberg-Malcolm, R. (1996). How can we know the dancer from the dance? Hyperbole in hysteria. *International Journal of Psychoanalysis*, 77: 679–688.

Ritvo, S., and Solnit, A.J. (1958). Influences of early mother–child interaction on identification processes. *Psychoanalytic Study of the Child*, 13: 64–85.

Riviere, J. (1929). Womanliness as a masquerade. *International Journal of Psychoanalysis*, 10: 303–313.

Riviere, J. (ed.) (1952). *Developments in Psycho-Analysis*. London: Hogarth Press.

Robertson, J. (1962). Mothering as an influence on early development. *Psychoanalytic Study of the Child*, 17: 245–264.

Rogow, A.A. (1979). Dora's brother. *International Review of Psycho-Analysis*, 6: 239–259.

Rose, J. (1978). 'Dora': Fragment of an analysis. *m/f*, No. 2, pp. 5–21.

Rose, J. (1982). Introduction II. In J. Mitchell and J. Rose (eds), *Feminine Sexuality: Jacques Lacan and the école freudienne.* London: Macmillan (pp. 27–58).

Rosenfeld, H. (1985). The relationship between psychosomatic symptoms and psychotic states. In *Yearbook of Psychoanalytic Psychotherapy, Vol. 1.* Emerson, NJ: New Concept Press.

Rosenfeld, H. (1987). *Impasse and Interpretation: Therapeutic and Anti-Therapeutic Factors in the Psychoanalytic Treatment of Psychotic, Borderline, and Neurotic Patients.* London: Tavistock Publications; Hove: Routledge, 1990.

Roussillon, R. (2011). *Primitive Agony and Symbolization.* London: Karnac.

Rubinfine, D.L. (1962). Maternal stimulation, psychic structure, and early object relations. *Psychoanalytic Study of the Child*, 17: 265–282.

Rycroft, C. (1956a). The nature and function of the analyst's communication to the patient. In *Imagination and Reality.* New York: International Universities Press, 1968.

Rycroft, C. (1956b). Symbolism and its relation to the primary and secondary process. In *Imagination and Reality.* New York: International Universities Press, 1968.

Rycroft, C. (1958). An enquiry into the function of words in the psycho-analytical situation. In *Imagination and Reality.* New York: International Universities Press, 1968.

Rycroft, C. (1968). *A Critical Dictionary of Psychoanalysis.* London: Nelson.

Safouan, M. (1974). In praise of hysteria. In S. Schneiderman (ed.), *Returning to Freud: Clinical Psychoanalysis in the School of Lacan.* New Haven, CT: Yale University Press, 1980.

Sandler, A.-M. (1963). Aspects of passivity and ego development in the blind child. *Psychoanalytic Study of the Child*, 18: 343–360.

Sandler, A.-M., and Godley, W. (2004). Institutional responses to boundary violations: The case of Masud Khan. *International Journal of Psychoanalysis*, 85: 27–42.

Sandler, J., Holder, A., Kawenoka, M., Kennedy, H.E., and Neurath, L., (1969). Notes on some theoretical and clinical aspects of transference. *International Journal of Psychoanalysis*, 50: 633–645.

Sandler, A.M., and Sandler, J. (1994). Theoretical and technical comments on regression and anti-regression. *International Journal of Psychoanalysis*, 75: 431–439.

Sandler, J. (1960). The background of safety. *International Journal of Psychoanalysis*, 41: 352–356.

Sandler, J. (1972). The role of affects in psychoanalytic theory. In *Physiology, Emotion and Psychosomatic Illness.* Ciba Foundation Symposium 8, New series. Amsterdam: Elsevier/Excerpta Medica.

Sandler, J. (1976). Countertransference and role-responsiveness. *International Review of Psycho-Analysis*, 3: 43–47.

Sandler, J., Dare, C., and Holder, A. (1973). *The Patient and The Analyst: The Basis of the Psychoanalytic Process*. London: Allen and Unwin.

Sandler, J., Sandler, A.M., and Davies, R. (eds) (2000). *Clinical and Observational Psychoanalytic Research: Roots of a Controversy*. London: Karnac.

Scarfone, D. (2005). Laplanche and Winnicott meet . . . and survive. In L. Caldwell (ed.), *Sex and Sexuality*. London: Karnac (pp. 33–53).

Scharfman, M.A. (1980). Further reflections on Dora. In M. Kanzer and J. Glenn (eds), *Freud and His Patients*. New York: Jason Aronson.

Schmale, A.H. Jr. (1962). Needs, gratifications and the vicissitudes of the self-representation. In *The Psycho-Analytic Study of Society, II*. New York: International Universities Press.

Schmideberg, M. (1971). A contribution to the history of the psychoanalytic movement in Britain. *British Journal of Psychiatry*, 118: 61–68.

Schneiderman, S. (ed.) (1980). *Returning to Freud: Clinical Psychoanalysis in the School of Lacan*. New Haven, CT: Yale University Press.

Searles, H.F. (1959). The effort to drive the other person crazy. In *Collected Papers on Schizophrenia and Related Subjects*. London: Hogarth Press; New York: International Universities Press, 1965.

Searles, H.F. (1960). *The Nonhuman Environment*. New York: International Universities Press.

Searles, H.F. (1962). Scorn, disillusionment and adoration in the psychotherapy of schizophrenia. In *Collected Papers on Schizophrenia and Related Subjects*. London: Hogarth Press; New York: International Universities Press, 1965.

Searles, H.F. (1965). *Collected Papers on Schizophrenia and Related Subjects*. London: Hogarth Press; New York: International Universities Press.

Searles, H.F. (1979). *Countertransference and Related Subjects*. New York: International Universities Press.

Segal, H. (1964). *Introduction to the Work of Melanie Klein*. London: Heinemann.

Segal, H. (1979). *Klein*. London: Fontana/Collins.

Sharpe, E.F. (1930). The technique of psycho-analysis. *International Journal of Psychoanalysis*, 11: 361–386. Also in *Collected Papers on Psycho-Analysis*. London: Hogarth Press, 1958.

Sharpe, E.F. (1943). Memorandum on her technique. In P. King and R. Steiner (eds), *The Freud–Klein Controversies 1941–45*. London: Routledge, 1991 (pp. 639–645).

Sharpe, E.F. (1947). The psycho-analyst. *International Journal of Psychoanalysis*, 28: 201–213.

Sharpe, E.F. (1958). *Collected Papers on Psycho-Analysis*. London: Hogarth Press.

Sherman, M.H. (1983). Lytton and James Strachey: Biography and psychoanalysis. In N. Kiell (ed.), *Blood Brothers: Siblings as Writers*. New York: International Universities Press.

Shields, R.S. (1962). *A Cure of Delinquents*. London: Heinemann.

Sklar, J. (2011). *Landscapes of the Dark*. London: Karnac.

Slipp, S. (1977). Interpersonal factors in hysteria: Freud's seduction theory and the case of Dora. *Journal of the American Academy of Psychoanalysis*, 5: 359–376.

Smadja, C. (2010). The place of affect in the psychosomatic economy. In M. Aisenstein and E. Rappoport de Aisemberg (eds), *Psychosomatics Today: A Psychoanalytic Perspective*. London: Karnac (pp. 145–161).

Smith, S. (1977). The golden fantasy: A regressive reaction to separation anxiety. *International Journal of Psychoanalysis*, 58: 311–324.

Sodré, I. (2005). As I was walking down the stair, I saw the concept which wasn't there: Or *après-coup*: A missing concept? *International Journal of Psychoanalysis*, 86: 7–10.

Sperling, M. (1950). Children's interpretation and reaction to the unconscious of their mothers. *International Journal of Psychoanalysis*, 31: 36–41.

Spiegel, L.A. (1951). A review of contributions to the psychoanalytic theory of adolescence. *Psychoanalytic Study of the Child*, 6: 375–393.

Spitz, R.A. (1945). Hospitalism. *Psychoanalytic Study of the Child*, 1: 53–74.

Spitz, R.A. (1951). The psychogenic diseases in infancy. *Psychoanalytic Study of the Child*, 6: 255–275.

Spitz, R.A. (1959). *A Genetic Field Theory of Ego Formation*. New York: International Universities Press.

Spitz, R.A. (1962). Autoerotism re-examined. *Psychoanalytic Study of the Child*, 17: 283–315.

Spurling, L. (2008). Is there still a place for the concept of 'therapeutic regression' in psychoanalysis? *International Journal of Psychoanalysis*, 89: 523–540.

Steiner, J. (1993). *Psychic Retreats: Pathological Organisations in Psychotic, Neurotic and Borderline Patients*. London: Routledge.

Steiner, R. (1985). Some thoughts about tradition and change arising from an examination of the British Psycho-Analytical Society's Controversial Discussions (1943–1944). *International Review of Psycho-Analysis*, 12: 27–71.

Stern, D. (1985). *The Interpersonal World of the Human Infant: A View from Psychoanalysis and Developmental Psychology*. London: Karnac.

Stewart, H. (1966). On consciousness, negative hallucinations and the hypnotic state. *International Journal of Psychoanalysis*, 47: 50–53.

Stewart, H. (1992). *Psychic Experience and Problems of Technique*. London: Routledge.

Stewart, H. (1996). *Michael Balint: Object Relations Pure and Applied*. Hove: Routledge.

Strachey, J. (1934). On the nature of the therapeutic action of psychoanalysis. *International Journal of Psychoanalysis*, 15: 127–159.

Strachey, J. (1959). Editor's introduction. In S. Freud, *Inhibitions, Symptoms and Anxiety*. London: Hogarth Press (pp. 77–86).

329

Strachey, J. (1963a). Joan Riviere: Obituary. *International Journal of Psychoanalysis*, 44: 228–230.

Strachey, J. (1963b). *Jubilee Dinner Speech. The British Psycho-Analytical Society: Fiftieth Anniversary*. London: The British Psycho-Analytical Society.

Strouse, J. (1980). *Alice James: A Biography*. London: Jonathan Cape, 1981.

Sutherland, D. (1980). The British object relations theorists: Balint, Winnicott, Fairbairn, Guntrip. *Journal of the American Psychoanalytic Association*, 28: 829–860.

Szymborska, W. (2003). Homecoming. In R. Bowen, N. Temple, S. Wienrich, and N. Albery (eds), *Poem for the Day: Two*. London: Chatto & Windus.

Temperley, J. (1975). *The Marriages of Female Hysterics.* Conference paper, Group for the Advancement of Psychotherapy in Social Work, November.

Thomas, D.M. (1981). *The White Hotel*. Harmondsworth: Penguin.

Tonnesmann, M. (1989). Editor's introduction. In M. Tonnesmann (ed.), *About Children and Children-No-Longer: Collected Papers 1942–80*. London: Routledge (pp. 10–25).

Tower, L.E. (1956). Countertransference. *Journal of the American Psychoanalytic Association*, 4: 224–255.

Trombley, S. (1981). *All that Summer She Was Mad: Virginia Woolf and Her Doctors*. London: Junction Books.

Veith, I. (1975). *Hysteria: The History of a Disease*. Chicago, IL: University of Chicago Press.

Wilden, A. (ed.) (1968). *The Language of the Self: The Function of Language in Psychoanalysis*. Baltimore, MD: Johns Hopkins University Press.

Williams, P. (2012). Incorporation of an invasive object. In P. Williams, J. Keene, and S. Dermen (eds), *Independent Psychoanalysis Today*. London: Karnac.

Williams, P., Keene, J., and Dermen, S. (eds) (2012). *Independent Psychoanalysis Today*. London: Karnac.

Winnicott, D.W. (1940). Children in war. In *Collected Papers: Through Paediatrics to Psycho-Analysis*. London: Tavistock Publications, 1958.

Winnicott, D.W. (1945a). The evacuated child. The return of the evacuated child. In *Collected Papers: Through Paediatrics to Psycho-Analysis*. London: Tavistock Publications, 1958.

Winnicott, D.W. (1945b). Primitive emotional development. In *Collected Papers: Through Paediatrics to Psycho-Analysis*. London: Tavistock Publications, 1958.

Winnicott, D.W. (1948a). Paediatrics and psychiatry. In *Collected Papers: Through Paediatrics to Psycho-Analysis*. London: Tavistock Publications, 1958.

Winnicott, D.W. (1948b). Reparation in respect of mother's organized defence against depression. In *Collected Papers: Through Paediatrics to Psycho-Analysis*. London: Tavistock Publications, 1958.

Winnicott, D.W. (1949a). Birth memories, birth trauma and anxiety. In *Collected Papers: Through Paediatrics to Psycho-Analysis*. London: Tavistock Publications.

Winnicott, D.W. (1949b). Hate in the countertransference. In *Collected Papers: Through Paediatrics to Psycho-Analysis*. London: Tavistock Publications, 1958.

Winnicott, D.W. (1949c). Mind and its relation to the psyche–soma. In *Collected Papers: Through Paediatrics to Psycho-Analysis*. London: Tavistock Publications, 1958.

Winnicott, D.W. (1951). Transitional objects and transitional phenomena. In *Collected Papers: Through Paediatrics to Psycho-Analysis*. London: Tavistock Publications, 1958.

Winnicott, D.W. (1952). Psychoses and child care. In *Collected Papers: Through Paediatrics to Psycho-Analysis*. London: Tavistock Publications, 1958.

Winnicott, D.W. (1954a). Metapsychological and clinical aspects of regression within the psycho-analytical set-up. *International Journal of Psychoanalysis*, 36 (1955): 16–26. Reprinted in *Collected Papers: Through Paediatrics to Psycho-Analysis*. London: Tavistock Publications, 1958.

Winnicott, D.W. (1954b). Withdrawal and regression. In *Collected Papers: Through Paediatrics to Psycho-Analysis*. London: Tavistock Publications, 1958.

Winnicott, D.W. (1956a). The antisocial tendency. In *Collected Papers: Through Paediatrics to Psycho-Analysis*. London: Tavistock Publications, 1958.

Winnicott, D.W. (1956b). Primary maternal preoccupation. In *Collected Papers: Through Paediatrics to Psycho-Analysis*. London: Tavistock Publications, 1958.

Winnicott, D.W. (1957). *The Child and the Outside World*. London: Tavistock Publications.

Winnicott, D.W. (1958). *Collected Papers: Through Paediatrics to Psycho-Analysis*. London: Tavistock Publications; reprinted as *Through Paediatrics to Psychoanalysis: Collected Papers*. London: Hogarth Press, 1975.

Winnicott, D.W. (1960a). Countertransference. *British Journal of Medical Psychology*, 33: 17–21.

Winnicott, D.W. (1960b). Ego distortion in terms of true and false self. In *The Maturational Processes and the Facilitating Environment*. London: Hogarth Press, 1965.

Winnicott, D.W. (1960c). The theory of the parent–infant relationship. In *The Maturational Processes and the Facilitating Environment*. London: Hogarth Press, 1965.

References

Winnicott, D.W. (1962). Ego integration in child development. In *The Maturational Processes and the Facilitating Environment*. London: Hogarth Press, 1965.

Winnicott, D.W. (1963a). The capacity for concern. In *The Maturational Processes and the Facilitating Environment*. London: Hogarth Press, 1965.

Winnicott, D.W. (1963b). Dependence in infant-care, in child-care, and in the psycho-analytical setting. In *The Maturational Processes and the Facilitating Environment*. London: Hogarth Press, 1965.

Winnicott, D.W. (1963c). Psychiatric disorder in terms of infantile maturational processes. In *The Maturational Processes and the Facilitating Environment*. London: Hogarth Press, 1965.

Winnicott, D.W. (1969). The use of an object. In *Psycho-Analytic Explorations*. C. Winnicott, R. Shepherd, and M. Davis (eds). London: Karnac, 1989.

Winnicott, D.W., Mannoni, O., Green, A., *et al.* (1978). *Donald W. Winnicott*. Buenos Aires: Editorial Trieb.

Zetzel, E. (1968). The so-called good hysteric. *International Journal of Psychoanalysis*, 49: 256–260.

Index

Abraham, K. 26, 35, 37, 38, 40
Abram, J. 214, 223
absence: concept of, Independent views on 13; role of in analytic encounter, Independent views on 16–18
abstinence, rule of, classical 232
acting out 135, 162, 191, 217, 221, 247, 252, 258; in analytic situation 225, 229; as communication 71, 187, 225; explosive 99, 187–8; and integration 191; and regression 229; of silent patient 227; transitional space valuable in preventing 182
active technique, analyst's use of 224
Adler, A. 268, 298
aesthetic experience(s) 92, 102
aesthetic moment(s) 91–2, 103
aesthetic space 103
affect(s): in analytic situation 173–91; definition 178; dissociated from object 173; occlusion of, by unconscious phantasy 138; as part of primitive system of ego 185; psychoanalytic research on 137; and psychoanalytic situation 173–91; role of, in reconstruction 188–9; unconscious 182 [existence of 173]
affect theory 138–40, 142, 174, 184
aggression, in genesis of hysteria 264

aggressive sexual phantasies, primitive 250
agony, primitive 124
alone, capacity to be 58
Alpert, A. 117
ambivalence 39, 43, 164, 169, 187, 285–7
anaclitic needs 108, 120; infant's 109, 112
analysis: facilitating environment for 71; futility in 125–6; goal of 56; parameters within 143, 156, 217 18, 221, 225, 243, 247, 259; as projection, by patient into analyst 56; training 50, 169; wild 36, 162
analysis of self, regressions as resistance to 98
analyst(s): act of freedom of 156 [as agent of therapeutic change 192–206]; as bisexual transference figure 286; early, psychological disturbance of 44–6; emotional position of, in psychoanalytic situation 175; emotional responses of 53; as environment-mother 98; ethical seduction of patient by 217; as good object 17; idealization of 17, 56; laughing in sessions 157; as mirror or receiver 55; need-recognizing function of 231; need-satisfying function of

as analyst's resistance 51; in analytic encounter, Independent views on 16–18; concept of 50–5, 140; expressive uses of 143; Independent views on 24, 50–69; indirect 240; indirect and direct uses of 63; indirect use of 64; as multi-dimensional phenomenon 16; objective 141–2; Object Relations view 52; theory of, contributions of Independent analysts 55–69; as tool 176; and transference, as unit 200; unconscious, professional 102; usefulness of 140; vicissitudes of 59

counter-transference interpretations 143

Cournut, M. 12

Cromwell, O. 26

cumulative trauma 8, 83, 183; aetiology of 113–19; concept of 104–20

Darwin, C. 26

Davies, R. 86, 267–9, 272

dead father 133

death: fear of 279; phenomenal 126

death drive 138, 304

death instinct 105, 174, 182, 211, 212; Kleinian concept of 42

Decker, J.S. 289

defence(s): analyst's, against impact of analytic relationship 55; against breakdown of ego organization 122; fear of breakdown as 145; hysteria as 281; of intellectualization 175; manic 168; patient's, interpretation of 99; primary 138; psychic 78; against psychosis 264; psychotic illness as 124; secondary 267

defence mechanism(s) 66, 105; of adolescent period 278

defence organization, failure of 122

deferred action: *see Nachträglichkeit*

delusion(s) 61, 66, 90, 188, 201, 252, 269, 292, 303

delusional transference 232

dependence, absolute 120, 123, 145

depersonalization 81, 123

depression, at end of analysis 67

depressive anxieties 184, 228

depressive character, hysterical 245

depressive character structure 244

depressive position 105, 129, 159; concept of 39; of newly qualified analyst 166

Dermen, S. 4, 5

desexualization of psychoanalytic theory 267

destructive drive, in genesis of 264

Deutsch, F. 278, 279

development and après-coup 215

developmental lines, concept of 41

developmental psychology, observational 75

Devine, H. 27

didactic analysis 27

Dimen, M. 223

displacement 66, 260, 280, 284

dissociation 98, 99, 116, 177, 180

dissociative seizures 265

divalence 266, 284–8; concept of 270

divalent stage in female development 266, 270, 287

Donne, J. 159

Donnet, J.-L. 215

Dora (Freud's patient) 6, 9, 26, 266, 273–88, 294

dream(s): analysis of 276; traumatic 108; unknowable navel of 269; waking in consulting room 168

dream interpretation, symbolic, in child analysis 37

dream thoughts 94; as sensory images 211

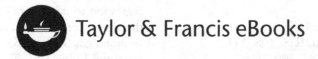

9781138579057